Nathan B. Gatchell II

1965 - Sept.

WEEK IN YANHUITLÁN

ROSS PARMENTER

Week in Yanhuitlán

with drawings by the author

THE UNIVERSITY OF NEW MEXICO PRESS

THE PUBLICATION OF THIS BOOK IS MADE POSSIBLE
BY A GRANT FROM THE FORD FOUNDATION

MANUFACTURED IN THE UNITED STATES OF AMERICA
BY THE UNIVERSITY OF NEW MEXICO PRINTING PLANT
ALBUQUERQUE, NEW MEXICO
LIBRARY OF CONGRESS CATALOG CARD NO. 63-21374
First Edition

TO GABRIEL AND GUADALUPE BLANCO

CONTENTS

ILLUSTRATIONS

To contemplate and to pass on to others the fruits of contemplation.

—Motto of the Dominican Order

I

MONASTERY IN MEXICO

I FIRST SAW THE MONASTERY at Yanhuitlán in September 1948. The bus from Puebla had been descending, crossing and climbing out of mountain valleys for more than six hours, when suddenly, after climbing through still another pass, it rounded a curve and there, spread out below, was a valley different from any of the previous ones. It was sensationally red. And rising from the nearest village was a construction so massive it suggested a dam.

It was a church, as I found when the bus serpentined down. But we passed through the collection of thatched huts at its feet so fast that I could note only its sand-pink color and its disproportionately small tower. Craning my neck to look back, I saw it had extensive outbuildings. But what struck me most was something I had seen in no other Mexican church—stone tracery in the high windows of the nave.

In Oaxaca, where I had been headed, I later saw some postcards of a large church. The tracery of its side windows provided a clue. Could this be the huge building the bus had whizzed past on the way down? The girl at the counter said it was. And she pronounced the name of the place Yan-wheat-LAN, using the soft Spanish *ah* sound in the first and last syllables. I was especially grateful for the identification, for Yanhuitlán was not on the map.

BACK IN NEW YORK, I discovered George Kubler's *Mexican Architecture of the Sixteenth Century*. I seized on it eagerly, for at that time I was working on my first try at a book on Mexico. It had the title *Stages in a Journey* and three of the stages were accounts of visits to buildings—the

1

fortress monasteries at Ixmiquilpan, Cuilapam and Huejotzingo. All were erected in the era covered by Kubler. Besides helping me with my particular buildings, his magnificent study opened my eyes to how many other monasteries the Franciscans, Augustinians and Dominicans built in Mexico. In the incredible eighty-year period following the Conquest, they blanketed the country with religious establishments. Kubler cited no fewer than 273, with nineteen being of the first class. The one at Yanhuitlán, as I was sure it must, belonged in the first class.

By this time Mexico was in my blood and its architecture was my leading interest. So in planning my next visit two years later I sought the means to visit as many of those top nineteen monasteries as my itinerary would allow. Since I was going back to Oaxaca, taking in Yanhuitlán would be easy. It was on the way. All I would have to do would be to get off the bus, visit the monastery and pick up another bus later in the day.

IT WORKED OUT as I planned. First class buses do not ordinarily stop at Yanhuitlán, but my driver paused at the village long enough to let me off.

The monastery was on a rise on the left side of the highway. I could see why two years before I had thought of a dam. The church's vast northern flank was braced by damlike buttresses; and the two at the corners were so massive they had arched passageways running through them.

I mounted the steps to the church. When I saw its front doors were closed, I asked a boy how I could gain admission. He told me to follow the outbuildings to the corner and then to turn left until I saw the visitors' entrance.

I found it easily. In response to my knocking, an attendant came to the door. He was wearing a straw sombrero, and, after I told him I was a tourist, he did something that charmed me. He took off his sombrero and put on his visored cap, thereby transforming himself from a native of the village into an official guide.

He was a man in his fifties with an attractive smile that revealed particularly fine teeth. Having been struck by the good teeth of so many country Mexicans, I congratulated him on his. Again he won my heart. He admitted they weren't real.

The monastery was even more magnificent than I had anticipated. The major features—the cloister, the church, the stairways, the corridors, the public rooms—were all grander than I expected. And there was a wealth of minor detail that was lovely. In the cloister vaulting, for instance, the bosses all were different. So were the medallions carved over the doors of the cells.

After the tour I asked permission to eat my lunch in the quiet of the cloister. A huge cypress was growing from its center and, as I sat in its shade chewing on a ham-filled roll, I couldn't help feeling that the neglected cloister, with its dappled sunlight and chipped balconies, was a friendlier place than the rest of the establishment. Elsewhere I had sensed something cold in the grandeur, as if the monastery embodied a slightly arrogant spirit.

Still, I had not absorbed all I wanted. So, after giving the guide part of my lunch, I asked for a second glimpse of the church. He escorted me willingly, and this time, being less excited, I was able to isolate some of the details and to analyze why the church created its particular effect. Those high traceried windows were much larger than most windows in Mexico's sixteenth-century churches. And they were empty of any glass. Thus the light flooded through them, and the ceiling, instead of being lost in darkness, was the lightest part of the building. It was magnificently vaulted and all the ribs and their interspaces had been washed a dazzling white.

The high altar reached almost to the ceiling in the night-blue apse. There were many other elaborate gold altars lining the sides. And the ceiling under the choir loft was unusually splendid. It was of wood and the beams intersected to form a network of hexagonal coffers. From each sunken hexagon hung a carved pendant.

All around were fascinating religious figures—primitive, yet full of pathos and drama.

I would have enjoyed a long stay, but no one had been able to supply definite information about the afternoon bus. Not wanting to miss it, I felt it would be safer to get out on the road to wait.

As it was the siesta hour, few people were about, but every now and then a man or woman would come along. Not one passed in front of me without saying "Con permiso." I was both charmed and amazed. Never in my own country had I known people to carry good manners to the point of asking permission to pass on the open road.

After a while an Indian youth came by. He had something unusual for an Indian—wavy hair. Since he stopped to chat I wanted to be pleasant, so I decided to compliment him on his waves. That meant searching for the right word in my pocket dictionary. *Ondas* was what I found. As I spoke the word I pointed with an approving smile to the deep undulations of his thick, glossy hair. He understood and was pleased. In our halting way we got along very well. He told me the town had movies every eight days. They were shown in the school. Children, he said, were admitted for half price.

Soon another youngster came along. He was tiny and I felt sorry for him struggling under the weight of the two big tins of water he was carrying, hung like balances from a pole across his left shoulder. I was terribly thirsty and, although I knew it was risky to drink strange water, I accepted the boy's assurance that the water came from a spring in the mountains and was pure. He ladled some out in the half shell of a gourd. It was cool and marvelously refreshing.

The youth with the wavy hair, I learned, was Cutberto. The smaller boy was Ricardo, and he wasn't to be pitied so much after all. He was sixteen, but because he was so small he was able to get into the movies for half price.

Presently a seller of cones came along. I was glad to see his familiar pushcart, so I hailed him. I bought cones for Cutberto and Ricardo. Each cone was surmounted with a little pile of pale lemon sherbet. A few more children appeared. I ordered cones for them too. More children emerged. More cones.

The total had reached about eighteen or twenty when adults began appearing. They graciously accepted cones too.

One old man asked if I was interested in *idolos*. Thinking they were in his pocket, I said yes. But his wares were at home, and I felt a pang of guilt as he limped away to get them, for the poor man had a club foot.

The cones made for friendliness so the time passed quickly. The people asked me where I was going, how old I was and if I was married. I was glad to tell them all I could, for it was easier for me to speak Spanish than to understand it when they rattled it back.

As we were talking, a bus appeared circling down from the hills. It was the one I must take for Oaxaca. Just as it arrived, the crippled old man returned with his idols. I did not have the time to look at them, and I felt badly that I could not even reward his pains for fetching them. But the bus was honking. I boarded hurriedly, waving good-bye to every one as I left.

BECAUSE I stuck to my plans on that 1950 visit, not only did I visit Yanhuitlán, and revisit Ixmiquilpan, Cuilapam and Huejotzingo, but I also visited the sixteenth-century monasteries at Acolman, Actopan, Etla, Cuitzeo and Yuriria. I came back to the United States fairly bursting with a sense of their importance. Clearly, they were the progenitors of the missions in New Mexico, Texas, Arizona and California. And whereas the missions had been built at a later period among poor tribes at the outposts of the Spanish empire, the Mexican fortress-monasteries were built during Spain's golden age among civilized Indians in the chief population centers of one of the wealthiest territories ever conquered for a European monarch.

The building of the Mexican monasteries is one of the great stories of the New World. And I knew it was virtually unknown to the general public. I felt proud that in *Stages* I had suggested the main lines of that story. I had the newspaperman's excited joy in having a major scoop.

Yet what did I walk into the day after my return? The first rejection. And what a rejection! No part of the manuscript, said the editor, was even "salvageable." But since I had a lot more work I wanted to do, I pitched in and began my revisions. After four more months of writing and re-writing, I began submitting the book again.

Subsequent editors were less damning, but still the verdict was "No." So many mentioned the problem of finding a market that it became apparent to me that the fact that those sixteenth-century monasteries were unknown —which I thought had been an advantage—was actually a handicap. Trade publishers, I saw, were only apt to take manuscripts dealing with interests already established in the public mind.

As the rejections continued to mount, I kept asking myself why I was so anxious to get the manuscript published. Was it merely vanity? There was an element of that, I had to admit. I think there is in all author-ship. But that was not the whole explanation. As I sifted my motives I saw two of the strongest were honestly altruistic. Because I thought those monasteries were so marvelous I wanted to bring their story to the outside world. And because I felt so deeply indebted to Mexico—for all it had done for me, for all it had taught me—I wanted, as a sort of thank offering, to communicate to others my particular vision of that beloved country.

I continued to work on my book. I polished, clarified, rearranged, cut, simplified. And at times, I must confess, I felt as if I were a hurt animal licking its wounds. However, my morale always shot up whenever I found the means of making a section more nearly the way I wanted it. Yet the manuscript continued to draw rejections. Each rejection drove me further in on myself, and by early 1953 I was struggling with a deep sense of failure. The subject matter, I felt, was the most wonderful literary material I had ever dealt with. Yet apparently I had not been able to make it living and vivid for others.

We can often see our own difficulties more clearly when we see similar difficulties plaguing others. And I gained some hints when I saw a playwright's struggles to impose integration on something so complicated and many-faceted as the Salem witch trials.

Stages dealt with six major episodes selected from three different journeys to Mexico. The half-dozen locales were all different. There were time-breaks between each episode. And of necessity there were several sets of characters. My material, then, lacked the basic unities of place, time and action.

Perhaps, I said to myself, I've been defeated by selecting material impossible to integrate.

Out of this thinking emerged the idea that if I were to write a successful book about Mexico it would be wise to confine it to a single town, and preferably to a single visit to that town. Then my unity of place, time and action would be in the material itself. Since I seem fated by temperament to write in a reflective manner I decided, too, that it would be better to make the visit a short one.

But which town should be the locale of my second try?

The candidate emerged from discussions of the first try. Friends, to console me for failing to place it, explained that readers were not interested in buildings. But knowing my intentions, I felt their criticism—"too much architecture"—was like saying a book about botany had too much about plants. Peggy Glanville-Hicks, the composer, was the friend who illuminated the problem. She said architectural description unsupported by illustration was hard to read. "Make more drawings," she urged.

Till then I had drawn only the features impossible to visualize without pictures. Spurred by her encouragement, I began drawing other details. I had little confidence, for I had never been to art school and, besides the preliminary sketches, all I had drawn had been heads of friends and some plants. But the new drawings gave me a lift. By turning out better than I expected, they showed me I had more artistic skill than I thought.

It was this extra bit of confidence that, because it made the project feasible, flashed that project into my mind: To go back to Yanhuitlán and spend a week drawing its monastery.

The idea pierced through my discouragement like a ray of reviving joy. All sorts of arguments rushed in to support it. I never got sick from drinking Ricardo's water, so I knew the town water was pure. And I knew the people were friendly. I knew, too, that the villagers were aware enough of the importance of their monastery to accept my drawing it as a sufficient reason for my being there.

In other words, the way was clear for undertaking the project as a personal adventure. And perhaps . . . .

Perhaps it would give me my book. Vicariously, I could take the reader sketching with me, and I could describe the monastery in the course of telling how I made the drawings. If my pictorial evidence was convincing, an account of one of those monasteries might suggest to a wide public the story of them all, and of the wave of evangelization that cast them up. And perhaps, between the lines, the account would enable me to convey the essential things about Mexico that I want those unfamiliar with the country to know.

II

PREPARATIONS

No SEGMENT OF EXPERIENCE, no matter how well rounded, stands in isolation from what has gone before. So Yanhuitlán's story—because of certain integral elements—requires a few glimpses of preparations in other parts of Mexico.

First, the permit. The monastery was under the jurisdiction of the Instituto Nacional de Antropología e Historia, and I knew that, unless the Institute gave me permission to draw the place freely, my whole project would be impossible. I was in no hurry to get to Yanhuitlán for, to admit the truth, I had many fears. Nevertheless, before doing anything else in Mexico, I wanted to make sure I would be free to head for the village when my courage was finally screwed up.

As soon as I stepped off the plane, I telephoned my friend Elizabeth Borton de Treviño and asked her to line up an appointment at the Institute.

Jorge Enciso, the sub-director, said he would see us at noon, for Elizabeth was to come along so her more perfect Spanish would prevent mistakes in comprehension.

The Institute was formed in 1939 by the merger of a number of government agencies, including the Dirección de Monumentos Coloniales. When I had first visited the Institute in 1950 I had been shocked at its shabbiness. It was on Córdoba, a street that must have been fashionable in the days of Porfirio Diaz, for it was lined with mansions that represented Mexico's Victorian style at its worst. The Institute was then at No. 73, a two-story house built in the likeness of a battlemented castle.

Knowing the Institute's excellent work in restoring pre-Columbian and colonial monuments, and having seen the money poured into handsome modern buildings for other government agencies, I had been saddened at such depressing evidence that, in the governmental family, the Institute was so poor a relation.

As Elizabeth and I drew up, the Institute looked more run down than ever. Perhaps it was because on this venture I was determined to use my eyes as I had never done before, but I saw everything with uncanny clarity. The runty castle had no curtains at its windows and the sashes needed paint. Inside, there were no rugs, walls were peeling and the dark wood had still less luster. And the three or four old wrecks who were hanging around! Had they wandered in from a Salvation Army hostel, or were they actually on the payroll?

The receptionist was sitting in front of an old-fashioned time clock, his newspaper spread out on the empty desk in front of him. He looked up from his reading to indicate that we would find Sr. Enciso's office if we went down the corridor and ascended the carpetless stairs to the second floor.

Sr. Enciso gave an impression of urbane and cultured elegance. He was slim, handsome and well tailored, and the comb tracks showed neatly through the slicked down waves of his silver hair. He bade us be seated on his sofa, a massive affair whose black leather covering was cracked and badly scuffed.

I was tremblingly anxious to get the permit. Sr. Enciso immediately set my mind at rest. The Institute, he said, would be happy to have me make drawings of the monastery. And he called for a young man and instructed him to prepare a letter to that effect. The wait for the letter gave me the chance to ask questions. I seized it gratefully for I wanted to round out my knowledge of the government's relationship to monasteries like the one at Yanhuitlán.

Actually, I knew quite a bit. I knew, for instance, that 1859 was the year Mexico suppressed the monasteries; and that this step was taken shortly after Juárez' Reform Law of July had confiscated all ecclesiastical property except church buildings. And I knew that the Constitution of 1917 had completed the expropriation by nationalizing the churches too. But what had happened between the two great seizures? And what happened after the nationalization swept more than 12,000 churches into government hands?

The mind, at the point of crystallization, is like a saturated solution. Drop in a few more facts, and, lo! all sorts of jumbled particles suddenly present themselves in an ordered pattern. That is what happened with the additional facts Sr. Enciso gave me, and this is the pattern that emerged.

The French invasion followed the suppression of the monasteries. Then came the interlude of Maximilian and Carlotta. By 1867, when Maximilian had been executed and the last French soldier driven out, the country had too many pressing concerns and was too poor to do anything about the deserted monasteries. They continued to deteriorate. Bit by bit, though, Díaz established stability, and his long dictatorial regime brought an enforced order to the country which was accompanied by a degree of prosperity. Toward the end of this period Mexican scholars and historians began to be concerned for the fate of the neglected buildings.

Little was done for them in a tangible way, though, until the setting up of the Dirección de Monumentos Coloniales. This, according to Sr. Enciso, was in 1915. But even then the Dirección could do little, for this was the period of the Revolution. Two years later, the problems of the Dirección became much more acute when all the nation's churches were declared government property. The Revolution continued. But by the '30s order had been re-established and in 1934 a law was passed to protect the nation's colonial treasures. It appointed a commission to study them and to decide on the work necessary to preserve them.

What work had been done for Yanhuitlán, I asked.

In the early '40s President Avila Camacho appropriated 100,000 pesos for the monastery, Sr. Enciso said. The Institute used this money between 1945 and 1947. The work was directed by Agustín García Vega, an engineer, who had crews of from five to twenty men to help him. The work, he said, was mostly to make the monastery safe to enter.

As Sr. Enciso spoke, a picture flashed on my mind. In Pablo C. de Gante's *La Arquitectura de México en el Siglo XVI* there is a photograph of the monastic church rather like one of those "blitz" pictures that became familiar during World War II. Only in this case it wasn't a bed that stood exposed in a frame of shattered masonry. It was the church bell. It was exposed so pitifully because some force that suggested a direct hit had destroyed the outer corner of the belfry. When I had visited the monastery in 1950 the tower had been repaired. Probably, I thought to myself, reconstructing it was part of García's work.

"Has the Institute done any work there since 1947?" I asked Sr. Enciso.

"It would like to," he replied. "But you see," and here he raised his shoulders with a gesture of sad resignation, "there is no money. . . ." At this point the young man brought in my letter and Sr. Enciso signed it.

Bringing Elizabeth had perhaps been a mistake. It made me guiltily conscious of taking up two persons' time, and, once I had my letter safely in my pocket, I felt I should release them both. I certainly wasn't going to ask Elizabeth to wait around while I pored over any books. But I had brought some tracing paper and I wanted, if possible, to make a quick tracing of the monastery's plan.

I would not have to make it myself, Sr. Enciso said. Then came the crowning act of his courtesy. He promised that if I returned at noon the next day Felipe Pineda, who was in charge of the Institute's plans, would give me a tracing.

THE NEXT DAY was Saturday and I was back before noon. I asked the receptionist at the time clock for Sr. Pineda. Looking up from his newspaper, he said Sr. Pineda was not in. I protested I had an appointment. The receptionist referred me to the Salvation Army hostelers, who were behind the counter in an adjoining room.

Sr. Pineda was gone for the day, they said, and would not be back until nine or ten o'clock Monday morning.

The casualness of Mexicans about time has been a stock source of humor, and many North Americans have made comic capital of their difficulties in getting Mexican workmen to complete their work by the dates promised. Thus perhaps I should have turned away, laughing the incident off as another instance of a national characteristic. But I was too disappointed to find the situation funny. I had a plane to catch at eighty-thirty Monday morning and Sr. Pineda's return would be too late for me to get the keenly wanted plan.

I didn't want to give up. If Sr. Pineda had gone, perhaps he had left something for me, I suggested to the men. They shook their heads. No plan of a monastery? I asked. Again heads shook. Not a plan of the monastery at Yanhuitlán?

The name of the place seemed to stir some faint bell in the mind of a discouraged-looking old man who needed a shave. He hauled himself from his seat in the corner and made his way to a filing cabinet. There he picked up a wandlike scroll, which he brought to me and asked if this was it.

How glad I was that I had been honestly disappointed and not humorously superior! When I unfurled the scroll I found, not one, but two beau-

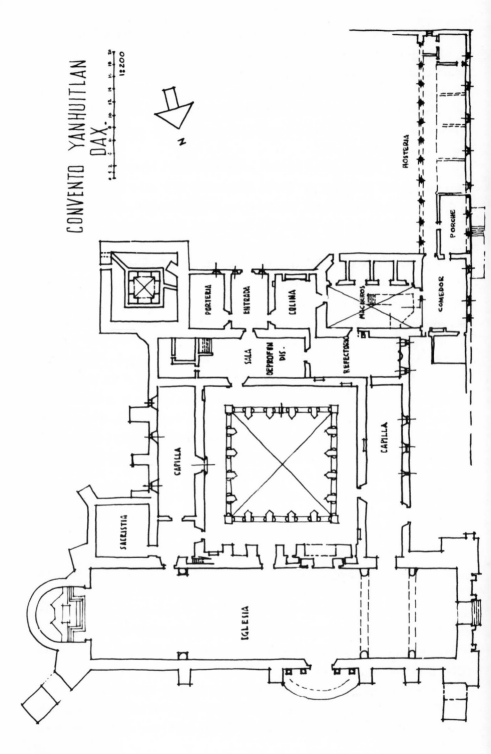

CONVENTO YANHUITLAN OAX.

1:200

N

PORTERIA
ENTRADA
COCINA
SALA
DEPOSITO EN DIS.
REFECTORIO
MACHEROS
HOSTERIA
COMEDOR
PORCHE
CAPILLA
CAPILLA
SACRISTIA
IGLESIA

12

tifully traced plans. One showed the ground floor, the other the second floor. And they were in a scale so large they extended almost two feet. They were far finer than anything I had expected. Sr. Pineda had been better than his word.

I thanked the old man effusively and triumphantly made off with my treasure.

ANYTHING SO PRECIOUS needed protection. So I spent the next hour scouring the city to find a cardboard tube in which to keep the tracings. A drafting supply store sold me a green one. And that night, armed with my green tube, I headed for Elizabeth's for dinner. I particularly wanted to show the plans to Luis, her husband. Receiving the plans had stepped up my excitement about my project and unrolling them before Luis would be a way of convincing him that this was a wonderful building I was going to study.

Here is a reproduction of the Institute's ground plan.

As can be seen, the wording was in Spanish. Clearly the vast section on the left marked *iglesia* was the church. The *capillas* on either side of the cloister, of course, were chapels. The *portería* on the right of the monastery entrance, I knew, was the porter's lodge. Thanks to visits to other monasteries, I was aware that the *sala de profundis* was the friars' hall of meditation. The *cocina* was the kitchen, conveniently placed so that food could easily be brought into the refectory, where the friars ate. But what about those enclosures at the lower right-hand corner?

In poring over the plan at my hotel, I had turned to my pocket dictionary and found the word *hostería*. It meant inn. So that barlike wing was where passing travelers found accommodation. The *comedor* was the dining room for the travelers. The fact that there was a different dining room for the secular visitors showed that they did not eat with the friars. So far, so good. But what was the partitioned space marked *macheros?*

Luis knew. He had been the paymaster for a mining company and he had spent many months in remote villages. *Macho* he explained, was a word for a male mule and *macheros* were mule drivers. The puzzling area was the stable of the inn.

Luis, knowing I was green, volunteered some advice: "There are two ways you can approach a Mexican village. You can either go through the Mayor, *el Presidente Municipal,* or you can go through the priest."

MY VACATION scheme was as follows: to go first to San Cristóbal de las Casas, my furthest point south, and then to work my way north in easy stages, with an especially long stop at Oaxaca before proceeding the 75 miles further north for that momentous, but left for the last, week in Yanhuitlán. I mention the route because along the way I picked up more of my story elements.

In San Cristóbal, for instance, I got an addendum to Luis' sage counsel about how to approach a Mexican village. I also got some vital historical facts about Yanhuitlán. The Danish archeologist, Frans Blom, was the source of both.

Blom had established a library and regional museum in his home. When I learned the famous Mexicanist was not averse to visitors from north of the border, I paid him a call. A shock of white hair, humorous Nordic eyes of piercing blue, sandals, old jeans and the lean figure of a cowboy made up the outer picture. Inwardly, he was all enthusiasm for the finds he was making in the neighborhood. But he was eager to help other scholars. When he heard where I was going, he went to his shelves and pulled down a folio volume. It was a publication I had not known existed: the National Museum's *Códice de Yanhuitlán*.

"Here," he said kindly, "take this off into a corner and browse through it. No one will disturb you."

I could only skim through it. But I quickly came upon a fact that made my eyes light up. Yanhuitlán was part of the feudal estate given to Francisco de Las Casas. This excited me, for I had read Cortés' letters. Las Casas was a cousin of Cortés, who had come to Mexico in 1523, bearing Charles V's letter naming Cortés the Governor of New Spain. Thereafter Las Casas had been one of Cortés' most trusted captains. The story I remembered best was how Cortés dispatched him to Honduras to arrest another of his captains, Cristóbal de Olid, who, instead of settling Honduras for Cortés, had proved treacherous and seized it for himself. Las Casas had the misfortune to have his ship wrecked on the shore where Olid was encamped. Olid captured him, and when Las Casas refused to join in the seizure of Honduras, Olid imprisoned him. Olid also captured Gil Gonzalez de Avila, the leader of another expedition that had converged on Honduras.

The two captured captains kept warning Olid to guard them well, for they were determined to kill him. And one night Las Casas got his opportunity. Olid came near him as he was cutting his nails with a paper knife. Las Casas sprang at him, seized him by the beard and stabbed him with the letter opener. Such a weapon did not kill Olid. But it precipitated a revolt. Olid, in his turn, was imprisoned. The next morning the two captains tried him and jointly sentenced him to death. "The which sentence was carried out on his person and his head was struck off."

What had made that story stick so imperishably was the small, but curiously vivid detail of the captain using a paper knife to pare his nails. And as I turned back to the *Códice* I savored the correlation. When the Conquest of Mexico was completed and the land and its people were divided, Yanhuitlán—my town—had been given to that watchful captain who had been engaged in that crude manicure when the chance came to square accounts.

In those days it was almost standard practice for captains to seize for themselves the lands they had been sent to claim for their superiors. Cortés himself had done this to the Governor of Cuba, who had sent him to Mexico. Las Casas, then, in refusing to join Olid in slicing up Honduras, had remained extraordinarily loyal to his cousin. No wonder he was rewarded with one of the richest plums Cortés could offer.

A few pages further in the *Códice*, I grew excited a second time. The monastery, I knew, was established by the Dominican Order, but I did not know when or how. The book had the missing information.

The first Dominicans came to Yanhuitlán in 1529 and stayed only a year. Four or five years later a new group arrived. The friars of the second lot stayed longer and they were zealous in destroying idols and uprooting the old religion. Such disregard for long-treasured beliefs roused the animosity of the natives. The friars' interfering ways, too, were resented by the ex-captain, Francisco de Las Casas, now a lord of the manor. The combined hostility of Francisco and the Indians, in fact, finally made it so hot for the friars that in 1541 they withdrew.

Not until Francisco died and his more pious son, Gonzalo, succeeded to his estates did the Dominicans come back. The *Códice* placed their return in 1548 or 1549. They started building the sumptuous monastery in 1550.

It was as Blom was accompanying me to the door that he gave the parting counsel about what to do if I should try to approach the town through the alternate to the *presidente*.

"If you go through the priest," he said, "be sure to take him something to drink. They all like a nip of the bottle."

DESPITE my earlier artistic bravado, I had a gnawing fear that I did not draw well enough to do justice to the monastery. This had played a role in my decision to leave Yanhuitlán to the last, and it led me to do some warm-up drawings in San Cristóbal.

The tower gate of El Carmen, which picturesquely blocks the vista down one of the streets off the plaza, was a trial subject. I began the sketch from the spot where the tower had first struck me as being beautiful. From there I was able to draw all the proportions, as well as the twin bell openings, the windows and the archway that straddles the street. When this was done, I found that from so far away I could not make out certain features. I moved closer so I could see the puzzling elements well enough to depict them intelligibly.

At the point where I could discern the details I found the proportions had altered. The archway was far larger and I could see the top of the tower only by cricking my neck looking upward.

So that's the trick, I said to myself as I made a mental note of a lesson that was to prove valuable. If you want to get proportions right, you must start from a distance.

WHENEVER a story strikes us with a particularly haunting impact, I think it is because it sets up reverberations in our own anxieties. And perhaps this accounts for the impact of a story I collected in the plane between Ixtepec and Oaxaca. I say this because I was then not only on the verge of an unknown situation—which always engenders anxiety—but I had never experienced any kind of solitary danger. My boyhood had been exceptionally sheltered and as a child of anxious parents I had absorbed much of their timidity about what was not "safe." As an adult I had continued to live in cities among people I knew. And even in the army there had always been one's fellow soldiers.

At all events, here is the story. It was told by an Ohio businessman beside whom I was placed by the fortuitous seating of air travel. He represented a U. S. company in Tapachula, which is at the end of the plane line on the border of Guatemala. What prompted the story was my question as to whether any other North Americans lived in Tapachula.

"Well, there's my wife," he said, "and one or two others. And now there is one less. There was an odd guy there, a navy veteran. He looked perfectly normal and he was the picture of health. But he wouldn't have anything to do with the rest of us Americans. He insisted on living in the hills. We called him 'Nature Boy.' But the natives got him. They must have thought he had money on him. They went at him with machetes. Almost killed him. He had to be taken to Mexico City."

IN OAXACA I made a copy of the permit I would soon have to surrender. The letter was addressed to the *Encargado del ex-convento de Yanhuitlán*. I smiled at the term: the caretaker of the *ex-convento*. An officially anticlerical government scrupulously calls these places *ex*-monasteries.

The letter warned the caretaker that the bearer had an interest in the monument under his charge. "Therefore," it said, "you will be pleased to supply him with the information that he solicits with the object that his visit will be the most profitable possible."

The name of the caretaker, I read, was Blanco—Gabriel Blanco. I wondered if Sr. Blanco was the old man with the interchangeable hats who had guided me through the monastery three years before. Thinking about him gave me an idea. Why not take three bottles? One for the *presidente municipal* and one for the priest, as I already planned, and one for the caretaker.

I TOOK THE LIQUOR problem to Oscar García Quintanilla, a big jolly miner from Monterey, who had received his engineering training at the University of Kansas. He was familiar with the Mixteca Alta, the high northern region of Oaxaca in which Yanhuitlán is situated.

"Take sacramental wine for the priest," he said, "and mezcal to the caretaker and the municipal president. In that part of the country they all drink mezcal."

"Be sure to keep your money in two pocketbooks," he added. "Keep only a few pesos in the pocketbook that people see you use. Keep your real money in another wallet hidden somewhere about you in a safe place."

Up till then I had always found Mexicans honest, uncheating and trustworthy. But never having been alone in a remote village, as the miner had, I decided it would be prudent to take the precaution he suggested. In fact, I was grateful for the tip because I was going where there would be no such thing as a bank, and I would have to carry more cash on my person than usual—enough to last a whole week, with an extra sum in case of an emergency.

SOMETIMES I SPECULATED about where I would stay, for I was sure there was no hotel in Yanhuitlán. My thought was that either the priest or the municipal president would know of a family that would take me in. I liked the idea of living directly with the people, and I hoped there would be children in the family.

The plan of the monastery's second floor showed cells around three sides of the cloister. Consciousness of those cells began to influence my first idea about accommodations. Perhaps the quarters would be too cramped living with a family in a small house. Such an arrangement would allow no privacy, no chance to have any quiet periods by myself. Then the idea of a cell came to me.

That's what I'd like best, I said to myself, a cell. I'd like to have a cell as a private room and take my meals with a family.

The thought of that cell grew in my mind. In it I would have space to leave my drawing things lying around unmolested. And perhaps, in some mysterious way, living in the very place where the friars had lived would enable me to make contact with them—to feel the presence of their amiable ghosts perhaps, or to come into some insight of their lives or natures.

MOST OF US in the United States take bathrooms too much for granted. I know I had, for when Baltasar Tarasco, the genial hotel manager, brought the matter up, I realized that in all my thinking about living in Yanhuitlán I had not given toilet facilities a thought.

"*No hay baños en Yanhuitlán*," he said jokingly, meaning there were no bathrooms there.

His comment prompted me to put three further things into my bag: a towel, a cake of soap and a roll of toilet paper.

The final item of my equipment was something no one had suggested to me. It was my own idea. Mexicans, I had found, both young and old, love *dulces*. So I had gone to a candy shop and bought almost six pounds of hard sugar candies. Each sweet was individually twisted in a bit of cellophane, and the girl had followed my instructions of putting them in seven paper sacks, one for each day of the week.

III

ARRIVAL

WEDNESDAY, SEPTEMBER 23, 1953, was the day I arrived in Yanhuitlán. Because of the habit of noting times at significant thresholds—a habit carried over from my training as a reporter—I know the exact minute. For as the bus pulled to a halt in Yanhuitlán, I consulted my watch. It was 10:48 A.M.

If I was noticed at all, the picture I presented in getting off the bus was that of a medium-sized fellow in an open shirt, a tweed coat and a pair of army suntans, who was carrying a lumpy orange brief bag in one hand, and in the other a loudly striped market bag, with a green tube projecting from one corner.

There were no villagers nearby and I was relieved to find myself alone. I had never stood on a threshold quite like this before and I wanted a moment to realize the situation. Perhaps I had never fully believed I would carry out my scheme, for I remember saying to myself incredulously, I'm really here.

Then I lifted my head and took a deep breath so I could let my spirit break out of the small shell represented by the bus and spread out into this vast pantheon of valley and sky. Gray clouds were moving north, and I had the sense that never had I seen so great an expanse of ragged overcast.

The town, I knew, was 7,350 feet up, and as I drank deeply of the mountain air I also drank deeply of the quietness. The distinctness with which I could hear a few birds and, far off, the crowing of a rooster underlined the silence of the village. In a place with any overall hum such tiny sounds would not have carried so far.

Memory plays strange tricks. I would have sworn I had forgotten that little cantina with the red brick porch, and that twisted sapotal tree at the foot of the steps leading up to the monastery. But when I saw them again I

19

knew they had persisted in that curious realm of the mind that holds those things which are not repressed completely, yet which can only be recalled when seen again. They had been part of the scene when I had stood at the same spot three years before, waiting for the bus to take me away; and I recognized them with a curious sense of the lost past leaping to life.

Just as vividly, I recognized the unusual coloration of the valley. Red, white and green—the colors of Mexico, but here the shades were as if on a flag that was old and a little dirty. Earth red in the valley and up to a remarkably even line along the eroded hillsides; rock white, and therefore tinged with gray, in a wide band of exposed limestone above the red line; and tea green where small trees covered the crowns of the hills.

By this time the bus had disappeared. The link had been cut. So, taking another deep breath, I started up the steps, feeling I was heading into one of the great adventures of my life.

The front doors of the church had the massive shutness of things that haven't been opened for years. But I knew where the porter's lodge was, so I made my way around the south wing until I came to the entrance door. It too, was shut. Not only shut, but padlocked. I knocked a number of times, but got no response.

The eminence on which the monastery stands is so high, extensive and overgrown that it suggests a natural rise. In actuality, though, it is man-made. It is a vast platform, whose existence helps account for the monastery.

It was not merely millionaire's folly that led the Spaniards to build so sumptuous a monastery in this place. I have indicated in the story of the nail-paring captain that Yanhuitlán was a rich reward for a conquistador. It was such a plum because it was the greatest population center of the Mixteca and nearby rivers contained gold. Wealth and an ample labor supply had enabled its pre-Conquest rulers to build this enormous terrace as a platform for their temples and sacred buildings. Since the Spaniards wanted gold more than anything else in Mexico, and since it became their policy to build monasteries where there were large native settlements, Yanhuitlán was a logical place for a major establishment. Since, too, the Spaniards tried to stamp out the pagan religions by building Christian churches on the sites of the old temples, the platform was the natural choice for the church.

These facts, however, were not in my mind as I stood at the door. My concern was rousing the caretaker. After a fairly long wait, I decided to seek help in locating him. I walked to the eastern edge of the platform and found myself looking down into the patio of a one-storied house. I was at its roof level because the house was built flush against the platform on the ground below. The situation can be grasped by a glance at the plan on page 60. There the shape of the platform is shown by the broken line and the house into whose patio I was looking is indicated by the number 6.

There was a woman in the patio hanging up some laundry. I called down to her and asked if she could tell me where I could find Señor Blanco. She was the first villager I had spoken to and I was relieved at her cordiality. She said she'd send her son up to guide me.

I got out a sack of candies in readiness for the boy's arrival. He proved to be a ten-year-old, and, when he had looked in the sack to see what it contained, he put in his hand and pulled out a fistful of candies.

It taught me a lesson. Apparently, when it came to *dulces*, the children of Yanhuitlán were not so polite as children in other Mexican places. I made a mental note that if I wanted my supply to last a week I'd better not offer free access to the sack again. In future, I said to myself, I'll hand them out one by one.

As it turned out, the boy did not have to do any guiding. While I was speaking to him, a man came hurrying towards me. His appearance was a little incongruous. Everything about his clothing was North American, including his black and gray lumberjack sweater-coat. But over that coat—and it was this that gave the touch of incongruity—he was wearing a native sarape, a blanket about the size of a bath mat, which he had got over his head by a slit in the center.

The man was Sr. Blanco. And Sr. Blanco was not the old man with the interchangeable hats, but a younger man of a more Indian type.

To my surprise, he knew my name. Ignacio Marquina, then head of the Institute, had written about my coming and he had been watching for me for almost a week. I think he was as excited as I was, and I was grateful for that advance warning from the Institute. It meant there was no need to explain why I had come, and it disposed of a difficulty I had envisaged—that of overcoming the suspicions of a reluctant minor official.

How long did I propose to stay? he asked. A week, I said.

I think that surprised him, for probably he had expected I would come and go like most sightseers, staying no longer than a day at the most.

Where would I stay? he asked. Perhaps I could live in one of the cells, I replied.

That is impossible, he said. There are no cells you could live in. Some are in ruins and the priest has all the rest.

But apparently a solution suggested itself to him, for he took my bags and started towards his house. On the way he confided his problem to me. He had an extra room, but it had no bed.

On excursions to the Isthmus of Tehuantepec I had slept in the open on the cement terrace of a cantina, so this did not faze me. I told him I didn't need a bed. If he could lend me a *petate* I could sleep on the floor.

His house was at ground level not far from the southeast corner of the platform. Because this corner was eroded we were able to descend along a sloping path.

His front door was one of several wooden doors set in a long white-washed wall. Inside, the house consisted of two rooms, one leading into the other, with both aligned parallel to the street. The first room was lit by the front door, but the other was pitch black—or so it seemed to me after coming in out of the light. In the darkness I stumbled over a tiny kitten and almost fell against a sewing machine. The kitten darted away with a frightened squeak.

By the time I had righted myself, my eyes were accustomed to the dimness. I noticed calendars on the wall and, in one corner, a big double bed. It looked thoroughly uncomfortable, for it was a factory-made affair with metal end-boards. And there was no mattress on the sheet of chain mail that did for springs—only a straw mat and a roughly woven blanket of black and gray wool.

A small, slim woman of about thirty-five came into the room and I was introduced to Señora Blanco. She had braided hair, tiny gold earrings studded her pierced ears, and she was wearing a rust-colored dress with a dark-blue rebozo over her shoulders. Her nice dry hand returned a firm clasp and I liked her immediately. The news that I was going to occupy their spare room seemed to strike her agreeably.

The extra room was at the corner of the long wall, two doors down from that of the Blancos. When I was shown in, I realized it was part of an adjoining house, and I knew it was constructed of adobe, for although its front was coated with white stucco, the unfaced side along the lane revealed the underlying bricks of brown mud. The caretaker explained the house belonged to his mother, who was living in a ranchito a little way out of the village.

It was true, the room did not have a bed. But against the wall opposite the door was something resembling a high altar. It was a crude wooden counter that had been salvaged from a store. And flattening his hand on it, the caretaker asked if I could sleep there.

"*Por supuesto,*" I replied, and I was able to say "of course" with such good-humored alacrity because it was decidedly better than my expectations. And the floor in this case would have been a real trial, for it was paved with square bricks so hard, worn and ancient that at first I thought they were cobbles.

As the caretaker went off to fetch something, I said to myself, I may not have a cell, but it does look like a chapel. And the notion came from the whitewashed chapels with the beamed ceilings I had seen in pueblos in New Mexico. The impression was heightened by the little benches against the wall and by the round-arched opening at eye level in one of the panels of the wooden doors. The peephole was fitted with a flap and it let in the only light when the doors were shut.

The caretaker returned with a wooden coat hanger. But when he looked around at the bare walls he saw nothing to hang it on. Off he went again and returned with a nail and a hatchet, which he used to drive the nail into the wall. Thereafter he made a number of trips back and forth, fetching the things he felt I needed to make me comfortable. So I could have facilities for washing, he brought a round tin basin and a bucket of water. But he warned me the water in the pail was not drinkable. On his next trip he returned with drinking water. It was in a gin bottle, precariously capped with an inverted tumbler.

Besides the counter and the benches, the only other furniture in the room had been a small table. Thinking I might want to write at it, Sr. Blanco brought a small wooden chair for my convenience, and a freshly laundered patchwork cloth for the table's adornment.

As the arrangements were being made, I met another member of the family: a cream-colored mongrel, whose long tail arched up over his back. His name surprised me. It was Bobby. And Bobby trotted back and forth with his master, looking curiously into my room as we worked, but not daring to enter.

"Bobby's an American name," I said. "How did you happen to call your dog that?"

Then it came out that during the war years, when many Mexicans had been imported into the United States to work in the fields because the armed services had depleted the civilian manpower, Sr. Blanco had gone to California. He had worked as a *bracero*—a term for a day laborer derived from the fact that a laborer is one who works with his *brazos*, his arms. Sr. Blanco had been in California for two years and there he had heard many dogs called Bobby. A touch of nostalgia had led him to give his dog a Yankee name.

"How long have you been in charge of the monastery?" I asked.

"Since October 4, 1950," he replied. This led us to compare notes, and we realized we had missed each other by just a month on my first visit.

"Has a North American ever lived in Yanhuitlán?" I asked.

"No," he replied. "There have been tourists who have passed through, but no one has ever stayed here."

"And how many people are there in Yanhuitlán?" Without hesitation, he gave me the figure: 2,200. Then he went for the final load, the bedding.

I had suggested a *petate*, a thin mat made of interwoven strips of palm leaf that I knew Indians generally slept on. But the caretaker went me two better. He returned with three *petates*. Somewhere, too, he had found two clean sheets. And I knew where the roughly woven black and gray blanket came from. Their own bed. As he smoothed the blanket over the sheets he said happily: "Wasn't it lucky? I just bought the blanket yesterday."

Something in me dissolved. They had owned the blanket only a single night and yet here, in all sincerity, he was saying it was a stroke of luck they had it to give to a stranger.

If I had been back in the United States visiting a friend, I would have refused to accept the sacrifice. And I know no better way of conveying the spirit in which it was offered than to report that something in the man's bearing checked the refusal in my throat. To have even made a comment would have violated something. But my heart knew its own gratitude.

Where did I propose to eat? the man asked me.

"Perhaps you know a family that would give me meals."

"My wife could cook for you," he said, "but the meals would be very simple."

My limited Spanish vocabulary, lacking the words for stern-faced or frowning, obliged me to answer in an almost Biblical way.

"Better simple meals served with smiles than elegant dinners served with a face of stone."

I think that helped put him at ease about the fare he and his wife could offer, so the matter was settled. To tell the truth, I was a little disappointed that I would not be eating in a family where there were children, but I was relieved the arrangements were so easily made. I could not quite let it go at that, though.

In the United States most of us are anxious to be prompt in paying our own way, and we have come to calculate our exchanges too much in terms of dollars and cents. Thus, largely so he would have the assurance I would gladly pay the rate he proposed, I asked him how much my room and board would be.

"For the room," he said, "*nada*," and he wigwagged his hand to underline that there would be no charge.

For the meals . . . and here he paused to think. Then he broke into a smile and said "Let us decide on that *más tarde*." This meant later, and I knew it would be tactless to press the matter.

Since I had done most of my unpacking by this time, I gave the caretaker his bottle of mezcal and showed him the bottles I had brought for the other men. Could he give me their names? The priest, he said, was Lorenzo Hernández Krauler. The municipal president was Venustiano Rodríguez.

Elation and excitement were my uppermost emotions, but I must have felt more insecure than I realized, for I was anxious to lose no time in getting those goodwill-generating bottles into the hands of the two most influential citizens. I did not feel free either to settle down or to lift pencil to sketch book until I knew both men were aware of my mission and had given their approval. Accordingly, I asked Sr. Blanco if he could tell me where I could find them.

I think he was a little surprised that I should consider the distribution so urgent, but he was willing to do more than tell me where the men were. If I'd just wait while he took his own bottle home and told his wife where he was going, he'd take me to them.

Before we started off he drew the two wings of my front door together and when the two screw eyes met he hooked a padlock through them, clicked it shut and, with the faintest suggestion of ceremony, handed me the key. "*Su casa*," he said, meaning "your house."

I had been a little incredulous when Sr. Blanco said Yanhuitlán had 2,200 inhabitants. It seemed so much smaller than that. But when a block's walk brought us to the plaza I discovered why the village had struck me as tiny. I was accustomed to towns laid out in front of their principal churches. Thus I had assumed there was little more to Yanhuitlán than the few reed huts along the highway.

But in the plaza I saw that this village did not follow the usual pattern. It was laid out at the rear of the church. The single-storied, whitewashed buildings that surrounded the plaza were modest enough, but at least they were more substantial, and suggested a somewhat larger village than the huts. They made me willing to accept Sr. Blanco's breakdown of his total: 800 people in the center of the town and 1,400 in the surrounding ranchos.

Because the highway had been built in front of the monastery, the accident of being behind had saved the plaza from falling victim to modern progress. It had retained its ancient peaceful character. And that character was quite different from that of most Mexican plazas. The rule is a bandstand in the center with formal plantings in the triangular spaces between the paved walks that run like the stripes of the British flag. But this plaza had no formal planting. It was grassy. Its only paths were dirt footpaths. And it had no bandstand. The central object was a large circular fountain, and around this fountain grew a ring of beautiful old ash trees whose branches seemed to join hands with the rhythmic grace of the life-size pink dancers in one of Matisse's most famous paintings.

As we passed the fountain, I apologized to Sr. Blanco for all my mistakes in Spanish. *"Al contrario,"* he replied, "I am the one who should apologize to you for not speaking *any* of your language."

The sentence was simply spoken, but it filled me with wonder. Talk about Old World courtesy. Could any gentle, elderly European scholar have designed a sentence so perfectly calculated to set a New World visitor at ease? Yet its framer was a man of predominantly Indian blood, who had been brought up as a *campesino*, or, as we might put it, a sharecropper. Perhaps he did not realize it, but it was a landmark in our relationship. It ended forever any difficulty of communication between us.

The north side of the plaza was bounded by a long, whitewashed building, and the arcade in front of it, with its thick square pillars and its twenty-one arches, suggested a California mission. The building contained the school, the jail and the municipal offices. It was to the latter we went.

El Presidente had gone for the day and would not be back until the morning. But I met El Síndico, the second highest official. His name was Vicente Gutiérrez and he was a dignified little man wearing a correct black suit. Sr. Blanco told him about my purpose in the village and about the recommendations of the Institute. So I felt covered as far as the municipality was concerned, even if I hadn't delivered my bottle.

The building housing the school and the municipal offices was severely plain, but it was well constructed and its rooms, judging from the Presidente's, were spacious. Walking back through the red-tiled arcade, I asked Sr. Blanco when the building had been put up.

"1862," he said.

The date was an interesting one. It was the year of the French Invasion, and that invasion, I knew, had plunged Mexico back into warfare, thereby cutting short the brief period of peace and reconstruction after Juárez and his followers had defeated the Conservatives in the terrible Three Years' War.

"Then it was shortly after the suppression of the monasteries," I said to Don Gabriel. For that suppression had been one of the first steps of the reconstruction.

I think he was surprised at my alertness to the era. Perhaps, too, he was pleased that I was acquainted with his country's history. It led him to tell me more.

"Yes," he said, "the municipal building was constructed when Juárez was trying to do things for the people. And do you know where the money came from?"

I waited with proper expectancy.

"From the sale of eight silver candelabras taken from the church," he said.

"Do you mean to say eight candelabras raised enough money for this whole building?"

"Yes. They were big and very sumptuous, and they were plated with gold."

I had read of the looting of the monasteries after the suppression of the religious orders, but this was the first instance I'd come across of the loot being used to such constructive purpose. Looking at the sturdy, serviceable building, I didn't begrudge the loss of the candelabras.

The jail occupied only one room. Glancing through its wooden grid, I saw it was empty.

Diagonally across from the arcade, at the foot of the old stairs leading up to the monastery, was a large open booth. It had a beguiling name: La Providencia. As we passed it, Don Gabriel waved a cheery greeting to the owner, a plump, jolly man who was leaning over the counter on his elbows.

Then we headed for the monastery, hoping for better luck in delivering the other bottle. Across from the entrance, a tin-roofed shelter jutted from the ruined end of the stone precinct wall. This makeshift garage housed a modest sedan. I pointed to the gray Ford and asked Sr. Blanco whose it was.

"It's the priest's," he said. "He's the only man in town rich enough to own an automobile."

The plan of the second floor of the monastery on page 296 indicates cells on three sides of the cloister—small ones on the west and south and large ones on the east. The first large one stands by itself, but the other three open onto a joint passageway. These the priest had taken over for his personal quarters. When we gained admission, I saw he had cut doors through the dividing walls in order to have an apartment of three interconnecting rooms. The center one was his parlor. It had whitewashed walls, a high, beamed ceiling and a floor of unglazed red tiles.

Glass in the windows, a bit of red Persian rug on the floor, a calendar on the wall, a cuckoo clock, a bentwood rocking chair with curlicues in its arms and a handsome modern radio were all I had time to observe before my attention was claimed by the priest himself.

In Mexico a man's mother's name is preserved in his own by being tacked on after that of his father. I knew therefore that, in having the name Lorenzo Hernández Krauler, the priest was the son of a woman named Krauler. That indicated what Don Gabriel had confirmed, a German mother. Yet I saw no hint of the Aryan in his appearance. He looked wholly Mexican, for he had swarthy skin and black hair that was cropped very close. He was short and cheerful and the compact rotundity of his body filled out his black cassock as smoothly as if it were the skin of a grape. He accepted the bottle of sacramental wine and said my project of drawing the monastery was agreeable to him. He didn't show the least interest in it, though. Nor did he offer any help.

He had been the priest of Yanhuitlán for sixteen years, he said, and he was leaving that afternoon for Oaxaca.

"Is he leaving for good?" I asked Sr. Blanco as we left his quarters.

"Oh, no," he replied, "he drives to Oaxaca every week. It's livelier than Yanhuitlán."

"What does he do there?"

"I don't know, but he owns two houses."

Descending the monumental stone stairway to the barrel-vaulted Hall of Meditation, we saw two Mexicans who were searching for a guide to take them through the building. They were truck drivers on their way to Salina Cruz, who had stopped to see the monastery.

The caretaker asked if I wanted to return to the house or to come along while he showed the truck drivers about. Wanting to familiarize myself with every corner so I could decide what to draw, I elected to be part of the tour.

The truck drivers were not really interested in the place, and after Sr. Blanco had swung open the large wooden doors from the cloister, it was incomprehensible to me that the two men could be so little impressed by the vastness of the white church with the beautiful ribbed ceiling and the high gold altars. A cursory look and they wanted to leave. Passing back through the cloister, their roving masculine eyes caught a glimpse of the priest's plump little maid in the upper gallery.

"*¿Hay monjas?*" they asked rather hopefully, meaning are there any nuns here? That Sr. Blanco and I could chuckle at the query in the same way showed us two bonds in common: similar humor and shared knowledge.

We both knew that because it was a Dominican friary there had never been any nuns there; that the idea of nuns in a male house, in fact, was a scandal. We understood, too, why the drivers had made the gaffe. In Spanish-speaking countries the word *convento* is used for both male and female establishments. Knowing they were visiting a *convento*, the men easily thought about nuns when they saw the pigeon-plump little maid.

It was almost two o'clock when the truck drivers left, and as the caretaker was locking up, I noticed the priest had already taken off for Oaxaca. His improvised garage was empty.

Since it was lunch time, I went to my room to wash. I poured some water from the bucket into the gray graniteware basin and then unwrapped my *extra gigante* bar of Palmolive, carefully saving the pale-green paper to serve as a soap dish. As I was drying my hands, the caretaker came to the door and gave me a benefit of his stay in California.

"Dinner is served," he said in a tentative English that he was delighted to hear was absolutely correct.

When I got to his house I was somewhat taken aback. An upright wooden chair, the mate of the one Sr. Blanco had brought to my room, was drawn up to the table, and there, on an embroidered napkin, was a single plate of rice soup. It looked tasty, but I felt uncomfortable that they had not set places for themselves. I asked them if they wouldn't eat with me.

"No, you eat," said the man. "We will eat later."

There was a spoon of blue tinware beside the white soup plate, so, seeing there was no help for it, I picked up the spoon and began. The second course consisted of boiled squash and I was surprised to see that the yellow flower had been cooked along with the vegetable. I ate it, flower and all.

I used the blue spoon, for there was no sign of a fork. With the third and final course—a few chunks of meat—I had to use the blue spoon once more, but this time as a knife, for there was no sign of that utensil either.

Sr. Blanco sat on the bed alongside the table. His wife, whose name was Guadalupe, sat on a wooden block beside her portable tin stove. They were so friendly and chatty, so much at ease, that I began to feel less awkward about eating in solitary state.

The little cat came to my shoe, looked up with cold, demanding green eyes, and went, "whah, whah."

"How old is the kitten?" I asked.

"Six months," said Sr. Blanco.

"What's its name?"

"She hasn't got a name."

"You give me a little time," I said. "When I get to know her character I'll give her a name."

Bobby stood on the other side, also looking up. But the dog was a figure of silent dignity, with hopeful gratitude, rather than imperiousness, in his gentle face. I gave them each a shred of meat. Meanwhile I met the two remaining members of the family, a little brown chicken and a young black turkey the same size as the chick. They too had the run of the bed-living-dining-room-kitchen.

Since I wanted to tell Sra. Blanco about our morning, I picked out the gaffe of the truck drivers as the most amusing incident. Apparently Sr. Blanco wasn't sure his wife understood my Spanish, so he added: "They asked if the cura's maid was a nun." Perhaps it was an even better joke than I realized. At all events, Lupe laughed heartily. And I knew that from then on we would always be bringing her back the jokes from our excursions.

Since I did not want to delay their dinner, I excused myself after I had eaten and went to my room for a treat I had been promising myself since my arrival—a siesta. Lying on the counter, as if I were a knight on a sarcophagus, I observed how the spaces between the ceiling beams were spanned by closely packed sticks about the size of kindling wood.

I did not fall asleep immediately, but, oh, the blessed silence! And lying there I had an experience that reminded me of a harpsichord recital I had heard in New York. As the tiny, rippling notes had begun I had experienced more than the beauty of their delicate sounds. I had felt, too, an easing of

WEEK IN YANHUITLÁN

tension. Why, I had asked myself, should this feeling of relaxation be induced by this music? The spirit of Couperin perhaps had something to do with it, but as the sense of ease and refreshment grew even deeper, the explanation came to me.

In a big city, where there are many noises, we defend ourselves against the ugly sounds. We build up noisebreaks, as it were, almost the way farmers erect windbreaks against damaging winds. But because we set up those noisebreaks unconsciously, we are not aware of the effort involved in rearing and then holding them firm. What was happening to me in that concert hall was this. I was so eager to hear every last little sound of the feathery instrument that I was welcoming what I heard, instead of excluding it. And I realized the extent of the strain of the struggle against unwelcome sound in the relief I felt when I was no longer engaged in it.

I was not hearing Couperin on the harpsichord in that brick-paved room with the whitewashed walls, but the silence of Yanhuitlán was having the same effect. It was so deep, so prolonged and so unbroken that, realizing there were no ugly noises to resist, I was shifting from the braced tension of excluding the sounds around me to the relaxed eagerness of welcoming them for the joy they brought. And in that spirit I fell asleep.

IV
THE FIRST DRAWING

In my advance thinking about drawing the monastery, I had thought especially about where to begin. Taking only myself into account, I wanted to start with something easy, some relatively simple details. The windows with the stone tracery, being unique features, suggested themselves. But then I remembered the reader. Details would be meaningless to him until he knew the total layout and could tell where those details belonged.

Obviously, then, my first drawing would have to be a big over-all one, an introductory sketch that would give a good general idea of the main edifice. This meant I had to find an angle which revealed the largest number of the monastery's most significant features.

I knew the angle would have to include the church's west front, so after my siesta I took a sketchbook and headed for the highway. From the southwest, the monastery, with its vast ruined outbuildings, looked decidedly picturesque. But, alas, the pages of my sketchbook were only nine inches by twelve. I did not have space enough on the page for a mass of buildings so spread out—that is, if I was going to carry out my intention of drawing everything on a scale large enough to be intelligible.

From the south, too, it was impossible to see the damlike buttresses, pierced by the high-arched passageways.

From the north, however, not only could one see those characteristic buttresses, but the church presented a compact, easily understood appearance. What is more, it made a composition well suited to a sketchbook whose tall pages were hinged spirally at the top. The north angle won.

Because I intended to dash off hundreds of drawings, I had equipped myself with four sketchbooks. The first brown one was earmarked for DE-

TAILS, while on the cover of the blue one I had printed WHOLE VIEWS. It was the blue one I had under my arm. My only other equipment was a soft pencil and a razor blade.

Fortunately, such things were easy to carry, for once I had found the general area from which I wanted to depict the church, I still had to locate the best spot from which to work. This was complicated by a particular requirement. My plan while in Yanhuitlán was to make pencil sketches that would later provide the basis for line drawings in pen and ink. And I had established a limiting principal. I was not going to use a hint of a shadow. Thus I had to discover where the solidity and character of the forms displayed themselves in such a way that they could be conveyed by outline alone.

A little way up the road from the brick cantina, the west front could still be seen almost head on, while enough of the northern flank was visible to reveal the buttresses. When I was in a position where the linings of the arched buttresses showed enough to suggest the thickness of the piers, I knew I had the best location. But if the spot was fine for visualizing, it was hardly ideal for sketching. One step back and I'd be in a deep ditch; one step forward and I'd be on the open highway. But not enough cars were passing to make proximity to the road a real problem. More serious was the fact that there was nothing to sit on. Not a rock, not a stump nor a fallen log. Still, I was more interested in my task than my comfort, so I began to sketch standing up.

This position was all right as long as I was merely blocking in the masses lightly. But when it came to drawing lines that required pressure to make them dark, I found I could not hold the sketchbook sufficiently steady. Sitting on the ground and bracing it with my knee was the only solution, so I started the next stage, seated like a tailor, on the shoulder of the road.

The façade, being seen almost flat, was fairly easy, but I had considerable difficulty with that northern flank. Not only was it at an angle to the picture plane, but, because it was retreating into the distance, I had to draw it in perspective. And sitting had lowered my eyes by about three feet, aggravating the chief drawback of my chosen spot. It was so much below the church that the edge of the pre-Conquest platform obscured the church's base line. I was like a man in the front row of a theater watching a dancer whose feet were cut off by the footlights.

I must explain, too, that I had an irrational notion carried over from figure drawing—that it was cheating to use instruments. In New York something had prompted me to put a little plastic ruler in my bag, but because of my feeling of the sanctity of doing everything freehand, I had deliberately not brought it out with me. Thus I had no straight edge to help me with the building's straight lines. The wavering of my hand in trying to draw long perpendiculars increased my difficulties. Being preoccupied and nervous I was in no mood to talk as I was struggling to get all those uprights correct.

As luck would have it, two curious villagers came and stood nearby just as I was having the most trouble. In rubbing out mistaken lines, I had worn the pencil's eraser to the brass and I was anxious to keep at the drawing till I had it right. Still, I didn't want to ignore the men. So when they proved too polite to come close enough to look over my shoulder. I interrupted what I was doing, got up and took the half-finished sketch to show them. That satisfied the taller man and he walked away, but the shorter man, whose name was Vicente Cruz, was a chatty soul.

He sat down beside me as I resumed work. He knew one or two English phrases because he had received some correspondence lessons from the Hemphill School in Los Angeles. He tried them out in the course of telling me he was making an excursion to a nearby town.

As he talked, I nodded occasionally and said "*Sí*." But I was too absorbed in my task to pay much attention, and, to tell the truth, I was relieved when the sight of his approaching bus led him to shake hands and make a hurried departure.

What made the buttresses so difficult was that so many of the verticals were so close together. I hated the mess I was making as I kept rubbing out lines that were improperly placed. Yet often the substitute ones did not seem any better. Despite all the smearing, though, I kept working doggedly to make the pencil lines have the same relationship to each other on the paper that the building lines had to each other on the obliquely seen flank.

My eagerness to achieve exactitude was dictated by knowing the subtle way a perfectly drawn outline can reveal the nature of a form. I knew that northern flank provided an opportunity for such a revelation and I knew that if it was outlined correctly my drawing would suggest what I wanted to convey: that the church was built of stone and had been standing there for almost four hundred years. I was anxious, too, to suggest the massive weight that had made the corner buttresses necessary. They were not part of the original plan. But the pre-Conquest platform, made of rubble, had not been sufficiently stable to sustain the ponderous tonnage of the monastery. The platform had settled under the crushing weight, and that settling had caused the church walls to crack. The corner buttresses were added to shore up the splitting walls so the whole fabric would not come crashing down.

What to call those monumental bracers? The arched spaces between the walls and the outer piers suggested the term "flying buttresses." But it was ironic to think of those pachyderms ever taking to the air. Stepped, or perhaps perforated buttresses, I decided, would be better.

Meanwhile, hadn't I drawn the perforation in the furthest buttress too tall? I had it almost reaching the first step. I sketched it in lower, and saw the effect was right. Finally, the whole flank was approximately correct.

I breathed a sigh of relief and turned to the carving of the façade. Because it was surface ornament that could be sketched in roughly, I worked more freely. Since it gave me little trouble and I felt more relaxed, I thought about the interlude with the chatty Vicente.

In imagining my project in advance, I had envisioned myself knocking off sketches almost as a sideline and spending most of my time getting to know the villagers. Yet how differently it had turned out. Here I had been so absorbed in my drawing I had almost ignored the first villager who had gone out of his way to be friendly. Clearly, too, drawing was going to be harder and more engrossing work than I had anticipated.

And the time it was taking! I had been at this first drawing two hours and still it wasn't completed. I glanced at the sky. It had been a little chilly all day and the gray blanketing clouds were continuing northward. It was past five. Would the light last long enough to allow me to finish the brick belfry? Even now the cornices and the mouldings were a little hard to see. But my hand seemed to move with greater sureness and I had got the belfry's proportions right in the first blocking in.

My attention being focused on the right-hand tower, I noticed two black lines across it that puzzled me. They weren't structural, for the lower one crossed in front of the little window. But from such a distance I could not make them out. My first impulse was to omit them, but since I wanted my drawings to be reliable records, I changed my mind and put them in.

Then I held the drawing off at arm's length. On the whole, I was pleased with everything except the way the line depicting the edge of the platform obscured the foundation. The church looked cut off at the ankles.

After a moment's thought, I exclaimed explosively: This isn't a photograph! Why not go up to the platform and draw in the base line from there?

The decision was clarifying and liberating. I saw that it didn't matter if I could not see the foundation from the road. What I wanted was the effect of reality; not just what a camera could take from one fixed position.

When I got to the top of the steps I saw five young women in a circle, feebly tossing around a soft volleyball. They had bobbed hair and were dressed like North American girls, but one would have to travel far in the United States to see girls of their age having so pleasant a time playing such a kindergarten game.

Wanting to be friendly, and acting on the assumption that everyone likes to see a sketch of something familiar, I asked permission to show them my drawing.

"*Que lindo,*" said one, meaning how fine.

"*Muy bonita,*" said another, meaning very pretty. They thanked me for showing it and resumed their gentle tossing.

Revising the drawing meant erasing the old uneven line that had represented the edge of the platform. Then I lowered the verticals till they gave the right appearance and began drawing in new lines to indicate the level ground.

Being much nearer the church, I saw that the black lines which had puzzled me were iron bands. I noticed, too, that the stones at the corner clasped by the bands differed from most of the building stones. They were as pale as pink hand lotion, whereas the other stones of the tower were the same sand pink as the rest of the monastery. The paler stones, too, were much less weathered. Then I remembered De Gante's photograph of the shattered belfry. This was the tower whose corner had been reconstructed. Those iron bands, I realized, had been bound around it for extra security.

As I was putting the finishing touches to the new base line, Sr. Blanco, the caretaker, came around the corner of the church. He expressed approval of the drawing. Standing by as I finished up, he looked humorously at the five Graces tossing the ball and made a comment that gave us another laugh over the truck drivers' gaffe. He dubbed them "*Las Monjitas*"—the little nuns.

Up close, the church was more overbearing than it had been from the distance. The two great pylons of masonry on either side of the heavily carved façade seemed almost menacing. And there was an off-balance effect because of the absence of any belfry on the left. Thinking perhaps the left pylon had once supported a tower matching the one on the right, I asked Sr. Blanco if this was so.

"No," he replied. "The front of the church was never completed." Then he surprised me with further information: the brick bell tower with the tiled dome was not part of the original scheme. It was added later.

"When?"

"In the eighteenth century."

Pointing to the iron bands, I asked if repairing the tower had been part of the Institute's work. "No," he said. "The work was done by the people of the village."

I asked for the details, and, as one trained to gather facts for a scrupulous newspaper, I was delighted at the preciseness with which he told the story.

The Institute, he said, did not start showing an interest in the monastery until 1944—that is, until after the opening of the highway to Oaxaca had changed Yanhuitlán from a remote and inaccessible village to a town on one of the principal roads of the Republic. The damage to the tower was done before the highway was built.

It began in 1931 when an earthquake caused a crack in the pylon. Then in 1939 the outer corner gave way and about a third of the belfry came crashing down. The tower stood in ruins for three years and then the town undertook its repair. An old priest from Oaxaca, José Santa Cruz, planned the reconstruction and supervised the labor. He was able to do both because he had been an engineer before taking holy orders.

Although the project took five months, it required only about three hundred dollars. It cost so little because the only money that had to be laid out was for materials and for the salaries of a few skilled masons. The rest of the labor was free, for the men of the village—and there was hardly one who did not pitch in—donated a day's work each week until the job was finished.

V

PUESTA DEL SOL

BACK IN MY ROOM, I had an urge to clean up my sketch, so I went to the striped bag which contained my drawing things. As I fished into it for the soft eraser, my fingers closed on the little plastic ruler. It presented a mighty temptation. Perhaps, I rationalized, it was all right to use a ruler *after* a sketch was done. I decided to weaken.

Because the room was already dark, I had to take the work to the front door. Here the light was clear and golden for, not long before, the sun, which had been obscured all day, had broken through the clouds.

Sitting on the threshold, I contentedly erased the false strokes. And as I used the transparent ruler to make the straight lines clearer and firmer, I blessed the last minute thought that had led me to pop it into my luggage. The notion that I could have got along without it, I saw, was a sign of my inexperience with architectural subjects. In using the ruler, though, I found to my surprise that my eye was pretty good. My uprights were nearly all true perpendiculars and my freehand straight lines bowed very little.

I was so intent on my corrections I scarcely noticed the approach of a young fellow with a little boy skipping beside him. But when I looked up and saw them almost in front of the house, I called out: "*¿Quiere ver mi dibujo?*"—do you want to see my drawing? And I rose to meet them half-way.

"*¡Qué milagro!*" the youth exclaimed. What a miracle! And I lowered the sketchbook so the little boy could see it too.

The small boy was wearing a sombrero and a bathmat-type sarape, but the older boy was dressed with the slightly modified formality of a city dweller visiting a small town. And that, as it turned out, was what he was doing. He came from Puebla. His name was Alfonso Cruz, and he was visiting his aunt in Yanhuitlán.

"Are you brothers?" I asked. "No, cousins," they replied.

So that explained the pride and hero worship in the small boy's attitude. He was out walking with his cousin from the big city.

"What is your name?" I asked the youngster. "Eliel," he replied.

"And how old are you?"

"Ten."

"He is the son of my aunt," amplified Alfonso.

"And how old are you?"

"Seventeen."

"Do you go to school in Puebla?"

"Yes, but now we are in vacations." And I knew he meant the ten or eleven free days that Mexican students have after celebrating Independence on September 16.

Sr. Blanco emerged from his house and came toward us.

"Good afternoon, Don Gabriel," said Alfonso.

My ear caught the appellation with delight. I already felt so friendly toward the caretaker that Sr. Blanco seemed too formal, yet I did not want to take the liberty of calling him simply by his first name. Don Gabriel was my solution.

The sky overhead was growing pink with the light of the setting sun. As a city man too cut off from the wonderful shows of nature, I was excited by the prospect of a sunset behind the western hills. Couldn't we go to see the light? I asked, pointing to the glowing sky. Everyone was willing and we climbed the slope to get an unobscured view.

In the ruined wall that extends from the south of the monastery is the rectangular gap shown on page 247. It was to the edge of this gap that Don Gabriel led me. And how my heart leapt at what I saw! The sky was coral, and because the sun had already disappeared behind them, the hills looked like cutouts of blue serge.

And what superb cutouts! Sweeping up from the southwest, the magnificent line of hills stretched as far north as the eye could see. Almost directly in front of us were five noble peaks. Wanting to memorize them, I asked Don Gabriel to name them one by one.

The first, which rose steeply from the valley floor in the south, was Jazmín. It was the closest and in the days before the Spaniards, it had been

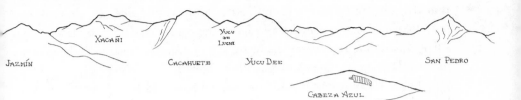

a sacred mountain. Here, Don Gabriel said, the villagers found *ídolos*, masks, jade beads and other evidences of religious ceremonies.

"Are there any tombs on it?" I asked. He pointed to two little lumps that broke the natural line of the long slope to the top. Those mounds, he said, covered tombs.

The second impressive peak, which had three tips to its flat-topped crown, was Xacañi.

The third was Cacahuete, and I smiled at the aptness of the name. It meant peanut and with a little imagination one could see the two vast pods.

Yucu, said Don Gabriel, was the Mixtec word for hill, and the fourth peak was Yucu Dee. Then with a quizzical look he asked if I knew what they called the little hill between it and Peanut. Naturally I didn't, and I gave him his opening.

"Yucu de Luchi," he said triumphantly. It meant baby hill. Couldn't I see how it looked like a *niño* between its parents?

The fifth, and in some respects the finest of the peaks, the most symmetrical of all, was San Pedro.

Don Gabriel then pointed to the foreground hill which had the gravel pit scooped out of it. Its Mixtec name was Deeque Ticue, he said, but the Spaniards called it Cabeza Azul, or Blue Head.

Dropping my eyes from the brows of the hills to nearer objects on the valley floor, I saw a large, walled enclosure with an arched gateway which stood at the end of a dirt road. The enclosure looked like a cemetery and Don Gabriel confirmed my guess by calling it a *campo santo*.

The dirt road, which was about a half-mile long, ran directly toward the church. And the brick cantina stood at the point where the road met the highway. Scattered around the cantina were the thatched huts, many embowered in trees. And surrounding the cemetery and extending all the way to the foothills were open, cultivated fields.

It was peaceful, spacious and beautiful. And though I did not think of it at the time, perhaps our group had its own picturesqueness. Anyone behind us would have seen the two boys, the tourist and the pointing guide silhouetted in the ruined gap against a sky that, having lost its fieriness, was turning the more subtle colors of mother-of-pearl.

As we chose places to sit, Don Gabriel indicated two stone stumps embedded in the edge of the gap. They were the stumps of pillars, he said. Then he directed my eyes to the walls of the gap. On each side was a corbel supporting just enough of the remains of an arch to allow the imagination to picture what had once been there. Even before Don Gabriel traced them, my mind's eye saw those three arches supported by two central pillars. And as the vision of them flashed before me, I imagined them framing the sunset. What we were seeing, I realized, would be still more beautiful if viewed through the white stone purity of those three lost arches.

Even in the daytime the framed view would be lovely, with the white clouds piling up splendidly behind the tea-green hills. But clearly the arches had been set up in the west primarily because of the sunsets. This loggia, then, which was now like a place where a tooth had been knocked out, had been planned especially to enhance this view.

I do not know which I felt the most keenly: the regret at its destruction, the thrill at the thought of its beauty, or the awe at the architectural imagination that had conceived such a stroke. And all my feelings were compounded in a bittersweet awareness of how much others had loved to come there too—especially in the evening when, at the setting of the sun, the serene arches had lent still more solace to the tranquilizing hills.

As we sat there with our feet dangling over the edge, we felt that ancient solace, and in our contentment we did not feel the need to talk. But knowing Alfonso was also an outsider stirred my curiosity as to when he began coming to the village.

His first visit, he said, was at the age of two. Then, through the facts he volunteered, he dramatized how isolated a pocket in the mountains this high valley had been until just a few years before.

"When I first came," he said, "there was no highway. We had to take the train. We got off at Parián. It was a long way from Yanhuitlán. We made the rest of the trip on horseback."

"How long did you have to ride?"

"Nine hours."

The railroad, then, had bypassed Yanhuitlán with a vengeance. But as I looked out over the valley I felt selfishly glad that there was no railroad to disturb its peace, or to blacken its fields with long trails of sooty smoke.

But what about the days before railroads? I asked Don Gabriel if Yanhuitlán had not been on the main road to Oaxaca in colonial times.

It was, he said. The road was called *el camino de las diligencias.*

The diligences—the word conjured up eighteenth-century coaches drawn by teams of horses.

The railroad to Oaxaca, I knew, had been built by a British firm and it had been opened in 1892. So that was another reason for the shrinking of Yanhuitlán. Sixty-one years ago, this town, which had been on the main artery of commerce for more than three hundred years, suddenly found itself nine hours away from the new route through which all the traffic was flowing. No wonder it lost out to towns nearer the railroad.

We fell into silence. But because I was less composed than the others, I was the one who started talking again.

"What do you call it," I asked (and I had to resort to the nearest equivalent I could phrase in Spanish), "when the sun goes to bed?"

"Puesta del sol," said Alfonso.

And we sat there until the last color had gone from the sky.

Alfonso and Eliel walked us back to Don Gabriel's house. There they politely shook hands to say good-bye.

"Hasta mañana," said Alfonso as he took my hand. I knew this meant "until tomorrow." I did not realize it also meant I had made a friend.

The Blancos' all-purpose room was lit only by a candle standing in a small tin can on the table. I was surprised at how much illumination the candlelight gave and at how beautiful it was. It transformed the drab room, with its ugly brown beadstead, into something Rembrandt might have painted.

The meal Lupe served was perhaps the simplest I ever ate. It consisted of a roll and a cup of very feeble coffee. I was tired and hungry, yet my feeling was not of disappointment for getting so little. On the contrary, I felt gratitude for getting so much. I was touched that out of their poor store they could spare me this.

As I broke off pieces of the roll, I wondered why I had such a deep sense of appreciation. It was partly because I eat so often in restaurants and this was a meal served with the utmost kindness in a home. It was also partly because of the bread itself. There was no competing flavor, not even that of butter, and as my teeth sank through the dry white center, meeting resistance at the crust, I was able to realize with a new keenness just what bread tasted like, and how good it was. Perhaps even more important, I had a sense of the symbolic nature of bread.

"Our daily bread"—the phrase I had often mumbled unthinkingly—was infused with new meaning. It was not just a vague metaphor for all food. Quite literally, it was the tangible substance I was savoring in one slow bite after another. And I could see why Jesus felt it was enough to ask. As I ate, too, I had a sense of the goodness and the wonder of the Giver of Bread.

Meanwhile, the little cat was being anxious about her daily bread. She was sitting at my shoe, looking up and uttering that unpleasant-sounding, imperious "whah, whah." I was all for giving her a piece, but Don Gabriel put out his leg and used the side of his foot to sweep her away. Back she came. She went "whah, whah" again and I gave her a bit of roll.

"You shouldn't encourage her," said Don Gabriel. "She's dangerous. The other day she leaped right onto my cheese as I was lifting it to my mouth."

Having finished her bread, the kitten began whah-whahing again. Suddenly I had an inspiration.

"I have it," I said. "The name for the cat."

"What?" asked Don Gabriel.

"Hambre."

Lupe and Don Gabriel laughted heartily, for *hambre* means hunger. And all three of us knew the hitherto anonymous kitten had irrevocably found her name.

At this meal I felt less uncomfortable about the Blancos not eating with me. I knew Lupe enjoyed sitting near the warmth of her charcoal stove, and Don Gabriel was at ease on the bed beside me. Nevertheless I was pleased when he agreed to take some coffee.

He was amazed that I did not want any sugar. He must have taken at least seven spoonfuls himself. I saw the chance of translating an American joke into Spanish.

"I see you like a little coffee with your sugar." It hit them just right, and I loved the way they chuckled.

Nearly everywhere I had traveled in Mexico I had been astonished at the people's artistic gifts. Each town seemed to have a specialty. Uruapan's was lacquer work, Azompa's pottery, Teotitlán del Valle's sarapes, and so on. I loved the regional arts and crafts, and one of my chief curiosities about Yanhuitlán was to discover what its people made.

Pottery? I asked. The answer was in the negative. Basketry? Again no. What about weaving? Three women made clothes, but there were no weavers. Any woodwork? No. Leatherwork? No. Not even a shoemaker? Only a man who repaired shoes.

Having exhausted most of the handicrafts, I turned to another field in which I had found Mexicans gifted. Surely, I felt, a number of villagers were musical. But again I drew a blank.

"Life here is very monotonous," said Don Gabriel. "There is little diversion."

"What do people do in the evenings?"

"They go to bed," he replied. "They are all *campesinos* here. They get up very early in the morning. They work all day in the fields. At night they are tired and ready for sleep."

"What are their crops?"

"*Maíz, trigo, frijoles, alpiste.*"

The first three were easy to translate—corn, wheat and beans. But what was *alpiste?* Don Gabriel tried to suggest it by approximate things I might understand. I offered guesses to learn if I was getting warm. But it was no use. Finally he got down his dictionary, which might show a picture.

To look up the word, he was obliged to bring the red dictionary close to the candle on the table. As he searched through the book the light shone upward on one side of his face.

It is curious how memories of paintings heighten our powers of seeing things. In that beautiful chiaroscuro I got an unforgettable picture of his face—the thick black hair, the coppery skin, the heavy eyelids, the somewhat knobby nose and the expression in which melancholy and tranquillity were almost equally blended. It was as if among the candlelit studies of Georges de la Tour one had suddenly come upon a portrait of an American Indian.

The picture broke up as he found the word. There was no illustration, but with the aid of the definition I learned *alpiste* is a birdseed grown to feed canaries.

As he put the dictionary away, he confided with a sigh the chief drawback of his life: "*Falta de libros.*" And since the lack of books was something I felt sharply in the army, I both knew what he missed and was drawn closer to him through learning how much books meant to him.

Wanting to let them have their own meal, I suggested I would like to retire.

As we left his house, we stepped into total darkness. It took me aback. I had not realized that Yanhuitlán, being without electricity, had no street lights. But Don Gabriel had prepared himself by bringing a flashlight. He lighted me to my room and held the beam on the padlock as I unlocked it. He kept it shining in the room, too, until I lighted the candle, which he had brought over in the morning. Like the one in his house, it stood in a can half full of sand.

As he snapped off the flashlight, he insisted that I keep it in case of need. And before he left, his forethought led him to do one more thing. He took a sturdy log from the corner of the room and showed me how to brace the door shut by lodging the log's butt in a sunken seam before a paving brick a little higher than the others.

Was it necessary to set up such a barricade, I asked. Yes, he said. And with wishes for a good night's sleep he left.

Before going to bed, I turned to my diary. When the ten lines allotted were filled, I thought of a heading to summarize the day. "Received Kindly in Yanhuitlán" is what I wrote. In the upper right-hand corner I also put two numerals. The days of my vacation were limited. As a means of treasuring each one, I was counting them carefully. This was number twenty.

VI

THE WINDOWS

DURING THE TOUR with the truck drivers, a decision had crystallized: that I should devote my second day at the monastery to drawing its windows. This idea developed because on that tour I became aware that the fenestration was one of its most fascinating aspects. The windows with the tracery were only part of the story. The other windows, although smaller and less important, were almost equally unusual. And they were nearly all different. The unknown designer of the monastery, it seems, was a man who got bored if he ever did anything twice in the same way.

The second day, however, did not fall into neat chapter divisions like the first. The strands of drawing and living were interwoven. And because I was so eager to learn all I could of the town and the monastery, I often laid aside my sketching to follow the threads of exploration that were offered. So this chapter is not going to be a concentrated architectural study. There were incidents before I even started drawing. In the course of my work I was taken clambering over the roof of the church and poking into such corners of the town as its school and its post office. And after I had drawn the last window I was introduced to one of the regional games.

The day began for me at a quarter to seven, and just as I finished dressing, Don Gabriel came over to see if I was ready for breakfast. Though there was a nip in the air, he was not wearing his sarape over his checked sweater-coat. I saw why when I got to their room. The sarape, looking more than ever like a narrow mat, was on the bed. With a pang, I realized it was the couple's only covering through the chilly night.

There was no lack of warmth in their cordiality, though, and for breakfast Lupe produced a cup of hot milk, a fried egg and some tortillas.

To make the egg go as far as possible, I did what I had often seen Mexicans do with sparse delicacies. I put small bits of it in the center of a tortilla and rolled up the disklike corn cake into a sort of cigar which I proceeded to eat. The scraps of egg made a flavorsome filling for the nourishing but rather tasteless tortillas. When all the white was gone, I used what remained of the yolk as a spread for a final tortilla.

Don Gabriel was sitting at his usual place on the bed. He was both more lighthearted and more curious than he had been the day before. He asked what sort of work I did in New York. When I said I was a music critic, he proudly told of his musical experience in California. He had seen two operas, *Aïda* and *Romeo y Julieta,* and one—and was the word for it operetta?—*El Soldado Chocolate.*

Then he asked how I had slept on the *mostrador.*

Very well, I said. Actually that counter had been damned uncomfortable. But because it had struck me as funny, I could not resist telling them one incident. I had climbed onto the sarcophagus at eight o'clock. The gods, finally, were kind and I dropped into a very long, deep sleep. When I woke I was enormously relieved. Bright daylight was showing through the arched peephole in my door. The fear of an awful night vanished. I had slept through it. Gratefully, I got up and opened the door—only to find it was a mere eleven P.M. The brilliant light was that of the moon.

One thing I did not reveal was my nightmare. I dreamed a mob of villagers had stormed my room. They battered and pushed on the wooden doors. For a while the log bracing the doors held. But when it gave way, the doors were burst open and I was overwhelmed.

While I was finishing my egg-smeared tortilla, a man came to the Blancos' front door. I could tell Lupe was buying some meat from him, because she took the coppers to pay for it from a small cardboard box that was on the table.

How long, I wondered, could that white box bear the strain of my extra rations? They seemed so poor I was fearful that by evening they would find themselves in the position of not having the money needed for my food. Thus, after allowing enough time to elapse so they would not see a connection between their buying the meat and my thinking, I once more brought up the question of payment.

They had not had time to calculate how much my meals would cost, they said.

Couldn't I give them ten pesos a day? The peso was then worth about twelve cents, so this was roughly $1.20 in United States currency. I suggested the round figure so I could give them the money on the spot and be sure they were at least that much ahead.

Oh, no, they replied. That was too much. And again they asked me to postpone the matter.

It was a few minutes before eight o'clock when Don Gabriel and I set off on our second attempt to deliver El Presidente's bottle. The sky, I was relieved to see, was a flawless blue. The overcast of the day before and the chilliness of the night had given me the idea that perhaps, because of the village's great altitude, its weather was always raw and damp in the rainy season. But that cloudless, sun-filled sky proved this notion was wrong. Obviously it was going to be a beautiful day.

With the sun out, the plaza was lovelier than ever. The grass had an almost golden greenness, and, in contrast, there was the dark shade of the ash trees that grew like the Matisse dancers in the inner circle around the fountain.

Two men were sweeping the long, handsome portal as we entered the municipal offices.

El Presidente was not there, and he was not expected until ten-thirty or eleven. But the trip was not wasted. Returning, I looked up at the back of the monastery. Struck by the slanting early morning light, the complex of buildings had an aspect difficult to describe. It was not transfigured the way buildings sometimes are in afternoon light, but because of the brightness and the clarity, and the complete lack of shadow, it was revealed as I had scarcely ever seen a building revealed before.

How often, as a writer only for the printed page, I have envied playwrights. So much of their work is done for them by the stage designer. Thus all the playwright has to do is to order the curtain up and the playgoer gets not only the physical setting in its entirety, but, what is more important, he gets it with the instantaneousness of vision in real life.

It is that power of instant communication of scenic impression I envy most. For when the element of time is introduced—and inexorably words take time to read—much of the reality of visual experience escapes. So with my vision of the monastery in that particular eastern light I gained the things described below, but I gained them in the space of a moment—and not in the time it takes to tell about them.

I think all people from time to time have a flash of vision in which they see a scene or an object, not merely as one of the hundreds of images

that make up the visual subject matter of their daily lives, but as a distinct picture, as something isolated from the commonplace as if it were depicted in a work of art. In looking up toward the back of the monastery I received two such picture visions. Both were of parts of the monastery that I knew I must draw before my visit was out.

One was of the steps leading up to the archway giving onto the platform—a drawing shown on page 168. The other was of the monastery from the rear, with its apse bulging out like a semicircular tower from the curtain wall of a medieval castle—a drawing shown on page 89.

In addition, I gained a sharp sense of difference of hue between the scattered chocolate-colored stones in the apse and the sandy pink which was the prevailing color.

In the hexagonal window of the sacristy I gained another odd window for my collection.

And I gained an essential realization about the monastery. Because it stands so high and unobstructed, because it has such large, unadorned wall spaces, and because its many-leveled, simple forms are blocklike in their opposing planes, it is a marvelous receiver of light. Not only is it interesting in all lights, but, as illumination strikes those opposed planes and massive forms from varying directions, the monastery is constantly changing in aspect, looking almost startlingly different at different hours of the day.

WHEN HAD MY SKETCHBOOK out ready to start a drawing I found myself faced with a dilemma. My personal urge was to do nothing but windows, and I was looking forward to an easy day. But the voice of my conscience had been inconsiderate enough to raise the question of the reader once more. What good, it asked, would a series of window frames be to the reader, if he did not know where the windows were?

The question was hard to brush aside. It looked as if, before anything else, another general view was obligatory. But I hated the idea, for I was itching to sketch the finest of the traceried windows.

Finally I said to myself: The deuce with the reader. Yesterday I spent a whole afternoon doing a difficult over-all drawing to please him. Today I'll please myself first. Before I do anything else, I'll make a drawing of that window as it was in its days of perfection.

Here is the window. The shoulders of its two round-arched lights, like Atlas, support a circular tracery head. Anyone could make the design in that head by cutting two S's in half and disposing the halves in inverted and reverse positions above and below the horizontal diameter. Yet see how fanciful the effect is. And how original, for the curves of the tracery suggest the Gothic, yet the embracing arch is Romanesque, and the twin lights are Moorish.

Once this drawing was out of my system, I was emotionally ready to make the larger drawing for the reader. But I wasn't ready physically. I had drawn the window standing up and it had underlined the lesson of the day before: You are handicapped in making a drawing if you don't have something to sit on. Getting a chair was feasible, for the big embracing side view I wanted to draw was not far from my room. So I headed down the slope, fetched the hard wooden upright chair and began to work.

The window with the scrambled S's is the first window of the side wall. And actually there are four windows with this basic design. The second one is obscured in this sketch by the cypress tree growing from the cloister. The other two are in the corresponding positions in the northern wall of the church.

But, alas, not one of the four exists in a perfect state. The one shown in this sketch and its opposite number across the church are both filled in. Stones and crude masonry block the twin-arched lights and more stones are packed into the graceful interspaces formed by the half S's of the tracery.

Don Gabriel said this blocking up was done during the War of Independence. Then he gave me the story. Shortly after Hidalgo launched the uprising against Spain, Royalists seized the monastery as a stronghold. They held it through the war, consolidating their position in 1812 when they beat off three different attacks by insurgent forces. José Maria de Régules, a rich landowner from nearby Nochixtlán, was the Royalist leader, and while he was besieged he ordered the filling in. The windows give onto the choir gallery and he had soldiers quartered there. He wanted the openings sealed so his men would be safer from gunfire.

The third window of the flank has tracery of a different kind—two simple voids shaped like teardrops. The fourth window has no tracery at all. As I was drawing it, I asked Don Gabriel if that vacant window had ever contained decorative stonework that had been knocked out at a later date. The condition of the other windows made this supposition reasonable. But he said the window had always been the way it was. At the time I felt regret that the architect had not designed some beautiful tracery for it too, but three days later, when drawing the church interior, I was to see the logic of leaving that window space as unobstructed as possible.

52

This drawing of the monastery's southern flank went far more easily than the drawing of the front had gone the day before. Very little erasing was necessary and, when I took an arm's length view at the end, I saw only one thing wrong. I had made the entrance too narrow. Don Gabriel had been watching the work as it progressed, and I called his attention to the disparity between the narrow door in my drawing and the somewhat wider one in front of us.

"But you are right," he said. "The door originally was as narrow as you have made it. See those little squares in the corner? They show how the door was made wider. The priest had the old sides of the doorway cut away so he could drive his automobile in."

Humor mingled with outrage in my feelings. "Did he want to use the entrance hall as a garage?" I asked.

"Yes," said Don Gabriel. Then he added with considerable satisfaction: "The Institute put a stop to that."

At this moment a bird whirred in front of us. It went so fast I could hardly discern its form, but I shall never forget the vividness of its breast. It was not much larger than a sparrow, but it flashed an underside as pink as a flamingo's.

"*La Venturilla*" exclaimed Don Gabriel excitedly. "It's a prophecy."

The bird, I have since learned, was a vermilion flycatcher, but then I knew neither its English name nor its Mexican superstition. That belief,

Don Gabriel explained, was that if the bird flies past and you see only its dark wings, it is a sign of bad luck; but if the bird shows you the pink of its breast you are in for good luck.

I'm not one to hold much with omens, but I felt a thrill of elation. The bird had shown me what I had not realized till then: my coming, ultimately, would prove a stroke of luck for Don Gabriel. And the realization that the bird spoke truly for him gave me an unshakable conviction that it also spoke truly for me. I knew there was a blessing on my venture. Suddenly I felt more lighthearted.

Having contented myself by drawing the window of the S's as it was in its glory, I decided my obligation to truth meant I should draw the two unblocked tracery heads as they actually were.

The one on the left shows the head as it exists on the northern side. Circumstances led me to draw it only in outline, for when I went around to make the sketch I found the window in shadow and so high up that the molding was hard to discern. Working on a half S in isolation, I was reminded of a cup hook, and this window, it will be seen, has three of its cup hooks left.

The other drawing shows the tracery head in the window that had been obscured by the cypress when I made the general sketch. I was able to include the central ridges of the molding because Don Gabriel led me up to the roof of the cloister where, because I was closer, I could see more clearly. This window has only two remaining cup hooks, but, being the lower ones, they show one of the beauties of the design: the way the moldings flow into each other.

Such phrases as "tracery heads" and "twin lights," however, are examples of words I found later. As I was making these drawings, my concern was with the particular lines, curves, uneven terminations and space-shapes created by the carved and fractured stones before me. I was not thinking of words. And this directness of perception was one of the characteristics of the whole Yanhuitlán experience. Ever so many things that came in through my eyes were carried straight to my consciousness as pure visual images without being verbalized at all.

The level of the cloister roof is shown by the line cutting across the cypress in the sketch a few pages back. Being that near the nave windows, I decided to take further advantage of our position to study something which had been brought to my attention in making the earlier drawings and which had puzzled me from below because I could not quite make it out: the molding which both framed the windows and filled the space between the recessed tracery and the wall. The study device I used was to draw a section.

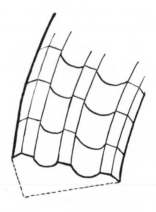

It was not a complicated molding. It curved outward in a concave arc, with the depression between the inner and outer frames being divided into a two-lane trough by a ridge down the center.

Perhaps its remoteness from any of the themes I had anticipated was a blinding factor, but as I was sketching that bit of molding I had no awareness that I had come upon what was to be one of the developing themes of my book. That is, drawing as a means of controlling the eye; directing the eye as a means of learning to see better; seeing better as a means to vision in the large sense, and the enlargement of vision as a means to a heightened awareness of life. But this is flashing far ahead. I was not even thinking of my book at the time. Nevertheless, I realized that drawing enough of the molding to fix its structure in my head had taught me a number of lessons.

For one, it emphasized the eye's tendency to skitter. From below, the frame made by the molding had been a relatively narrow border. The reason I could not discern the particular ins and outs of its ridges was not because I could not see them—for I could—but because I couldn't keep my eye sufficiently concentrated on so small a piece of banding to make out its planes. I had to climb to a point where the parallel lines of the banding were wide enough to allow for the shifting play of the eye without having the eye skittering away from the frame altogether.

The second lesson came from looking at the frame as a whole after I had carefully drawn one section of it. What had been hard to observe before was now easy to see. My eyes had grown no keener, but because of my intellectual grasp of the molding's plan I was able to take it in better. This showed me how knowledge aids vision. The eye, as an organ, is wonderfully acute. In most cases it is the mind's inability to interpret what the eye brings it that makes us purblind.

The third lesson obliges me to reveal that not only had I never been to art school, but I had never taken even an elementary course in architecture. If I had studied architecture formally, I would have known what I became aware of then: the importance of moldings in nearly all ornamented buildings.

I thought of some of their uses. With their graceful lines, moldings take the curse off ugly, unavoidable projections; they form cornices to save walls from ending too abruptly; they heighten the beauty of tracery, and, as in the instance before me, they form handsome frames at the same time as they fill awkward transitional areas.

When I had lined up these functions, I realized I'd been observing the effects of moldings all my life without ever analyzing what brought those effects about. And this led to a further lesson about observing: We have a tendency to receive impressions without any consciousness of what is creating them. Thus some modern windows can seem blank to those who have never stopped to realize that the absence of molding is the cause of the particular effect of blankness. Or, as in this case, the molding that was present played an important part in the impression I received from these nave windows, yet I had hardly been aware of that molding's existence until the problem of reproducing the window made me see I must include the molding in the sketch.

When Don Gabriel saw I had finished the section, he suggested we complete the ascent by going up to the roof of the church. I agreed happily. The nave window with the teardrop tracery was still to be drawn, but I was ready for a break.

IN THE DRAWING of the monastery's south side, near the bell tower, is a little stone pillbox that looks like a water tank. Actually, this is the exit to the spiral staircase that bores up the narrow shaft below it. Reaching the roof meant climbing this staircase. As we corkscrewed up, Don Gabriel told me that rebuilding the stairs was part of the reconstruction done by the Institute. With the pride of one who had counted them all, he said the spiral had sixty steps.

One of the amusement parks of my boyhood had a large slide of polished wood, which, because of great rounded swellings to make the descent more exciting, was called "Bump the Bumps." I was irresistibly reminded of that slide when we stepped out onto the roof. Here the major "bumps" were the domes of the rib-supported vaults that rested like inverted saucers over the four bays of the nave. The way they look in profile can be seen in the frontispiece.

Mexican towns are nearly always divided into administrative units similar to our wards. They are known as *barrios*, and the first thing Don Gabriel did on the roof was to show me the *barrios* of Yanhuitlán. Taking me to the façade gable, he pointed to San Pedro, the finely peaked hill he had identified the night before. The *barrio* at its foot had the same name as the hill. It consisted of perhaps three reed shanties. Then he pointed straight ahead to a hillock beyond the cemetery.

"That's San Sebastian," he said. What I saw on the little rise was a ruined adobe chapel. There were no houses.

Pointing a little to the south, he said: "That's Santa Rosa." Here I saw only a few thatched huts. Then he pointed further south and said: "That's San Bruno." Since I could see nothing but ploughed fields, I checked to make sure I was really following his index finger.

"I can only see two trees," I reported. "That's right," he said. "That's all there is left."

"What happened to these *barrios?*" I asked. "They were wiped out in the cholera epidemic of 1830."

"How many people were there in Yanhuitlán before the cholera?"
"Sixteen thousand."

His answer staggered me. Obviously the village had once been larger than it was now—the size of the church proved this—but I had no idea that as late as 1830 it was still a bustling community of 16,000. And cholera had been the great decimater! Looking out over the serene valley it was hard to imagine that any settlement so tranquil and apparently unscarred could have ever been subjected to so terrible a visitation.

The *barrio* Don Gabriel showed me from the north side of the church was Ayuxi. It consisted of the ultimate houses on the village's longest north and south street. A little beyond the last house on a slight hill was a small chapel. It was called El Calvario, Don Gabriel said. It was the shrine of El Señor de Ayuxi.

I knew El Señor was one of the chief holy personages of the town, for in Oaxaca I had been told that the fiesta in his honor was the major fiesta of Yanhuitlán. My interest perked up. Might I have the luck of having his fiesta fall within my stay? Half hopefully, I asked him which was his sacred day.

"May thirty-first," Don Gabriel replied. That meant his next fiesta was more than eight months off. The hope that had flickered promptly expired.

Don Gabriel then directed my attention to the hills enclosing the valley beyond the chapel. The quarry where stone was obtained for the monastery, he said, was in those northern hills.

At no point could I see any big pocket where man had dug stone out of the mountains, but there was plentiful evidence of a different kind of human activity. The hills were pitifully naked. One could see how, in the days when the population was dense in this valley, those hills had been cultivated right to their summits. In the course of that cultivation the sod cover had been broken up and all the restraining trees had been cut down. The inevitable had ensued. Over the years the rains had washed down the unbound earth so that now there was no soil anywhere except in the flatlands of the valley.

Cholera, I knew, had not been the only agent of depopulation. The whiteness of those upper slopes showed the forces of erosion, quite literally, had scoured the hills to the bone. Clearly, people had left the valley because it was no longer able to support them.

When Don Gabriel and I reached the eastern end of the roof we saw another "bump"—the half dome that joined the semicircular apse to the church. And that curved roofing made the apse look more than ever like a silo that had been sliced in two.

Being so high up enabled us to look down on still another "bump"—the dome over the sacristy, which, as the plan on page 12 shows, nestles in the angle where the nave is joined by the conventual buildings.

Our position at the back of the church gave us an excellent view of the plaza. And since the center of the village was spread out below, I paused to make a rough plan.

Don Gabriel gave me the names to fill in. The street in front of the municipal building was called Calle de la Plaza. The street on the far side of the fountain, that bound the plaza on the east, was named Porfirio Díaz after the Oaxacan general who had been President of Mexico for thirty years. The street bounding the plaza on the south was Calle de la Paz. And the roofless building that faced the wide Street of Peace was a chapel called La Pastora.

The longest north and south street of the village—the one that led out to El Calvario—was Hidalgo, after the priest who started the War of Independence. My room was in the house at the corner of Hidalgo and the first street south of Peace. The street, Don Gabriel said, was too small to have a formal name. It was just Callejón, which is Spanish for lane.

In walking along the roof line of most sixteenth-century churches in Mexico, I had felt I was pacing a battlement. This was because the majority had fortresslike crenellations. But Yanhuitlán had no castellation, not even a parapet. In circling the roof we had walked unguarded along the tops of the walls. I had been a little nervous, being so near, as it were, to the cliff's edge.

Nervousness of a different kind beset me when Don Gabriel started back over the domes. Surely such delicate shells were not safe to walk over. But he assured me they were, so I followed him. At the apex of the first one, I had the opportunity to see that my feeling about the thinness of the shells was justified. There was a round hole here and one could look right through it into the church below. I estimated the dome could have been only nine inches thick.

The domes were perfectly symmetrical, smoothly rounded and neatly covered with brown bricks of uniform size. They gave me a new admiration for the builders of the church. And I recalled something I had read about the early days of Spanish building in Mexico. In some cases natives at first refused to enter the new high-vaulted churches. The curved arch being unknown to them, and never having succeeded themselves in spanning wide spaces, the Indians could not believe the buildings were safe. To them it

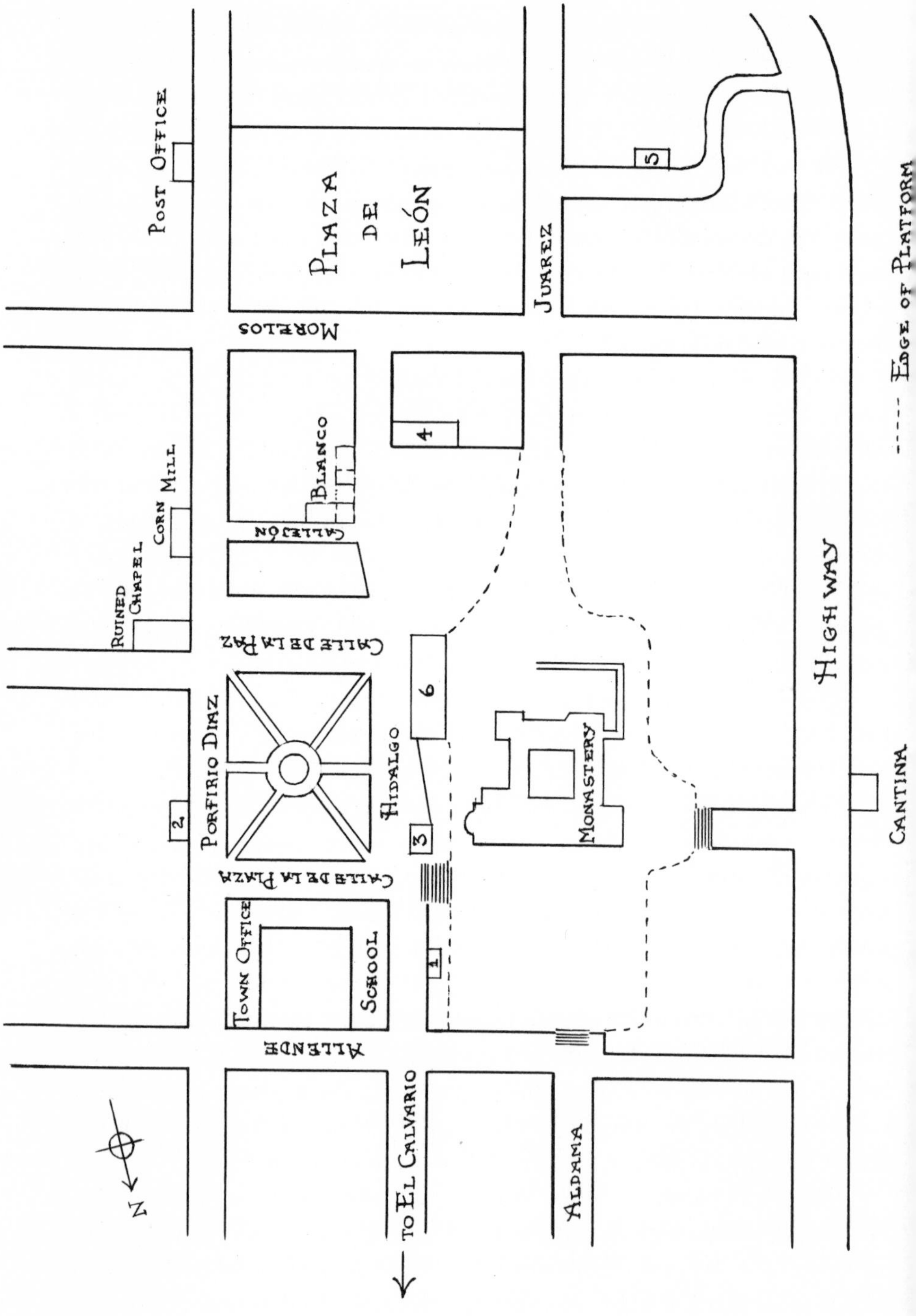
Post Office
Plaza de León
Juarez
Morelos
5
4
Blanco
Callejón
Corn Mill
Ruined Chapel
Calle de la Paz
6
Porfirio Diaz
2
Hidalgo
3
Monastery
Highway
Cantina
Edge of Platform
Calle de la Plaza
Town Office
School
1
Allende
To El Calvario
Aldama
N

just wasn't logical that such expanses of heavy stone could be safely supported over interiors, which, in contrast to their own, reached such dizzy heights. The ceilings, they were convinced, would come crashing down on their heads.

If they felt this about being underneath, I thought, how much more timid about walking over these domes they must have been than I was. And when repeated experience showed them such walking was feasible, how they must have been awed at the engineering skill of these men who could throw so thin a dome over so high a space and yet make the dome so strong that men could stand on top of it!

Before we descended, Don Gabriel showed me the bells in the corner tower. There were four of them. A very big one hung unmovably from a great beam. So did the other large one. But the two smaller bells were of the type that swing on a bar and can be made to ring out with a fine clatter by being pushed in such wide arcs that they finally swing over the top of the bar in complete circles. I saw, though, that the priest had rigged up a system whereby he could ring one of the smaller bells without having to make the effort of climbing to the belfry to push it. Tied to its clapper was a rope that went down to the upper level of the cloister.

A short rope dangled from the clapper of the great bell. Don Gabriel took hold of it and gave it a quick yank so the clapper hit the wall of the bell. It emitted a fine deep note. Then he began ringing it regularly.

Since bells are generally rung for a specific purpose, to call people to church or to sound an alarm, I wondered what the people of the village would think to hear the sudden sounding of the big bell. Then with his other hand Don Gabriel took hold of the rope from the clapper of one of the smaller bells and began ringing it too. Surely, I felt, the people would soon start streaming from their houses from all directions to find out what was up. But no one stirred. Meanwhile Don Gabriel went on contentedly ringing the bells and I discerned that he was creating a regular sound pattern: bong, bong, bong on the big bell, and then eight clang, clang, clangs on the small bell. It was lovely the way the last of the three bongs of the big bell would persist through the higher, briefer clangs of the small one.

The whole building seemed to quiver in delight at the awakened bells. The joy seemed communicated elsewhere too. The winds of the valley had blown seeds to the roof. Those which had found lodging between the stones had sprouted and I would have sworn the roof-line plantlets were dancing to the brazen music.

When Don Gabriel had exhausted the pleasure of the bells, he bade me look at the date on the largest one. It was 1877. That was eighteen years after the law suppressing the monasteries. It was a year when I thought the church was probably at its lowest ebb. How then did it acquire so fine a bell at a time when it was so poor? And my curiosity was further aroused when Don Gabriel said two of the other bells had the same date. The bells had gold and silver in them, he said, and were cast in Yanhuitlán.

"Who cast them?" I asked.

"The Dominicans."

"But I thought they had been expelled in 1859."

"Oh, that was when the law was passed. The friars did not leave until about 1890 or '91."

This was so surprising and he was so well informed that I pressed for more information.

"Did the secular clergy take over as soon as the friars left?"

"No. For ten years there was no priest here at all."

"Do you know who was the first secular priest?"

"Apolinar Zamora. He came about 1901."

"And how long was he here?"

"Twelve years. But during the Revolution the people tried to kill him."

"Did they actually attack him?"

"No. Friends warned him of the plot. He hid in a private home, and in the darkness of the night he escaped."

The village that lay so peacefully at our feet, then, had experienced at least one of the flare-ups of swiftly murderous fury that I had read often occurred in Mexico.

How curiously the story contrasted with the monastery, especially with the cloister below. And looking down I was struck by how the gray quadrangle was framed by its red tiled roof. From above, too, I was in a better position to appreciate that roof tiling than when I had been standing on it. Pointing to the sleeve of my sports jacket, I showed Don Gabriel how the tiles below were set in a similar herringbone pattern.

The roofing of the cloister, he said, was one of the things the Institute restored. In the years of neglect most of the original beams had rotted away and the ceiling had fallen in.

When we were down on the lower roofs again, I found I could get the best view of the teardrop window from the dome over the sacristy, and it was from there that I made my drawing.

This window was the same height and width as the cup hook window. When I began to frame it, I saw it also had identical outer molding. Understanding that molding better, I was able to draw it more accurately. The molding, I noticed, was flanked with two buttresses that projected very slightly. Did the other windows have them too? I looked and found they did. And they added considerably to the beauty of the design. Another instance of receiving an impression without awareness of one of its important causes.

I did some verbalizing as I sketched this window, and, as I became more aware of its features, I became dissatisfied with the word "teardrops." It merely described the tracery head's unusual voids. "Mask," I decided would be better. And suddenly I exclaimed to myself: I've got it. Now I know what that tracery suggests: the visor of Pallas Athene's helmet.

Something else happened as I worked on this window. It grew on me. I became aware that its apparent simplicity had deceived me. By the time I was nearly finished I knew I had been taken in by the rhythmic curves of the scrambled S's. The other window was more flamboyant, but surely this one was more chastely beautiful.

Don Gabriel sat on the dome nearby as I sketched. The expression of melancholy I had seen in his face the night before had been replaced by one of perfect contentment. When he caught me looking at him, he smiled back; and when, after my final stroke, I asked him if he were ready to help deliver the presidential bottle, he got to his feet with cheerful alacrity.

For the third time we found El Presidente was not in the municipal offices. We decided to try his home. But since we were passing the school, Don Gabriel asked if I wouldn't like to look in there first.

Because of the Independence Day holidays, the children were away. Thus the long room to our left as we passed in under the central archway was deserted. All I could see were some benches and, at the far end, a cluttered stage with a valance hanging from the round-arched proscenium.

The large open courtyard was deserted too, and the posts supporting the basketball hoops looked a little desolate. We did meet one of the teachers, a soft-spoken young man named José Ortiz. He had a broad, high cheekboned face, and I was struck immediately by his air of quiet intelligence. I asked for the main facts about the school.

It was not a rural school, he said with a touch of pride, but one classed as *semiurbano*. It had been "federalized" in 1925.

"In the regime of Calles?" I asked. He nodded, and I could tell from the way his face lit up that he was delighted at finding a North American who was aware of one of modern Mexico's great achievements: the nation-wide educational campaign carried out by the government after Obregón and his successor, Calles, had ended the anarchic period of the Mexican Revolution.

The school, he said, had five women teachers and two male teachers besides himself. There were 300 pupils, who ranged in age from youngsters of seven to boys and girls of fifteen or sixteen. The education they received was *primaria*, which took them only as far as a United States public school. Young people who wanted any high school education had to go to Oaxaca, which was seventy-five miles away.

As Don Gabriel and I emerged from the school we met Alfonso, the courteous seventeen-year-old who had watched the sunset with us. We shook hands, of course, and I invited him to accompany us to find El Presidente.

When we turned the corner into Hidalgo I noticed a tin sign by a door of one of the houses on the left side of the street. (Marked 1 in the plan on page 60. The sign indicated those who lived there sold orange soda. Wouldn't Don Gabriel and Alfonso first like a *refresco?* I asked. Since by this time the day had grown hot, there was a pleased acceptance.

The house, or rather the front room of it, turned out to be a little store. A long barricading wooden counter divided the front from the back and behind it were a number of shelves and bins. Dried macaroni, a few cakes of soap, candles and some packs of cigarettes were the items I noticed.

A little boy disappeared to fetch the owner. And who did he turn out to be? None other than the object of our search, El Presidente. And he was not at all the elderly, rather portly self-important person I expected. He was a compactly built man of thirty-eight with a pleasant face, and eyes whose whites were tinged with brown.

Don Gabriel introduced us, telling him my reason for being in the village. To prove my seriousness, I showed him the drawings I had completed. Then I gave him the bottle. He was, I judged, a man of few words, for he did not seem impressed one way or another. But as we finished our orange drinks he reciprocated my present of the mezcal by refusing to accept any money for the three bottles of pop.

There was one more window I wanted to draw before calling it a morning. It was the small circular one over the doorway to the entrance hall. Its intriguing feature was its filling. What would have been glazing bars—had there been any glass—formed an ornamental cross. It resembled the Iron Cross of Prussia and I thought such a cross was called Maltese. To check this, I consulted Helen Stuart Griffith's *The Sign Language of Our Faith*, the booklet of church symbols I had brought with me. Miss Griffith set me right. A Maltese cross, though it also suggests four converging spearheads, has straight sides. This cross, having curved sides, was a cross patée.

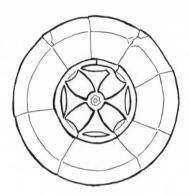

My appreciation of this window also grew as I sketched. And the closeness of observation necessitated by drawing led me to notice a feature that had escaped me before: the carved flower at the center of the cross. There was a similar flower in the corresponding position on the reverse side—as I discovered when I went in to check.

Just as we were ready to leave for lunch, four Mexican travelers showed up. This meant Don Gabriel had to stay and show them around. Again I welcomed the opportunity of tagging along, and on this tour I was struck by a new development in my observing. I noticed relationships.

The mind, it seems, can only absorb one new wonder at a time. On my previous circuits of the monastery, when everything was relatively unfamiliar, I tended to go from one splendor to another as if I were viewing a series of independent pictures in an art gallery. But by this time I knew the main features well enough to take them in at a glance. Thus my eyes, no longer being needed for close inspection, were freer to rove more widely. Several times they caught two features at once and I saw how wonderfully these were planned in relation to each other.

In the church, I was struck by the beautiful effect when, looking through the handsome side door of the nave, I glimpsed the sunlit cloister. A pale-green apricot tree stood in the dappled light filtered through the dark cypress, and fruit tree and cloister looked lovelier for being seen as an adjunct to that cathedrallike interior.

In the upper gallery of the cloister I happened to look up at the bell tower we had visited earlier in the morning. Here was an additional instance of one thing being enhanced by its relationship with another. The mellow brick-red tower rearing against the intense blue of the sky was framed by the second floor arcade. Under those arches, that somewhat incongruous tower looked more beautiful than it had ever done in isolation.

A third lovely relationship led into my theme of the day, for one of the elements was a window. It was circular and as we turned into the southern cell corridor I was struck by the way it framed an enchanting view of the hills at the far end of the passageway.

The window is marked A in the plan on page 296. By looking at it, the reader can understand the window's other relationships. There he can discern that, besides being planned both to light the corridor and to provide a charming vignette at its end, the porthole was also planned to light the grand stairway.

When we came to the stairway, we saw a diamond of light projected on the wall below the circular window. Naturally, I looked to see what sort of magic lantern was creating so striking an effect. It was another window, this one near the barrel-vaulted ceiling in the wall facing the porthole. And it was printing its diamond shape across the stairwell because the two o'clock sun was striking right through it.

The sun, then, was pointing up that not only were two of the windows lighting the stairwell different in shape, but they were ingeniously planned so that their contrasting shapes could sometimes be seen as neighbors, even though the windows were at different levels in opposite walls.

At the foot of the stairs, one of the Mexicans slipped Don Gabriel a tip. And, when we got outside, I had occasion to see how ungrasping the caretaker was. One of the other travelers, not knowing what his friend had done, also extended his hand with some money, but Don Gabriel shook his head.

"I have it," he said, showing he had already received his tip. But the second traveler, I was glad to see, insisted Don Gabriel take his money too.

For Mexicans, lunch, or *la comida* as they call it, is the big meal of the day; and Lupe certainly outdid herself for this one. It began with consommé filled with five-pointed stars. Then came lamb with squash and fried potatoes. Next, an egg beaten in tomato sauce. Again I ate it by rolling bits in a tortilla. Everything was served in one of the white soup plates, and this time my all-purpose utensil was a spoon of *white* tinware. Three courses, I felt, were surely enough. But Lupe produced a fourth: kidney beans that had been boiled till they formed their own black sauce. And this meal also had a dessert—a banana.

Such a *comida*, I was sure, was enough to exhaust their poor fortune, so again I asked about paying them. After all, this was my fourth meal and surely they now could judge what the extra costs were going to be. Lupe began to calculate with Don Gabriel's help. But it didn't seem to work, so he turned to me and said: "We have decided we would rather you paid us all at once at the end of your stay."

Wanting to make sure there was no misunderstanding, I asked: "Then you would prefer it if I never mention money until I leave?"

"Yes," he replied. "We have confidence in you."

I smiled at the term, and was glad they felt I was not the sort who would run out on them.

Since I had not shaved that morning, I asked Lupe if she would heat some water for me. Don Gabriel said he would bring it over when it was ready. I put in the waiting time by writing some of the postcards I had brought with me. I had not thought to bring a mirror, though, so when Don Gabriel arrived with the hot water in a little clay pitcher I asked if he could lend me a mirror. He returned with one the size of a calling card.

I did not want to slop my suds over the floor, so I took my basin of hot water to the threshold of the door. Sitting there in the warm sun was very pleasant, and by holding the mirror in my left hand and shifting it from one section of my jaws to another I managed to see well enough to scrape all the stubble clean.

There were interruptions, though. First, Don Gabriel came over lugging a thin quilt stuffed with straw. His idea was to place it on top of the boards of the counter to serve as a mattress. I was grateful for this thoughtfulness, and I smiled when, after arranging the bed softener, he patted it and said, "For your siesta."

The other interruptions were of the type I'd been hoping for. The spectacle of the gringo in his undershirt sitting on his doorstep shaving was something passing children could not resist. When two small boys paused, I saw my opportunity.

"*¿Quieren dulces?*" I called out. And they came forward like little squirrels for the candies. My one exaction in return was their names. The one with something especially winning about him, a firm-set sturdy youngster of about six, was Paco. He had a bullet-shaped head and I set him down in my memory book as the little tough guy, for it was easy to imagine him as a middleweight fighter some dozen years hence. The other boy, who was shyer and a year or two older, was Raul.

Two little girls paused, their thumbs in their mouths, as they saw the boys getting candies. Did they want some too? I asked. And they came scrambling forward. The smaller one was Sarita and the older was Angelita. The only thing that distinguished them was size, for they both had identical big black eyes, pigtails, bare legs and the same short cotton dresses.

A rather homely young woman carrying her little son, Hugo, also came by. How her smile transformed her face, and she gave me such a smile when I offered her candies too. Being older than the children, she was bold enough to give voice to her curiosity. Was I a doctor? When I said no, she asked if I was interested in buying *"cerámicas antiguas,"* meaning items of pre-Conquest pottery. After this she apparently felt she had asked all the questions warranted at that time. She gave me another smile, bid me a cordial *adiós,* and walked on, Hugo dangling at her hip.

As the shave was just about finished, Don Gabriel, the ever thoughtful, was back again. Was there anything I would like Lupe to launder for me? I had worn one of my suntan shirts for several days, so I gave it to him thankfully, along with a handful of candies for himself and Lupe.

Then I climbed onto the padded altar for a blissful siesta. Knowing I had completed the windows of the south side and thereby indicated their duplicates on the north, and realizing my drawing of the day before showed the big rectangular window of the front façade, I was able to drop asleep with a good conscience. Only three windows remained to be done—those at the back—and I was sure they would be easy.

It was almost four o'clock before I woke and I decided I'd better mail my postcards before I started drawing. Did a place as small as Yanhuitlán have a post office? I sought out Don Gabriel and he said it did. He volunteered to take me there.

The route he chose took us by La Pastora, the ruined chapel we had seen from the roof of the church. The chapel, Don Gabriel said, was built in the eighteenth century. Did I want to go in? *"Sí. ¿Cómo no?"* I answered, proud of being able to use the colloquial "Yes, why not?" that I had heard others use when faced with something perfectly agreeable.

The chapel was made of adobe and because there was no longer any roof to protect the mud walls from the rain, the tops of those walls were already rounded and worn down unevenly by the slow attrition of water.

The shallow, partially domed apse that protected the altar was of stone and therefore still intact. A Spanish crown was carved at the apex of the chancel arch. Beside the crown, sculptured in the same scale, was an eight-pointed star.

"That's a symbol of Santo Domingo," explained Don Gabriel. And he made it plain why the star of the founder of the Dominican order should be set over the non-monastic chapel. St. Dominic, he said, was the patron saint of the village.

Rain had washed away much of the wooden retable's paint, but not enough to obliterate the blue, white and yellow color scheme. No figure was left in the central niche, but the glass that had protected it was still there. The retable itself was naïve provincial Baroque. It was far better than some of the altar pieces I had seen so carefully preserved in the pueblo churches of New Mexico. Altogether the little chapel must have been quite charming. I felt sad to see it disintegrating.

"When did the roof cave in?" I asked. "In 1927."

"Why was it never rebuilt?"

"The people here are very liberal. They don't care about religion. Haven't you noticed how little they think of the *convento?*"

Don Gabriel's words made me realize he was right. I had seen little evidence of local interest. El Presidente had betrayed no sign of civic pride at my attention to the monastery; and, when I had shown my drawings to people who had approached as I sketched, the response, almost invariably, had been, not what a wonderful thing the monastery was, but how amazing that someone, by a few pencil lines on paper, could reproduce it recognizably.

How different from what I had anticipated! And I felt some of my book collapse, for in New York, when I had thought about the kind of story this would make, I had conceived the village's devotion to its great church as a unifying and developing theme.

The post office was a block further south on Díaz. If it had not been for Don Gabriel I would not have been able to find it, for it was in a somewhat dingy house, which, like all the other houses of the village, was of a single story. It was shut. In the United States that would have caused a North American to turn away with the realization he'd have to come back tomorrow. But the running of federal offices, it seems, is not so strict in rural Mexico. Don Gabriel knocked hard on the closed door and called out for Don Patricio.

WEEK IN YANHUITLÁN

The postmaster indicated from within that he was coming and finally opened up. He was a little old man with a parchment-colored face that was crosshatched with innumerable small wrinkles. His last name was Ramírez. After shaking hands, he went behind his partition and formally received the postcards through the arched opening in the bit of frosted glass that is the hallmark of a post office the world over.

On leaving, I said something to Don Gabriel about the old man being very poor.

"You don't have to feel sorry for him," he said. "His daughter is married to Felipe Cruz Soriana, one of the richest men in Yanhuitlán."

More interesting than the post office was the huge open space in front of it. Don Gabriel said it was Plaza Antonio de León.

The name rang a bell with me, for outside my hotel window in Oaxaca had been a statue of General León, epaulettes on his shoulders and bicorne in hand.

"Wasn't he the Mexican patriot who was killed defending his country against the invasion of the United States in 1847?"

"Yes," Don Gabriel replied. "He was also one of the heroes of *Independencia*. It was General León who finally forced the royalists to surrender the monastery in 1821. He was the liberator of Yanhuitlán."

Although the open space honoring the liberator was called a plaza, it was a medieval village green if ever I saw one. Low houses on all four sides held it in rectangular shape. But there was nothing else to give it formality; no pavement, no trees, no benches and no municipal statue. And I could see why its grass was so short. Some sheep and one or two burros were cropping near the post office, and in the northwest corner was a flock of white goats.

Don Gabriel said the big event in this plaza was the annual bullfight. The villagers created a rustic bullring by enclosing an arena with temporary fencing like farmers' snake fences in the United States.

The thought of the bullfight brought another flicker of hope. If my week did not include the fiesta of El Señora de Ayuxi, perhaps it might include this.

"When do they hold the bullfight?" I asked. "On the day of St. Dominic."

"And when is that?" "August fourth."

Another hope dashed. I had missed the fiesta of the village's patron saint by seven weeks. It looked as if the weekly market, then, was the only festal occurrence I was likely to encounter in my chosen seven-day period. Yanhuitlán's market, Don Gabriel said, was on Monday. And I stored the day in my mind as something to look forward to.

The first of the three back windows I wanted to draw was the porthole lighting the grand stairway which, from within, had provided the vignette at the end of the cell corridor on the morning's tour. The window lived up to expectations. Even indicating all the divisions between its stones, it was easy to draw, for it was in good condition and its form was simple: a wide collar of plain molding encompassing a narrower circle of molding hardly more complex.

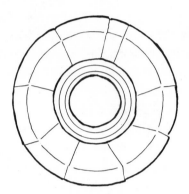

The stone frame was finely finished and it looked well, set as it was in the somewhat rougher stonework of the plain wall. I was interested in how much molding was lavished on a relatively small aperture. Clearly the designer was not content with merely providing a round void that would carry out its interior functions. He also wanted the window to be handsome from the outside.

I have indicated the position of the sacristy, for its dome was one of the "bumps" we had seen from the church roof. A glance at the plan on page 12 will show how the square chamber is fitted into the angle between the eastern end of the church and the conventual buildings. The last two windows on my agenda were those piercing the sacristy's free sides. Needless to say, they were not alike.

The first one I tackled was the window in the south wall. Inside, it must have presented a simple diamond, like the second window of the stairwell, but outside, as I discovered when I started to draw, it was anything but simple. Here was another instance of the designer being as concerned with outward appearance as with inner shape. The window was almost all

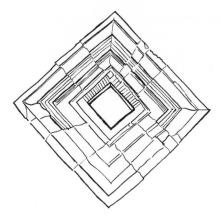

molding. And not only was that molding complex, but it was badly shattered, which meant many of its parallel lines were chipped and out of line.

Only an hour or so of daylight remained. Obviously I could not draw every line of it, so I decided to compromise—to draw the top chevron in detail, and only to indicate the lower one.

Even doing the upper half of the window required more time and patience than I expected. As I counted bands within bands and struggled to indicate contours, I smiled at one of the day's ironies. For a man who had never drawn a piece of molding in his life, I was certainly having a baptism of fire. By the time I reached the point when I felt I could leave the rest of the window vague, I was genuinely tired. Drawing was more of a day's work than I realized.

My final problem was the hexagonal window in the east wall of the sacristy, which is shown in its position in the sketch on page 89. The mold-

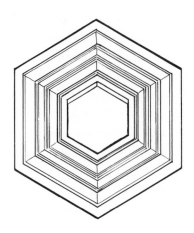

ing of this window had even more bands than that of the diamond window, and the destruction here was so much worse that even the principal bands were difficult to count. What a punishment that window must have taken from shot when the monastery was besieged! All the irregularities of the breaks, plus the depth of the inlay gave me a feeling of defeat. Being as weary as I was, I could not draw even half of it in its present state. So this time I decided on a different compromise: ignoring all the destruction and drawing the window as it might have looked on the designer's drafting board.

While working on this second sacristy window I had a companion. My friend Alfonso had reappeared, this time his city appearance modified by a sombrero with a sharply upturned brim so wide it almost hid the peaked crown.

When the drawing was finished, he suggested a walk. Cries and an occasional shout led our footsteps to the village green. It was here I encountered the regional game. Alfonso said it was called *juego mixteco* and that it went back to pre-Conquest days.

It was a form of handball. But it did not have North American handball's resemblance to squash. It was closer to tennis—with four or five men on each side. The chief differences were that the players used their padded right palms as rackets and the net was imaginary. The server would bounce the ball on a rock and then whack it over the nonexistent net. A fellow on the other side would try to whack it back, either on the fly or after it had bounded. The scoring, too, was like tennis and the serve would pass back and forth at the end of each game.

The ball was easy to miss and since there were no walls to keep it within the court area, the players spent fully as much time chasing the ball to the far corners of the green as they did in actual play. This meant the game was not much fun to watch. Neither the delays between serves nor the need to keep chasing the ball, though, seemed to mar the enjoyment of the participants.

The players were pleasant-looking field workers, but a certain country roughness about them helped me to understand why the city-bred Alfonso had gravitated to me. He was clearly better educated and gentler than they were, and probably had found few companions of his own age in the village. I saw, too, that the energetic players were men who would probably feel tongue-tied and ill at ease with a stranger like myself. And this led me to a rueful conclusion. Because the strictness of Mexican custom ruled out the companionship of girls, Don Gabriel and Alfonso would probably be my only friends during my stay.

As the light began to fail, the players missed the ball more often, and therefore spent more time retrieving it. My attention wandered to the white goats at the edge of the green. Some were kids hardly a month old. What a delight it was to watch all four tiny feet leave the ground as kid after kid hopped into the air out of sheer joy of living.

The changing sky prompted Alfonso to ask: "Shall we go and watch the sunset?" The words were right out of my own mind. I was pleased, though, that the suggestion came from him. It showed he had enjoyed the previous evening as much as I had, and that he, too, wanted a repetition.

We collected Don Gabriel and the three of us repaired to our gap in the ruined wall. The sun had already gone and clouds had gathered in the west. But the clouds seemed anxious not to let their skirts drag on the hill-tops, so there was a space of clear sky that showed a little salmon pink over San Pedro. But the pink soon disappeared. Accordingly, the chief color interest lay in what happened to the greens of the valley. When we arrived the trees and fields, though differing a little in density, were the same emerald shade. But as the light ebbed the trees grew dark as olives. This meant their forms, which before had been merged in the common hue, came to stand out sharply; for, magically, the fields had turned a milky jade.

"Whee-wheet," sang a distant bird, and contentment descended upon us. The alteration in the relative values of shades of green—a difference standing in the same relation to technicolor as *juego mixteco* to tennis. But what a pleasure in a movieless life, where a visit to watch the sunset is as big an event as a picture show!

The Blancos' bed looked thinner than ever when I entered their room for the evening meal. Had they given me their quilt too? If so, it had been given cheerfully, for Don Gabriel sat on the almost bare springs and chatted with the best goodwill in the world.

Dinner consisted of a cup of hot milk, an egg cooked in tomato sauce, tortillas and another helping of kidney beans—only this time the frijoles were mashed. In the course of the meal I saw the same two white soup-plates and the same two tin spoons—one white and one blue. And then it dawned on me: the reason they served me separately. It wasn't because they preferred eating alone after I had gone. It was because they didn't have three of everything. And that was why Don Gabriel sat on the bed. They only had items in pairs, and they had given me their other chair.

That night I had another dream. It was very different from the first one. I dreamed about the death of one of my father's friends, but I transformed him from a chartered accountant into a man with many Mexican employees. His widow was overwhelmed by the way they turned out for his funeral and at all the sweetness and goodness they showed her out of their gratitude and affection for the man they had worked for. She was wondering how she could ever write to thank them.

I was not so surprised as she was at their goodness and kindness. These were qualities I knew well. But we discussed the problem of those letters. I remember my very words—and I remember them so clearly I think I must have spoken them aloud in a moment of wakefulness as I turned on that counter vainly seeking a comfortable position.

"What you need," I said, "is a good Spanish-speaking stenographer."

VII
THE DOORWAYS

THE FACTS OF LIFE oblige me to open this chapter with an indelicate matter. My digestive system, fortunately, had been working satisfactorily in Yanhuitlán. From time to time, therefore, it had been necessary to dispose of what the medically minded call human waste. My practice had been to take my roll of toilet paper and retire among the bushes in the secluded corner formed by the priest's garage. The situation was not ideal, so I counted myself in luck on the third morning when a call from nature woke me about five o'clock, which was so early no one was up and about. Thus I could relieve myself not far from my front door without the embarrassment of being caught in the act. Also, because no long hike was involved, I was not thoroughly wakened, and I could climb back on the counter for another forty winks.

As it happened, I didn't get up until seven-thirty. And when Don Gabriel arrived with some fresh water I told him of my stroke of luck in the early call.

"Oh, but you should use the patio," he said solicitously. I had visions of a tiled terrace and a beautifully kept garden suggested by the patios of California houses. Naturally I protested.

"It is perfectly all right," he assured me. "Look, I will show you." He opened the door in the back wall of my room. To my surprise, it led into a larger empty room. By going through that room and out its side door we came to the patio. It was a large unkempt weed patch shut in by adobe walls —clearly a place that would not be desecrated by a little night soil.

I don't know whether or not the Blancos had begun to borrow from neighbors, but when I got to my place for breakfast I found some new utensils. For the first time the setting included a knife and fork. And the comestibles included *two* eggs.

It was at this meal that I first began hearing of the glories of California. For when Don Gabriel saw Lupe serve the two fried eggs in the white soup-plate he was reminded of his breakfasts in California when he used to eat *six* eggs. He cooked them himself, he said, on a two-burner kerosene stove which he had in his shack. And did I know that in California when it got cold and they were afraid the orange crop might be nipped with frost they made great clouds of black smoke that kept the trees warm? And did I know that they sprayed the oranges with a solution that saved them from the insects? The insecticide was so strong that pickers had to use special soap to wash it off their hands.

Another additional feature of this breakfast was a meat course. As I cut off a little chunk for Bobby, the cream-colored mongrel, Don Gabriel tested his memory and asked if "meat" was not the English word for *carne*.

Hambre, the kitten, was living up to her new name. She, too, was after food, and crying for it in her imperious way. Did she eat meat? When I was assured she ate anything, I cut a chunk for her too.

Lupe had served beans for lunch the day before and beans for dinner. This was the first time she also served them for breakfast. And since Don Gabriel was thinking of English equivalents for Mexican foods, he asked what we called *frijoles*.

I knew these dark red beans were kidney beans, but my tongue was tied by not knowing the Spanish word for kidney. Finally I hit on a scheme. I drew a little kidney and then pointed to the area of my anatomy where the organ was located.

"Oh *riñón!*" he exclaimed. Then he turned to explain to Lupe that in the United States they called her beans *frijoles riñones*. She laughed in delight at the aptness of the term. And I saw the possibility of many further jokes in telling them U. S. names for different features of their lives.

"Would you like another cup of hot milk?" Don Gabriel asked. If anyone had ever told me I would accept hot milk at breakfast as an acceptable alternate for coffee I would have told him he was quite wrong. Yet here I was doing it with pleasure. And I lingered over the second cup, for at this meal we all felt more relaxed.

Having completed the windows in a single day, I was reassured about having sufficient time to finish my project in the five days remaining. A result of this relaxation was a new sharpness of vision for small details. I realized this by the way I caught things I had looked at but not seen. Don Gabriel's feet, for instance. His blue pants were factory made, but he was wearing peasant sandals. The flame in the rose-colored glass on a bracket in the corner provided another example. It had been burning all along, but at this meal I noticed Lupe had arranged some fresh flowers in front of it. And behind it were religious postcards, splayed like a loosely held poker hand. One version of the Virgin was the iconlike Our Lady of Perpetual Help, and in the place of honor was Nuestra Señora del Sagrado Corazón, holding a flame-crowned heart in front of her child as if it were a toy.

In our easy mood we exchanged some vital statistics. I furnished the information that I was not married, that my father and mother were dead and that two sisters were my only close relatives. From them I learned they had been married seventeen years. Don Gabriel's parents were living, but all his brothers and sisters had died. And Lupe's father was dead, but her mother was still alive. Did Lupe have any brothers? Five. Any sisters? And here Don Gabriel answered for her in a tone that mingled envy with humor. She had six. As one of seven girls in a large family, Lupe expanded with visible pride.

For both personal and literary reasons, my first visit to Yanhuitlán had been in the back of my mind ever since my arrival. The personal reason that kept it there was the hope that by enjoying some of its experiences over again I could recapture some of its happiness. My literary reasons sprang from another idea I had for my book. I had conceived it as a following up of the main elements of that afternoon. I could achieve continuity, I felt, by telling more about the things and persons encountered on the first visit. Thus my hope was not only to give more details about the monastery, but also about the youth with the wavy hair, the old man who had gone limping off to get his idols, the spring where the village water came from, and perhaps to describe what it was like when the motion picture truck came to town and young and old crowded into the school to see the weekly movies.

Accordingly, I questioned Don Gabriel about those earlier elements. The answers led to a series of disappointments. Movies no longer came to the village. The spring was too far away to visit. And because the father of the boy with the wavy hair had been killed by an automobile on the highway, the friendly Cutberto, now fatherless, had gone to Mexico City to try to support himself there. As one element after another was shorn away, another hope for my book collapsed.

What about the old caretaker, was he still in Yanhuitlán? No, he had gone to the capital too. But at least I learned his name. It was Angel Martinez. And since Don Angel was in our thoughts I couldn't resist telling about his two hats.

Knowing the limitations of my vocabulary, I decided to act it out in pantomime. Getting to my feet, I pretended to knock at the monastery entrance. Then I took the part of the old man, raising his sombrero, finding the visitor was a tourist and hastening to change into the visored cap of the official guide before starting the tour.

The Blancos laughed till the tears rolled down their cheeks. And Don Gabriel relived his enjoyment by acting it out for Lupe in his own fashion. He didn't engage in any such hat-changing nonsense himself. He had this —and he pointed to his badge, which resembled a policeman's shield. No wonder I had never noticed it, for it was pinned on his shirt so the pocket hid all but the crest. It was his only official designation. And he laughed all over again at his predecessor's *uniforme.*

THE FENESTRATION, as the reader knows, was the feature of the monastery that first caught my interest. During my circling of the friary, however, I had grown increasingly aware that it was endowed with a second set of stone frames more elaborate, more beautifully designed and even richer in variety of design than the windows. I refer to the doorways. And it was the doorways I had set as my assignment for this third day in Yanhuitlán.

In his *Mexican Architecture of the Sixteenth Century,* George Kubler points to the puzzling fact that in a great many monastic churches in Mexico the door of popular use is not, as one might expect, the door in the west front, but the door on the north side. He suggests that the Indians, being newcomers to Christianity, were really freshly converted gentiles, and traditionally the north is the direction associated with gentiles. Whatever the reason, many of the northern portals are unusually splendid. The Yanhuitlán church provides an outstanding example, and its northern portal was the first of the doorways on my list.

Some of the essential facts about the doorway may be observed in the frontispiece. There one can see how it stands between two of the flush buttresses of the northern flank; how it directly faces an archway at the head of steps leading up to the platform, and how the platform on this side forms a spacious courtyard.

I already knew the doorway quite well, for its design incorporates one of the nave windows and the day before, in drawing the tracery head with

WEEK IN YANHUITLÁN

the three cup hooks (page 54), I had sketched a part of that window. Because of this familiarity I knew just how I intended to go about making my drawing. I planned to take advantage of the trick I had learned while sketching that tower in San Cristóbal. I was going to start from a long way off to make sure I got the proportions right, and then I was going to move closer to fill in the details.

I wanted a view of the portal that was squarely centered. This meant the logical place for starting to work was under the northern archway. The archway was directly in line with my subject and it was as far back as I could get. Once there, however, I did not begin sketching right away. The drawing of the day before had taught me how knowledge aided vision, so I determined to grasp this doorway intellectually before I did anything else.

First, I imposed on myself the discipline of deliberately moving the eye from one defined point to another. Then I made an effort to fix the pattern in my mind by verbalizing it.

The central interest, I said to myself, lies in three arches—the almost flat arch of the doorway, the more deeply bowed arch of the conch shell, and the semicircle topping the window. As well as growing more acute in their bending, the three arches diminish in width.

The arches, I saw, were contained between uprights. Words came easily for the uprights that flanked the door and the shell. They were Corinthian pillars extended by finials. But how to describe the tall outer uprights that framed the whole composition? Suddenly I had it: bedposts.

Because I needed the aid of a central axis, I used my ruler to draw a line down the center of the page. Even with the axis, I found myself unsure of my ability to judge the spacing of the uprights on either side. This was a serious matter, for I knew that to re-create the effect of the doorway, I had to have the verticals set up properly and they had to be exactly right in relation to the horizontals.

To my surprise, I found gauging the respective heights of the doorway's crossbands comparatively easy. Accordingly, I established the horizontals first. After that, blocking in the rest of the portal was not so hard. And using marks along the edge of a piece of paper, I checked to see if I had the matching uprights equidistant from the center line. After a little shifting, I saw the result was pretty good.

My solution led me to wonder if an Oriental would have gone at the difficulty in the same way. "Perhaps," I said to myself, "I solved it as I did because reading has accustomed me to move my eyes horizontally. A

Chinese, used to reading up and down, probably would have found it easier to establish the uprights first."

Having isolated the disciplined left-to-right eye training I had absorbed in the course of learning to read—and seeing how accidental and exceptional it was—I was swept again by my old regret that as a boy no one had given me training in how to direct my eyes so I might be more skillful in observing the world around me.

Behind me, at the foot of the steps, was a public faucet mounted on a cement stanchion shaped like an obelisk. Happening to look around, my attention was arrested by a young fellow making his way toward the faucet. He caught my interest so sharply because, like Ricardo of three years before, he was carrying two big tins, hung like balances from a pole across his shoulders. Could it be my little friend who had got into the movies for half price?

When he reached the faucet and began filling his tins, I saw he could not have been the youngster who had given me water from just such tins on my first visit. Even in three years Ricardo could not have grown into so husky a youth. Besides, Ricardo didn't have this boy's striking eyes. They were the sort that would fill a girl with envy—very large and a velvety brown, and shaded by long, heavy lashes.

Disappointed, I turned back to the last adjustment of my proportions. But even when his tins were filled the youth did not go away. He stood there so long that I was puzzled. An explanation finally dawned on me. Perhaps he was like the men who had stood near me the first day. Perhaps he, too, wanted to see my sketch, and yet was rooted in his place because, on the one hand, he was too shy to ask to inspect it, while, on the other, he was too polite to come to look without asking. Since the work had reached the point where I was ready for a little outside approval, I acted on my hunch and suggested he might like to see my drawing. He smiled and nodded, so I took it down the steps to show to him. Then he went away with his heavy tins of water, apparently well content.

Though it had taken almost an hour, the blocking in of the doorway had not been made more difficult because I was standing. Of necessity, the guidelines had to be light, and neither neatness nor exactitude of outline was essential. But in the next stage—the filling in of detail from up close—I knew precision was required. This, in turn, meant my hand had to be sure, so I decided I'd better fetch my chair, for there was nothing raised to sit on in all the wide expanse of the churchyard.

After I was seated I faced a new dilemma: whether to draw the portal in its ruined state, or to draw it as it was before bombarding cannon had battered it so cruelly. The tracery head being shown unbroken reveals my decision. I drew the design in its original purity because I found, when it came to the actual depiction, I could not bear to record the destruction.

The bedposts were the most badly damaged elements, but I was able to reconstruct them because the destruction was different on each side. Thus I could fill in a missing section on the left by drawing there the same swelling or contraction visible on the right. In other places, I could fill in the right by borrowing from the left.

I began the details from the bottom and, carefully and painstakingly, I started working up. Since where the details were to go had been established by the guidelines, the task of reproducing them was largely mechanical. Patience, I found, was the chief requisite. I needed it in constantly checking with my eyes to see that I kept my details in proportionate scale with the structural members. For remember I could see these things large, which here are shown small. Also I had to impose a mental patience on the bodily impatience of the hand, which of its own nature seemed to want to move quickly.

Don Gabriel, accompanied by Alfonso and little cousin Eliel, came along. Naturally, formalities being what they are, I had to stop to shake hands. When I resumed working they disposed themselves on the grass around me. I was too absorbed to talk, but I enjoyed the sound of their chatter. I particularly enjoyed Eliel's laughter, and the laughter pealed out with many varieties of delight when the child caught two green grasshoppers and decided to pit them against each other as if they were fighting cocks. To fence them in he hunted for long-stemmed dandelions, which he used as the timbers of his miniature arena. But the grasshoppers were not disposed to fight. And Eliel had to go after them when, instead of attacking each other, they hopped over the prone stems of his interlocked dandelions.

It was another beautiful day and, though there was a degree of tediousness in reproducing all the details of the ornamental stonework, I am hard put to describe the contentment I felt as I sketched and my three friends relaxed around me. It arose partly because the task of drawing was engrossing enough to exclude all cares, but not so engrossing that it eliminated the feel of the sunshine and the little winds, or the sounds of Eliel and his older companions.

As the sun grew hotter, the three of them retreated to the shade of the

WEEK IN YANHUITLÁN

church, and there Eliel drew Alfonso into a new game. He insisted on being lifted by the legs so he could be a wheelbarrow. What speed they managed before tumbling, and how Eliel squealed with happiness when Alfonso grasped his legs so firmly that he was carried forward as if he were not a wheelbarrow, but a swan diver.

We had the churchyard to ourselves, but every now and then someone would pass by. One I recognized was José Ortiz, the courteous schoolteacher.

"*Buenos días,*" I called, happy to greet someone other than the three-some who were my companions. He came over, shook hands and expressed pleasure in the drawing. He was cutting across the atrium because he was going to the highway to catch a bus. He was making, he said, a *viajecito.*

I smiled at the term. It meant a little journey, with the smallness being indicated by the *cito* added to the word *viaje.* It was the first time I had heard this particular diminutive, though I had noticed Don Gabriel made any number of things smaller by adding *ito.*

Another passerby was the plump, jolly owner of La Providencia to whom Don Gabriel had waved as we had passed his booth after our first effort to deliver the presidential bottle. This time Don Gabriel introduced his friend. His name was Felix Palma.

The need for patience increased as I got near the top of the drawing. I had been sketching for a long time and anxiety to be finished was trying to hasten my hand. I realized, too, that in starting my heavy penciling from the bottom I'd made the mistake of a man who, by starting to paint a floor from a doorway, paints himself into a corner. It is true, I could retreat by lifting my hand completely, but for this detailed work I had to support my wrist on the paper. Thus I couldn't go on working at the upper details without smudging the lower ones with my palm. I should have begun at the top and worked down. A new lesson learned about drawing.

As the sketch neared completion, I was struck by something curious. The doorway looked more beautiful on the paper than it did in fact. This puzzled me. Surely, I said to myself, adding those imaginary restorations could not have made that much difference. Then I realized I had put the cart before the horse. It was not that I had drawn the doorway more beautiful than it was, but previously I had not recognized the degree of the portal's beauty.

Why had I failed to appreciate it properly? For one thing, I had approached it so objectively—so much as if it were only a matter of elements, proportions and details—that I hadn't even stopped to wonder if it was beautiful. Then I had been so busy putting it down on paper I hadn't paused to allow myself to respond to it aesthetically. Another explanation, even more telling, arose from something physical—the portal's size.

This was no neat little doorway such as a motion picture star might order for the front of a Spanish-style house in Hollywood. It was a design more than one hundred feet high. And that window was not just a fancy stair light on a second floor landing that the designer had incorporated into his pattern. It was a large window high in the nave of a church. What had happened, I saw, was that in the drawing I had reproduced the design of the doorway on a sufficiently small scale so the eye could take it all in with one gulp. Thus I could appreciate the balance, the harmony and the compactness of the design in a simultaneous moment of apprehension. In front of the portal itself this had been impossible. When I looked at the doorway, the window high above was out of eye range. When I looked up at the window, I lost the door. But here, on the paper, doorway and window were together in a space where their relationships could be appreciated. And I saw that to be fully sensible of such a portal one first had to abstract the whole design in the mind, so that one could bring one's knowledge of the total design to one's inspection of the parts.

Later I was to become aware of another and more subtle factor that had stood in the way of my immediate appreciation of that magnificent portal. There are always many elements that contribute to our delighted apprehension of a work of art. One of the most important elements—though often one of the least recognized—is the element of style. Thus when we respond, say, to the nave of Canterbury Cathedral, we respond not only to its intrinsic beauty, but to its Gothicness. And how much we are thrilled by that nave is conditioned by how much we love the Gothic style. Being at home with the style through familiarity with many examples of it, in turn, conditions our love.

To take an example from music. Many musical beginners love Tchaikovsky, but find themselves indifferent to Bach and Handel. It is partly because they feel at home in the Romantic style whereas they feel like tourists in a chilly place in the Baroque. But the man who knows and loves the Baroque style will love Handel and Bach—and respond to them with heightened intensity for the very Baroqueness that makes the neophyte uncomfortable. And so it was with my response to that portal.

Its style is Plateresque, a peculiarly Spanish style that derives its name from the fact that its motifs suggested to early critics the work of *plateros*, or silversmiths. One of its characteristics is applied ornamentation that bears little relationship to structural realities. When I began the drawing, Plateresque was not a style with which I had much familiarity, nor one in which I was accustomed to find especial beauty. Thus on my first exposure to the doorway I was not predisposed toward it by its style. On the contrary, I had to find it beautiful in itself before I could see that the style in which it was composed was a style that made possible a distinctive beauty within its particular range.

Alfonso's reaction to the finished drawing was the same as to its predecessors: *"¡Qué milagro!"* Don Gabriel was admiring too, but less awestruck; and as usual he added something helpful. Pointing to the arch of the doorway, he asked if I had noticed the *diamantes*. By these he meant the ornamentation cut in the three concentric arches of the door frame. I had indicated it by a series of little rectangles, but, truth to tell, I had not examined it at all closely. Stimulated by his question, I looked at the rectangles more closely. I could see why he used the word diamonds.

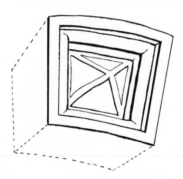

Each rectangle, or panel, was like a stone box containing a countersunk pyramid. And the finish of the workmanship was so fine that each pyramidal diamond point was embellished with a little rib along the ridges where the planes of the faceting met.

"There are diamonds all over the monastery," said Don Gabriel. "They are like the artist's signature."

Next he pointed to the coat of arms on the raised disks on either side of the conch shell. Did I know whose coat that was? I didn't.

"Philip the Second," was the reply. And it gave me gooseflesh to realize this church had been built during the reign of the king who had launched the Armada against England. The building was coeval with Drake, Sir Walter Raleigh and Shakespeare.

The monastery, I knew, had been commandeered as a fortress in two of Mexico's major wars. The day before Don Gabriel had told me its role in the War of Independence: how Régules, the rich landowner had blocked up its choir windows and resisted three attacks in 1812, and how León had finally captured it for the insurgents in 1821. And in Oaxaca I had learned something of its role in the War of French Intervention. When Maximilian, Napoleon III's puppet Emperor, arrived at Veracruz in 1864, French troops, despite two years of fighting, still had not conquered all of Mexico. Díaz held the state of Oaxaca. Maximilian sent French troops to uproot him. They succeeded in doing so, and in conquering the state they seized Yanhuitlán as a strong point to occupy as a fortress. They held it until the autumn of 1866, when Díaz, having escaped from his French jailers and rallied his troops, forced the surrender of the Count de Gants and a squadron of French hussars who were barricaded in the monastery.

Seeing the portal's chipped cornices and its battered pillars (some so badly fractured they had been filled in with concrete), I asked Don Gabriel if the damage had been done in the War of Independence or the French War.

"In neither," he said. "It was done in 1876—in Díaz' rising against the re-election of Sebastián Lerdo de Tejeda."

So Yanhuitlán was involved in still a third nineteenth-century war. And that beautiful doorway had been damaged so badly not in a major conflict for independence or national sovereignty—not in something that might make the price worth the sacrifice—but in a struggle between two political rivals to inherit Juárez' power.

It was sad, but also a little ironic. Part of the scheme of the first Spanish colonizers was that the monasteries built to serve as centers of conversion should be so constructed as to be capable of serving as forts. In fact, the building of fortress-monasteries had been the chief measure taken to protect the colony against Indian uprisings. Yet what had happened? In most places the Indians had remained peaceful, while the white men had used some of their fortress-monasteries, including this one, as bases for blasting each other.

Consulting my watch, I saw it was exactly noon. The drawing had taken three hours, but there was still time for one more before lunch. As a relief from the slow, painstaking work on the north portal, I wanted something fairly big and simple that I could draw boldly and freely. Why not the monastery from the rear—the aspect of the building I had seen in a flash of picture-vision the morning before? The idea was no sooner entertained than accepted. When I told Don Gabriel my plan, he insisted on carrying the chair; and, followed by Alfonso and Eliel, we made our way to the plaza.

Whenever I sketch anything I have seen with the particular flash of vision I'd had with the back of the monastery, I have found the drawing emerges with almost miraculous ease. And it happened again here. Having glimpsed the rear as a picture the day before, transforming it into a picture-in-fact was almost child's play. During the blocking in I hardly made a false stroke, and my hand was sure and steady when I began to draw the darker lines.

The apses of most sixteenth-century Mexican churches are rectangular or polygonal. I knew therefore that Yanhuitlán apse was unusual in being semicircular. As I tried to suggest the smoothness of its curve, I became aware of another of its distinctions. It was constructed of carefully dressed stone, laid in beautifully even courses. The planes of the sacristy were equally clean, for it, too, was constructed of carefully finished blocks set in level courses with fine joints. In a flash, I recalled the rough stones of irregular shape embedded in mortar that form the backs and sides of most Mexican conventos. Yanhuitlán, then, was not like them. A few have façades of cut stone, and some façades are made to seem smooth because a heavy

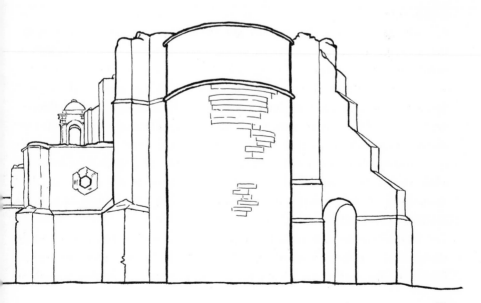

coating of plaster conceals the imperfections of the stonework, but most of them are of rubble construction, with the rubble clearly showing everywhere except at the front. But Yanhuitlán, I realized, had no need of such plastering, front or back. And a shift of my eyes confirmed what I had sensed without sharp realization: The adjoining monastic complex is also built of ashlar masonry. This is almost unheard of; and the use of finely cut stone for the outbuildings too sets Yanhuitlán apart still further.

The edge of the monastic platform, and the sheer wall rising up to it, are better preserved at the rear than at the front. As I drew from the lower level of the plaza, I realized the edge of the platform was obscuring the foundation, as the front edge had done with the western façade two days earlier. Thus in my sketch the building did not look as tall as it actually was. But this time I decided not only to leave in the platform edge, but to exploit it. The way it cuts off the base with a clean line is characteristic of the plaza view.

Being in the plaza was very pleasant. As a bird-starved city dweller, I loved the sound of the birds that peeped and chirped in the trees surrounding the fountain. So, just as there had been contentment as I drew the north portal, there was contentment as I drew here too; and it was enhanced by the children who were playing about in the tranquil, trafficless square. Two of the little boys were pointed out to me by Don Gabriel as being the sons of El Presidente. Arturo, who might have been the lad who went to fetch his father from the back of the store, was about ten. Jorge was about eight.

Because of my desire to relive my first stopover in Yanhuitlán, my eyes had been peeled for the man with the pushcart who sold ices. I had seen no sign of him, so I was greatly delighted when, glancing up from my drawing, I saw a member of his tribe approaching the plaza. This was a different man and he did not have a cart, but I knew the wooden bucket he was balancing on his head held *paletas*. And the children were already assembled for the party! What luck!

The man's popsicles were orange, lime and vanilla, and I asked each child to pick the flavor he wanted. How they hovered over the bucket after it had been placed on the ground and opened up! And as I knew they would, further children materialized. Arturo, El Presidente's older boy, if I remember correctly, wanted orange, his brother Jorge wanted lime. Thereafter the distribution became so wholesale I lost track. But when everyone seemed accounted for, and when I had seen that even two little girls in the corner of the park, who were too shy to come forward, had received their ices, the *paleta* salesman told me I owed him for sixteen.

Glancing around to make sure no one was overlooked, my eye was greeted by an entrancing spectacle. Eliel had retreated to the shade of a skimpy casuarina tree and he was sitting there, cross-legged, eating a vanilla ice from the stick in his right hand, while with his other hand he held an orange popsicle in the deepest shade the casuarina offered. He had snitched two and he wanted the orange to melt as little as possible in the time needed to eat the vanilla.

THE NOVELTY of Lupe's lunch was a fresh napkin for the tablecloth. The un-novelty was the presence of tortillas and frijoles. And at this meal the bits of stewed meat in the sauce were recognizable. Unmistakably, they were kidneys.

"*Riñones*," I said, delighted to show off the new Spanish word I had learned through the beans that morning. "*Si*," smiled Lupe.

As I ate, I had the sense of gratitude that I had felt at each of their meals. I think it was this that prompted me to ask Don Gabriel if they had a grace in Spanish. With his aid I wrote it out: *Gracias a Dios, que me vas a dar de comer este día. Bendice mi comida.*

The first sentence I understood right away, but the second stumped me. I asked Don Gabriel what it meant. Nothing he said seemed to elucidate the meaning, so he took to pantomime. He stood up, and light dawned when he gestured like a priest giving a benediction.

After lunch, as I was shaving in the doorway, I heard a little voice say "*Adiós*." I looked up and saw Angelita, the older of the two little girls to whom I had given candies the day before. She had resorted to speech as a desperate measure, for in my absorption with my shaving I had failed to notice her as she passed. I knew it meant she was in the market for a candy, so I gave her a caramel, which was the type in the latest bag I had opened. She departed, and the red ribbons in her pigtails were bobbing as she skipped away.

More little squirrels were about, as I discovered when I heard childish voices calling me from the safety of their own doorway, which was in a house catercorner from Don Gabriel's. The ringleader looked like Paco, the six-year-old bantamweight of the day before. I showed I had heard them by waving in reply. Then, apparently regretting their boldness, they vanished back inside the house. But I was pretty sure they would reappear. They did.

But they did not have the nerve to come over to my doorway. So I decided to take a handful of caramels over to theirs.

As I drew closer, I saw there were five of them, three boys and two girls. All five retreated to the inner courtyard as I reached their house. The girls never came forward, but Paco and the two other boys did. I gave them each a caramel and added two extra ones for their timid sisters. *"Gracias,"* the boys called back as they turned on their heels to make delivery.

I returned to my room for a siesta. But I did not sleep long and by two-thirty I was ready to draw more doorways. As I was locking my door, I saw Lupe was locking hers. Her arms were full of flowers, beautiful mauve lilies, which she called *reginas*. She was taking them for one of the altars, and she wanted to find Don Gabriel to be let into the church. She thought he was up by the monastery. We went to find him together, and we came upon him, sitting in the gap of the ruined wall, poring over the book on symbolism which had helped identify the cross patée. Its drawings had fascinated him, and he had asked to borrow it.

THE FIRST DOORWAY I wanted to draw in the church was the one that had looked so beautiful the day before as it framed the apricot tree standing in the dappled sunlight of the cloister.

The position of this doorway is shown in the plan on page 12. It is midway down the nave on the south side. The plan shows, too, that no pillars or side aisles break up the interior. Thus, even though I was indoors, I had no difficulty finding a position of good visibility far enough back from the door. The church was forty-five feet wide.

When I had picked my starting point, I solicited Don Gabriel's aid in moving one of the church's benches to it. Having something to sit on from the start, I could rest my sketchbook on my knee. So the book was supported through the blocking-in stage, which had not been true with the north portal. The comfort made the work much easier; and, since this doorway was also something I had seen in a flash of pictorial vision, my hand had the same sureness it had in drawing the monastery from the rear.

With this doorway I was not interested in establishing the exact center till the freehand blocking in was complete. Lupe, having arranged her flowers, returned as I began to do the centering. She watched as I placed a piece of paper across the rough sketch. When I marked the two edges of the doorway and folded the paper to get the middle crease between the marks, Lupe was tickled. It was just the way she found her centers in sewing.

The only real difficulty I had with this drawing was taking the pesky lines of the molding around the corners of the archway. Parallel lines close together are hard enough to draw freehand, even when they are straight. In curves it is almost impossible not to run them together. I had to do a lot of erasing. As I concentrated on these fine inner lines, I realized I was learning another lesson about the importance of molding. That wide, many-banded molding was certainly an important element in the beauty of that doorway. My special difficulty in getting the lines around the corners made me painfully aware, too, that the arch was not a semicircle. That would have been so much easier.

Flipping back a leaf of the sketchbook to the morning's drawing of the north portal, I took a closer look at the curve of the door frame there. Since it wasn't a semicircle either, my eyes were opened to one of the characteristics of the Yanhuitlán doorways. They were not mere compass-drawn half circles. They were more subtly beautiful than that, and each one, I was to find, had its own particular curve.

This doorway, with the crowned woman in the niche at the top, was not white like most of the doorways of the establishment. Though the hues were faded, the doorway still gave evidence of an early color scheme. The molding I had such trouble drawing was ochre and black. The side pillars were olive green with sepia plumes painted on them as if the great feathers were floating upward in a spiral. The statue and its shell niche were gold and there was a lot of terra cotta in the shadows of the various moldings. There was also painting on the flat surfaces in and around the doorway. Big flowers sprawled up the sides, and on each side of the queen's niche was a Gothic rose.

Don Gabriel said all the church was once painted like this doorway. "Then when did they do all this whitewashing?" I asked, including the ceilings and the walls in a sweeping gesture. "In 1831, after the cholera epidemic."

This amazed me, for the white was so clean I had unhesitatingly concluded it had been applied in the wave of anticlericalism in the late 1920's when Calles had ordered all priests to register as foreign agents.

Don Gabriel studied my drawing. He pointed out that here, too, were diamonds, though only on the pedestals of the pillars.

Then he asked if I could identify the crowned woman in the shell-like niche. "The Virgin Mary," I replied promptly. "No," he said, "that's Santa Catalina."

Catalina is the Spanish version of Catherine. But Don Gabriel did not give me a chance to inquire which St. Catherine was represented, for he swept on to say that what she held in her right hand was her sword.

I blushed to realize how little I had speculated about what I had sketched in. It was true I had the excuse that, as Don Gabriel pointed out, the sword was broken. But that hardly seemed enough. And I blushed even more when he drew my attention to the lump at her feet. It was something I had not even noticed.

"That's her father's head," he said, and with this clue I could see the lump was wearing a turban.

"Her father's head!" I repeated incredulously.

"Yes," said Don Gabriel. "She cut it off."

It seemed hard to believe the Catholic Church would canonize a woman who had killed her father in such a fashion, so in the pause following Don Gabriel's dramatic announcement, I pressed him to tell me which St. Catherine it was. He didn't know. But he said he knew her story. She dated back to pagan times, he related, and she was a princess who, along with many of her people, was converted to Christianity. Her father, though, stoutly remained pagan. Not only this, he persecuted her fellow Christians. Finally, to save her coreligionists, she hacked off daddy's head.

More incredulous than ever, I asked Don Gabriel who had told him this story. "The priest," he said.

I was right to be skeptical. Later, when I was back in New York, I tracked down the saint. She was St. Catherine of Alexandria, a virgin of royal descent who lived in the fourth century. She was a famous bluestocking in her day and was said to have confounded not only the Emperor Maximin, but fifty pagan philosophers too. The head at her feet was symbolic of her victorious debate. The sword was the instrument of her martyrdom, for legend has it that, after the spiked wheel on which she was to have been killed miraculously split apart, her angry executioners took up a sword and finished her off that way.

The other doorway in the church I wanted to draw was the one nearer the altar leading into the *sagrario,* which is the distinguishing local name for the *capilla* on the eastern side of the cloister. This doorway, too, appears in the plan on page 12.

Lupe had stayed in the church with Don Gabriel as I had completed the other doorway, and she stayed with him through the drawing of this one too. It was good to have her in the party, for previously I had felt Don

Gabriel and I had left her out of things. Part of my pleasure in sketching in the high cool church was hearing them whisper together as they sat on a bench beside me.

Suddenly I heard more than whispering. It was music, and I looked up to see that Don Gabriel had gone to the little harmonium. He was pumping it with his feet and running one hand up and down the keys. He didn't know how to play, but he was having a good time, and I was delighted at the boyishness in his attitude. From the way he broke off, I knew he had done it partly to startle me, partly to show off the organ and partly for the sheer fun of making a noise in the almost oppressively quiet church.

After the north doorway and Santa Catalina's, drawing the smaller *sagrario* portal was like running one hundred yards after training for the mile. It went so easily I had sufficient mental freedom to speculate as I drew. Those finials on either side of the shell certainly looked like candlesticks. Then I remembered one of the most interesting parts of Pál Kelemen's *Baroque and Rocco in Latin America.*

In the Spanish colonies, he wrote, native sculptors often reproduced Spanish objects and designs in the most unexpected ways. They would be shown a silver plate, say, etched with a foliage design. Then not knowing— or perhaps not caring—that such a design had been created expressly to embellish a small household article, they would carve a large version of it to decorate the wall of a church. The style of this doorway was fairly pure Plateresque, but perhaps those candlesticks betrayed its colonial origin. They might well be the work of an Indian, who, unrestricted in his mind by European art conventions, had decided the altar's sticks, with their candles included, would serve very well as models for the finials he knew he had to carve to flank the shell.

The shell itself was even more interesting, and its raised lines, like the narrow bands of the candlesticks, were picked out in gold. Naturally, this shell led me back to my drawing of the shell over the north portal, and I saw that the two were in different positions. On the larger doorway the hinge of the scallop was at the top; here the hinge—and it was much more realistically depicted—was at the bottom. This shell, in consequence, radiated upwards. The orientations recalled something else in Kelemen: how he shows four shell portals where the positions also vary. And remembering his photographs—all of eighteenth-century churches—I realized that in a later era these shells over the doors became so large and cavernous that they engulfed the portals. In some later churches one sees entire doorways stand-

ing in massive shell niches the way Santa Catalina stands under her golden shell in her niche at Yanhuitlán.

When the unblocked mind is making discoveries, it generally does not stop at one. And something else flashed into my memory—a sketch I had seen in leafing through the Griffith book.

"*Por favor*," I said to Don Gabriel "the sign book." Almost feverishly I leafed through it till I came to the sketch I remembered. It was the third illustration of the "Shields of the Apostles." And my memory was correct. It *was* a scallop shell on that shield. And the name of the apostle confirmed my hunch. It was St. James the Greater, and I knew that St. James, or Santiago as he is called in the Spanish-speaking world, was the patron saint of Spain.

The shells were used in the designs, then, because the Spanish builders wanted to impress the attribute of their patron saint upon this great church they were putting up in this colony. Greedy for more information, I turned to the reading matter under the shield. Here the book provided another revelation—the reason for the scallop shell's association with James. Tradition says St. James crossed the Mediterranean to preach in Spain. The shell is a symbol of "pilgrimage by the sea."

Excitedly I turned to Don Gabriel.

"See," I said, "these doorways have shells because shells are the symbol of Santiago." He was as delighted at having the explanation as I was. And this was another landmark in our relations. Up to this time, he had been the one who had been doing all the explaining. But here was a case where I had been able to point out something significant to him. We were growing in our knowledge of the monastery together.

Realizing the symbolism of the shell, I thought how apt a decoration it was for this particular foundation. To build it the Dominicans had embarked on wider and far more unknown water than St. James. The church, in very truth, was the result of a long pilgrimage by sea.

Since Lupe had been so obliging about admiring my artwork, I asked her if she wouldn't show me hers. Could I see her mauve lilies on the altar? This meant passing under the shell doorway and going into the *sagrario*.

The flowers, divided among four vases, looked lovely on the far end of the chapel; and, to her pleasure, I told Lupe so. Yet there was no disguising that the flowers were dwarfed by one of the glories of the monastery: the life-size representation of the Descent from the Cross that fills most of the wall space above the altar.

Because the figures are colored realistically, it suggests a painting, but actually it is a huge marble bas-relief. It shows St. John and the three tearful Marys at the foot of the cross, while four men work to lower the dead Christ. The action is depicted at the point where the men have all but Jesus's left hand free. A workman high on the ladder sustains the weight of the body in a sling, and two other men steady the dangling body, while the other workman uses pliers to wrench out that last nail holding the transfixed hand.

It was massive and a little crude, especially in the modeling; and the colors applied to it—yellow, blue, red, green and white, with a few gold lines—were anything but subtle. Yet it had what Bernard Berenson has singled out as the most essential attribute in a work of art—the power to stimulate the tactile consciousness. Not only did it tell its story, but it made one aware of the reality of the scene by making it almost physically palpable. In imagination, one could feel the weight of the limp body in the sling. One could share the awkward position of the yellow-clad Nicodemus on the ladder, and with him one could grasp those feet. One could cherish that head the way Joseph of Arimathaea was doing as he lifted the winding sheet that fell back over his blue robe. Above all, in the way the nail extractor held the arm he did not want to damage further, one could feel the force of his prying on that nail.

What a contrast with the other chief work of art in the *sagrario!* The other was a canvas filling the lunette over the door at the other end of the barrel-vaulted chamber. It was a crudely allegorical painting, done mostly in blues, white and tan. It showed a small triumphal car with gold wheels and a blue chassis. An angel was at the driver's seat and the animals he was urging on were not, as one might expect, a pair of horses, but a lion and an ox, while above them flew an eagle holding in his beak a ribbon extending from the chariot. Angels and cherubs hovered round the honor seat at the back, but what was occupying that seat seemed to me even more incongruous than the unexpected draft animals. It was not a human or divine figure, but a golden sunburst mounted on a stand resembling the stem of a chalice. I knew it was a monstrance, but it did seem odd to find a bit of altar furnishing sitting where one was accustomed to seeing Bacchus.

I asked Don Gabriel if he understood the allegory. He said he didn't. The date of the painting, I noted, was 1861, and I shrugged it off as characteristic of the taste of the period.

My fancy was caught, though, by a figure against one of the side walls.

It was a Jesus in a violet cloak mounted on a papier-maché ass, as if he were riding into Jerusalem. It had the naïve quality of folk art, and I stored it in my mind as one of the religious figures I would draw when I had completed the architecture.

Though virtually stripped now, the *sagrario* clearly must have been an important part of the friary. The Descent from the Cross was proof of that. I asked Don Gabriel why it had been so splendid. His answer made everything intelligible. It had been the foundation's chapter house.

"Don't you see the benches?" he asked. And he pointed to a feature I had not noticed: long, unbroken stone banquettes that went around the room. As I understood their function, I had a vision of the friars ranged along the benches as the solemn business of the monastery was conducted.

Leaving the chapter room, I noticed further evidence of the care to give it splendor. Its dark wooden doors were sumptuously carved. Not only were all the panels filled with rich foliage ornamentation, but the central panel of each door was recessed in the shape of a cross. The crosses were as heavily embossed with floral carving as the rectangles surrounding them.

The plan on page 12 shows that in being outside the carved door we were near the sacristy. Because sacristies are robing rooms where the priests' vestments, the altar linens and the sacred vessels are kept, they are often imposing. The fact that I had missed this one on my first visit to Yanhuitlán had not troubled me, for I had not known it was there. But in the meantime handsome sacristies had so often been high points in visits to other Mexican monasteries that I had come to realize that the sacristy of an establishment is nearly always one of its showplaces. With this particular vestry, too, sitting on its dome, drawing its diamond and hexagonal windows and sketchings its rear flank nestling beside the apse had made me sharply conscious of its existence. And its exterior aspects had been striking enough to give promise of a fine interior, so I asked Don Gabriel if we could go in. He shook his head. The priest kept his personal things there and only the priest had the key. I knew that El Cura was in Oaxaca.

By this time it was nearly six o'clock. Two important stone doorways remained undrawn. But I was willing to let them go until tomorrow. They were both in the cloister, and the cloister was the subject I had chosen for my fourth day.

VIII
THE RISING OF THE MOON

THE PATTERN OF THE EVENING was identical with that of the two previous ones. Once more Alfonso came at six-thirty, and with Don Gabriel we again went to watch the sunset. Lupe served hot milk and frijoles for dinner. As before, there was a little conversation at the end of the meal. And at eight o'clock Don Gabriel lit me to my room, and presumably to bed.

But I found I was not disposed to stretch out on that sacrificial altar so early. The night air was balmy and it was so dark that Don Gabriel could not see me flying in the face of his courtesy. So I betook myself up the slope across from my room and decided to sit for a while under the stars. They were bright and clear in the charcoal blackness of the sky and the Milky Way arched overhead in a decisive band.

The stars have a way of inducing detachment, and as I lay back to look at them a question began to form in my mind.

I had a distinct sense of being let down. In its lack of local handicrafts, Yanhuitlán was perhaps the least artistic town I had visited in Mexico. No fiesta was scheduled during the period of my stay, and the ordinary days had an almost unbelievable uniformity. The people were less expansive than I had expected. And I was being cut off from any exploring or idle adventuring by the physical requirements of my self-imposed task. There was no getting around it, drawing was manual work. And it took time. It took mental concentration, too—so much, in fact, that there was hardly a sign of the significant reflections I thought might arise from the experience of living in such a village. In brief, my great adventure was turning out to be a very tame affair.

The question that formed was this: Why had I thrown myself into this mild project with such crazy intensity? There had been something almost obsessive in my behavior. With that realization, what had not been in my awareness at all suddenly became obvious. I had been under compulsion. My failure to think more objectively in advance of some of the realities that would be involved in the visit was proof of this. My irrational determination to get that permit from the Institute before I did anything else in Mexico was further evidence. Just as surely, the disproportionate, almost trembling anxiety I had felt about the permit showed something blindly emotional had been underlying my request for a favor I had every expectation of receiving.

Those rejections, those rejections. . . . They must have hurt me even more than I had acknowledged. Otherwise why should I have tried to bury myself so deeply in a Mexican village?

I had discovered Mexico right after World War II when I went there as a miserably dislocated veteran. The rhythm of its life had brought a new music into my own. Five times I had returned, and on each visit my happiness seemed richer and more perfect. This gave me the clue to the motive of flight in my compulsion. I was fleeing from the unhappiness of failure to a place where I was sure happiness lay. But why had failing with one manuscript given me such a feeling of desolation?

I had asked myself the question many times. Already I had penetrated through several levels. I had taken it past the disappointment of four years' labor gone for nothing, past the dashing of so many hopes, past feelings of attachment for one particular brain child, until I had become aware that my whole self-confidence was involved. If I had failed in this work, where the material seemed so good, surely I would fail in all others. In other words, I had reached the point of knowing my dejection was caused in large part by loss of confidence in my literary gifts.

As I sat there in the darkness, I saw, with sudden effortlessness, a deeper explanation.

It is an attitude perhaps less common than it used to be, but I look on the profession of the writer as a vocation. I had chosen it, rather than medicine, the ministry or teaching, because I felt my gifts, such as they were, had made me more fitted for it than the others. And it was a decision I had made more than twenty years before. What that failure had done to me was, not just to make me question whether or not I had a certain skill—that was relatively unimportant—but to make me feel that perhaps I had based my whole adult life on a false assumption. Its truly undermining effect, then, was that it had shaken one of the chief faiths sustaining me—faith in the rightness of my vocation.

I had been fleeing from more than the unhappiness of failure. I had been fleeing, too, from the unhappiness of heart-corroding doubts.

This insight revealed that coming for material for a new book only partially explained my pilgrimage. And, as I recalled the book plan, I realized I had better wipe it off my slate.

A good book does not necessarily need intense physical action. External action and variety of interest, of course, help any story. But the mind has its own drama, and a book almost devoid of outward excitement can be an absorbing and moving record if it deals with some significant inner drama. But what was I going to obtain at Yanhuitlán?

Already I had lost my two hopeful themes. The one about the people's love of their church had gone up in smoke when I had discovered the church was not a focal point inspiring unified devotion. The other one—the re-encountering of familiar characters—had vanished when I found so many friends had gone away.

Unless, then, there was some alteration in the day-to-day patterning of the visit—and I saw no indication of such change—I obviously was not going to get what I sought. Faced with this ultimate disappointment, I sized up the situation by saying to myself: If more doesn't happen in the town—or inside me—it won't be much of a book.

With that ruefully humorous verdict, I resigned myself to abandoning the idea.

For most of us, fortunately, periods of brooding and grief seem to have natural limits. They can sweep back over us on later occasions, but when specific bouts have spent their force we find our attention being claimed once more by things around us. And this happened here. My mind, through for the moment with pursuing its disappointments, turned once more to the outer world. I became aware that an overcast of clouds had advanced to cover the stars. Now there was not even starlight. God, it was dark!

Suddenly I heard a mysterious noise. It induced an irrational wave of fear. Frozen into stillness, I listened more carefully. The noise suggested an animal cropping the grass. I heard the snuffling and the biting and tearing by the teeth. I though of that scene in Traven's *The Treasure of Sierra Madre*, where two Americans, seeking work in Mexico, had found themselves stranded on the black road overnight and were terrified when they heard an animal moving near them. They climbed a tree and spent the night in wakeful agony, dreading the beast, only to discover when daylight came that it was a peaceful burro grazing in a pasture. Probably this animal was only a burro too. But I did not like the idea of anything so big being so close.

One fear tends to beget another. Suddenly I remembered that poor navy vet at Tapachula—the one they called "Nature Boy." Remembering how the natives had sneaked up on him and attacked him with machetes, I felt I was a fool to be sitting there in the pitch-black, equally exposed.

I beat a retreat. But I still did not want to go to bed, so I got my chair and set it up a few steps from my door. From there, if I heard any stealthy steps, I could easily reach my room and barricade myself behind those braced doors.

One or two people passed along the ridge of the slope where I had been sitting. I knew of their movement only by the flashlights they carried. Even though they were against the sky, it was impossible to see them as anything but bobbing lights.

Someone without a light approached. It must have been a young man, for only a youth could have whistled that loudly. And it occurred to me he must have been whistling with such false bravado because he, too, was afraid in the dark.

The whistler passed. A little later, down the street where he had gone, I heard a dog bark. It was a quiet, unvoiced "huff" addressed obviously to owners. And it was a single "huff," as if the dog did not want to call attention to itself, lest there be prowling enemies. A door opened. A gold rectangle was thrown across the black street. The dog entered and the rectangle of light disappeared as the door closed.

A phrase welled up from some part of my subconscious—"ancestral night." I couldn't remember where I had read it, but I was sure whoever coined it had in mind just such darkness as was all around me. Then another phrase came to me—"nightfall." And the fact that the darkness should seem so strange to me revealed a basic element in human history that I, as a city-dweller, born after the invention of electricity, had never properly realized. The significance of nightfall—this was what I had forgotten, or, indeed, never known.

In our electrified cities, the lights come on so rapidly that we are hardly aware of the nightly coming of the dark. Because it scarcely affects our lives, we lose our consciousness of the ancestral night into which the earth keeps rotating. But in Yanhuitlán such forgetfulness was never possible. Nightfall was always a major factor in life. And with that realization came another. The era of electricity is only a drop of time in the ocean of man's history. And since Edison, the fraction of the earth that has been electrified is small in relation to the whole surface of the globe. Those of us who know well-lit cities, then, are history's freaks. What has become so common to us as to make unrelieved nightfall seem strange is, in actuality, the thing which is *un*common in human experience. For the vast majority of mankind, through endless centuries, the coming of night has always been what it still is to the people of Yanhuitlán.

I thought of Lupe's room and of how beautiful it looked each night in the soft, transfiguring light of the candle. And I saw that its beauty did not come only from the light. The light derived its beauty in large part, from the darkness. And it was not simply a matter of contrast. One loved the light not merely because it was golden while the darkness was black, but because the golden radiance created an area of safety and peace from which the blackness was excluded. One loved the light not only for what it was—for what it represented and for what it made possible—but for what it was not. It was not the ancestral night outside into which the earth had turned.

But even as I had been sitting there the darkness seemed to have been alleviated. At first I interpreted it merely as the adjustment of my eyes. Holding up my hand, though, I saw from its vague whiteness that the sense of more light was not just an illusion.

The moon, the moon! I said to myself, for I knew this barely perceptible foreglow was proof that it could not be too far below those eastern hills. Excitedly I scrambled up the slope to my old place so I could have a house-free vantage point to see the spectacle.

Because Yanhuitlán is fitted lengthwise into the northern end of its valley, the hills on the east run just as parallel with the main street as the hills on the west. So I knew the profile I was to watch stood exactly across from the crests where I had seen the sun disappear.

As yet, though, hills and sky were equally black. But as the familiar profile began to be faintly discernible I knew the sky was less black than it had been. Soon the lightening was so apparent that, as well as seeing the undulating line of the crests of the hills, I could see the black frontier of the overcast that hovered not far above. Then a beautiful silvery grayness began to come into the intervening band of clear sky. As the free space grew more crystalline, the blackness of the hills became velvety. Suddenly the lowering clouds were edged with pearl. Then the moon's aureole—a strong bright gold—showed above the velvety profile. As the aureole grew brighter, the pearly under lines of the clouds turned to gleaming silver. And at 8:37 the first bright corner of the moon pushed up behind the hills. Soon I saw it was the left corner, for the right side had been nibbled away.

Lopsided, very big and lime gold, the moon took thirteen minutes to rise entirely free of the hills. Then how it transformed the valley! Where there had been total darkness I could see to write. And I cast an enormously long shadow. The most striking difference, though, was in the monastery. The cypress growing from the cloister was preternaturally black. So were the windows. But the tower and the flat walls facing the moon were as if painted with phosphorous. And those moonlit flanks made sharp angles with the dark walls that were in shadow. So I discovered something else about the monastery. The marvelous receiver of light was as notable for its reception of moonlight as for the way it took the sunlight. Indeed, as I saw the moonlit monastery standing so dramatically against the dark western sky, I got the impression that the architect who had designed that cubelike corner, those unadorned walls and the curve of that rounded apse must have had a special thought for how they would look in the moonlight.

The period of glory lasted only ten minutes. It was so beautiful I had the feeling of being caught up into a purer, more ethereal world that I have experiencd in listening to Mozart. But soon, as I knew it must, the moon climbed into the overcast. The cloud deck was so heavy it obscured the shining disk completely. But although it became dark once more, this darkness was not total. A grayness was in it, for the moon, though it could not be seen, was providing enough diffused light to make basic forms perceptible.

I was standing exactly where I had been when that wave of fear swept over me. Yet now I did not feel at all afraid, and because of this I was able to apprehend a significant distinction. It is not the darkness that makes us panicky when we have imagined a lurking danger; it is the not being able to see.

Fear was not the only feeling that had gone. Depression had vanished too. It was as if the discouragement churned up by the remembered rejections had been cleansed away by the rising of the moon. That magical radiaance, which had flooded the landscape with silver, had wrought the same sort of change in my heart that it had wrought in the valley. From the depths of darkness it had brought me though an interlude of seraphic beauty to a mood of comfortable grayness in which I felt relaxed, at peace and ready at last to join the rest of Yanhuitlán in sensibly going home to bed.

IX

THE CLOISTER

EACH MORNING I had heard the beat-beat-beating of an old gasoline motor somewhere back of my room. It usually began about six o'clock and I had learned from Don Gabriel that it operated the machine that ground the villagers' corn. On my fourth morning it was already running when I woke at six-thirty. And it was responsible for the sight I saw when I looked out the peephole to greet the new day. There were three women, and a little boy in a poncho, all coming from the mill. They made a marvelously harmonious group, for they were carrying their cornmeal in little sacks slung over their backs and supported by leather straps across their brows.

They made their way up the slope and proceeded in single file along the edge of the platform. Because my room was low and they were high, they formed a frieze against the horizon. The uniformity of the three female figures, the backward-flowing drapery of their wide skirts, and the youngster, obliged by his load to bend in the same attitude as the women, gave me a fresh sense of one of the most remarkable characteristics of Mexican countryfolk. I think it must be because of some harmony in their inner relationships, for, when they are in a group, either in repose or in activity, they seem to fall naturally into compositions so rhythmic and well unified that they cry out for rendering by an artist.

Breakfast began with a cup of hot chocolate. Then came a dish in which kidneys were mixed with eggs and potatoes; and there was a green sauce to go with it. Tortillas served as bread. When I had finished the main dish, I was so full I declined the inevitable frijoles. But I did accept a cup of tea. It looked like ordinary orange pekoe, but it had a totally different taste. It was *cedrón*, Lupe said, and its delicate juniper flavor was pleasant to linger over.

Don Gabriel began telling me more of the glories of California. Did I know how many different ways they served meals there? You could eat sitting at a counter in drugstores. You could even drive up to a restaurant in an automobile and be served in your car. The time he remembered best was when he went into a huge dining room with some other Mexicans and sat down. They waited and waited for someone to bring them their dinner. But no one came. Did I know why? He waited for my guess.

"Was it because you were Mexicans?" I asked, suspecting discrimination. "No," and he laughed merrily. "The place was a—how do you call it—a cafeteria."

Lupe, who must have heard the story many times, laughed again at the thought of her Gabriel being kept waiting. I laughed, too, for I had never stopped to think how incomprehensible a vast, gleaming cafeteria would be to a Mexican male who had never heard of self-service.

"Were the people of California kind to you?" I asked.

"Yes, but they sometimes made fun of us. Do you know what they called us?"

His expression showed a joke was coming.

"*Estufas.*" Fortunately, I knew the Spanish words that made me see the humor. An *estufa* is a stove. The reader, who remembers that *bracero* means a man who works with his arms, can see the humor too if he realizes that a *brasero* is the Spanish word for the type of stove we call a brazier. With the two words, *bracero* and *brasero*, being so similar, one can readily see how Californians used one instead of the other.

Since I had set myself the cloister as my assignment for the day, my thoughts were turning toward it. Did Don Gabriel know when that big cypress was planted there? It was about the time the monastery was completed, he said, for it was meant to be symbolic of the growth of the friary. If I'd wait a moment he would give me the exact date. Then he got out some typewritten pages and began searching through them. His hunting produced the year. It was 1573.

Did the typed sheets have other historical facts? They did, and he showed them to me. They turned out to be sections copied from books that had passages about Yanhuitlán. And his answer to my next question gave me new insight into his attitude to his work. Those sheets had not been furnished by the Institute as a sort of course in what he should know as a

WEEK IN YANHUITLÁN

guide. He had acquired them by typing them out himself. He agreed to let me borrow them.

After returning to my room I visited the patio. Since many of the weeds growing there had bright flowers, I paused to pick some. I came, too, on a rusty old talcum powder tin which I retrieved for a vase. When the bouquet was placed on the little table, I was delighted at how much color the flowers brought into the severe room. They seemed just what was needed to bring charm to the whitewashed walls, the beamed ceiling and the brick floor.

Since Don Gabriel was the only one with the keys to the cloister, I could not start my day's drawing until he had finished his breakfast. To put in time, I turned to his typed material.

I had the information he had passed on about the sieges of the monastery in the War of Independence, the War of the French Intervention and the rising of Díaz against Lerdo. But it also gave me something fresh. The monastery, it said, had been the scene of a battle between a Liberal leader, Col. Rafael Cataneo, and a Conservative one, Capt. Rafael Martél. The Liberals won.

That was not much to go on. But it was enough, for the date of the battle was given—April 13, 1858. It confirmed what I had guessed from the Liberal and Conservative labels. Yanhuitlán had been in a fourth war— the dreadful civil war of 1856 to 1859 known as the Three Years War. This was the war that the Liberals, under Juárez, finally won; the war that was followed by his Reform Laws that suppressed the monasteries, and the war that paved the way for the confiscation of those silver candelabra that financed the construction of Yanhuitlán's municipal building. It also paved the way for the French Intervention. Because the Conservatives would not accept the decision of battle they invited Napoleon III to send an army to defeat their Liberal president and to give them a Conservative emperor.

One of Yanhuitlán's Liberals, I read, had been executed by a French firing squad in 1863, because, as municipal president, he had defied the conquerors. He was Justo Rodriguez. This was doubly interesting, for Yanhuitlán's school bears his name and he was the man responsible for that fine building in the plaza.

A sound like a sudden rushing of wind made me look up. Goats were being chased down the slope by a man in a sarape. It was over in a moment and, perhaps for the very fact that it was so momentary, it startled me into the sort of vision in which one sees a scene forever. For I have found that generally what prints a scene on the mind indelibly is neither length of exposure nor intrinsic importance, but the way it is seen. And with indelible vision I saw that flock of goats racing diagonally down that slope, the man in pursuit.

A moment later it happened again. And again the enduring image was caused by the nature of my perception, rather than by the momentousness of what occurred before my eyes. The vision was none other than Eliel, the happy ten-year-old, who the day before had tried to make the grasshoppers fight in an arena of dandelions. He passed on a perfectly routine errand, but to this day I can see the handful of wheat stalks he carried in one hand and the sickle he had in the other.

Together with the man chasing his goats and the women bowing under their loads as they returned from the mill, Eliel made the third entrancing

CHURCH

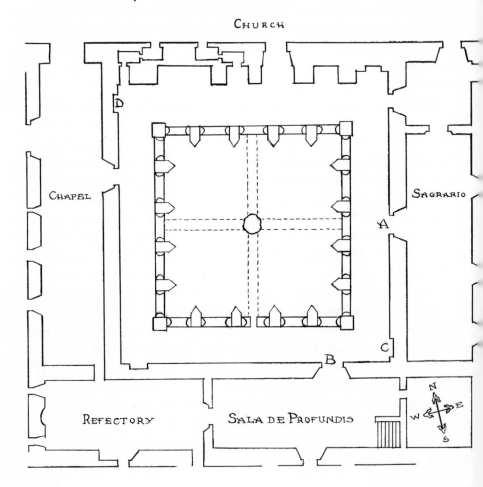

film sequence I'd seen that morning by accidentally looking out of my doorway. Then I realized that on previous occasions the same vantage point had provided other sequences which had left an impression of equal charm, but no precise pictorial memories.

The lost images set me thinking. I had just had evidence that things which make accidental inroads into our consciousness can be seen sharply. But on the whole we do not see what we do not look at; and whether we look or not depends to a large extent on whether we consider a subject visually significant. The monastery, I had felt from the beginning, was in that class. But I had hardly looked at the passersby because I had not considered them on the same visual level. Yet now I knew two things. They were very much worth looking at, and my doorway opened ideally on a fascinating passing parade.

One of these mornings, I said to myself, I'll just sit here and watch.

That I had no time that particular morning was made plain by Don Gabriel's arrival. Together we made our way up the slope. Passing the priest's garage, I noticed from its emptiness that, although it was already Saturday, the *cura* was not back from Oaxaca.

Arriving at the monastery, Don Gabriel unlocked first the door to the entrance hall and then the grilled wooden gates that led into the cloister. At that particular hour the cloister suggested an heraldic field. The morning sun was parting the quadrangle diagonally with a bend sinister. The corner near us was black with shadow, while the far triangle, bounded by the west and north sides, was in blazing sunlight. The huge cypress enhanced rather than interfered with the scene, for its boughs did not branch out till the great column of its trunk cleared the railings of the upper gallery. The bole of the cypress is indicated by the irregular disk in the center of the plan opposite.

The hyphenated lines that form a cross leading away from the cypress represent the brick walks that subdivide the cloister's garden. The square frame, which contains the letters B, C, A and D, indicates the covered walks that surround the garden. And the lines that connect the pointed buttresses show the guard walls that confine these stone-paved ambulatories.

My chief task for the day was to make a drawing conveying the cloister as a whole. But since this presented a problem I did not know how to solve, I decided to start where I left off at the end of the chapter on the doorways —that is, by sketching one of the cloister's two stone portals. The transitional drawing would take at least an hour, and during that time I was sure the solution of the major problem would present itself.

113

This confidence arose from the mysterious way in which drawing problems often solve themselves. If, instead of forcing yourself to begin, you remain within proximity of your subject, sometimes studying it closely, but more often merely noticing it casually, at a certain moment the way to depict it to best advantage will suddenly present itself. Frequently it will come when you are thinking of something else, and it generally comes in the form of a sketch already drawn in the mind's eye that merely needs to be reproduced on paper.

The doorway I wanted to start with is marked *A* and the plan shows how it once linked the cloister with the former chapter room where Don Gabriel and I had seen Lupe's lilies. But now the areas are no longer interconnected, for the doorway has been blocked up. Fortunately its frame has not been harmed.

The classical doorway was less complicated than the three I had drawn the day before. But making the drawing was not so easy as it looks. The first difficulty was getting far enough away to judge proportions. The cloister walks had struck me as being generously wide, but now I muttered against their narrowness and against the guard wall that would not let me get further back than twelve feet. Perhaps, I thought, I could get a better view from the opposite side.

Garth is the technical name for the garden part of a cloister, and I went to the garth through the opening which gives admission to it on the south side. From where I wanted to draw I met a second difficulty—that damn cypress. Standing squarely in the center of the garth, and being monstrously thick, it totally blocked the view of the doorway. Clearly, then, the farthest back I could get was in front of the tree. And here I encountered a new difficulty, or rather an old one in a new aspect. The upper part of the doorway was visible, handsomely framed by the arched opening between the buttresses, but the lower part was hidden by that frustrating guard wall.

Still, there was no help for it. Accordingly, I started to work with my back to the tree. Despite what I had learned about the advantages of drawing while seated, I began standing up. But that did not satisfy Don Gabriel. He insisted on hunting up a wooden box and bringing it for me to sit on. Upended, it provided the ideal height, and, as I saw how much easier it made the work, I blessed him for his thoughtfulness.

As I sketched, Don Gabriel tore out weeds that had grown in the earth plots of the garth. Some of the weeds caused a stinging itchiness; nevertheless, he went at them bare-handed. He also brought some of the flowers to

show me. One was blue and I recognized it as a periwinkle. But the odd yellow flower was a species I had never seen. Though its scale was miniature, the flower suggested a fat purse hanging from the girdle of one of Chaucer's merry wives. And when Don Gabriel pressed back the roundish sack of its lower petal, the flower opened like a purse too.

At this point, Alfonso entered the cloister. Lupe had told him where he could find us. Polite as always, he shook hands. Then he joined the inspection of the unusual flower. When he asked if I knew what it was called, I could tell he felt its name was especially good. I gave him his cue by inquiring.

He did not answer *calceolaria mexicana*, which I have since learned is its scientific name. Instead, he gave its popular name, *bolsa de Judas*. And because I knew *bolsa* is a word Mexicans use for a number of carrying devices, including their pocketbooks, I could share his delight in its graphic aptness. And my pleasure was heightened by a sense of antiquity. The purse of Judas must have earned its name when the wallets it suggested were in general use.

By this time I was accustomed to Alfonso. He was a lad of exceptional composure and spending the day quietly with us in or around the monastery was his idea of almost perfect contentment. Thus I took up my sketching again with the knowledge that he would feel neither slighted nor hurt in not being given more attention.

In the final stage of blocking in the doorway, I had to guess at the part obscured by the guard wall. Just how far down, I asked myself, was that unseen threshold? When I thought I had it placed at the right level, I sketched it in. Then I moved forward to start the details.

The wall, which had been such an obstruction, suddenly became an advantage. Its flat top furnished something I had not had in making any of the previous drawings—a drawing table. And provided I stood, it was the perfect height. Carried away by the pleasure of such an unwonted facility, I didn't pause to check my proportions. Instead, I plunged eagerly into the task of defining the details. And having that stone surface to support my sketchbook, I bore down more heavily than usual with my pencil.

The exactness of vision imposed by drawing made me aware that each pillar had a secondary ripple, an extra profile flat against the wall that echoed the profile of the doorway's projecting parts. I mention it because, small as the detail seems, it served to crystallize the difference between spontaneous and induced vision.

Before I moved forward to draw the doorway's details my vision of the portal had been purely spontaneous. That is, I had absorbed only its total impression. And in this case, as so often happens, the vague euphoria of aesthetic response had kept my vision from growing more exact. The mind loves total impressions, especially if the effect of the whole is pleasing. But often this fondness for the over-all effect prevents the eye from observing something it is quite capable of perceiving. My mind, operating spontaneously, had blinded me thus when I had looked at the nave windows and not seen the molding, and now it had done it with the ripple. But again careful examination had induced vision of the part in question by making my eye note what it had the power to see.

Then it dawned on me that similar ripples had also echoed the pillars of Santa Catalina's doorway and the shell doorway. This was doubly instructive. It showed that, if you do not reflect on what your eye takes in, you can have little conscious awareness even of something you have seen clearly enough to draw. It also illustrated the role memory plays in vision, for I realized the two previous encounters with the ripple were what had made me see it so sharply now.

The next step was one of correlation. The three recurrences made me recognize the ripple as a stylistic trait of the monastery's doorways. It was a conclusion that delighted me. It underlined that we do not need to live in a world in which what we observe depends solely on the spontaneous whims of the undirected eye. By the purposeful exclusion of total impressions, by the summoning of memory and by using the mind's power to classify, we can induce all sorts of vision, which, once obtained, makes us permanently more observant.

But in making a drawing, excluding total impressions can have a baleful effect—as I discovered when I held my finished product at arms' length and compared it with the actual doorway. In concentrating on small details at close range, I had not realized a basic miscalculation. I had made the doorway too narrow.

I felt both stupid and disappointed. But I decided the damage was done. All that firmly drawn detail could not be erased without horrible smearing. If I was ever going to correct the drawing, the correcting would have to be done in the ink version back in New York.

The drawing shown provides the correction, and my mistake has served to increase my respect for this particular doorway. In the overly narrow pencil original the arch is squeezed into a semicircle and the portal looks like a Renaissance doorway that follows the classical model too slavishly to be of much interest. But in this more accurate representation one sees that the doorway has a character of its own. I think it is the arch that turns the trick. Its amplitude prevents the design from being too academic. And being made aware of the importance of the arch's particular curve, I noticed this arch differed subtly from those of the three previous portals.

That circle in the pediment is a thick, projecting disk on which something was to have been carved. But the work was never done. The disk has not been left blank, though. A gold monstrance has been painted on it. Other parts of the portal have been touched up with paint too. Pink and ochre are the chief colors, but also there are some green veins on the pillars, streaked on, presumably, to make them seem like marble. This painting was much cruder than the fine work on the doorway of Santa Catalina and Don Gabriel confirmed that the colors were applied at a later date.

The eye is a roamer by nature and it is never comfortable if it is fixed on one spot for any length of time. Thus, in the intervals when I had looked away from the doorway, my eyes had wandered about the cloister. These haphazard glances, as I expected they would, stimulated my subconscious, and by the time the doorway was finished I knew effortlessly how I should go about suggesting the cloister as a whole.

The four sides were practically identical, so a view of one would be sufficient to indicate all. Again, since the five arched openings in each side were alike, I knew I did not have to draw all five. The three central ones, with hints of their fellows, seemed enough. My only problem, then, was to locate the threesome I wanted. The south side was cut by the entrance into the garth, and, being in the shade, no sunlight glared from it. It was the logical candidate. So I took my upended box and went to find the best vantage point.

The sketch that had formulated in my mind's eye showed the trunk and boughs of the cypress creating a pleasant confining line on the right. Thus all I had to do was to find the position in actuality where the tree's line bounded the arches as it did in my visionary sketch. I found the spot in the northeast corner of the garth and from there I made this drawing.

The cloister lacks the airy lightness of an arcaded cloister—that is, one which has only pillars between the arches—but its openings take up the entire width between the buttresses, and because those prism-shaped buttresses are so cleanly beveled and handsomely capped there is little impression of crudity.

Those buttresses make the cloister an over-all success. Actually, the two floors are very different. The top one is constructed of brick, its flat ceiling is supported by wooden beams, and its shallow arched openings are without any fine trimming. The lower one, on the other hand, is built of stone; it has a ribbed vaulting, and its high-arched openings are trimmed with half pillars at the sides and finely carved molding over the top. Yet the buttresses tie these disparate stone and brick stories together, and they do it so successfully that the total effect is one of unity.

The buttresses, too, provide bold and prominent verticals, and these decisive verticals play a multiple role. Like the upright stakes of a basket, they provide a strong skeleton for the composition, and by dividing the identical sides into balanced compartments they enhance the symmetry of the design at the same time as they save it from flatness and monotony.

This evaluation of the cloister is the result of later analysis and reflection. As I was drawing it, I was too absorbed with the problem of getting

WEEK IN YANHUITLÁN

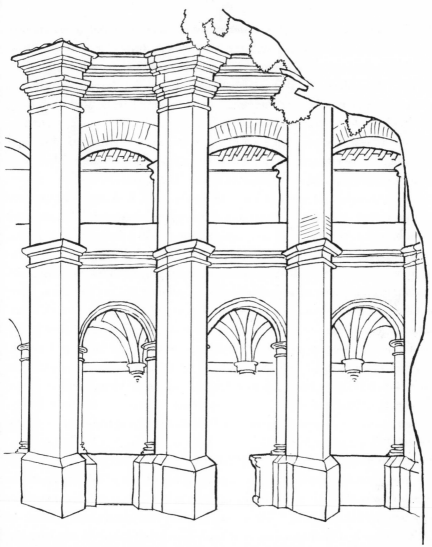

my lines in the right places to be concerned with how the designer got his effects. At one point, though, my absorption was broken by the clanging of a bell. Looking up to the gallery, I saw the priest had returned. For there he was, dressed in a black cassock, tugging on the bell rope he had strung down from the belfry to save himself the trouble of climbing the tower.

A minute or two later he descended to the garth, nodded to Don Gabriel and gave a large key to Alfonso. With the key went some instructions. Then he disappeared. Alfonso explained the key was for the wicket door in the north portal, and he excused himself while he went to open it. There was to be a Mass, and he was going to assist the padre.

The rib vaulting over the lower cloister walks deserved to be treated in more detail. So, on completing the south side, I turned to this new problem. Again my task was made easier by the identical nature of the four sides of the quadrangle. It was also facilitated by the drawing I had just finished. I knew my drawing suggested three essential facts: that each alley was divided into a sequence of square bays; that the bays corresponded to the arched openings, and that each bay was roofed with an identical canopy of ribbing. Thus I was aware I could give an idea of the whole if I drew a close-up of the vaulting of a single bay.

This drawing was made in the southeast corner, looking north. But the position is hardly material. The roofing of each ambulatory can be conjured up in the mind by imagining this pattern repeated five times in diminishing size as it retreats toward a central vanishing point. What makes this vaulting more elaborate than that in most sixteenth-century Mexican cloisters is the double cross. The usual pattern—that is, where there is vaulting at all—is composed only of the single X-shaped cross of the groin ribs. In Yanhuitlán, though, there is also a right-angled cross. Personally, I rather prefer the simpler vaulting. Here, where the rib moldings are so thick and heavy, the extra cross makes a rather clumsy effect. Still, it is another detail that makes the monastery more lavish than most of its Mexican rivals.

Another touch of distinguishing splendor is revealed in the drawing. In most monastic cloisters the round bosses at the intersection points of the ribs are left plain. At Yanhuitlán each boss is carved. It will be seen, too, that all three bosses are carved differently.

The Saturday morning Mass must have lasted about half an hour, for I was midway through the drawing of the vaulting when Alfonso returned. How many had attended? I asked. His answer confirmed Don Gabriel on the lack of religious fervor in the village. The priest's bell summoning the faithful had drawn only eight people.

Alfonso stayed with us while I finished the drawing, which took about twenty minutes more. Then, just as the three of us were turning to leave for lunch, we heard a knocking on the great wooden doors between the church and the cloister. It was wonderfully expressive knocking that conveyed a combination of fear, desperation and pleading.

Don Gabriel went to the doors to investigate. When he got them open, out darted an elderly woman. How relieved she was to be released! Talking very fast, with innumerable exclamations of *gracias* tumbling over her narrative, she explained that she had remained behind to say a few prayers

after Mass and then had found herself locked in the huge vault after Alfonso
had shut the north door. She knew the cloister was generally deserted, so
she had feared she might have to knock there for hours. What good luck
that we were there! And she wasn't shut up in the church until the next
day!

"Gracias, gracias," she said as she bobbed again and again. And she
was still saying it as she made her way down the vaulted cloister towards
freedom. When she was safely out of earshot the three of us rocked with
laughter. What a reward for piety!

It was not the only break in our plans, though, for as we were leaving
a second time a rich Spaniard arrived with his chauffeur. He was a cigar
magnate who wanted to be shown the monastery.

Alfonso left anyway, but Don Gabriel was stuck. As usual, he asked if I wanted to come on the tour, but this time I declined. I wanted to check the bosses to see if they were all different. I found they were not; but the variety was considerable nevertheless. There were nine different patterns.

Two were of stars, and later I was to learn why the star is one of St. Dominic's attributes. It has become associated with him because of the legend that while his godmother held him at the font for his christening, she saw, as the water was poured upon his head, a brilliant star shining on his forehead. I was to learn later, too, that of all kinds of stars, the one most commonly associated with the saint is the eight-pointed one. This had been demonstrated already in La Pastora, the ruined chapel. And it was demonstrated still further in the cloister, for only four bosses carried the twelve-pointed star. But there were six with the star of eight points.

The chief heraldic motif of the Dominicans is an equal-armed cross with a fleur-de-lis tipping each arm. I had noticed it all over the monastery

and it formed the basis of two of the boss patterns. The cross with the lances occurred eight times, while the cross with the stars vastly increased the preponderance of the eight-pointed star. I found that this pattern recurred fourteen times.

The other five patterns all were flowers.

There were forty-eight bosses altogether, and a little additional variety was provided by the fact that not every recurrence of the same design was banded in the same way. Some encompassing rings were like coils of rope, some were plain and some were dotted with little rings.

After the cigar magnate had gone, Don Gabriel and I finally got home. The first thing we told Lupe was the story of the old woman who got locked in the church. Don Gabriel mimicked the relief and delight of the woman, her prayers knocked clean out of her head. And Lupe laughed heartily.

I recalled how we had laughed several times over the truck drivers who had taken the priest's maid for a nun; and how this incident had provided

still another laugh when Don Gabriel had called the bell-tossing girls the "little nuns." I recalled, too, the several laughs over the former guide with the interchangeable hats. The old girl locked in the church, then, would be like her predecessors. She, too, would be good for several more laughs. And this made me aware of something fundamental about village life. In a little place where nothing much happens, a humorous incident is treasured. Not only is it saved to pass from neighbor to neighbor, with fresh enjoyment at each telling, but it can be repeated several times between the same people and arouse delight each time. And this seemed still another endearing characteristic of Yanhuitlán: it was a place where a little joke could go a long way.

Up to this meal the food Lupe had served had all been palatable—and oh, how welcome!—but, in all honesty, I couldn't claim that anything had been superbly tasty. At this lunch, though, there was something of that order. It was a rich, thick, dark red sauce that transformed a few chunks of lamb into something ambrosial. Obviously, tomatoes formed the basic ingredient, but it also contained herbs unknown to me which gave it a subtle overtone of most delicious flavor. Not only did I eat all that came with the meat, but I asked for a little more so I could mop it up with my tortillas.

Afterward, when I was shaving on my front doorstep, Don Gabriel came over with my shirt. Lupe had laundered and ironed it beautifully. He also brought something else; some pink and white flowers arranged as a bouquet in a medicine bottle.

"I thought you might like these," he said, placing them on the little table so they balanced the bright weeds in the talcum powder tin.

Occasionally among human beings there are some moments of understanding so perfect that both parties know better than to spoil them with

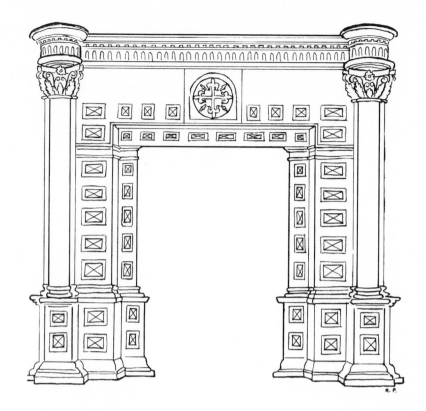

verbal acknowledgment. This was one of them. Don Gabriel had never brought flowers to my room before. I saw he needed the assurance of my own gesture in picking the weeds to be sure that I liked flowers well enough to understand his bringing them. I saw, too, that it must have been the weeds that led him to show me all those flowers in the cloister in the morning, including the *bolsas de Judas*. All I said, though, was *gracias*. But I think from my tone he knew as well as I did that this was another landmark.

AT THE END of the "Doorways" chapter, when we turned away from the locked sacristy, I mentioned *two* doorways in the cloister. One was the door with the triangular pediment, which I had drawn in the morning. The other was the doorway leading from the cloister to the *Sala de Profundis*. And it was this second doorway—to me the most marvelous one in the establishment—that I had set as my major task of the afternoon.

One can readily see why Don Gabriel called it the doorway of the diamonds. It fairly blazes with those pyramids, countersunk in stone boxes; here the designer indulged his passion for the diamond motif most lavishly.

This doorway is marked *B* and the plan (page 112) shows it presented a problem similar to that of the classical doorway. That is, it could not be viewed in its entirety from any distance because its lower part was obscured by the guard wall between the buttresses. Having made a miscalculation in the morning by trying to block in a doorway that I could see only partially, I decided I would not even try to start from a distance. So I placed my sketchbook on the guard wall and began the drawing at the range of only a few feet.

Utilizing the flat top of the wall meant that for the first time I could block in with table support. It proved wonderfully liberating. Even though my pencil had soft lead, I could sketch much more lightly. Also, it was easier to work patiently since my left arm was freed from the tiring task of holding the book. I was freer, too, to step back from the work. As I checked and re-checked my proportions, I rubbed out the incorrect lines.

Being faint, they were easy to erase. And this brought home another lesson about the mechanics of drawing. A pencil with a hard lead, in making light lines, would have saved me all the messing of the paper that had complicated the effort of getting the buttresses right in drawing the church. I had been foolish not to bring a hard pencil, and I made a mental note to see if I could get one in the village.

With this diamond doorway I resolved not to make the mistake I had made with the classical one, so I did not let myself start filling in the details until I was sure each main element was in correct scale with every other element.

Don Gabriel had taken his leave shortly after letting me into the cloister, and this was one reason I did not feel hurried. Being alone, I could take my own time. And I think the cloister itself was a major factor in enabling me to draw with slow, patient exactitude. I had been immersed in it long enough for its varying influences to have worked on me.

Under ordinary circumstances, when a man is in a building for very long he needs two things if he is not to feel confined—space and windows. This two-storied cloister certainly cut me off from the spaciousness of Yanhuitlán's valley, and, in the sense of openings looking outward, it was utterly windowless. Yet I did not feel at all imprisoned, because the cloister provided for the two psychological needs in its own way. Not only did its amplitude make it seem roomy and unconfining, but, being open to the sky at the center, it provided space of a particular kind—space upwards.

And those openings on all four sides, both upstairs and downstairs, gave the illusion of windows. One had open frames to look through, and that was enough, even though all they gave onto was each other.

Thus the cloister, by the allowance it made for human needs, created an environment in which one was psychologically comfortable. But this was only the beginning of its influences. Others arose from the way it excluded the outside world. First, those high walls excluded it visually, so the eye could see no far distances to tempt the foot to wander. Neither could it see any coming and going of people to arouse the gregarious instinct to join them, either vicariously by watching them or in fact by going out among them. Second, by being at the heart of the monastic building block, the cloister excluded the outside world physically. Those distracting vistas, those interesting people, and that tempting activity were not just on the other side of a thin wall. The cloister was moated, as it were, by wide surrounding halls that seemed to absorb even the influences emanating from the things that could not be seen. Third, and perhaps most important, the cloister, by providing an environment of symmetry, harmony, balance and order, excluded the factors of the world that probably do most to keep us agitated in the deepest levels of our being—its multiplicity, variety and irregularity.

Yet the cloister did not exclude the world altogether. It allowed for flowers and trees. It let in birds and their songs. It let in sunlight and it let in that element which is the most eternal of all the features of our physical universe: the element more eternal than the hills, the deserts and the seas— the sky.

As I outlined each rectangular panel of the doorway and drew in the X's to indicate the diamond faceting, I could understand why the monks of the Middle Ages had the patience to illuminate those manuscripts so beautifully. I had not come to the cloister either to meditate or pray, but from the way its particular environment was aiding my tranquility and concentration I could appreciate fully for the first time why the cloister as an institution was one of man's most wonderful inventions for the development of the spiritual life.

Running along the top of the doorway was a fluted frieze that curved out over small half drums on top of the pillars. In the drawing it seems to be an integral part of the doorway, yet actually it is only one segment of the frieze running around the whole cloister. With the finish and beauty of this segment in mind one can get a better idea of what that frieze, suggested on page 119, is like. I also point out that the half drums topping the pillars of the doorway are really corbels supporting the ribs of the vaulting, as shown on page 121.

With these elements correlated, the cloister can be more perfectly imagined and the way the diamond doorway is integrated into the basic design can be more fully appreciated. For ribs spring in three directions from these half drums that seem to belong completely to the doorway; and curving up and forward over the door is a canopy of ribs similar to the one I have shown. This canopy, too, is joined in an unbroken sequence to all the other canopies that roof the walks.

After completing the frieze, I turned to the Dominican coat of arms over the lintel. Because it retains most of its original paint, this particular representation is the most stunning version of the arms in the establishment. Because of its paint, too, it shows the colors of the order—black and white. The black stands for mortification and penance, the white for purity and faith. The coat also shows how those symbolic colors are traditionally distributed. Each arm of the cross fleury is half black and half white, with the color depending on the field beneath. Thus the overlap on the black gyron is white, that on the white gyron is black.

The capitals of the pillars were the last details I tackled. Working on the volutes, the flowers between them and the vaguely acanthuslike leaves, I had a fresh experience of memory coming to the aid of vision. These capitals, surely, were like the capitals on the classical doorway which I had drawn that morning. And with this correlation came another memory, for I

realized the similar sets of capitals were charming but naïve versions of the Corinthian order. Were the two sets identical? I went back to the other doorway to check. They weren't. The carver had varied the flowers. The flower in the diamond capital was like a rose. The flower in the classic capital was like a cosmos. And the carver was naturalistic enough to see to it that the differing flowers had different leaves.

There is a subtle difference between a discovery you make for yourself and one that is pointed out to you. The latter can be exciting and interesting, but somehow it does not bind you to the thing revealed the way a self-discovery does. A discovery about a part, too, can have a mysterious effect on one's feeling for the whole. It can transform something, which before seemed merely interesting, into an object of wonder. Thus finding the variety in those flowers on the capitals stepped up my feeling for the whole cloister.

Suddenly I remembered those other flowers on the bosses. One was perhaps a narcissus and two were other species of roses. And could the others be dahlias? Why, the whole cloister was a garden of stone flowers!

I wanted to communicate my excitement, and happily Don Gabriel returned at this point.

"¡Mira!" I said, taking him by the arm. "Flores diferentes." And I showed him first the rose of the diamond door and then the cosmos on the classical door, and I pointed out the differing foliage too. Carefully as he had observed the cloister, he had not noticed this particular difference.

"Look too," and I showed him the rough sketches I'd made of the five different flowers on the bosses of the vaulting. "Un jardín de piedra." And though the parallel was unspoken, the understanding about living flowers that had developed between us earlier in the day was a factor behind

129

our investigation of the stone flowers. We studied the sketches with the consciousness of a community of interest and with an equal feeling of kinship for the flower-loving sculptor. Having been made aware of the flowers of the village, too, I could readily see why Yanhuitlán had inspired that sculptor to carve so many flowers of his own.

"Those aren't the only flowers in the cloister," said Don Gabriel. Then he pointed to one of the half drums supporting the ribbing. His finger made me see something I had not noticed before. At the point where the corbel tapered into the wall was a flower resembling a daisy.

I turned my eyes to the other corbels to see if they also terminated in flowers. Those that were not broken off did. And the flowers varied.

I had hardly time to absorb this new facet of the decoration, when Don Gabriel asked, "Have you noticed this one?" And he was pointing to the alcove where he kept the register book for visitors.

The alcove (marked C, page 112) was wide, quite shallow and surmounted by a flat arch. It had an ornamental stone frame, studded with what I had taken to be a series of lumpy knobs.

Looking more closely, I saw each knob was a rose. And each rose had a budlike center and two rings of petals. I had not previously distinguished the knobs as flowers, partly because I had never really looked at them, and partly because of the whitewashing of the cloister. In that wholesale operation the roses had been swallowed up in the all-prevailing whiteness. They had been made cruder, too, by the whitewash that diminished their definition by filling the crannies between their petals.

So fine a frame gave the the clue that in monastic times the alcove had housed something more worthy than a bottle of ink, a ten-cent pen and a

scuffed old register. Don Gabriel confirmed this. With a gesture that took in the whole back of the recess, he said it had once been covered with a painting, or perhaps a bas-relief. There were similar alcoves at each corner and each had contained graphic subject matter for meditation. The friars, he said, would come from the church and walk counterclockwise around the cloister, stopping at each alcove to pray or meditate on whatever was pictured in the recess.

"How do you know they went counterclockwise?" I asked.

"Look, I will show you," he said. And at this point, so that what he demonstrated will be easily intelligible, turn again to the cloister plan on page 112. There, at the church end of the east walk, indicated by a squared notch, is the alcove towards which Don Gabriel led me. It was identical with *C*, the alcove that held the register. When he continued the counterclockwise direction by turning left, we saw, straight ahead, a third rose-studded alcove. This one (marked *D*) was whitewashed and pictureless like the others, but it contained two statues of women that had been taken from somewhere else in the establishment.

The women's robes had lost most of their gold and both statues had seen better days. The lady tipped to one side by a broken base, suggested a Mater Dolorosa, but Don Gabriel said she was Santa Elena. The other held three little balls in her right hand, which later enabled me to identify her as Clara of Monte Falco, a thirteenth-century Italian abbess whose cult was officially approved in 1624.

Standing in front of the lady saints, we could see down the west ambulatory. Sure enough, there was an alcove at the end of that walk too. But instead of taking me down it, Don Gabriel proposed that we turn our backs on the holy ladies and reverse our direction. As we retraced our steps, the wall we approached had a blocked doorway, but no alcove. When we continued clockwise and turned into the east walk we faced a blank wall.

Reaching C and looking west, we saw still another blank wall. The demonstration was convincing. The alcoves can only be seen at the end of the walks if one is strolling against the clock.

The alcoves opened my eyes to yet another refinement of the cloister as an invention to aid the spiritual life. A complete cloister, with its end walls properly painted or sculptured, does not stop with providing an environment that fosters meditation. It also furnishes the subject matter and places it in such a position that one is forced to keep running into it.

I cannot truthfully say, though, that this Yanhuitlán cloister had given me the impression of being strongly spiritual. The afternoon sun had reversed the bend of shadow across the quadrangle from sinister to dexter, and the light, that was now caressing the north and east sides, was more mellow than the morning light had been. In that warm, lazy sunlight, the cloister certainly did not vibrate with evangelical fervor. Nor was there any indication of devotion to the thirteenth-century ideal of monastic poverty. On the contrary, with its beautifully finished details, with its air of luxury and leisure, and in its remoteness from the reality of the civilization into which it was set, it reminded me of an institute for advanced studies built for graduate seminarians by some alumnus who had become a millionaire. An alumnus, I might add, who had since gone bankrupt, leaving his gift to fall into disrepair with no endowment to sustain it.

At this moment the priest passed by. Having done his ecclesiastical duty for the day, he had doffed his cassock in favor of tan pants and a pink shirt. Looking like a plump and self-contented little Buddha, he was smoking a cigarette in a holder long enough for Theda Bara. Below the pudgy hand that held the elegant holder was a gorgeous gold wrist watch. Hardly, I thought, a very sacerdotal figure! Yet one that in so worldly a cloister was not altogether out of keeping.

Alfonso had said he would join us in the afternoon and he turned up just after the priest had passed. Since I was still excited about the ingenious alcoves, I asked Alfonso if he knew about them. He didn't; so I took adtantage of his lack of knowledge to point them out. As Don Gabriel had done with me, I showed him how he always walked towards alcoves if he went counterclockwise; and always towards blank walls if he walked the other way. The demonstration was a great success. Having been guided about Yanhuitlán so much, I derived satisfaction from playing the role of guide for a change. I especially enjoyed guiding Alfonso, for he responded to the alcoves with the same delight as I had done, and there are few satisfactions in life as sweet as guiding someone to something about which one is enthusiastic and having the person react with equal wonder and delight.

Don Gabriel, I had noticed, apportioned his guidance in direct ratio to the degree of interest he detected in his charges. When he saw Alfonso and me so intrigued with the alcoves, he could not resist capping them with a final wonder.

At the top of the plan of the cloister (page 112) one can see four little chambers cut in the thickness of the wall between the church and the cloister. They seem to peck at each other like two pairs of lovebirds.

Don Gabriel took us into the chamber nearest the church entrance. It was like entering a closet, though there was a small window on the left that was blocked with loose stones. Don Gabriel told us to keep our heads close to the window. Then he disappeared. A few moments later we could see him through the chinks in the stones. He had entered the neighboring chamber from the church.

He asked us to forgive his sins.

Alfonso and I turned to each other and smiled. We both understood. The chambers were confessionals. Arranged as they were, the friars could hear confessions without leaving the cloister; and the townspeople, their sins duly repented, could obtain their absolution without entering the monastery.

THE CLOISTER 133

Don Gabriel had had his way. The confessionals outdid the alcoves.
And when we returned to the cloister I saw I still had not exhausted the
flowers of that stone garden. Around the entrance of each confessional was
a narrow frame of low-relief blossoms. They were conventionalized in a way
that combined art and piety. Being squeezed into rectangles, they fitted neatly into the border, and, in buckling under the pressure, the middle petals
formed a cross.

X

THE EVENING OF THE FOURTH DAY

WHEN I WAS A BOY my parents were always concerned about my associates. The memory of this made me think Alfonso's aunt might be worried about the strange *gringo* her nephew was hanging around with. I felt it would be a good thing if she saw my work so she could be convinced I was an honest citizen.

"Perhaps your aunt would like to see my drawings," I suggested to Alfonso after we left the cloister. When he agreed, I offered to take them to her.

My motives were not all altruistic. In the four days I had been in Yanhuitlán I had not been inside a single home except Don Gabriel's. I wanted to see how the people lived, and taking the drawings to Alfonso's aunt would be a way of seeing what her house was like.

The house is marked *No. 2* in the plan on page 60. Its position facing the plaza indicated a family of some consequence, but the house itself was as simple outwardly as all the others of the village, and, like them, was a flat-roofed, single-story building. The front door led into a rather bare, whitewashed room that was scrupulously clean. The doors that gave off it were shut and Alfonso left me there while he went to fetch his aunt. All I had time to notice was a very large sepia photograph in a heavy gilded frame and a closed sewing machine which was covered with a coarsely knitted blue runner.

Alfonso returned with a young woman, who carefully closed the door of the adjoining room behind her. She looked too youthful to be the boy's aunt, but I knew that in Mexico many girls marry at an early age.

"*¿Su tía?*" I asked inquiringly.

No, not the aunt, but the aunt's daughter.

"Then your cousin." And both heads nodded. I was introduced and I found the young woman's name was Acela. Her mother, she explained, was not at home. I was disappointed, but I asked Acela if she would like to see the drawings. She looked at them and thanked me for bringing them, but she did not invite me in. I took the hint and turned to leave.

Alfonso checked me. Would Don Gabriel and I be watching the sunset? he asked. It hadn't been planned, but I said "Yes." I could tell it was the answer he hoped to hear. Relieved, he promised he would come for us in about half an hour.

Walking home I chuckled over my sociological investigation. In closing that door so carefully behind her, Acela had firmly thwarted me, even though I had not shown my hand directly.

It serves me right, I said to myself. I shouldn't have been so nosy.

This watching of the sunset was a little different. We all knew it was Alfonso's last evening, and that he had to head north the next day. Thus our watching had in it some of the sadness of the ending of things. There was also some of the sadness of parting. But our awareness that it was the last such evening we would be enjoying together brought some of the compensations that often come on such occasions. Because tomorrow one of us would be leaving the valley, we had a heightened consciousness of its physical beauty. Because our companionship was soon to be broken, we knew its sweetness as we had hardly known it when it was something we could count on from day to day. And because there was to be a leave-taking, there was an acceleration of the ordinarily slow processes in which friendships are formed.

Alfonso had to be back in Puebla to resume school on Monday. He told us he would be graduated in three months. He wanted to be a pilot in the air force and he had already put in his application for training. In January he would go to Guadalajara to enter the army's flying school.

School led our thoughts to sports. Alfonso's favorite was basketball. Don Gabriel liked to run. My love was swimming.

Alfonso asked about my books.

The process of learning a new language is a mysterious one. You struggle along on one level for a long time without apparent improvement and then, without any transition, you suddenly find yourself on a different level. You are surprised at your new volubility. And so it was with me that evening. I was able to tell them what the books were about and how I came to write them. And I noticed one thing especially about my speech. It was much easier for me to differentiate the vowels "a" and "o" at the end of words. Previously such words as *hermoso* and *hermosa,* the masculine and feminine for beautiful, had seemed so alike that it was difficult for me to differentiate them. But this evening I could articulate them clearly, even though I often got my genders wrong.

I asked some questions about Yanhuitlán's municipal government. How long, for instance was Don Venustiano's term of office? Don Gabriel and Alfonso seemed undecided as to whether it was every two or every four years that the *presidente* was elected. And what were the duties of the *síndico,* the second highest officer? He was responsible for the natural resources of the village, and from what they said about his connection with the state government I gathered he was also a sort of attorney general. The man who worked at the old-fashioned typewriter in the municipal office, they said, was the secretary of the administration. Was there a village council? Yes. It had eight members. And were there any policemen? Yes, twelve, but they did not have any uniforms. They were more like watchmen. There was practically no crime. The jail for the men was empty and the town had abandoned its old jail for women.

We were able to talk without any feeling that we were distracting each other from the sunset, for truth to tell, it wasn't much of a spectacle that night. The baby pink in the clear sky behind the hills had quickly deteriorated into a pale brown, and therefore there was a slow diminution of the light without any dramatic change of color. And as it grew darker the silence grew more profound. When a distant burro broke the stillness with a few hee-haws the sound carried for miles.

Later a small gold light came on in the little refreshment stand at the place where the busses stopped. But no cars passed.

We were not disappointed that the sunset was not better. The ending of this particular day, in fact, seemed especially right. Its mood of subdued melancholy, permeated as it was with a sense of peace, and made gentle by a feeling of harmony and affection between all things in the valley, consorted very well with our own. We strolled away from the ruined wall, knowing that we and the world about us were fundamentally in tune.

Bobby, the dog, came out to greet us as we neared home, and at supper Hambre wanted some of everything: some of the thin, crisp sweet bread that was served with the hot chocolate, some of the tortillas, preferably with a little fried egg on it, and even some of the mashed frijoles. When I had finished eating, Don Gabriel again escorted me home, and this time he insisted on lighting my candle. It was just eight o'clock when he said "good night" and bid me sleep well.

Taking the tin holding the candle to the counter, I spread out my sketchbooks. In the soft glow of the candlelight, I gloated over my drawings. I had now done nineteen. Those of the cloister, being the latest, were the ones I studied most lovingly. Using my eraser, I began rubbing out the lines that had become superfluous. Smudging was almost impossible to avoid and a few of the heavier lines were hard to eliminate. I certainly needed that hard pencil.

Since it was still early and the counter was no temptation to retirement, I decided to take a little air before committing my body to the boards.

The night was mild and, because the moon had not yet risen, it was almost as dark as the night before. There were more stars though, and in the plaza I could see a light burning in La Providencia, the corner stall run by Felix Palma.

Perhaps, I said to myself, he might have a hard pencil. At all events, it's a good excuse for a visit.

"*Buenas noches,*" I said on arriving, and he returned the greeting in a tone different from any I had heard from a city shopkeeper. It gave me the feeling that one reason he liked having his booth on the corner of the plaza was because it enabled him to chat with most of the strangers who visited the village. I got the distinct impression that selling was a service he was glad to render, but he did not consider a purchase essential.

His plump and pretty wife was leaning over the counter beside him. Her name was Lucina and she, too, was cordial. I learned, in fact, that there was even a hint of nostalgia in her greeting. For six years she had been a maid in the home of an American engineer in Mexico City. They had been happy years and it gave her a taste of the old life to talk with a North American again. They presented their children. The two little girls were black-haired, pretty and tubby, like their mother. Graciela, the older, was three. Trinidad, the younger, was two. Jorge, the boy, was just one. As we chatted, a hoarse little radio played softly on one of the back shelves. A coal oil lamp furnished the light.

The Palmas did have pencils and fortunately their leads were so hard they barely made a mark.

My eye also lit on something else. The desire to give the Blancos a present had been growing in me. But what could one get in Yanhuitlán? Hanging in clusters by their wicks were candles. Obviously, they would be useful. I bought three. A pile of oranges prompted another purchase. Lupe had served practically no fresh fruit and an orange would be refreshing on the way home.

After paying for the orange, I said good night and started back. But I paused at the circumference of the stall's illumination so I could have light enough to peel the orange.

Three men and a boy, their sarapes lifted over their mouths against the night air, came along the road and stopped when they reached me. Since they watched the peeling with such interest, I had no alternative but to pass the orange around when the last of the rind was removed. And that was the end of my bit of fruit!

The segments had been accepted without a word, but then the leader, an old man who looked thin and cold, broke the silence by asking for money. Tourists in Mexico are often asked for alms. But this was the first time in my four days in Yanhuitlán that any such request had been put to me. The absence of beggars, in fact, was one of the town's admirable features.

Perhaps, I thought, these people were poor strangers, passing through, who still had a long way to go before reaching their own village. I gave the old man a peso. For an individual beggar this represented a large donation, but I explained it was to be divided among all four of them. The old man understood. Then the dark silent group, muffled in their sarapes, the boy trailing behind, resumed their passage through the town.

Having given my orange away without a taste of it, I went back to the stall to buy another. Felix gave it to me. Then he handed me a second.

"But I only want one," I said.

"The other is a present," he explained.

As I was thanking him in touched amazement, another villager tugged at my coat. He was angry.

"La Policía," he said. And I realized he must have been one of those twelve men who had municipal power, even if they did not have uniforms. He quickly made the cause of his anger clear. I should not have given those men any money.

"It is against the law to give money to beggars," he said. "There are no beggars in Yanhuitlán. Here everybody is contented. We don't want it to get around that people can get money by asking for it. We don't want beggars to come here."

There was no fooling in what he said and for a time I thought he was going to take me to the municipal authorities. But he said he would let me off with a warning this time. On no account, though, was I to do it again.

It was a sobering experience. Not only did I respect the individual villager for taking his police duties so seriously, but I felt the municipal attitude he represented was still another reason for counting Yanhuitlán an admirable village. I apologized.

Strolling home, I looked up at the rear of the monastery. Each night it had been so deserted its windows had been cavelike in their blackness. But now two of those frames on the second floor were soft golden rectangles. I was startled. Who could be in the monastery at this hour? Of course, the priest. He was back, and those were the windows of the cells he had made so comfortable. I wondered if he were listening to his radio.

That I reacted with surprise to the unexpected light made me realize something fundamental about the village. None of its houses had windows. During the days one did not notice their absence; the doors were so big and the sunlight so bright. But at night . . . . And the absence of windows, I saw, was a major factor in the blackness of the nights. Not only were there no street lamps, but no windows to allow any internal light to escape.

A few steps more and a familiar sound arrested my attention. "Scrunch, scrunch," was the insistent note, with an occasional variation as if large teeth were seizing and pulling up clumps of grass. This time I did not feel frightened. The sound was coming from somewhere in the plaza. I went to investigate. It wasn't an animal at all. It was the bubbling of the water from the stone post in the center of the circular fountain.

The discovery gave me the true measure of the night quietness of Yanhuitlán. It was so profound that such tiny, watery sounds could carry a great distance. Even two blocks away they had startled me by sounding so near I had imagined a large, snuffling animal almost at my hand.

By the time I got back to my room I was ready to retire. But on the counter, retiring and falling asleep were not simultaneous occurrences. Yet I felt happy lying there and began singing quietly to myself. The tune that came spontaneously was one with many emotional associations. When I recognized it, I began singing its words—with one significant but explicable change. In my version it began.

O little town of Yanhuitlán,
How still we see thee lie.

Then with a rush came the unforgettable picture of what was just outside my door.

> *Above thy deep and dreamless sleep*
> *The silent stars go by.*

It was uncanny what those words, underlined as they were by music, did to my awareness. Yanhuitlán and Bethlehem—the one that was near helped me to imagine the one that was far, and the one that was far gave me a new consciousness of the one that was near. For surely they could not have been very unlike.

The music changed and brought the words: "Yet in thy dark streets shineth the everlasting light." They told me something about Yanhuitlán, though I could not understand just what. I felt that in this village, too, there was the paradox of something shining despite the physical darkness.

My memory garbled the second verse, but the remembered reference to the angels keeping "their watch of wondering love" had a curious way of taking my vision of Yanhuitlán into a new dimension. I can best describe it in terms of a certain trick that has been used in motion pictures. The camera seems to back away from a town until it becomes only a spot on the globe and then the globe retreats into the distance till it comes to be indistinguishable from the other stars. And even though I'm skeptical about angels, that reference gave me a sense of divine Providence watching over the universe in which Yanhuitlán was so tiny a speck. Considering my stumbling over the second verse, I was startled at the ease with which I sang the third.

> *How silently, how silently*
> *The wondrous gift is given!*
> *So God imparts to human hearts*
> *The blessings of his heaven:*
> *No ear may hear his coming;*
> *But in this world of sin,*
> *Where meek souls will receive him still,*
> *The dear Christ enters in.*

Suddenly my whole concept of the hymn changed. I saw its association with Christmas had blinded me to its true character. I had classed it merely as a carol, lumping it with "The First Noel" and "Good King Wenceslaus." Yet here in this third verse I recognized a significant statement about the nature of the mystical experience. Substitute the words "the presence of

God" for "the dear Christ" and the verse is perfectly intelligible to mystics of all religions—Hindus, Buddhists, Moslems, as well as Christians.

And note the qualification for the experience—meekness. That gave me the clue to the nature of the paradoxical shining I felt in Yanhuitlán. Its people had the attitude of spirit that made it possible for them to receive and, in turn, to give off the mysterious light.

My memory failed me on the final verse, but after a little reconstructing of well-known phrases I got the first four lines.

> *O Holy Child of Bethlehem,*
> *Descend to us we pray;*
> *Cast out our sin, and enter in;*
> *Be born in us today.*

Understanding the symbolism of the "Holy Child"—it was another version of the "dear Christ"—I also saw the significance of the first part of this plea. I balked, though, at the theological word "sin." Then an idea dawned.

Could it mean "hardness of heart?" Could it mean the accumulated results of hurt pride, the bitterness of disappointment and the frustration of self-will? In other words, could it be the result of the things that we do to our hearts through our own attitudes?

The notion that sin and hardness of heart could be synonymous led to a new comprehension. Perhaps our falling from grace is only partly voluntary. For against one's own wishes, the heart, imperceptibly, hardens in a noisy, hectic city where there is scarcely enough time for friendship and none for sunsets; where the mind is disassociated from the body and occupied too much with the struggle to meet deadlines; and where one lives with the unremitting realization that many people, both within one's circle and without, are tense, unhappy and at war with their environment.

Thinking of the influences that harden the heart led me to consider those that soften it. What were they? Love, of course; awareness of the interest and wonder of the physical world; appreciation of one's blessings, and, as a result of these, an indwelling sense of gratitude. The list showed me I was on the right track. Since these are recognized virtues, there was justification for the interpretation of their absence as "sins."

Was the hymnist, then, saying: "cast out our lack of love, our inappreciation and our ingratitude?" It seemed to be a justified construction of his meaning, and I was construing it thus as I fell asleep, still humming the tune.

XI
THE CHURCH

Sᴜɴᴅᴀʏ ᴡᴀs ɴᴏᴛ ᴀ ᴅᴀʏ ᴏғ ʀᴇsᴛ for the corn mill. It began beating away at its usual hour. And since a hard bed doesn't tempt one to remain in it after waking, I was up and almost finished dressing by seven o'clock when Don Gabriel came around for his morning greeting.

Knowing Mexicans put on their best clothes on Sundays, I knew in advance that my host would show up wearing something clean and different. But I hadn't quite expected the vision he presented. He was all in pink. His trousers were pale pink and his shirt a dark pink; and, perhaps because of these hues, I noticed for the first time that the narrow band around his sombrero was orange. Since he arrived bearing two tins of water hung scale-fashion from a yoke across his shoulders, he made one of the pleasantest sights imaginable.

"*Como una rosa,*" I said, congratulating him on his ensemble. Though his coppery skin did not betray it, I think he blushed a little. But I could tell he was pleased that his Sunday finery had not gone unnoticed.

The water in my bucket was fresh, but he insisted on throwing it out and giving me still fresher water from the tins he was carrying. Then he departed, but soon he was back again. This time he brought orange juice. Breakfast, he explained, would be a little late. He hoped I wouldn't mind.

A moment after he left, a big black turkey with a blue head and red wattles strutted in front of my door. The magnificent bird was calling attention to itself by a gobbling noise, and its tail feathers were fanned out proudly.

The Grand Marshal! I exclaimed. Now's my chance to watch the parade.

A brother and sister were next. The girl was wearing a burgundy-colored sweater-coat. The boy was in white with a red cap. They were holding hands. Scarcely had they passed when along came a barefoot woman in a pink dress, with a navy-blue rebozo. She was returning from the mill, and she was carrying her corn dough balanced in a basket on her head. She crisscrossed with another woman wearing an orange apron and a black rebozo, and I could tell the other woman was on her way to the mill, for her basket, whose handle was slipped over her arm, was empty.

After these peasant-type women came a young woman who might have been a schoolteacher. Her bobbed black hair was uncovered. She had shoes and stockings. She was wearing a gray sweater and a pink skirt and she was clutching a book at her waist.

Then, advancing from one direction or another, came a black dog with four white paws and a white tip to his long black tail; a tall man in blue jeans with a peaked sombrero and a long sarape over his right shoulder; a sandaled boy with pans of water hanging from a yoke over his shoulders; a barefoot woman in white, with a black rebozo draped over her back, who was carrying a clay pitcher; a boy in a red cap, who was pushing sacks in a wheelbarrow and whistling happily; a man with a gray beard and a very old straw hat; a . . . .

I break off because a mere listing of the people and their clothing does not give the right effect. One must also envisage the routes they took. Those routes, as they appeared from my door, formed a large flattened-down, reversed Z. The bottom line was the road to the plaza. The diagonal was the path that had been cut across the red earth of the eroded slope as a short way to the upper street. That high street ran on the same level as the platform of the monastery, and it was while the people were on the top line that they were silhouetted against the sky. And at this line, as well as the transient profiles of those who passed, there were the unchanging profiles of the beavertail cacti which guarded a corn field.

Now the procession can be resumed. As the whistling boy pushing the wheelbarrow started up the switchback to the upper street, new characters appeared on the other two levels. One who came along the lower street was a pigtailed girl in a blue dress. Since she was small, her adult-sized blue rebozo was looped in large folds to keep it from dragging on the dirt path. She had a big shallow oval basket and because it was empty she was carrying it in the most manageable way—that is, flattened against her side. As she retreated towards the plaza, a trio moved in a counter direction along

WEEK IN YANHUITLÁN

the upper level. A woman with a white dress and a black rebozo led the three-some. Behind her was a girl in a red dress and a faded wine rebozo. Both the woman and the girl had their corn dough balanced on their heads in soft straw baskets that suggested chunky cyclinders. The third member of the party was another girl, who like the woman, was dressed in white. Her rebozo had slipped from her black hair and was hanging down her back. She was carrying her corn at her hip.

Presently, the woman in the orange apron reappeared from the mill. She was doubly laden. The basket over her arm was filled with corn dough and she had more dough in a cylindrical basket that hung on her back by a tumpline that passed across her forehead.

As she moved up the switchback, Don Gabriel returned. I pointed to the basket hung from her forehead and asked its name. A *tenate*, he said. I was glad to have the term, for I had noticed such baskets widely used in the village. They had caught my admiration. Less limp than cloth sacks, but more flexible than wicker baskets, they served the same purposes as our brown paper bags; yet they were more sturdy and were not destroyed if a little moisture soaked through. And I have since learned they were one of the ingenious inventions of the ancient people of Mexico. Like others of those domestic inventions, they were in use before the Spaniards came and have survived the passing of the conquerors.

The brown hen and the small turkey were pecking outside the Blancos' home when we went in for breakfast. Hambre, the kitten, was inside, but I was quickly told she had just returned. It seemed she was starting young to see life. For a second night running she had been out all night.

As I began breakfast I asked Don Gabriel to repeat the grace he had told me two days before. Again I copied it out. But this time I was not collecting it as a local folk usage. I sought its text because I wanted to say it. I went over it several times, and when I had committed it to memory, I spoke it aloud. And I might add that thereafter there was never a meal at he Blancos when I missed saying it. Feeling its need was an index of how grateful I felt for those meals. And sometimes I saw the irony of it. To think hat I should want to say grace before a cup of hot milk and a tortilla when o often I had sat down to seven-course dinners without thinking I was getting any more than my due.

That I, a seasoned newspaperman who had given up saying grace at he end of childhood, should also feel no self-consciousness in saying it loud before two people whose language I spoke haltingly—well, that was an index to the Blancos. It showed the extent of their influence that within four days so much uneasy sophistication should drop away. It showed something else too. Appearing ridiculous is one of man's greatest fears. That I could say that grace before them with none of that fear proved how completely I had come to trust their human understanding.

As I was finishing my meal, there was a discreet rap at the front door. It was the meat man who had come around while I had been eating my first breakfast. This time I felt more at ease in the household, so, instead of letting the transaction take place quietly behind my back, I came to the threshold of the front room and frankly watched. The meat had just been cooked, for it was still warm. After the man had cut some for the Blancos they produced their own scales so there could be no swindling in the weighing. Such home weighing, I could see, was customary, for the man's smile and the tip of his hat as he left showed his feelings had not been hurt.

Lupe put the meat in a small basket which she hung on a hook that dangled from the ceiling on a short chain. When she withdrew her hand, the basket hung like a wicker chandelier in the center of the storeroom. The kitten, who had also come to watch the transaction, looked up wistfully at the basket. Don Gabriel gave her a shove with the side of his foot. Without his words I knew she was the reason for the elevated storage place. Even Hambre could not leap that high.

Was there a slaughterhouse in the village, I asked. The answer was no, the butchers did their own killing. And how many butchers were there? Three.

THE TASK I had set myself for the day was drawing the interior of the church. It was the crucial assignment of my project. That interior is the chief glory of the monastic complex, and I was all too keenly aware that if I did not get at least one drawing that gave an idea of its glory, I would fail in my mission. Without it the series would be as incomplete, say, as Bernard Shaw's *Saint Joan* with Joan left out.

Without it, too, my words alone would never carry the necessary conviction. Who would ever believe that in a Mexican village of eight hundred people, in a town not even on most maps, was a Renaissance church of such splendor that it deserved a book-length study—who, I repeat, would believe that, if he were not presented with the visual evidence to conquer his incredulity?

Is it any wonder, then, that I had shrunk from the task of trying to

WEEK IN YANHUITLÁN

draw that interior? How on earth was I going to convey an impression of that loftiness, of that splendid length of nave, of the effect of those gold altars in the great white building? How in the same drawing was I going to give an idea of both the vaulted ceiling and the lower parts? And how, in black and white, was I going to give any sense of color?

I had chosen a spiral campaign: general drawings of the exterior first; next, the relatively easy windows, followed by the more difficult doorways; and then, after that warm-up, a plunge into the second most important feature—the cloister. And now having swum in a lake, I had to try the sea. And I could not put it off any longer. Many features crowded the schedule for Monday and Tuesday, so if I was to leave at noon on Wednesday, when my week completed its cycle, I had to draw the church today.

With the outcome so uncertain, I was hot and cold with nervousness. Since I had to wait until Don Gabriel had his breakfast, and waiting in that state can be agonizing, I welcomed the diverting companionship of visitors. First there were two little girls almost dragging their younger brother, whose small arms were laden with the long stems of three scroll-type Easter lilies. As they passed I offered them candies and they came to receive them.

The other visitor was Bobby, the Blancos' dog. He had often come over with Don Gabriel, but this was the first time he had come by himself. I counted it quite a triumph, even though he was too shy to do more than stand at the entrance and look in. I broke a candy in half and offered it to him in my hand. He was wary and did not come for it, but he ate it when I placed it on the threshold. He ate the other half in the same way. Then, having decided that what I was offering was good, and that I was trustworthy, he took the third piece from my hand. He also stood still while I stroked and scratched his head.

Mexicans, as a rule, don't pat their dogs as we do, so I could tell this head-stroking was a new experience for the cream-colored mongrel. And the indecision of the gentle dog touched me in an odd way. I knew he liked the feel of it, and I sensed in him a hunger for the sort of affection it represented. Yet something in his stance communicated to me that he was wondering if it was right to allow himself to be petted like this.

Don Gabriel's arrival put an end to his dilemma and he came bounding along with us as we mounted the slope to the monastery.

As we entered the cloister we saw some strangers on the roof. They were throwing pebbles and pennies down, aiming to sink them in the barrel of rain water standing in the garth. Apparently they were rich youths with a car and they had been able to get into the monastery because it was open for the priest's coming and going.

The easygoing Don Gabriel was galvanized into action. He went after them, and in the firm dignified way he ordered them out I saw a new aspect of his sense of responsibility. No one, no matter how wellborn or affluent, was going to trifle with his monastery. *"Un gusto especial,"* he said, as he angrily picked up some of the pennies that had fallen near the barrel. And in the scorn of his tone I heard the voice of a man who respected cultural values and who looked down on such childishness in people old enough to know better.

Because I knew so much hinged on the drawing I was about to start, I felt once more on the verge of a significant threshold. Thus when Don Gabriel opened the doors from the cloister and let me into the church, my old habit automatically led me to note the exact time. It was 9:14.

I had already written off the choir gallery with the coffered ceiling on its underside. I knew I could not include it in my big general drawing, since it was at one end of the church and the main altar was at the other. But I did want to include, if I could, a bay of the vaulting, the high altar and part of one wall. That suggested a three-quarter shot. Accordingly, I went to the western end and from first one corner and then the other I tested the views looking toward the apse. Not a single oblique view satisfied me.

Neither the vaulting nor the apse showed at their fullest beauty from off-center, and, no matter which way I looked, I could not see a balanced composition that would include one of the side walls. The elaborate side altars, too, made for excessive complication.

There's no help for it, I said to myself. I've simply got to sacrifice the wall idea.

This decision made, finding the best starting place was easy. It had to be looking squarely down the central axis of the church; and, because of the old difficulty of establishing proportions, it had to be as far back from the altar as possible. The nave extended well over two hundred feet and I wanted to take advantage of its full sweep to judge the relative heights and widths. After all, there were going to be hundreds of tiny details to fill in and I wanted to be sure I had the framework, and all its different compartments, the right size.

The experience with the diamond portal the day before had shown how enormously helpful it was to have a support for one's sketchbook from the start, so I looked about for some sort of table. Luck was with me. In front of one of the side altars was a flat-topped candlestand about the height of a lectern. Could I use that, I asked Don Gabriel.

"*Sí. ¿Cómo no?*" he said. We went to it, and he unceremoniously knocked off the candle stubs left by the devout. I was about to lift it, but he insisted on carrying it for me, and he brought it back to my chosen spot under the choir loft.

When I laid my sketchbook on it, I was delighted to find its height was ideal. I would have to stand, of course, but the lectern was high enough so I could work at it comfortably without crouching or bending. Feeling for the first time like a professional, I laid out my equipment—a smudgy bit of art gum, a razor blade, my little plastic ruler, a piece of white paper on whose edges I could mark widths, one of my soft pencils, and the new hard one I had bought the night before from Felix. The final act of the ceremony was using the blade to refine the points of the pencils.

And here I find myself faced with a dilemma. If I present the finished drawing at this point I rob the story of suspense by anticipating the outcome. Yet if I don't present it here the narrative will be hard to follow. For ease, the drawing is given. But may I ask that you use your imagination to see the drawing as if it were your own vision of the church, and not the result of my finished sketching? I ask this so you will keep aware that through this chapter I was in a state of suspense. I had never in my life tried anything so ambitious. I knew the project stood or fell by whether or not I caught what I was after. And I did not know how the drawing was going to turn out.

To help you see it as your own vision, may I supply the chief colors? The vaulted ceiling is white. That triumphal arch framing the apse is sea green. The half-dome over the altar is night blue and its ribs are gold. The altar, too, is an old mellow gold—that is, in all its structural members. But the life-sized statues have the colors of life and the spaces I have left blank are filled with Renaissance oil paintings.

Shortly after I began drawing I heard the church bell. I hoped it meant there was to be a Mass. And five minutes later I saw my hopes were to be realized. The plump priest in his black cassock crossed the nave and opened the big wicket door in the north portal. Then he set about dusting the altar with a feather brush. With Don Gabriel's help, he next brought in pots of stiff, artificial gold flowers which he set in line on the gradine at the back of the altar.

Meanwhile, villagers began to assemble. An old man with a staff and a big bandage around his gray hair came and took a seat on the steps leading up to the green and gold pulpit that stood like a tall goblet on the left. The majority, though, were women and children. They either sat or knelt on the floor. A few took places on the three or four benches that were set choirlike on either side of the chancel. A very old woman in black, helped by a man and a woman, made her way slowly to a bench. A man in a mustard-colored shirt crossed himself as he entered the church, but instead of taking his place up front with the children and the women he stood at the right some way back.

As I was to learn later, it was the sixteenth Sunday after Pentecost. The liturgical color of the season was green, and that was the color of the priest's vestments when he emerged from the sacristy. He had one helper, a little boy with a white surplice over a rose cassock.

Since I was too far back to hear distinctly, I was irreverent enough to jot down: "9:55 mumbles begin."

There were about twenty-five women present, and one of them had her four children sitting beside her on the altar steps. Because their dark rebozos were drawn over their heads in the same way, the women all looked alike from the back. Only the teacher-type girl with the pink skirt and the gray sweater stood out. She was so vivid because her rebozo was peacock blue with a lemon fringe.

Three men came in late. A fourth followed a few minutes afterwards. The men remained near the door at the back. Other latecomers joined them until there were about ten men.

At 10:03 a little bell rang. The silence that ensued was so intense that I paused in sharpening my pencil. Distant as the people were, I was fearful the scraping of the razor blade on the lead might carry and give offense.

Having come to trust my eye, and having learned that any use of the ruler in preliminary stages had an inhibiting effect, I worked in freehand. Thanks to the supported book and the hard pencil, I could draw very lightly. The blocking-in went fairly easily. I indicated the vaulting with single lines and then I outlined the main horseshoe of the triumphal arch. This arch established, it was not too difficult to set the horizontal lines indicating the five stories of the great reredos.

The Mass ran its course and at 10:17 the priest covered the sacred vessels with a green cloth and bore them off to the sacristy. The altar boy followed, and the service was over.

Several of the villagers came back to have a look at my work. There still was not much to see in the faintly blocked-in apse, but I was glad to

151

show them the work of previous days. The drawings, I felt, were my surest means to winning their friendship and trust.

They gathered around in a three-quarter circle and I found the best method of exhibition was to take each sketch in turn and to swing it round the arc. The rings at the top of the book made it easy to flip the pages. Thus each drawing could be exposed as if it were on an isolated sheet. I held up the drawings, facing out, and moved them around the group at a slow rate. This was fine for the adults. Their eyes were all more or less on the same level. But even standing on tiptoe, Jorge and Arturo, the two sons of El Presidente, could not see drawings displayed that high. I had to give them a special showing at a lower level.

The boys, I noticed, had little fur collars on their brown jackets.

One of the villagers was the husky youth with the long-lashed, velvety brown eyes who had come to draw water for his tins the morning I sketched the north portal. I nodded to him in recognition, but Don Gabriel made a point of introducing him nevertheless.

"This is my nephew," he said. His name was Alberto, and he was the son of Don Gabriel's sister, who had died several years previously.

Don Gabriel remained a little while after the others had left the church. I remarked that the relatively small congregation for the Mass illustrated his point about the townsfolk not being very religious. The comment elicited an astonishing piece of information.

"They aren't all irreligious. Many don't come to this church because they are Protestants."

"Protestants in Yanhuitlán!"

"Yes," said Don Gabriel. "There are many Protestants." Then as if to prove his point, he added: "The principal of the school is a Presbyterian."

Protestants, I knew, had brought medical aid to some of the poorest and most isolated sections of Mexico, and because they had worked in such neglected, out-of-the-way places they had been unmolested. The eroded mountain valleys of the Mixteca Alta certainly were isolated before the coming of the highway. Yanhuitlán, then, was just such a place as I had heard about. It was interesting to put two and two together. And I hoped I would meet the school principal.

After Don Gabriel left, I resumed my sketching. The ribbing over the chancel suggested a gigantic cobweb that had been blown concave by a strong updraught. Having laid out the whole network in freely drawn, spidery lines, my task was to check the symmetry and to give the ribs their necessary thickness. Because of its central position, I began with the one line in the web that appeared to be perfectly straight. And it was the only rib I had time to solidify.

I had to suspend work because Alfonso's bus was leaving at eleven o'clock and I wanted to see him off.

THE BUS STOP, it will be remembered, was in front of the church at the foot of the long flight of steps leading down from the platform. When I got there a number of people were already assembled. A few were waiting in the shade of the twisted sapotal tree, but Alfonso and his party were standing in the full sunlight.

There were so many in his circle that at first I could not get them straightened out. I was especially taken by a firm, vigorous, matriarchal type of woman with kindly eyes that crinkled at the corners when something struck her as humorous. She, I felt, must be Alfonso's aunt. But I was mistaken. She was the Widow Isabel, a close friend of the family. The real aunt was a somewhat mousy little woman of about forty.

There were three young women in the group. Two, as it turned out, were the aunt's daughters. I recognized Acela from the visit to the house when I had been foiled in observing their domestic arrangements. The other daughter was Marta. They were going to Puebla too. Alfonso explained they were studying to be schoolteachers and their Independence Day holidays were ending at the same time as his.

Puebla, I knew, was more than six hours away. It seemed a long way for the girls to have to go for their training, but I realized that was a penalty of life in such a village. If you wanted anything more than primary education, you had to travel to get it.

The third young woman was a friend of Acela's and Marta's. Her name was María Luisa. She was a rather heavy, good-looking girl and I recognized her as one of the *monjitas* I had seen the first afternoon, tossing that ball around in a tame little circle.

Eliel, the happy ten-year-old, was in the group. Only this time he did not seem so happy. Perhaps he was sad that his cousin Alfonso was leaving. The boy had his slingshot with him, and every now and then he would break away, pick up a small stone and shoot it at a bird that had come to rest nearby. He never hit one, but from the way he yanked back the elastic and fiercely fired the stones I got the impression that he was taking out some of his feelings on the birds.

THE CHURCH

El Presidente and two of his friends arrived. They were taking an excursion in the opposite direction, for they were going to the nearer town of Nochixtlán. They paused to join our circle, and once more there was a mass showing of my drawings. Since the aggregate was considerably larger than the second day when we had visited his store, I think Don Venustiano was a bit more impressed.

Presently an open farm truck came along. Don Venustiano and his friend raced to it, were told they could have a lift, climbed in and were off with cheery waves to those of us remaining.

"Don Venustiano plays the cornet in the town orchestra," María Luisa volunteered. Then she added with a gleeful look, "Tonight there is going to be a dance."

"*Un baile!*" I exclaimed in delight. It was going to be in the school and they told me a stranger could come.

"I will teach you how to dance," said María Luisa. And they all laughed at her boldness.

At this point the sight of Alfonso's bus in the distance suddenly precipitated our farewells. I gave Alfonso a good Mexican hug, promised to send him a copy of my column from New York and then withdrew so I would not intrude on the family good-byes.

When the bus arrived, Eliel darted in to find places for his sisters and Alfonso. Some of the luggage was hoisted onto the roof. The two girls got on and went to the seats Eliel had saved for them. As Eliel got off, Alfonso, in boarding, gave him a hug. And I noticed that Alfonso was carrying some yellow flowers. They were *bolsas de Judas*. To see that they would survive the long bus ride to Puebla, he had their earth-clogged roots in a little plastic sack partly full of water.

"For his mother," the Widow Isabel explained after the bus had passed beyond waving distance.

The excitement over, we turned away a little sadly. And as I went back to the church I felt something had gone out of life. But I was deeply glad I had made the effort of going to the bus. It had given me the first chance to mix with the people in the friendly way I had hoped would have been possible sooner. I was excited, too, at the thought of the dance.

NEARLY EVERY DRAWING goes through the same three stages—the posing, the blocking-in and the detailing. When I resumed work I had definitely reached the third stage. The section I decided to detail first was the one I

WEEK IN YANHUITLÁN

had already started—the stone spider web over the chancel. I chose it partly because my mistake in starting the north portal at the bottom had taught me it is always better to start the heavy penciling of a big drawing from the top. But the top decision was also dictated by the fact that the rib-vaulting had an almost independent existence. Finishing it off would get its problems out of the way and this would enable me to turn to the rest of the drawing with less anxiety.

In the further work on the web I had the wedge-shaped interspaces to guide me. I knew if the wedges were right in their relation to each other the lines of the ribs would be correct. Another aid was the church itself. Because it was once more locked up, it was cool and utterly quiet. Thus I was physically comfortable and I was completely undisturbed. And the over-all beauty and the spaciousness had an influence that is hard to describe. It was a curious combination of exaltation and tranquility. The beauty seemed to lift and liberate the spirit, and, because there was so much space in which that spirit could soar freely without hitting anything jarring, the spirit came to feel more and more at ease in a flying area so much wider than its customary home.

The drawing of the rib-vaulting was turning out well, and I rejoiced that this was so, for it meant I would not have to make further drawings of the ceiling. I say this because of the particular nature of the Yanhuitlán roof. In some sixteenth-century Mexican churches, the chancel ribbing is more elaborate than the rest, but in Yanhuitlán the ribbing of the chancel is identical with that of the other three bays. Thus the concave spider webs over the other vaults have the same number of ribs springing from each corner as in the one I have shown; and in each of them those ribs, in intersecting, create an octagonal crown around the central boss.

The frontispiece shows the four shallow domes that cover the spider webs within. The dome at the front roofs the bay that contains the choir loft. The second and third domes roof the free part of the nave and the rear dome covers the chancel. This was the eggshell I was hesitant to walk over. The hole Don Gabriel and I looked through is indicated in my altar drawing. It is the dot in the central boss.

The reader, knowing that both the ribs and the plates over them are of stone, might have an uneasy feeling at seeing so heavy a ceiling looking so unsupported. This effect is deliberate. I have intentionally omitted the two beautiful fluted columns that help support those two corbels that seem to hang in space. I have done this because, being only half columns, they are inconspicuous. Also they are exceptional in that they are the only hint of columning in the whole church. All the other rib clusters spring from corbels high in the walls, like those shown near the angels in the corners. The result is that when one is in the church the ceiling has a hanging, floating effect.

Another look at the frontispiece will show how this interior effect of effortless insubstantiality is achieved. The additional thrust of those rib clusters is sustained by the big external buttresses that brace the bearing walls at the crucial points.

A decision I had to make while working on the ceiling was whether or not to draw the windows in the lunettes between the corner corbels and the ones seeming to hang in space. My verdict was to leave them out. They would only involve additional arched lines that, in making the drawing more complicated, would spoil the clear patterning of the vaulting.

Those particular windows are the ones whose absence of tracery I mourned when I was making the side view shown on page 53. The light was pouring through the great voids, and that light gave me the clue to their logic. Being inside, I could see readily that these were the windows that lit the chancel. Because they had no central stone pillars, no tracery heads, nothing in them obstructed the illumination. Thus they let in more light than the other windows of the nave. The result, achieved with such subtlety, is that the altar area has a greater brightness than the rest of the church. A trick, of course, but no wonder that towering gold altar catches the breath with a sense of luminous sanctity.

Once the ceiling was finished, I turned to the latticelike ribbing that decorated the quarter-sphere roofing the apse. Here again I left things out. There were studlike projections at each point where one rib cut another, and there was a golden star in each of the square meshes of the latticework. In the actual ceiling these details did not seem fussy, but I knew they would look like gingerbread in the drawing. I did not even try to draw them. I did take pains, however, to get the ribs and the interspaces correct. It meant a very careful adjustment of lines. And, though I sometimes cursed the side lines for running close together, I was thankful for those ribs. Foreswearing shadow, I had the problem of suggesting by line alone the curves of the interior of a sphere. Those ribs provided the lines that would help create the illusion.

When they were drawn, I was delighted with the effect. The half-silo form of the apse was unmistakable and I knew the drawing would not suffer from looking flat and planlike.

WEEK IN YANHUITLÁN

AT THIS POINT Don Gabriel came to say the midday meal was ready. I had reached an excellent place for a break, so I gladly shut up my sketch-book and we went home together.

Bobby confirmed my intuition of the morning. As I was eating, he came and stood under the table near my left knee. It was the position where he could be most conveniently stroked. I gladly obliged. But the Blancos expressed concern. They hoped he was not a nuisance. Assuring them I liked dogs made me want to tell them about a dog that had been a favorite of my parents. But what on earth was the Spanish word for dachshund? I decided a picture might give the idea. So I drew a rough approximation to one of the low-slung little hounds.

"¡O, salchicha!" they exclaimed. I laughed. *Salchicha* is the Spanish word for sausage.

Hambre didn't want to be petted, but she did want to be fed. As usual, she got a little of everything: some rice on a bit of tortilla, a shred or two of meat and some frijoles.

The coffee was strong, and as I was drinking it Don Gabriel produced an example of Lupe's handiwork at the sewing machine. He asked if I knew what it was. It looked like a white trouser leg, so I said: "*Pantalones con solamente una pierna.*" It was their turn to laugh. No, it was a case for his rifle. To show its excellence, he took his rifle apart and slipped the barrel into one compartment and the butt into another. Then he showed how Lupe had even thought of making a flap to cover the open ends. He was obviously delighted with the new acquisition, and she basked in his appreciation.

Lupe made most of her own clothes and some of his, he volunteered as further evidence of her cleverness. Was she, I asked, by any chance one of the three dressmakers in the village? I could tell by their expressions they were pleased by the implied compliment. But the answer was no; she just made things for the home.

Up to this time, I had taken a little nap after each lunch, but today I was more concerned with drawing than with sleep. So after shaving, I used the rest of the siesta hour to strengthen the altar's sketchy framework to make it ready for the details. This meant using my ruler to true the perpendiculars, and to see that I had achieved equality in all spaces of equal width.

THE CHURCH

The knowledge that on returning to the church I would move my stand nearer the front led me to think of some of the advantages drawing had over photography. A photograph taken from far enough back to get the widely embracing view of my sketch would lose the details that, thanks to the visibility of an advanced position, I was going to be able to draw in clearly. Another advantage was suggested by the uprightness of my verticals. The artist can tilt his viewing aperture upwards without causing the upper lines to slant together as they do in a photo. The artist, too, can penetrate intervening masses, like platform edges and guard walls. And the artist can leave things out. This last struck me especially as I looked at my wall-less sketch. And as I revised I saw there were advantages in not having the subject before one's eyes. Not being overwhelmed by the physical presence of the altar, I could be more detached and calculating.

It was pleasant working there. Inside, it was cool, shaded and tranquil and I had the little table with the flowers on it to support the sketchbook. Outside, there was bright sunlight and a stretch of lovely pale blue sky. Outside, too, the landscape had figures.

One I recall was a small black horse that galloped past my door, unbridled and unattended, and obviously exulting in its freedom. In contrast, how slowly those two little girls sauntered along the same roadway. Could it be they wanted to be sure they did not walk so fast as to miss a candy? I tested the hunch and the alacrity with which they came forward showed it was not lack of energy that had caused their feet to drag.

Then there was Serafina! *"¿Quiere blancos?"* she asked.

I was doubly caught off guard. She had come to the door so quietly that I had not noticed her approach. And she was so beautiful that for a moment I was dazed. She was a girl, probably about fifteen, of a pronounced Indian type. And it will be a long time before I forget those large eyes, the clear dark skin, the heart-shaped face and the black hair, parted in the center and perfectly combed—especially as she stood with the sunlight behind her.

"¿Blancos?" I stammered. *"No entiendo."* In explanation, she drew back the napkin from her little basket and revealed six eggs. I saw she had called them "whites" rather than "eggs" because no hint of brown stained their snowiness.

I was delighted at the opportunity of buying something for my host and hostess, but I was a little troubled about procedure. Perhaps it would be wrong to buy all six eggs at a swoop because then the girl wouldn't have any left. I had heard of Mexicans wanting to keep part of their stock in order to have the fun of making new sales. Accordingly, I compromised. I bought five. They were forty centavos each.

Lurking behind Serafina were two young girls. The little girls of the village were especially difficult to tell apart, but I was pretty sure I recognized one as Angelita, the child who had resorted to a loud *Adiós* when I had failed to notice her as she passed two days before.

I gave them all candies. After they had gone the idea occurred to me that the visit might have been a put-up job. Perhaps Serafina had been coached to run interference with the eggs so all three could get *dulces*.

Don Gabriel showed up a few minutes later. I gave him the eggs and, after he had taken them to Lupe, he let me into the church, helped me move the stand forward and, after being assured I was thoroughly settled, left me alone at my work.

I sharpened my pencils very carefully, for my problem was to fill in the details of that vast sevenfold screen that rose behind the altar. Sixteen life-sized figures, as many niches, innumerable cornices, moldings, bases and capitals and more than twenty-five pillars, some of them elaborately twisted —I blenched before the task. But after checking my proportions to see that I had all the compartments the right size, I screwed up my resolution and began. And I began it the way I have other large tasks: that is, I put the thought of the whole out of my mind and started with one small area.

The need to work downwards dictated the top story. In carefully outlining the baroque cresting I came to the cross. No wonder it hasn't been straightened, I said to myself. How could you ever get up there to fix it?

As I drew the ovals that held the coats of arms and the frames that held the oil paintings, I blessed my decision not to try to indicate what they contained.

Then came the first row of cornices with the problem of indicating the seven planes of the retable and the jutting cornices at each corner where the screen folded at a different angle. Next, the top row of figures. I thought they were friars, but, even though I was now about halfway down the church, they were still too high and far away for me to say with certainty.

Then another and more ornate row of cornices. It was slow, painstaking and almost entirely mechanical work. I found it tiring and I had to keep myself under firm control so I did not start putting in lines in a slapdash manner. The miters on the heads of the figures in the second tier showed that these men might be bishops.

One thing interested me as I worked: the contrast between the drawing and the reality. Even though I was leaving out a great deal of low-relief ornamentation, the sketch began to seem overly fussy.

But what would happen when I looked up from the "busy" drawing to the apse itself? All the curlicues were there—and more—yet the chancel was as serene and lofty as ever. How could this be? I asked myself. Why, with all that extravagant and varied ornamentation, isn't the effect of that apse fussy too? One explanation which presented itself was that the great shoe box of the church provided space enough to absorb that decoration. The other explanation that came to me was more subtle and is perhaps less acceptable to those who believe in aesthetic laws. But I had the odd feeling that all this elaborate, writhing ornamentation seemed to fit so placidly into the church because the church and the ornamentation had been together so long. They had grown used to each other.

As I was working on the third row of figures an elderly man with a bandaged arm entered the church from the cloister. He looked like an old shepherd, and I think this impression stemmed partly from his staff and partly from the fact that, instead of following most men of the village in wearing American-style trousers, he wore the white cotton *calzones* characteristic of the country Indian.

He was a touching figure as he went humbly to a side altar and lit a candle to the Virgin. After he had crossed himself and said a prayer or two, he came back to where I was sketching, and revealed it was not piety alone that had brought him to the church. "Would I like to buy an *idolo?*" he asked.

He was not the man with the club foot who had limped painfully home to fetch his idols three years before. But in my heart I welcomed him as the other's prototype. I felt I could make retribution for my involuntary meanness to the first man by buying something from this second one. I did not let on my mind was fully made up, though. That would not be part of the etiquette of Mexican bargaining. Instead, I asked him to show me what he had.

He produced a tiny head of olive-green stone.

At first glance the head seemed to be wearing a helmet and the carving suggested a little football player whose eyes had been bunged up in a particularly rough game. I was charmed by the vivacity of expression and when I turned the stone sideways I saw that, even though it was only an inch high, it also had a profile of irresistible character. I was totally captivated, but I retained a poker face.

"How much is it?" I asked, knowing the price he would set was higher than he expected to get.

Ten pesos was his starting point. *"Es muy caro,"* I said. It is very dear. I countered with five. He then dropped to nine. I boosted my offer to six and we settled for eight.

When I took out my wallet I found I did not have the exact sum. All I could offer the man was a ten peso note. He did not have so much as two pesos to make change. I thought quickly. I did not know the man from Adam, but my hunch was that he was just as honest as all the other Mexicans I had dealt with. Here was a chance to play my hunch that could cost me no more than two pesos. So I said casually, "Take the ten pesos and bring me the change." It gave him the perfect chance to vanish into thin air.

But the old shepherd did not betray my trust. About twenty minutes later he shuffled back into the church. I felt almost mean in accepting the two crumpled pesos from his calloused old hands. But I could not reveal I had tested him, and I could tell from his gratitude and the sweetness of his smile that he was very well pleased with the bargain.

After he had gone and I was back at my cornices, I smiled at the irony of the situation. An Indian had used a Christian church as a market place for the sale of a pagan idol. Could any of the Dominican friars have stirred in their graves?

How tedious the job was becoming! And as I put in one little careful stroke after another I realized that drawing details forces you into a curious sort of observing. You look at a thing in order to reproduce tiny aspects of it, rather than to absorb it as a whole. It is both a looking and a not looking.

The element of not looking comes in all the things you exclude as you work. You exclude color, atmosphere, the sense of the total effect, and you remove all personal response in order to make the pencil markings convey one or two particular lines and shapes on which you are concentrating. Insofar as you focus only on the appearance of the part, excluding for the moment all feeling for its nature, you look in a peculiarly uncomprehending way. It is both a looking by rote and a carrying of objectivity to the nth degree. But, oh, the curious effect once one has drawn an object in detail! Thereafter it is much so more fully visible.

The idea occurred to me that there might be some therapeutic effect in drawing details, and I wondered if any doctors had lit on the idea of prescribing such drawing for emotionally disturbed patients.

What a sigh of relief I huffed when I finally completed the retable! Next I turned to the triumphal arch. I had already decided to omit all the squiggly ornament that swarmed over it like heavy embroidery; so figures were my main concern. These went fairly easily, for I have had more experience drawing figures than architecture.

Don Gabriel returned when I was about halfway through. Lupe was with him and she looked charming, for she was wearing her coral dress and one end of her charcoal-gray rebozo was drawn across her breast and flung over her left shoulder. Having an especially long upper lip, she was not what one would call a pretty woman, but her broad-cheeked face was as open, practical and pleasant as one could hope to find.

I showed them the little head I had acquired. "How much did you pay for it?" was Don Gabriel's first question. "Eight pesos."

Lupe could not contain her laughter. "Eight pesos? Eight pesos—for that?" she asked incredulously, and went off into fresh laughter. It was laughter I loved to hear. It was utterly lacking in offense and yet so unreservedly candid. And it showed me I must have passed some milestone with her, otherwise she would not have felt free to respond in front of me with such unconcealed mirth.

I think Don Gabriel was amused too, but instead of laughing he took out his jackknife. He asked for the head and began trying to cut into it. The stone was so hard the knife could not even mark it.

"At least its genuine," he said, handing back the head. Then he explained that the fake heads sold to tourists were always of such soft stone that you could cut shavings from them. So my stone head, in addition to being so lively in expression, was older than the monastery. I felt that, in acquiring a Mixtec piece for so little, I'd got a bargain.

The figure I had been drawing when the Blancos arrived was the patriarch on the right side of the triumphal arch who seemed to be holding a book facing outwards as if he were showing one of his sketches. Did he represent St. Paul, I asked. Yes, said Don Gabriel, and the man on the other side, catching up his chartreuse cloak over his blue robe, was St. Peter.

"Who are the angels at the top?"

"Those aren't angels. They are archangels. That is San Miguel on the left and San Rafael on the right."

Both, I noticed, had blue tunics, but Michael's skirt was brick red, while Rafael's was yellow.

The archangels provided a chance for a joke. My host, of course, was named after Gabriel, the chief of all the archangels, So I asked: "Why isn't there a statue of the archangel named after you?"

He had an answer. "There isn't a place in the church sufficiently high."

"Can you identify all the figures on the retable?" I asked.

"No. Most of them are too far up. But they are in groups of four. There are the four *evangelistas,* the four *fundadores,* the four *doctores* and the four *padres de la iglesia.* The only one I know individually is the one turned sideways in the bottom row at the left. That is San Andrés. You can tell from his cross. It's like an X."

"Was there once a figure in that empty niche in the middle of the second tier?"

"There were two. Santo Domingo and San Francisco."

"Who removed them?"

"The priest," said Don Gabriel in a tone that seemed to imply: "What else would you expect from a man who tried to drive his car into the monastery?"

"You say both Santo Domingo *and* San Francisco were in the niche?" I asked, finding it hard to believe that the founders of the rival orders should be placed together. "Yes," he said. "There was a pact between the Franciscans and the Dominicans whereby the Franciscans agreed to let the Dominicans evangelize this part of Mexico in return for the Dominican agreement not to enter Franciscan territory."

A figure stood above the altar against a deep-red curtain. It was sustaining a banner and wearing the white robe and long black cape of the Dominican Order. I knew it must represent St. Dominic, since he was the patron saint of the church.

"Is that the statue that used to be in the niche?"

"Oh, no. Can't you see it is new? That is one the priest brought in when he hung up the red curtain."

'What did he do with the old centerpiece?"

"It's under the choir loft." And when he led me back to look at it, Don Gabriel pointed to a figure that had impressed me on my first visit—a life-sized skeleton wearing a crown and seated on a throne.

"Do you mean to say Death sat on the altar?"

"No," said Don Gabriel, laughing. "I mean the picture behind him."

It was a large canvas showing Jesus seated on the right hand of the Father, and above them hovered the dove of the Holy Ghost. As a lover of early music, I was especially taken by the two angels at the feet of the Divine Personages. One was plucking a lute and the other was drawing an arched bow across the strings of a viol. I was sorry the painting had been deposed, but at least it had not met the fate of some altar paintings and been destroyed.

Lupe left after we had examined the painting, but Don Gabriel remained until I completed my drawing.

What a load lifted from my spirit as I put in the last stroke of the altar steps! Not only was there joy at a long task finally over, but there was release from the fear that had haunted me since stepping from the bus. I had pulled it off.

Looking at my sketch, I knew it was the most beautiful drawing I had ever done. I knew, too, that it captured the church. A few spots needed fixing, but there was no gainsaying its success. I had faced my great test. And I had passed. In my hands I had the drawing that justified the whole series.

Glancing at my watch, I saw it was almost six o'clock.

No more than half an hour of light remained. And I had done only a single drawing! My plans called for two. And the second subject was especially significant. With the desperation of the overtired, I said to myself, I must at least get a start on it. And I must hurry, must hurry.

My feeling of almost panicky urgency increased when I examined the part I wanted to draw. It was already in shadow and I could not see it well enough even to decide how to start. Couldn't Don Gabriel open the front doors of the church to let in more light?

I do not want to identify the part here, for its story belongs to the sixth day. But I do want to record Don Gabriel's goodness. First, in an understanding way, he pointed out the magnitude of the beam that served as a Bunyanesque bolt. He also drew my attention to the big wedges that had been driven into the floor to insure that even battering rams could not

164

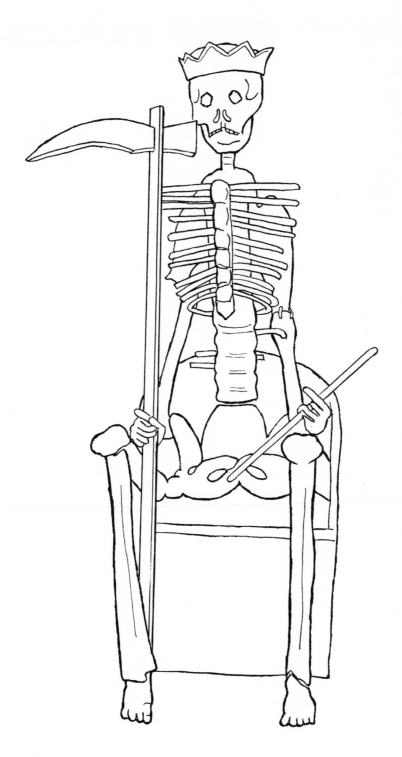

drive in those great doors. Then, when he had convinced me of the impossibility of my request, he said he knew a secret about the part. He wouldn't reveal it, but he promised that it would greatly facilitate the drawing.

"Leave it till tomorrow," he urged. "Come, let us go now."

As we came out of the monastery, we saw many people in the plaza and they had the look of a crowd slowly breaking up at the end of an entertainment. There were several men on horseback too, and the horses seemed tired, yet still excited.

"What went on?" I asked.

"Horse races," replied Don Gabriel.

With a pang, I realized the toll exacted by my drawing. It had caused me to miss something I would have dearly loved to see. But there was a consolation. I might have lost the races, but tonight there was the ball.

XII

EL BAILE

I HAVE TRIED to make each chapter adhere around a central nucleus, but this one will start exceptionally. The dance did not begin until nine o'clock and an intervening development needs recounting because it is part of the larger story. It was touched off unexpectedly by a casual question.

As Don Gabriel and I watched the slow dispersal of the villagers after the horse racing, we were standing under the arch at the top of the flight of stairs connecting the plaza and the church's large side court.

Projecting from the impost was the end of an old gray beam with a hole bored through it about the size of a man's wrist. My interest in that hole was so slight I hardly know why I inquired about it. Perhaps it was just my old reporter's habit of asking questions. Whatever the motivation, this query touched off the surprising development.

My casualness vanished the moment Don Gabriel explained the purpose of the pierced beam. It was to hold the upper end of an iron gate's turning pole.

"See," he said, "here is the socket," and he pointed to a hole in the stone at the foot of the gateway. This concavity, also the size of a man's wrist, was directly below the hole in the beam. Recollection of the doors leading from the cloister into the church made everything clear. Instead of being hinged, those doors pivoted on great wooden poles held perpendicular by being fitted into sockets in the lintel and threshold. This iron gate, then, also swung on a upright pole. And it must have been matched by another iron gate swinging from the opposite side, for projecting from the other impost of the archway I saw a second pierced beam end.

Remembering the archway where I had begun drawing the north portal, I asked Don Gabriel if it, too, had been fitted with iron gates.

"Yes," he said. And in his way of volunteering fresh information once a new line of investigation had been opened, he added that there had been an arched gateway at the head of the western stairway too, and that this now-vanished gateway had also been fitted with iron gates.

Iron gates standing free at three points on the rim of a platform sounded incongruous to me, so I questioned further. "Formerly," he said, "the whole monastery was surrounded by a wall."

A wall! Curiously, I had never thought of that. If there was an unbroken wall, naturally the iron gates would be useful. They could be shut to make the whole precinct inaccessible.

"How high was the wall?" I asked, for my curiosity was thoroughly aroused. "You can see for yourself," replied Don Gabriel. "It was as high as the piers supporting this arch." Looking at the piers, I estimated the vanished wall must have been about nine or ten feet high.

"Can you still see traces of the wall?"

"Oh, yes. Come, I will show you." And with that Don Gabriel and I began a walk around the edge of the platform. Where the wall had stood was apparent. It must have been almost three feet thick. And when we reached the northern end of the platform where the drop to the street was greatest, I realized that, from below, the flank of wall, with an extra ten feet added must have presented an impressive cliff of masonry.

As I envisaged that massive wall I had the strangest sensation. Up to this moment I had seen the monastery only as it stood before me—that is, an exposed, wind-swept, almost deserted monument, with one wing in ruins, that dominated a few huts in a valley, whose mountainsides were growing ever more barren. In other words, because of some freezing of my imagination, I had been unable to conceive it in any other aspect than the one it presented to the traveler in the 1950's.

Yet as those stones began to snap back into place in that wall—like a film record of a disaster run backwards in slow motion—my imagination unfroze. And as the walls rose to enclose the precincts, the dull gilt on the altars inside began to gleam with the highlights of new gold leaf, the white-wash dissolved from the walls, and the brick reds, the turquoise blues and the olive-, sea- and emerald-greens grew brilliant, transforming the church from a primarily white interior to a nave that was a mass of bright colors.

Why hadn't my imagination stirred like this before? Or putting it another way, what had suddenly liberated the imaginative faculty? As we continued our stroll around the platform in the gathering dusk, I received a clue.

Perhaps, I said to myself, my mind was struck in the single track of seeing the monastery only as it is now because the task of drawing it meant reproducing its physical appearance; and I could think of nothing except its present aspect because I had so much anxiety over whether I could achieve an adequate set of drawings.

This explanation was plausible, and it was confirmed by a converse realization. Since I felt all subsequent drawings would be relatively simple, the drawing of the church interior, by turning out successfully, had clearly put an end to that particular anxiety.

Anxiety, then, had been the block. Its presence had paralyzed my imagination, and its dissolution had freed my imagination. And I treasured my new vision of the high-walled monastery, with its quiet, sheltered, carefully kept grounds and its fabulously colored interior. Its vividness in my mind, where before no such concept had existed, seemed a particularly telling example of the way in which our perceptions are influenced by our inward states.

WHEN I FINALLY sat down at Lupe's table I had a full awareness of my weariness. Who could have thought one could be so tired just from drawing a picture. The warmth of that hot milk was like strength flowing back into me, and I am sure I never ate an omelet that tasted so delicious. This time, too, I did not turn down the stewed frijoles. I felt especially grateful when Don Gabriel inquired: "*¿Quesito?*" (meaning, "A little cheese?"), and then, hardly waiting for my affirmative, crumbled bits of the white cheese into the dark beans.

The Blancos had told me the village had three bread shops, and Lupe must have visited one during the day, for pieces of sweet bread were heaped in a bowl on the table. I took one resembling the convex side of a cockle shell. It was called a *capricho,* Don Gabriel said. It went very well with the black coffee, and by this time I felt revived enough to start planning for the dance.

I had broached the subject at lunch, asking the Blancos to go with me. They had demurred. When pressed for a reason, the fact came out. It was too expensive. They thought the tickets cost about five pesos each.

"But it will be my treat," I had protested, liking the idea of making it possible for them to attend. They still hesitated.

"Don't you like to dance?" I had asked Lupe, incredulously. Her answer was a "Yes, but. . . ." Finally, Don Gabriel had asked me to let them think it over. They had promised their verdict at dinner.

This being dinner time, I asked if they had made their decision. Lupe said yes. Don Gabriel would go with me, but she would not. I tried to persuade her, but she was firm. She would rather not go. I felt that part of her reluctance was shyness, but being convinced her feelings were sincere I did not press her further.

The decision made, Don Gabriel warned me to take very little money. There was danger of pickpockets, he insisted. All I should take would be enough to pay for the tickets and perhaps to buy some flowers from the girls who might be selling them.

Taking him at his word, I reached into my buttoned hip pocket and brought out the second wallet that the Oaxaca miner had advised me to keep in a secret place. It contained practically all the money I had and I realized the extent of my confidence in Don Gabriel by the spontaneous way I handed it over to him.

"Will you keep it for me?" I asked.

"Gladly," he said. And he took a key from a nail on the wall and used it to open a trunk by the bed. The trunk, I noticed, was a U. S. Army one. Don Gabriel explained he had bought it before leaving California—at a "surplus" sale.

Once he had put the wallet in the trunk, he locked it again and hung the key back on the nail. I laughed good-humoredly at his system. The trunk was locked all right, but the key was in full sight. Lupe and Don Gabriel laughed at the absurdity too. But he told me not to worry. *"Es seguro,"* he said. And I knew it was.

I returned to my room while Don Gabriel had his evening meal. As I waited, a knock sounded at my door. I opened it and found three villagers. I think they all had drunk too much and standing there in the inky darkness they put me in mind of the conspirators who gather so ominously outside the garden gate in the second act of *Rigoletto.*

"Una invitación especial," said one rather thickly.

"From El Presidente," said another.

So I gathered they had been sent by the Municipal President to escort me to the dance. They were men I had never seen before, and because they were so unfamiliar and mysterious, I did not trust them. But I tried not to betray this. I explained I had promised to go to *el baile* with Don Gabriel and that I had to wait for him because he was eating. Apparently this satisfied them, and, after obtaining a firm assurance I would come without fail, they took their leave.

Considering its usual darkness, the municipal building might almost have been said to be a blaze of light as Don Gabriel and I approached it. The illumination was soft and yellow, but it was unmistakably electricity. I was surprised, for it was my impression the town had no electricity. Don Gabriel explained there were two small Diesel-operated generators in the village that were used for special occasions.

The dance was in the long schoolroom on the left of the central archway. This was the room that had been bare and deserted when I had glimpsed it on the third attempt to deliver El Presidente's bottle. What a different appearance it presented now! Men and boys crowded the doors and windows. The benches ranged against the walls were all occupied. The village orchestra was on the stage at the far end. And the place was raftered with twisted streamers of red, white and blue paper.

The crowd at the entrance door opened up courteously to let us through, and a man had been alerted to serve as official greeter. His name was Refugio Rendón and he shook hands warmly as he guided us past the ticket taker into the big room. There Alberto, the handsome water carrier, came forward to shake hands, and I must say it was good to know at least one friend among so many strangers.

María Luisa and a friend of hers also came forward, and the other girl startled me by pinning something on my left lapel. It was a great bow of baby blue ribbon, with streamers a foot and a half long. When I looked more carefully, I saw a silver peso and a little bunch of pink and white artificial flowers wired neatly at the knot of the bow. I have treasured that decoration ever since, but at the time I was partly embarrassed, partly touched and partly amused.

The orchestra was not playing, so Alberto led me across the open floor to a place that was vacated for me on a bench on the south side of the room. I found myself sitting next to the Widow Isabel, whom I had met seeing Alfonso off. That was another welcome familiar face, and I greeted her with a cordial *"buenas noches"* and she replied with a smile and a friendly nod of the head.

The north side of the room was lined with the señoritas of the village. There they were, seated in a row. I knew the only thing to do was to smile at them as if I knew them all. They all smiled back and returned my *"buenas noches."*

Presently an elderly woman moved down our line with a tray loaded with white cups. Each had a tin spoon standing in it for stirring its contents. When the server got to us, the Widow Isabel and I did an Alphonse and Gaston about taking one. After we both had our cups, I found it was a hot apple punch mildly spiked with something alcoholic. It was good.

The punch was followed by a plate of wafers passed by a younger woman.

The striking up of the music, then, caught me with my hands full. But I was bound I was going to dance from the start, so I gobbled the wafer, asked the widow to guard my punch, and crossed the floor to ask María Luisa for the honor of the dance. I picked her because she was the only girl I knew. Fortunately, she was willing.

Other men advanced from the benches or from where they had been standing near the entrance, and in a moment all the girls were taken and María Luisa and I were engulfed in a mass of couples, all doing a tame little jigging sort of fox trot.

Perhaps María Luisa and I were not so inconspicuous as I thought, for when the process of circling the room brought us in front of the big north window, the boys peering in gave us a cheer. And what a jolly sight those brown-faced kids were! How they piled on top of each other outside I do not know, but their heads filled practically the whole window. Those at the bottom had their elbows on the sill. Some poked their heads in diagonally at the sides, and others must have been standing on boxes or tables in order to see over those on the bottom row. Most of them wore their sombreros and some had their sarapes pulled across their mouths against the night air.

More boys crowded the still higher windows on the south side, and some of them were sitting on the sills dangling their legs inside. They, too, grinned broadly as we passed, and I realized my decision not to hesitate about starting to dance had been a wise one.

I began to feel more at ease, and I saw that not all the people lining the benches were strangers. Some were villagers I had nodded to. One face was especially familiar. It was the plain woman who had stopped by my room and asked if I were a doctor. Despite the lateness of the hour, little Hugo was sitting in her lap. She recognized me, and her transforming smile seemed more ingratiating than ever as it beamed on me reassuringly. I asked María Luisa for the woman's name. It was Ester.

When the music stopped, the partnerships broke up as rapidly as they had formed. The girls darted back to their places along the north wall and the young men retired to seats, if they had them, or to the crowded standing room near the main entrance. Many of the men did not even escort their partners to their benches. I took María Luisa to hers and fully expected to sit beside her during the intermission. But she squeezed into a narrow place between two of her friends, leaving no room for me. Since neither of the other girls moved over, I realized it was not customary for young men and women to sit together between dances. Accordingly, I thanked María Luisa and retired to my place where the Widow Isabel was guarding my punch.

I had been seated only a moment when another woman offered me a second cup of punch. I explained I already had some. She protested it must be cold by now. Wouldn't I like a warm cup? I thanked her for her thoughtfulness but said I was *muy contento* with what I had.

I must say that, as we had entered, more attention had been paid to me than to Don Gabriel. In the excitement we had become separated. While dancing, though, I had noticed he had taken an inconspicuous place in the corner behind the men standing near the door. I went back to see him. Didn't he want to come and sit at the front near me? No, he said, he was very happy where he was.

"Just enjoy yourself and don't worry about me," he counseled. I took him at his word and returned to my bench against the south wall.

Next, I was offered a bottle of Spur, which was brought forward on a tray with a tumbler beside it. But I held up my punch to show I was well provided with drink. And as I sipped the punch I made a more careful examination of the now silent musicians who were picturesquely grouped under the round arch of the stage proscenium.

The orchestra was a six-piece one. Sure enough, Don Venustiano, the Presidente, was the cornetist, and we nodded and smiled at each other as our eyes met. The orchestra was mostly brass, for besides El Presidente at the cornet, there were three saxophonists, one of whom doubled on the trombone. The other two members of the ensemble were a blind guitarist and a drummer. The latter's drum was like something out of an African travelogue. I think they call it a samba drum, for it was a tall cylinder, bulging in the middle, that had its skin stretched over the top.

The drummer gave the drum a couple of introductory whacks with his hands, and on the third beat the music began again. Since being beribboned was a sort of introduction, I headed for the girl who had pinned the blue bow on my lapel and asked her for the dance. Her name was Elvira, and she, too, was willing. When I held her in my arms, though, I could tell she was nervous, so I decided to modify my style. The experience with María Luisa had shown me the girls of the village were not used to long, gliding steps; and sliding side steps, especially if they had to be executed going backwards, were almost fatal. Accordingly, to make Elvira as comfortable as possible and to spare her the embarrassment of finding her feet in the direct path of my own, I fell into the jigging walk, with the occasional half circling that was the common way of dancing. Round and round we all went and I was reminded of drivers in those circular cars that take erratic courses in amusement park rides. The one at home used to be called the "Dodge 'em."

To tell the truth, too, the schoolroom floor was not well adapted for gliding. It was of cement, and there were two areas, like wide bands across the floor, where the cement was broken up.

Elvira, as I had observed from her activity, was one of the three girls on the dance committee. Apparently she was the treasurer, for she carried the money that had been collected in a transparent plastic box. It was tied to her wrist as we danced. She wasn't taking any chances of letting it out of her hands.

At the end of this dance I knew I was not going to be able to sit with my partner, so I escorted Elvira back to her place, and deposited her between María Luisa and Ofelia, the other member of the committee. When I went back to my seat, the widow and I exchanged smiles. How well I remember her expression! My grandmother used to love going to parties and watching the young folks dance. This gave me insight, for the widow had just the expression my grandmother used to have. And the spark that passed between us had a special quality. The old woman knew no one in the room was paying any attention to her, but I could tell she knew too that I was one person who was aware of the good time she was having.

Perhaps the mutual understanding arose from our both having a consciousness of being outsiders. She was outside the world of youth and dancing because of her age; I was outside the village life because I was a stranger from a different country. Yet we were both being allowed to be within the circle of the warmth to which we did not fully belong. And I think that for her, too, the scene took extra vividness and sweetness from a double awareness that one was already partly outside it and it was something that would not recur very many more times in one's life.

A short, round-faced little man came over and shook my right hand in both of his. How was I and how was my drawing going? Clearly, he considered himself an old friend. But I couldn't remember ever having seen him before. I let him talk, hoping the mystery would clear up. It did. He was Vicente Cruz, the man who had come over and sat beside me as I was making my first drawing in Yanhuitlán. No wonder I hadn't recalled him. I'd been too engrossed in getting those buttresses right. This time I learned he was one of the teachers in the school I had since visited. Again he insisted on using some of his English phrases. "Dancing," he kept saying, very proud that he knew the word for the occasion. He was so naïve and unteacherish that it was hard to think of him imparting knowledge to a class.

His freeness with me encouraged one of his friends to join us. This was a larger man whose name was Pedro. He explained he was one of the local policemen. He had been drinking, but not enough to make him offensive. He was in the stage of being almost maudlin in his friendliness to Vicente and myself. And I might say he was the only villager on the dance floor who showed any sign of inebriation. The men who had brought my "*invitación especial*" were nowhere to be seen. I gathered they were in the other room on the far side of the entrance passageway, which seemed to be reserved for the men who were more interested in fraternal drinking than in dancing with the women.

While Vicente and Pedro were talking to me, the policeman, who had taken me to task for giving money to the strangers in the plaza, came over and recalled himself. All sternness had melted from him. In fact, he was so far from being angry that he was grateful I should remember him without any jogging of the memory. I was pleased to see I had been so completely forgiven, and I wondered in what other country one would find a cop coming to you and citing the fact that he had bawled you out as proof that you were friends.

Alberto came and joined us too, and he brought a younger boy with him. He introduced the lad as Nahum. "He is your brother," I said the moment I shook hands. I said it because Nahum had the same large, dark brown eyes as Alberto. Then I pointed to an older fellow nearer the front door, who also had the unmistakable family eyes.

"I think he is your brother too," I said.

"Yes. He is Saul."

A very dark-skinned young man in white stood on the far side of me. Since I did not want to seem rude in turning my back on him I made a point of speaking to him too. "*Buenas noches,*" I said.

He was a distinct Indian type. By Western standards his features were irregular, but he was very handsome nevertheless, and when he smiled his teeth were startlingly white against a skin the color of mahogany. His name was Juan. When I asked him what he was, he replied unhesitatingly: "*Un campesino.*" By some this has been translated as "a peasant." And his reply seemed to have an archaic ring, as if he had said just that. "A worker in the fields," though, is a more exact translation. Whatever the meaning, I was delighted to have this proof of the social equality of all members of the village. The highest was not above playing the cornet in the band, and the lowest was a welcome guest.

When the orchestra struck up again, I asked Ofelia for the third dance. This time I recognized the music. It was *Over the Waves*. I knew it from a very old phonograph record, and this provided the clue for the rest of the music. I had not been able to identify any of the pieces, but the style had been vaguely familiar. With the recollection of that old recording, I could put my finger on it. It was the sort of dance music in vogue when most phonographs had morning-glory horns.

Hardly folk music, I thought to myself. And the absence of the folk element sharpened my perceptions of other things about the *baile*.

Over the Waves is a waltz, so with this dance there was a little more stepping from side to side. Fundamentally, though, the partners jigged around in the same sort of human dodge 'em. The boys held the girls in the U.S. manner—right arm around the waist and left hands clasped a little above shoulder height—but both partners stood stiffly upright and they did not squeeze close together. It was dancing, then, of the same era as the music. By no stretch of a fanciful tourist's imagination could it be called folk dancing.

Ofelia, like my two previous partners, was wearing a U. S.-style printed cotton dress. All the other girls dancing had similar dresses. The young men wore factory shirts and belted, factory trousers. Thus the only hints of folk costume were the rebozos of some of the older women watching from the sides and the ponchos of the young boys crowding to look in through the windows.

Was there any hint of folk art in the decorations? Hardly. The streamers of crepe paper, which were draped in rafter fashion over the cord stretched the length of the room, were obviously cut from rolls bought from a store. The other decorations were purchased too. In form they suggested the trimmings for a children's Christmas party, for they were the tissue paper honeycombs that you buy flat, but which turn into three-dimensional shapes when you open them up and pin their flaps together. Large bells hung at regular intervals from the ridge cord supporting the paper rafters, and there were half bells and half spheres tacked against the walls in the bays between the streamers. But not one of the paper honeycombs was a Christmas red. They had been turned out from the factory with segments of white, green and the more orange red of the Mexican tricolor.

As I was dancing with Ofelia, I was thinking about whom I would dance with next. The fact that young men and girls did not mingle in social groups between dances meant I had not been introduced to any of the girls. Picking off the ladies of the committee had been easy. I knew María Luisa and through her I had bridges to her two colleagues. But who was to be next?

Could I go over to a Mexican girl I did not know and ask her to dance? If I did, would she accept? Or might I be embarrassed by her saying No? This was really a worse hurdle than the first dance.

Knowing it confronted me, I had been studying the different girls. There was one willowy girl in a plaid dress who looked as if she were a very good dancer. She would probably have the self-confidence to accept an invitation from a stranger. But mightn't she be a bit too sure of herself, and therefore bold enough to say No? There was a heavier girl in a mauve dress, with a face that was both exceptionally pretty and exceptionally kind. Surely she wouldn't say No. And there was a small plump girl with pigtails and a dark-blue dress printed all over with little flowers. She did not have as much poise as the girl in mauve, but her face was kind and humorous too. I didn't think she would refuse me. I'll try her first, I said to myself, and then, if all goes well, take the other two in reverse order.

Accordingly, after the next intermission I went to the girl with pigtails, who was sitting demurely on her bench, hands folded in her lap. Would she dance with me?

"*Sí. ¿Cómo no?*" she said with alacrity. And she was on her feet and in my arms as quick as you could say Jack Robinson. How I blessed her for making it so easy for me! And I found myself charmed by her combination of shyness with lack of shyness. Or to put it another way, she was shy without being timid. And her natural impulse to be friendly and ready for adventure was clearly strong, for she couldn't have had much confidence in her dancing ability. She was the stiffest and most awkward dancer yet. As soon as I realized this, I danced as much like the other fellows as possible to keep feet collisions at a minimum. And I felt so much gratitude to her for accepting me—and for showing me thereby that it was all right to ask the girls to dance—that I didn't care whether she danced well or not. It was pleasant just to be walking round with her.

Her name was Soledad, she told me. And perhaps she was more scared than she let on, for the moment the music stopped she broke from me and darted to the bench where she was immediately safely wedged between her girl friends. Ordinarily, I might have been irked in being left so unceremoniously in the center of the floor. But I felt that nervousness and not rudeness had precipitated her flight. She confirmed this by the smile she gave me when I went over to thank her formally for the dance.

The girl in mauve was Leonila. She was as friendly and agreeable as Soledad in accepting my invitation. She even tried to make a little conversation while we were dancing. Didn't I think Yanhuitlán was *triste?* she asked. She must have thought that, coming as I did from a big city, I found her village dull and slow.

"*Tranquilo,*" I replied, "*pero no triste, no triste.*" I think she was pleased, for I sensed she loved her village and it did her heart good that a stranger, who might have found the slowness of the town a drawback, had praised that essential attribute as a source of tranquility.

Because Soledad and Leonila had been so obliging, I had no hesitation in approaching the girl in plaid. Her name was Emelia and she turned out to be an even better dancer than I anticipated. There wasn't any step she couldn't follow, and she could glide with the music with complete ease. This was dancing that was pleasant for itself, as well as for its sociability, and I cursed those rough areas in the floor when the rotation induced by the mass movement of all the couples forced us to interrupt our smooth dancing as we got across the broken cement.

When I left Emelia, I discovered my place on the south side of the room was taken. A gray-haired man sitting on the benches in front of the stage signalled to me to come over and take the vacant place beside him. I did, which meant that for the first time I was seated looking down the length of the schoolroom. Like the others in this row, I could use the riser to the stage as a back rest.

The older man introduced himself as Gabriel Sánchez. The name rang a bell with me, for the Blancos had a number of advertising calendars on their walls and by this time the names printed in big type below the pictures had become familiar to me. Sr. Sánchez, I remembered, was a storekeeper who several years before had issued a calendar adorned with the Virgin of Guadalupe. Even if I hadn't been aware of who Sr. Sánchez was, I would have known he was one of the men of substance of the community. It was in his bearing. He was short and a little rotund, but nevertheless he had a native dignity that was impressive. His voice was rather deep and he spoke excellent Spanish in a measured cadence that made it relatively easy for me to understand him. He was wearing a gray business suit. I told him how much I admired his village. He, in turn, asked me about my work.

This intermission was longer than usual and when the orchestra resumed activity again, it did not open with the preliminary two blasts on the drum. Instead, there was a fanfare—followed by silence. El Presidente laid his cornet on his chair and came forward to the edge of the stage. We were in for some speeches.

Don Venustiano was clearly not an orator and after he had got hesitatingly through the part of his speech he had memorized, he pulled out his notes. I could not follow all he said, but at a certain point he called out the name of a villager. A tall man, who looked like something out of El Greco, stood up. And I gathered that this lean, handsome, rather melancholy man was the one who had been called on.

El Presidente consulted his notes again and read off the name of a señorita. One of the girls rose, came to the three members of the committee, collected a long ribboned bow like the one I was wearing, and went over to the man with the El Greco face. To my surprise, he dropped on one knee before her. Then she pinned the flowing decoration on his lapel. He rose, thanked her and everyone applauded.

Having seen the basic pattern of the ceremony, I was able to follow the next one a little more readily. El Presidente's introductory talk, I could tell, was in praise of a civic worthy, who was thereupon called to stand. Then he spoke of the girl who had been selected to bestow the decoration. She came forward, got the ribbon, and again the man kneeled before her. She was not a queen and she did not actually say the words, but it was as if she were proclaiming, "Arise, Sir Knight!" as she pinned the large bow on the man's coat.

Sr. Sánchez was the third man to be honored, and since his knighting occurred just in front of me I could watch the expressions closely. The girl selected to give him his ribbon was respectful, but not foolishly flustered about her task. He, in turn, received it in all seriousness. And I got an impression of a different attitude between the young and the old than I had ever received in the northern part of the continent. The dignified little man, I could see, saw the young princess in the attractive girl. She, in turn, saw the aristocratic quality in the plump little burgher.

Up to this point, the dance had seemed as sedate, proper and shall we say as unimaginative as a rural church social in the midwest. But this touch suggested May queens and courtly age bowing to youth and beauty.

Several other men were honored. Some of the bows were pale green, some were baby pink, some were mauve and several were blue like mine. All had artificial flowers at their knots. And these great party dress ribbons were not ridiculous because they were not considered ridiculous. And I began to feel a positive pride in my own.

A new introductory talk by El Presidente began to run on a little longer than the others. I caught such phrases as *"convento"* and "distinguished visitor" and I realized he was talking about me. Since I am ordinarily a rather shy person, the wish that sprang to my mind was a surprising one. I hope, I said to myself, I hope he'll ask me to make a speech.

Meanwhile, the saga of my virtues continued. When El Presidente reached the crucial point where the structure of the rhetorical introduction called for a flourishing announcement of my name—well, there was a pause. He leaned over the stage toward me and confided in a whisper he had forgotten it.

To make matters easy, I printed it in large letters and handed the bit of paper up to him. He studied it a moment and then filled in the missing link in his oratory. After that he added: "And now I will ask him to say a few words."

I was gratefully ready, for with the desire to make a speech had come the idea for one. I got to my feet and, even though I was aware I was embarking on a foreign language, I was not nervous. I knew that, with what I was going to say, faults in pronunciation and errors of grammar would be readily overlooked.

"*Gracias, Señor Presidente,*" I said, with a bow in his direction. Then I began:

"I have been in Mexico seven times, and on those visits I have visited nearly every part of the country. I have seen nearly all the famous towns." And here I told off the dearly loved names—Morelia, Querétaro, San Luis Potosí, Puebla, Guadalajara, Chapala, Guanajuato, Oaxaca, San Bartolomé de las Casas, Zacatecas, Campeche, Mérida, Lagos and San Juan de los Lagos and several more, for I wanted to build slowly to my peroration.

"Everywhere," I continued, "I have found many things I have loved. I have loved the colonial architecture, the pre-Hispanic ruins, the mountains, the valleys. I have loved the ceramics, the weaving, the markets, the band music in the plazas. . . ." And again I drew out the list.

"But above all I have loved *la gente.*" And I stressed the Spanish word for people. "And I have found that of all the people of all the places, the very best people of all the Republic are the people of Yanhuitlán."

And then I sat down, for a catch in my throat made it impossible for me to say anything further than "*mil gracias.*" A thousand thanks.

There was a silence and then applause. I felt abashed for having exposed my feelings so openly, but from the reassuring smiles I knew I had been understood.

When the music resumed, I asked María Luisa if she would dance with me again. She accepted readily and I was happy to be swallowed up once more in the crowd of jigging couples. Apparently, though, the end had come for my days as an ordinary dancer, mingling jokingly in the intermissions with the young men. When I returned to my place beside Sr. Sánchez, I found the tall man with the El Greco face sitting on the other side of me. He was introduced as Roberto Ramos. A little later another decorated worthy came over and room was made for him. He was Felipe Cruz Soriano, the rich villager married to the postmaster's daughter.

Don Felipe was pleased when I indicated I knew he sold *ropa y abarrotes*—clothing and groceries. I knew his position in the community because he was another man I recognized from his calendar.

When Don Felipe sat down, too, it meant I was one of four worthies sitting in a row—all with big schoolgirl bows and long ribbons. Clearly, I had gone up in the world. Now I was an honored guest, sitting, as it were, on the dais, even though in this case it was merely a row of benches at the the foot of the stage. The burghers, I observed, were too dignified to dance, but I did not let their flanking presences restrict me too much. I went on dancing whenever the music struck up, and one by one I picked off the most attractive girls of the village.

As I circled again and again, the other dancers became increasingly familiar. They were a healthy, pleasant-faced lot and I could see they were quite contented with their tame manner of dancing. Probably, I thought, if they saw our American cheek-to-cheek style, with girls in strapless evening gowns being hugged glidingly over hardwood floors, they'd be shocked.

As I got to know their faces better, I felt if we met on the street, we would automatically greet each other as if we had been introduced by mutual friends. One face, especially, stuck with me. It was that of a rather unsmiling young man, whose skin was somewhat lighter than most, yet whose face was most un-European. Something about it made me think of those giant heads that rise from the slopes of Easter Island. Searching for a phrase to suggest his appearance, I finally hit on a rough approximation—hatchetfaced.

During one of the intermissions, the row of worthies increased to five, for we were joined by Miguel Gómez, a dark-skinned, chunky man, who, I was to learn later, was a rich farmer who owned many lands.

All this time Don Gabriel had been sitting quietly in his corner. I was beginning to feel guilty about keeping him waiting so long, Accordingly, at eleven-thirty I turned to the men beside me and said I thought I should leave. It was late for Don Gabriel. They protested it was early and were firm about my staying. Their insistence made me decide to consult my host.

I went to him and asked if he was tired. No. Was he happy? Yes. Did he want to go home? That was entirely up to me. Since I really did not want to leave, I lit on a compromise. Pointing to my watch, I said I'd stay until midnight and then I'd be ready to go. That was agreeable to him, so I had another half-hour of dancing.

At twelve, somewhat reluctantly, I stuck to my promise. I got up to go. The four men of substance still said it was early, but they were willing to accept my decision. Instead of merely bidding me good night, though, they saw me home en masse. It was an almost embarrassing honor to be seen to my door by four of the leading citizens of the village, but I was pleased nevertheless.

I turned in. But two hours later, having a little difficulty sleeping on the counter, I rose and went outside for a while. The dance was still going on. Faintly I could hear the drumming, the three saxophones and every now and then the more brilliant sound of El Presidente's cornet. I wished I were still there. And I thought how beautiful the arcade of the school looked, glowing in its soft gold light on the far side of the black lacy screen of the plaza trees.

XIII

THE COFFERED CEILING

TRANSFORMED is too sweeping a word for the change that had come over the world the next morning. But certainly there was a difference. The atmosphere was as clear as if the earth had turned over a new leaf. And instinctively I knew the villagers and I had come into a new relationship.

The passing of a little girl in a maroon rebozo provided the first supporting evidence. This time she was not a figure in a parade. She was a neighbor. And when I gave a couple of candies to Paco, the little bantamweight, it was no longer like feeding a squirrel. It was a morning custom between a child and an adult who had taken a shine to each other.

My hunch that all the guests at the *baile* would recognize each other as friends was quickly confirmed. Paco had no sooner proceeded to the plaza, than along came the young man with the hatchet face. We had not exchanged a word at the dance, yet our greetings rose simultaneously. Not only this, he paused for a chat. His name was Herminio. We both agreed it had been a fine dance.

Don Gabriel was whistling as he came over, and the fresh water he brought was hot. Breakfast, he said, would be ready soon. I climbed to the top of the slope to wait. From this eminence I could see the morning mists lingering far to the south where the valley spread out. Because the haze-clad hills were a pale blue, one could maintain the illusion of covered slopes. But to the north the air was so crystalline, and the sunlight so bright, that the erosion showed as clearly as the wrinkles of an old man's face.

With some of its surfaces in clean-cut shadow and some in flawless light, the monastery looked marvelously serene. I realized I had come into a new relationship with it too. Because I had passed the test of the church interior, the monastery was no longer a formidable antagonist that challenged my skill. And I think it was the conclusion of the duel that made the monastery's imperturbability, which had sometimes suggested disdainful complacence, now seem like radiant composure.

Lupe's breakfast was generous. There were lamb's kidneys with the eggs, cheese with the frijoles, and a *capricho* with the hot chocolate. I was also offered an extra cup of chocolate, but I declined. This morning I was in no mood to dawdle over a breakfast beverage. I wanted to get on with the drawing I had started the night before.

Its story involves flashing back to my frustration in the church. Perhaps the desire to have the front doors opened gave the clue to the part of the interior I wanted to draw. It was something that would have been illumined by their opening—the coffered ceiling on the underside of the choir loft.

The intricate details were what I had not been able to see clearly. But I had discerned the basic design. The ceiling resembled a honeycomb in that it had an over-all pattern of hexagons. But the equal-sided hexagons were not staggered with beelike economy; that is, cells were not fitted snugly together along diagonal axes. They were set out in a rectangular grid which left diamond-shaped spaces between the walls that did not touch.

Because the hexagons and diamonds kept recurring in an unchanging geometrical relationship, I knew a small part of the ceiling would suggest the whole. All I would have to do, I felt, was to indicate the patterning of the network and to show in detail one hexagon and one diamond. This being the scheme, I resolved to prepare a network of hexagons in advance. Then, when I came to the church the structure of the pattern would be already drawn.

I began the network in my room after the stroll that had conjured up the monastery's vanished walls. I expected the task to be easy, for at school I had learned to make hexagons by the simple process of walking a compass around a circle and then using a ruler to link the six X's where the pencil arcs cut the circumference.

The drawback was that I did not have a compass, and I was trying to draw a series of hexagons by candlelight with only the marked edge of a small sheet of paper to swing around to approximate radius widths. I had the devil's own time. The horizontal sides were not hard to establish, but, oh, the sloping ones! Even if I got them the right length, the chances were they were not running at the right angle. And I had no protractor to help make each angle an exact 120 degrees. The errors showed up mercilessly when

I extended the wrongly angled lines and got very cockeyed diamonds. After many tries, and a little cheating, I finally achieved a balanced network— with the up-and-down hexagons standing in columns, flat edge on flat edge, and the horizontal ones running in rows, point to point.

It was this network I wanted to start filling when Lupe offered me the second cup of chocolate. Don Gabriel, knowing my feeling of urgency, agreed to take me to the monastery right away.

He led me first to the room marked *portería* in the plan on page 12. It was always locked and I had never been in it before. Once inside, I saw the former porter's lodging was now a storehouse. It was partially filled with fragments of carved stone and wood. Clearly, workmen from the Institute had carefully collected all the stray sculptured pieces that might be useful should there ever be enough money for an extensive restoration of the monastery. And there they were, kept under lock and key, lest villagers cart them off for firewood or building material. Don Gabriel picked up something that looked like a great wooden lampshade. When he turned it face up I recognized it as one of the coffers of the ceiling.

Then he went to a diamond-shaped box, with 60-degree angles at its sharp tips and 120-degree angles at its obtuse ones. Did I recognize it? he asked. I did. And in a flash I realized how the ceiling was made. Instead of being created by a network of intersecting beams, as I had thought, it was like a pavement of boxes.

Each hexagonal box was called a *casetón*, Don Gabriel said. And he set one flat on the floor, its wide opening uppermost. I anticipated his next

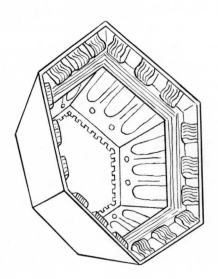
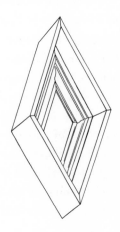

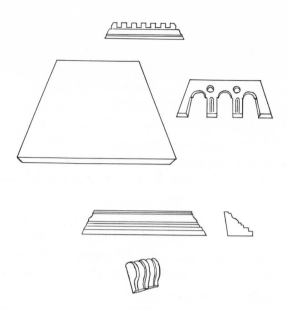

move by fitting the diamond box against a side of the *casetón*. He saw I understood. To form the ceiling, the boxes were nailed together and then hung, face down, from the beams of the choir loft.

Looking at the *casetón* and the diamond box on the floor made it easy to comprehend why the ceiling looked as richly ornate as it did. It was the way the boxes were lined. The diamonds contained pieces of molding mitred together to form a box within a box. The *casetones* were lined as the drawing shows. And everything was achieved by small pieces of wood being nailed in. Those three little consoles along each open side, for instance, were not chiseled from a solid beam. They were individual chunks tacked to the boards forming the sides of the coffer.

Don Gabriel then showed how the final fanciful touch was achieved. He picked up a couple of wooden objects suggesting clubs you might swing in

a gymnasium. They were examples of the pendants I had seen hanging like little stalactites from the centers of the diamonds and the hexagons. And I got a fresh realization of the exquisite detail of the ceiling when I saw the pendants were carved in a variety of flower and leaf shapes.

"What type of wood are they?" I asked.

"Cedar. The whole ceiling is cedar."

Don Gabriel then suggested we go up to the choir. There was lots of light in the gallery, he explained, and I could draw one of the *casetones* lying around up there on the floor. As for pendants, I could draw these—and he shook the two he had picked up.

His secret for facilitating the drawing was out. His plan was for me to draw the appearance of the ceiling rather than the ceiling itself. Because he knew I understood the basic patterning, he wisely calculated I could reproduce that appearance by working comfortably in a place where sample parts could be set up easily in a good light.

The route to the choir may be traced on the plan on page 296. First, we had to mount the grand stairway that can be seen in the lower right-hand corner. I went up lingeringly, for I had set this stairway as my project for the afternoon and I was on the lookout for drawing angles.

Once on the second floor, we entered the cloister gallery and made our way to the northwest corner. Here Don Gabriel bid me pause to examine the archway through which we had to pass.

We must have gone under that arch the day we climbed to the roof. So it was a shock to me to realize I could have passed anything so fine without noticing it. Lacking a set of doors, the archway, strictly speaking, could not be classed as a doorway. But it was certainly a portal. Battered as it was, I could see that, with its rose-studded molding and the niche above its Tudor arch, it was a worthy companion to the others. The monastery's series of portals, then, was more extensive than I had realized, and I had not completely covered it, as I thought, by my drawings of the third and fourth days.

Since the opening was jammed against the wall, the space at the designer's disposal was fundamentally awkward, but he had done wonders in getting a balanced composition. And I was especially struck by his ingenuity in managing the transition from one level to another. If he had placed all the steps on this side of the archway, the entrance would have been hardly as high as a man. But by cutting the top three steps from the upper level, the designer had managed to achieve both a handsome stair-

188

way and an arched passageway high enough to have dignity. Why, I wondered, when the space offered such difficulties, had such pains been taken
to create an imposing archway? After all, it was only an entrance on the
way to the choir gallery. What did it matter?

When we passed under the archway and came to the upper level, my
self-esteem received another knock. For here, on the right, Don Gabriel

pointed to another feature I had barely noticed: a flight of ten steps leading up to a pair of high wooden doors. But I did not feel quite so sheepish about missing the steps as I did about overlooking the arch. On that second day, I had little familiarity with the layout of the monastery. Not realizing where the choir was in relation to the upper cloister, I could hardly be blamed for not perceiving that the function of those steps was to lead to the choir. And Don Gabriel had not told me those wooden doors led anywhere in particular.

But his opening of those doors and the disclosure of the great choir loft beyond provided another instructive lesson in vision—namely, the role that comprehension of function plays in the ability to observe. The day we climbed to the roof those well-worn and partly ruined steps had seemed merely meaningless terraces we had stumbled over. Yet now, with the evidence indisputably before me that they led to the choir, I could see them clearly, and I could discern that they were risers leading handsomely to the scarcely noticed doors.

The progression of vision is generally circular. Observation leads to knowledge, knowledge to understanding, and understanding to keener observing. And the cycle worked in its usual virtuous way in this instance. Seeing the steps as the approach to an entrance made me realize that the chamber in front of them was a foyer. This realization, in turn, made me observe the dimly lit anteroom more closely. It had splendid height and a good barrel vault. And before that slot in the west wall had been sealed up it must have been much better lighted. Now it was in a sorry state, but clearly in palmier days the anteroom had been a spacious lobby in which one might pause with a sense of its impressiveness before going into the choir.

Don Gabriel warned me to proceed cautiously once we entered the gallery. I could see why. It was only partially floored, and what flooring there was consisted merely of thick planks laid over beams that in many places were exposed. The beams were embedded in the church's west wall and ran toward the altar. They were lengths of barely squared tree trunks such as might have provided the piles for a Cape Cod wharf. It was a little disillusioning that a ceiling looking so elegant from below should be hung from so crude a floor.

The inadequacies of that floor, however, provided one great advantage. The incomplete planking revealed the ceiling's reverse side. I had the oddest sensation. It was as though I had been taken behind the scenes in a factory of the future. Specifically, I felt I was in a great glassworks looking down into a mold for the casting of a mirror even larger than the one made by Corning for the Mount Palomar Observatory. Like that Corning mold, this was a sea of flat-topped humps, with the diamond-shaped humps having upright sides, while the higher hexagonal mounds had sloping ones. As in the Corning mold, there was a clear geometrical plan in the crisscrossing passageways between the humps.

It was those passageways that made my heart sink. My network of hexagons, so painfully prepared in advance, was not going to be of much use. The diamond and hexagonal boxes were not set flush together, as I had thought. They were divided by lanes of board.

I quickly resolved I would not make a whole new network. A border around one of the hexagons with a new diamond contiguous to the border seemed sufficient. Before I settled down to the work, though, there was something in the loft I wanted to inspect.

It was the church organ. And here I must explain that, because of its position, I was already aware of the instrument's splendor. It was in a spot where it could be seen readily from below. Its site is indicated in the plan on page 327 (No. 2), and the best way to visualize it is to imagine that altar niche against the north wall as an immensely tall fireplace; a fireplace so tall, in fact, that it reached the level of the choir gallery, which it adjoined at right angles. The organ was like an ornament on the mantel of that fireplace. And the mantel was made to seem part of the gallery because the wooden balustrade of the choir loft was built out to confine it too.

The organ was a mass of silvery pipes and golden scrollwork and the underside of the overhanging mantelpiece on which it rested was painted marvelously with bold floral designs that, happily, had not been covered in the general whitewashing of 1831. The designs were outlined in heavy brown lines and the breathtaking colors were turquoise blue and brick red.

Needless to say, a great baroque organ mounted in so prominent a position had often claimed my attention from below. Being familiar with the work of Arp Schnitger, the German organ builder, who lived from 1648 to 1719, I had sized up the Yanhuitlán instrument as belonging to his period. And that was the only impression I had expected to take away with me because I had not known it was possible to get to the choir loft.

It was not the ornate golden tracery alone that made me think the instrument belonged to the early eighteenth century. Another stylistic clue was the characteristic disposition of the pipes—the triangular bays at the

sides and the tall circular tower in the center. The figure at the top was characteristic too. "That's St. John the Baptist," said Don Gabriel helpfully.

The bellows to provide wind for the instrument was supported on a crude wooden stand to the left. Don Gabriel went to it, grasped the projecting handle and began to pump. "Try the organ," he said.

It had a single keyboard of four octaves and there were no pedals. I pressed down one of the keys and, to my surprise, a sound emerged. The missing pipe in the central tower and the general state of disrepair had given me the impression the organ was totally unworkable.

"Play some more," said Don Gabriel, pumping at the bellows. I pressed another key but, alas, it produced the same note. Then I ran my fingers up the scale and found nearly every key produced the same tone. It was like a snoring moan. The organ had eleven stops on each side. I pulled out the knobs, one after another, to see if they would alter the sound. But always the same moaning snore emerged.

It was discouraging, in view of the sweet, piercing, reedy sound the organ must have had once. And while I was at the keyboard I had an opportunity to see that the case was not as substantial as I had thought. The front wall with the baroque bulges was fixed, almost like a bow tie, to the sturdy frame that carried the organ's weight. But if the front was false, its painting atoned for the deception. The artist had chosen a black field to contrast with the gold superstructure, and painted on that black were great swirls of scarlet foliage.

But the drawing of the ceiling was calling, so I decided to get to work.

"¡Cuidado!" called out Don Gabriel, so I started back impulsively. He had reason for urging caution. The northern half of the loft was the most sparsely planked. And the wide spaces between the planks here made all too apparent one of the saddest things about that wonderful cedar ceiling. It was in ruins. Most of the northern part had disappeared; by looking down I could see that some of the casetones at the frayed edges were hanging precariously by ropes tied to the beams. If I had put my leg through the beams and given a stamp on the upper surface, I could have sent another big chunk of the ceiling crashing to the floor below.

Don Gabriel motioned me to look up at the webbing between two of the ribs fanning from the corner. Some of the stones of the webbing were gone and no trace of ceiling remained immediately below the blackened cavities left by the missing stones. The stones, said Don Gabriel, in coming loose from the vaulting had fallen straight through the gallery, taking flooring and *casetones* with them.

Once we were back in the more solidly floored area, Don Gabriel placed a *casetón* where I could sketch it, saw that I had a seat and then asked if I needed anything more. When I assured him I was all set, he left me to work alone.

Bird droppings were spattered all over the choir. But the fresh air came in so freely from the huge west window that the place was not a bit foul. It was easy to see, too, why the birds should like the choir. It was light, airy, sheltered from the wind and spacious enough for all sorts of acrobatic flying. Being so high above the church floor and yet still far from the rib-vaulted roof, I felt rather like a bird myself.

What a difference good light and a night's rest made! Giving the hexaagon a border and drawing a new diamond required careful measuring, and my means were as primitive as ever, but the work was pleasurable. As I did it, too, I got a fresh realization about the ceiling. Since its ornamentation consisted principally of moldings fitted into boxes, its carving was obviously not as remarkable as I had believed when I had thought the coffers were sculptured in solid wood. What was remarkable was the precision of the carpentry. Imagine getting each *casetón* and each diamond exactly the same size, with each side nailed to its mate at precisely the right angle! And they all must have been identical, otherwise they would not have fitted together in a gapless pattern with the seams running as perfectly straight as they did. Thus making that defective network the night before had not been a total loss. The cockeyedness of the diamonds when the hexagons were not geometrically perfect had enabled me to appreciate more fully the skill of the sixteenth-century carpenters.

When the hexagon was bordered and the new diamond placed, I began to fill in the details, using as my model the *casetón* Don Gabriel had propped up. The work made Don Gabriel's plan seem more sensible than ever. If I had been following my own plan, I would have been standing below the ceiling, constantly bending back my head to see the details I was trying to reproduce and obliged most of the time to hold my sketchbook as if it were a ceiling on which I was doing a mural. Also, with the wood being so dark brown and so high up, the details would have been hard to distinguished, even with the better illumination of morning sunlight. Here I could see everything clearly and at a comfortable angle, and I had a place to sit.

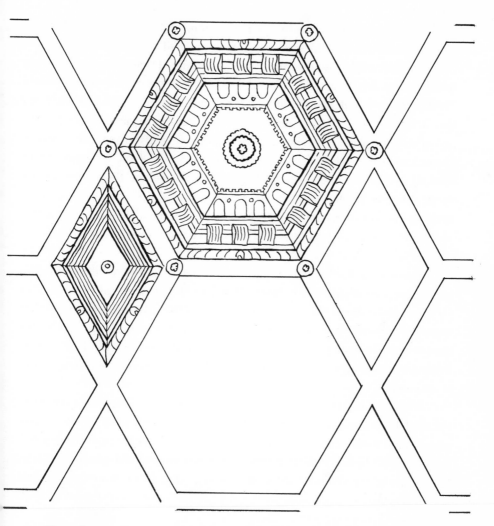

The scheme of my drawing was to present a section of the ceiling as it would appear to a person standing directly below it. Thus I filled in the details of the *casetón* as if it were lying flat. The work required careful observing and it took time, but it was relatively easy. Filling in the details of the plainer diamond was still easier. Then, taking the two pendants as my models, I drew a flower head in the center of each shape.

The flower heads, I thought, completed the task, but I decided it would be wise to go below and look up at the ceiling for a final check. Here I discovered a drawback to Don Gabriel's plan. Not having the actual subject before my eyes, I had gone blithely ahead without reckoning on an important element—the rosettes. But looking up at the ceiling I saw that there

THE COFFERED CEILING

was a rosette at each angle of each hexagon, and these rosettes were so placed that they also seemed to be at each point of each diamond.

Could I work the rosettes into the border I had left between my hexagon and my diamond? I found I could not. It was not wide enough. Then I noticed still another detail I had overlooked. Each sunken form was bordered by a ropelike molding which had been tacked on after the boxes were in place. Clearly, if I were going to get the pattern accurate, I would have to draw a second new diamond on one of the hexagon's other free sides. To bear the right relationship to the coffer, the new diamond would have to be far enough away to provide space for the additional molding and yet near enough that its points would be disposed to the points of the hexagon, with each set of points aiming squarely at a common rosette.

I went back to the choir to tackle this new problem, and as I worked to find the new diamond's correct placement, I felt more admiration than ever for the ceiling. Not only did it require such precise carpentry, but what extraordinary care had gone into the planning of each section! I also blessed the power of pictures to illustrate difficult subjects, for I knew that without a sketch an account of my struggle to comprehend the ceiling would be impossible to follow.

When the rosettes, the rope molding and the new diamond were completed, I breathed a sigh of relief. The major representation of the ceiling was done. I took pride in it because it made the patterning clear. But I knew such a head-on depiction, because it was void of shadow, hardly suggested one of the salient facts of the ceiling: that it was a composition in depth. What I had drawn might be a flat pattern printed on a piece of wallpaper.

The way to suggest the three-dimensional nature of the ceiling, I decided, was to give the reader a sketch of an individual *casetón* drawn from such an angle that its resemblance to a lampshade would be unmistakable. Thereupon I began the drawing used on page 186.

Having studied the *casetón* so closely for the major drawing, sketching its familiar parts from a new angle was fairly easy. And once more, the main job being finished, there was a lessening of tension. Accordingly, as I worked I was freer to think.

Every now and then I glanced up at the window of scrambled S's that let light into the nave on the far side of the organ. The window looked beautiful in its interior aspect, for its splayed jambs gave it a different framing than it presented from outside. And here the first thought came. When seen from outside it was part of that wonderfully handsome north portal, which I could recall vividly because of my drawing. That was a new merit of these windows. They were so designed that they were beautiful— and differently useful—on both sides. From without, this window seemed part of a big composition with the side door; from within, it was an interesting opening high in a blank wall that let light into the nave through an open screen of fanciful tracery.

Next my mind turned to the puzzling archway leading from the cloister to the choir. My original question recurred, but in a slightly different form. Why had such pains been taken to make that archway so impressive, if this gallery was meant only for a group of nondescript village choristers who led the congregation's hymn singing? Put that way, the question started many wheels turning in my head.

Anxiety over carrying out my project had held my imaginative powers in a sort of a paralysis, and I have shown how it was not until the completion of the church interior that my imagination was liberated sufficiently to start coming into play as an aid to my perceptions. What I need to say here is that my imagination was not the only blocked mental faculty. My memory, too, had been curiously paralyzed.

Actually, I had read quite a lot about monasticism, but the stunning impact of immediate apprehensions, combined with concern about getting them down on paper, had acted as a stone lid, making inaccessible to me the well of my memories. That question about the Tudor archway revealed that the apparently impenetrable lid was only a psychological barrier which, somehow, had vanished overnight.

My reading had made me aware that attending divine services was a monk's chief activity. I knew monks went to church many times each day, and that the routine was so rigid they even had to get up in the middle of each night to attend a service. I knew the Dominican Order was not a secluded one—i.e., that its members had duties out in the world as preachers, instead of being confined always to prayer and meditation in their monasteries. But, though they were friars rather than monks, I also knew they adhered strictly to the monastic routine of many services each day; that they were, in fact, perhaps the closest to the contemplative orders of all the active friars.

And as these facts came back to me, my memory brought a word. When the Dominicans went to church they sat in the "choir." My picture had always been of an area up front near the altar. But this gallery was a "choir." Could it have been the place where the friars assembled for their daily services? If it were, that would account for the attempt to make its approach impressive. Was there evidence that I was on the right track?

My memory yielded something else. In Querétaro I had visited the conventual churches of two nunneries, Santa Rosa and Santa Clara. Each of them had galleries placed like the one in Yanhuitlán—that is, at the opposite end of the church from the altar. And these galleries had magnificent gilded screens filling the whole open area between the gallery railing and the ceiling. Naturally such screens had invited curiosity, and I had been told the nuns attended divine services in the choirs and the screens were erected to keep them more secluded from the congregation in the church below. If nuns did their churchgoing in a choir loft, why not friars?

What evidence supported this? The obvious fact that came to me was that the choir was so easily reached from the cloister. And then came the clinching realization: the choir could not be reached *except* from the monastery.

All the stories I had read of visits to monasteries had described how visitors were excluded from the living quarters of the monks. If this ban held here too—and there was no reason to believe it didn't—then non-friars could not even gain admission to the choir. The corollary was that *only* friars could use it.

With the realization (since verified) that the choir was the friars' customary place of worship, I understood many things. I understood the pains taken with the rose-studded archway. I understood the loftiness of the entrance lobby. I understood why the gallery was so deep and spacious that it extended a quarter of the church's length. I understood the ornate splendor of the organ. And I saw, too, the logic of the choir's magnificent underside.

The choir being situated where it was, the members of the congregation in the nave could hear the friars chanting, but they could not see them. The cedar ceiling, then, was to impress on the lay worshippers below that, next to the sanctuary, the choir, where the friars worshipped so regularly, was the most sacred part of the church. I think, too, it was meant to be an outward manifestation, a sort of declaration that the friars were so precious and worthy of reverence that it was only fitting the underside of the area in which they chanted the Divine Office should be of such magnificence.

Again I blessed Don Gabriel's plan for drawing the ceiling. By the

WEEK IN YANHUITLÁN

accident of bringing me to the gallery, it had allowed me to get to know the monastery's choir. And I realized that had it not been for that accident I might have left Yanhuitlán not knowing I had missed a unit almost as important as the cloister.

And the wheels weren't through turning. The next occurrence combined memory *and* imagination.

I knew each service attended by inmates of religious houses had its particular name. The one shortly after midnight, for example, was Matins. The service in the late afternoon was Vespers and the final service before retiring was Compline. I knew, too, that Compline was the service particularly important to the Dominicans. They loved the last of the canonical hours because it was then they made a procession, chanting the *Salve Regina.*

As my reading produced this memory, a recollection from another area of my life rose to the surface. As a music critic I have heard so many settings of that hymn that I know its text. And as I glanced at the organ I had an uncanny experience. It was as if it were sounding in support of human voices. Not only that, I was hearing in my inward ear a particular setting of the hymn by Monteverdi. It seemed particularly apt, for Monteverdi's music might well have been sung in that choir and been accompanied by just such a Baroque organ.

As I heard the hymn, I imagined one particular friar among the singers. "Hail Holy Queen, Mother of Mercy," he sang, understanding the Latin as if it were his native Spanish. "Our life, our sweetness and our hope," he continued. And then a lump came into his throat. "To Thee do we cry, poor banish'd children of Eve." It was the word "banish'd" that caused the trouble. That was how he felt in Mexico. The lump grew larger as the words expressed his homesickness with sharpening exactitude. "To Thee do we send up our sighs, mourning and weeping in this valley of tears." Even the description of where he was—in a valley, ever so far from Andalusia. "Turn then, O Most Gracious Advocate, Thine eyes of mercy toward us and after this our exile. . . ." And remembering how I had felt in the army, I knew that friar could not find the tone in his throat for the rest of the words.

A bird flew in through the great, glassless west window. Its cheeping snapped me back to the present, and as I completed the drawing of the *casetón* my chief feeling was one of surprise. In view of the fact that I had been around the monastery for so many days, it seemed remarkable that this insight into the feelings of that homesick friar should have been my first imaginative vision into the human feelings of those who had inhabited the place in the three hundred years of its life as a religious community.

The *casetón* finished, I decided to draw a final illuminating detail. Accordingly I began the sketch of the two pendants, used as an illustration at the point where Don Gabriel picked them up.

As I was drawing, I heard footsteps on the stairs. It was Don Gabriel, and he had four U. S. tourists in tow. Since in my six days in Yanhuitlán he had never brought me into the choir before, and since in that time I had never known him to take any others there, I knew he had a reason for veering from his usual circuit. His introduction led me to suspect I had become one of his prize exhibits—a North American who thought the monastery was worth drawing from top to bottom.

XIV
THE TOURIST PARTY AND THE MARKET

THE TOURIST PARTY consisted of two middle-aged couples who had met in Mexico, found each other congenial and joined forces to make a two-car caravan. One couple came from Chicago, the other from South Bend. The women had fizzled gray hair and wore glasses and the men were wearing Hawaiian-style sport shirts. At first they suggested a cartoon from the New Yorker, but I quickly learned they were open minded, interested and alert. They were loving Mexico. It was the eighth visit for the Chicagoans, but the first for the South Benders, whose name was Stumpff.

"When was the monastery built?" asked Mrs. Stumpff. "It was started in 1550," I answered.

"Four hundred and three years old!" said the man from Chicago, looking incredulously into the vast church.

Were there other such monasteries in Mexico? they asked. "Not many quite so magnificent," I replied. "Yet this one is really not unique. In the sixteenth century, the Spanish covered Mexico with monasteries. Haven't you encountered any others on your trip?"

"Not like this," said the little lady from Chicago. "Are there any more on our way?"

"Which way are you headed?"

"We're going to Puebla tonight and on to Mexico City tomorrow."

"Then you'll pass one of the very finest. It's at Huejotzingo, just about twenty miles on the far side of Puebla on your way to the capital. This one is a Dominican monastery. That one is Franciscan."

"Oh we must stop there, dear," said the Chicago lady, turning to her husband. Then turning back to me she explained. "You see, my brother is a Franciscan priest. That means I'm especially interested. Could you write down its name for me?" After I had done so, Mr. Stumpff asked if they could see my drawings. Naturally I was happy to oblige. The final one, of course, was of the pendants.

"We are keeping you from your work," said the Chicago man, seeing their unfinished state. Turning to the others, he said, "Perhaps we had better get on with the rest of the tour."

We parted with friendly handshakes and the Chicago lady thanked me again for telling her about Huejotzingo. "We won't fail to visit it," she said.

After they had gone, I felt a pang. It had been good to speak English again, especially with such nice people. And as I completed the second pendant, I said to myself: I hope they are still in the church. Perhaps I can catch up with them.

The sound of voices coming from the *sagrario* reassured me. When I entered the chapel, I saw them all gazing at the allegorical painting that filled the lunette over the door. Don Gabriel was pointing to it and moving his finger from figure to figure. I could hardly believe my ears. When I had queried him on the allegory several days before, he said he did not know its meaning. Yet here he was explaining it! The lion drawing the chariot, he told them, represented St. Mark, the ox was St. Luke and the eagle was St. John.

Knowing the tourists did not understand much Spanish, he was relying on his pointing and the easily intelligible saints' names to make himself clear. And his tone was most authoritative. But in a gleeful aside to me, spoken rapidly, he said he had obtained the explanation from my book of symbols.

"Who is the angel driving the chariot?" asked Mr. Stumpff. "That's St. Matthew," replied Don Gabriel, giving the impression he had understood the allegory all his life.

The chapel completed their tour of the interior. "Have you got a little more time?" I asked. "Because I'd like to show you the north doorway."

"Is it worth seeing?" Mr. Stumpff wanted to know.

"Yes, and it won't take long. It just means returning to your cars by going around the back of the church."

They were game. And the route gave me the opportunity to point out other things too. As we circled the establishment, I called their attention to the windows—the porthole lighting the stairwell, the diamond and the hexagon of the sacristy, and, after we had cleared the apse, the repetition of the

Minerva mask window and the one with the scrambled S's. I told them the big arched buttresses had been added when the walls began to crack. And at the northern portal I rejoiced in their delighted response to the diamonds, the inverted shell and the arms of Philip II.

By the time we had reached the front steps, I felt that here, at least, were four North Americans who were convinced of the greatness of the Mexican mission effort—an effort which, in the second and third generations after the Conquest, had thrown up almost three hundred monasteries.

The two businessmen did not seem the sort who would find Mexico congenial. Curious, I asked why they did.

"It's so European," said Mr. Stumpff. "Both my parents were German and I've often been abroad. I like the atmosphere of Europe and I find it in Mexico. I had no idea so much of Europe had been transplanted anywhere on this continent."

"I think it's the pace," said the man from Chicago. Here you're not forced and rushed." And then he said something that surprised me—both in what it revealed of his inner nature and in the way it reflected how my particular project could strike an outsider. "You know," he said, "I envy you, staying here and drawing."

A satisfaction of the tour had been working as a team with Don Gabriel, for I had been able to pass on things he said which they did not understand. They knew there was no need to tip me, but they asked if it was right to offer something to him.

"It certainly is," I said.

"How much should we give him?"

"That's an embarrassing question to put to me. He's my friend. I'd like to see him get as much as he can."

"How much would you suggest?"

I thought quickly and then with a perfectly straight face proposed what I knew was an exceptionally big tip: ten pesos.

"That's more than we're used to giving," said Mr. Stumpff, "and our expenses are beginning to run us a little short."

In their currency, it was only about $1.20, which meant an average of thirty cents a head. It did not seem exorbitant, but I knew even half the sum would be a good tip, so I said,

"Well, just give him five."

And that is what they gave. And when they had gone I told Don Gabriel what a good Mexican I had been. By asking for ten I'd got him five. He laughed and said he was very satisfied. And the size of the tip led him to reveal something I had been eager to learn, yet unwilling to ask about—his salary.

The Institute, he said, paid him ninety pesos every fifteen days. That was just a little more than $10. His salary, then, was $5 a week. No wonder he was pleased with the tip. It was almost a day's pay.

BEING MONDAY, it was the day of something I had been anticipating with pleasure. So I had a quick answer when Don Gabriel asked what was next on the agenda. The market, I said.

"*Es muy pobre,*" he protested, and he spoke about its poverty so disparagingly that I got the impression he would rather not show it to me. But my drawing had already cut me off too much from village life, and I was not going to be deterred from seeing this aspect of it.

We walked to the arch at the back of the church where we had stood the night before watching the people disperse after the horse racing. It proved an excellent vantage point, for the market was concentrated at the corner of the plaza at the foot of the steps.

Those steps show in the plan on page 60. And the little building to the right (No. 3) was Felix Palma's stall where I had bought the candles and the hard pencil.

The market had four lanes. One was in the covered arcade that ran in front of the school. The other three were created by parallel rows of white awnings that had been rigged up along Calle de la Plaza. In the lane near the trees some of the vendors had stalls. But the majority had spread their goods out on mats on the dirt roadway. The vendors with the mats either sat on little boxes or on the ground beside their wares. In many cases, the improvised awnings consisted of Robinson Crusoe-type umbrellas—that is, squares of canvas held extended by X-shaped frames at the top of upright poles.

Sizing up the scene, I could guess why Don Gabriel felt I would not be interested. He had traveled in other parts of Mexico and thus he was aware that, as Mexican markets go, this one had little to offer in the way of variety of goods. It was a market for rural villagers. The supplies were limited and there were no thronging Indians in unusual regional costumes.

Raucous music was shattering the town's normally pleasant silence. It emanated from a loudspeaker on top of a panel delivery truck, which was parked in front of Palma's stall. Obviously an ancient phonograph was playing inside the truck, and between the hideously scratchy records came an over-amplified sales talk urging the villagers to buy Iris and Corona soaps. "None better," the voice kept repeating. "Iris and Corona soaps. The best in the Republic. None better. Iris and Corona."

"Where did the truck come from?" I asked. "From Oaxaca," he replied. "Now the highway is open, it travels from one village market to another."

I suppose the truck made salesmanship more efficient—but how much more charming the market would have been without it! Something sentimental in me made me resent the ugly modern note. It was the one thing out of key, for all the other out-of-town salespeople clearly had brought their goods from their villages in the age-old way—either on their own backs or on the backs of donkeys.

The evidence could be seen assembled on the terrace that projects like an intermediate stage two-thirds of the way down from the sheer back wall of the platform. On the ordinarily deserted grassy shelf was a collection of gray, black and chocolate-colored burros. They were grazing contentedly, even though most of them were saddled with stuffed sacking, a reminder that by nightfall they would be on the road again, loaded with goods so heavy and uncomfortable that the sacking was necessary to save their backs from abrasion.

When we descended the steps for a closer view, Don Gabriel further betrayed how uninteresting he considered the market by the speed with which he proceeded to conduct me through it. "Not so fast," I protested.

"*Es pobre*," he repeated. And then I hit upon a scheme that would enable me to linger. I could buy things.

We started at the head of the aisle under the arcade of the municipal building. If we had been in a Woolworth's in the United States, we would have been among the "notions." Most of the wares were displayed on improvised flat surfaces, some being the sides of cartons, others being boards, raised about a foot from the tiled walk. The articles included hooks and eyes, cheap earrings, thread, ribbons, elastic tape, mirrors and so on. Dangling from horizontal strings above them were red bandannas. The item I purchase as my excuse for looking over the notions was a wooden comb with teeth facing two ways. It at least was handmade, which most of the other things were not.

The comb, frankly, was a subterfuge, but there was one thing I definitely wanted to buy. I had seen no evidence that Lupe had a long-bladed kitchen knife with a good sharp edge. Knowing how useful such a knife can be, I wanted to get one for her, and I saw I could find one among the goods of the next section, which contained the sort of articles dime stores carry in their basements—hinges, sickles, hammers, flashlights and the like.

Because I wanted to linger in order to see as much as possible, the knife proved ideal for my delaying purposes. Don Gabriel was determined I was not going to be overcharged, which meant he would not let me buy several knives I examined because the vendors would not come down to his price. Finally we got one of stainless steel that he agreed was worth eight pesos. Searching for the knife allowed my eye to light on other things and one item gave me an idea for a present to take back to friends in Oaxaca—an old-fashioned can opener with an attached corkscrew. It was a peso and a half.

The arcade, I decided, must have been reserved for city products, for nearly all the goods here were manufactured items. They had probably been brought in by itinerant peddlers or assembled by villagers on trips to larger towns. The other two chief classes of goods—the homemade and the homegrown—were to be found in the three less sheltered aisles, out on the unpaved road, underneath the awkward, many-angled bits of canvas that provided shade from the sun.

I was on the lookout for attractive handicrafts. But the products revealed that the people of the other villages of the region were hardly more artistic than those of Yanhuitlán. I could not help reflecting on how completely the Mixtecs had lost the skills they had before the Spanish conquest. Here there were some straight-backed wooden chairs from Tlaxiaco, some heavy red-brown pottery from Santo Domingo Tonaltepec, and, from further south, some olive-green pitchers from Azompa and a few colored bowls from Oaxaca, but little else.

Most of the goods in the three short rows were foodstuffs. With them, purchasing served a double purpose. Besides helping me to hold back Don Gabriel, it enabled me to get things for his household. I passed up the potatoes, the onions and the inevitable piles of red and green chiles, but I bought some oranges, a few bananas and a handful of tomatoes. I couldn't, however, find any eggs. Don Gabriel said there weren't any.

"You mean there isn't an egg in the whole market?" I asked incredulously. He explained that chickens were hard to keep. An insect infested the ground and generally chickens died after eating the insect.

As he spoke, I realized the insect would also explain why Lupe had never offered me any chicken. In other parts of Mexico chicken is about the only flesh served, and I had expected it to predominate in my diet. But not a piece had I seen—even in soup.

Our oranges, tomatoes and bananas were hard to carry in our hands and when we came to the peanuts we obviously needed help. Needless to say there were no paper bags, so Don Gabriel asked an old woman from whom we bought some peanuts if she could lend us a *tenate*. She was perfectly agreeable, and we placed the larger things in the bottom of the flexible sack. Then she let the dark-brown peanuts dribble through her fingers till they covered the top.

To know a market woman who trustingly lent you a container in which to take away your purchases—this was a new experience for me, and I liked her confidence that she would get it back. Her name was Margarita and she had a battered, old brown face that made her all of a piece with her dark, scorched peanuts. Poor and toothless as she was, she smiled most winningly.

In the aisle near the trees one or two of the stands were tended by butchers, and their gobs, strips and chunks of purple-red meat either hung on strings or lay attracting flies on the counter. At one I recognized Saul, the elder brother of Alberto and Nahum of the family with the deerlike eyes. We greeted each other with the cordiality of people who had attended the same dance. Don Gabriel then introduced me to the young man's father, whose name was Lorenzo Palma. Since the boys were the sons of Don Gabriel's deceased sister, Lorenzo was Don Gabriel's brother-in-law. He was a tall, vigorous man and the fact that he needed a shave made him look like a handsome pirate. But he was friendly and courteous and I could see from whom the children had inherited their eyes.

After we had exchanged a few words with the butcher and his son, no further excuse remained for lingering at the market. Not wanting to seem unduly curious, I agreed to go home with Don Gabriel. After lunch, though, I had a fresh excuse: to return Margarita's *tenate*. Don Gabriel protested that I did not need to bother. He would do it. But I wasn't going to lose my opportunity, and I talked him into giving me the basket.

I would have sworn I could have made a beeline for Margarita, but when I got to the row in which she was sitting I found myself uncertain. The old market women sitting by their pottery, their tomatoes, their oranges, their chiles, their peanuts, looked so much alike. Fortunately Margarita gave herself away by her smile and the way she reached out for her *tenate*.

On this second visit to the market I saw that Don Gabriel and I could have bought a new *tenate*. They were for sale among the goods of the weavers of palm leaves. Besides the soft cylindrical baskets, these people had the sleeping mats known as *petates* and they had many hats. In fact, most of them were making hats as they sat by their wares. They interwove the long ends of the palm strips as if they were knitting.

Another previously overlooked section I caught on this second visit was the turkey counter. And counter is only a figure of speech. The people who had brought in their turkeys had neither mats, nor stands, nor awnings; nothing but the birds themselves. The gobblers were tied by the legs in knots of two or three, and their owners had taken the precaution not to kill them. After all, if they were not sold this Monday, living turkeys would keep better until next week, or the week after.

A dog fight began. And oh how I would have loved to have stood at a corner and made notes. But I knew I must not betray how the market fascinated me as a sociological manifestation. However, I did have one more pretext for looking around. The fact that after lunch was shaving time had reminded me I was still using the tiny mirror borrowed from Don Gabriel. There were mirrors among the notions, and I went to the arcade once more and bought a glass with a prop behind it. It was about the size of a frame a teenager would use for a photo of a favorite movie star.

After I got back to my room, Don Gabriel brought a jar of hot water and I returned his mirror. And what a surprise when I began to shave, using my new mirror! This was the first time in six days I had looked in a glass big enough to show my whole face.

I hardly recognized myself. The furrow between my eyes had relaxed. My eyebrows were bleached the color of straw. And seldom had I seen my cheeks as round and pink. But my eyes astonished me most. The green in them had been engulfed by a China blueness.

Zen Buddhists have worked out a series of sayings that carry the shock of surprise. They have done this because they have learned that often the mind has an extraordinary alertness when it has received an unexpected but harmless shock. My alertness at this point is an example. It was not so much the changes in my face that startled me as that I should find my face unfamiliar. This had never happened previously, because never before had I been so long in a place without mirrors.

Realizations came thick and fast. The first was similar to the one that flashed on me that dark night when I saw the era of electricity as only a drop of time in the ocean of man's history. The era of mirrors, I realized, was but slightly longer. Even though the looking glass is a fairly old invention, only in recent times have mirrors been cheap enough to become commonplace in most cultures. In other words, the majority of mankind through most of its history has lived in an environment as relatively mirrorless as the one in which I had been living in Yanhuitlán.

The mirror—what an unexpectedly large factor of difference between our civilization and earlier or more primitive ones! We are so used to the looking glass that it is almost impossible for us to realize how it has transformed life by increasing the individual's awareness of his physical appearance. Not only has it made people of all social levels so much more fashion-conscious, but it has enormously increased self-centeredness.

This last came to me through realization of the interconnection between self-consciousness and awareness of one's appearance. When a man can see others and cannot see himself, his self-image plays a relatively small part in his consciousness in proportion to the images of others. But what happens when omnipresent mirrors won't allow him to forget his own image? It is what happens with anything that is constantly before the eyes. What is in sight is in mind. Thus, when mirrors constantly remind one of what one looks like, it is hard to escape wondering how that outward appearance is affecting others. Also, since one's physical shell is very much a part of one's total being, repeated glimpses of that shell in mirrors cannot help but serve as constant reminders of the self as something separate and isolated. This makes it increasingly difficult to lose awareness of the self. But when a man goes for days without seeing much more than his hands, knees and feet, his awareness of his appearance automatically dwindles. This, in contrast, makes it increasingly easy to forget the self.

Mirrors as a factor in making people neurotic—this was the next theme my mind turned to. But its pursuit, like my shaving, was halted by an unexpected caller.

"*Buenas tardes*," he said. "May I introduce myself? I'm the principal of the school."

"The Presbyterian," I said, greeting him with delighted interest.

He was a man of twenty-eight, dressed in brown pants and a maroon corduroy jacket. His features had a slightly Oriental cast, and, considering he was slim and of only medium height, his speaking voice was unexpectedly deep. His name was Fausto Cervantes Velasco, and it turned out that he knew some of my Protestant friends in Oaxaca.

He apologized for not calling earlier, but during the Independence Day holidays he had been away on a brief vacation. He was single, he said, and liked to travel as much as possible.

Having known schoolteachers who had been opposed in their communities by the local priest, I asked if El Cura had attempted to interfere with anything he was trying to achieve in the school. Priests, he said, sometimes did try to keep the people "culturally blind," but the one here was easygoing. He never made any trouble.

"Has he ever co-operated with you in a project for the village's betterment?"

"No. He keeps to himself. All he does is conduct the routine services of the church."

After this Fausto took his leave, for he had not come for a long conversation, only to make a courtesy call. And I was grateful for the formality; he was the first adult in the village who had done such a thing.

I relathered my left cheek and completed my shaving. Then, since some warmth remained in the water, I decided I'd put the basin on the floor and wash my feet. When I got my socks off, there was hardly a line at the top level of my shoe. And the cleanness of my feet taught me something important about the monastery. That's the explanation, I said to myself. That's why the century-old whitewash in the church interior looks recent. It's because Yanhuitlán is so clean. If my feet don't get dirty here, the monastery doesn't either.

"*Buenas tardes,*" said another voice at the door. This time it was a tiny, high voice—Angelita. I knew she wanted a candy, so, holding my one washed foot off the floor, I hopped over and gave her a caramel.

As I was putting my socks back on, Ester, the plain woman with the transforming smile came by. Needless to say, she was carrying the infant Hugo. I gave them both candies, and this time we had more than the weather to talk about. There was also the dance. She had enjoyed herself and she could tell I had enjoyed myself too. My dancing, she said, was "*muy elegante.*"

X V

STONE HEADS AND THE STAIRWAY

AFTER ESTER LEFT, all was quiet and I brought my diary up to date. The thought of the days that were past led to plans for those that were to come. Should I stick to my resolution and leave the day after tomorrow? Checking my sketches, I estimated there was time enough in my allotted span to make the additional drawings I needed. But, when faced with the prospect of leaving, I found I did not like it. Actually, there had always seemed so much time ahead that I had hardly thought of the end.

Today was Monday, September 28, and I had to be back in my office in New York City on October 7. With a little calculating, I figured that if I pared down my revisits to Oaxaca and Mexico City I could stay in Yanhuitlán until Friday, October 2. If I stayed almost ten days, my title, "Week in Yanhuitlán," would appear to be unsuitable. But now this didn't matter. The book idea had collapsed. Snapping the diary closed, I decided I would stay till the last possible moment—if that was agreeable to the Blancos.

It was—as Don Gabriel assured me when he came over a few minutes later. And I think he was as pleased with the extension as I was.

Don Gabriel did not come with empty hands. What he brought was evidence of his mind and generosity working as they had done after my putting the weeds in the talcum can had shown him my interest in flowers. In this case, my purchase of the Mixteca head from the old man in the church had shown him I had an interest in the pre-Conquest civilization of the area. And he was following up this interest by bringing me three additional archaeological objects.

One was a jade bead that looked like a hard pea that had been slightly flattened in being drilled through. The second was a curious little bust of

flesh-colored clay. It represented a man with a face that seemed part dog and part death's-head. I judged he must have been a personage of importance, for he had round plugs in his large ears, an imposing breastpiece and a high headdress.

"It's a whistle," said Don Gabriel. He took the piece from my hand, put the headdress between his lips, and blew. But no sound emerged. Returning it to me, he said it didn't work because it was broken. Examining it more closely, I could see that the destroyed resonating chamber had begun at the breastpiece. Perhaps the whistle had once represented a whole figure.

The third object was another head. It was of a pink-gray, marblelike stone. I noticed the eyes were indicated by three crescent-shaped grooves, as with my little football player. But this head was considerably inferior to the first one. There was no real attempt at modeling and the nose projected only because the head was cut from a triangular piece of stone. Still, it did not lack expression. I could not help thinking it looked like Herminio, the young man I had called hatchet-faced.

The effect of the crescent grooves intrigued me. At one moment the middle crescent suggested an under lid of a vacant eye. Another look, and

t seemed to be an iris. Still again, it looked like the closed upper lid of a devout pilgrim, who, despite his piety, had dark circles under his eyes.

The head was broken, said Don Gabriel. The surface under the chin was a little rough, but I could not see why he was so confident the head was not complete in itself. I was not to understand, in fact, until my final day in Yanhuitlán.

Where did the head come from? I asked. From Jazmín, the sacred mountain with the tombs which we had seen from the monastery's ruined porch.

"Up there," said Don Gabriel, "people find such things lying on the ground all the time."

I offered to pay for them, but he laughed and said I could have them. They were of no value. Of no value to him perhaps, but to me they were evidence of an ancient civilization that excited my imagination. In a sense, they helped explain the sumptuousness of the monastery. Gold, the presence of a large population, and a previous religious site were not the only reasons for its grandeur. There was also the fact that this civilization had been flourishing in the region. A great establishment was felt necessary to eclipse what it was supplanting. I knew I could not learn much about the ancient Mixtecs on this visit, but I hoped I would find more of their traces before leaving.

After thanking Don Gabriel for the objects, I set them carefully on my little table. Then he escorted me to the monastery's *Sala de Profundis,* for he knew the great staircase was my project for the afternoon.

The monumental stairway rose at the eastern end of the long, barrel-vaulted hall. Its first flight, which began in the *Sala,* ascended into the stairwell under the rather flat arch, and climbed eighteen steps before reaching the first landing. The last of the long flight is shown in the lower right of the plan on page 296. The plan does not convey the force of that great stairway, nor what the centuries have done to its old stones, but it does show how the first landing fits into the southeast corner of the wall, how a shorter flight of steps leads up to another square landing, and how that second landing enables the stairs to turn once more, with a final flight of twelve steps completing the ascent to the second floor.

In ascending, the railing is always on the left, and that railing is especially striking for it consists of a wall ornamented with massive stone fleur-de-lis. My trips up and down the stairs, including those in going to and from the choir that morning, had shown me how I could get all the stair-

way's essential elements in a single sketch. The trick was to work on the first
landing. So it was there that I led Don Gabriel.

The railing, I told him, was the key to the graphic problem. When he
had difficulty understanding, I explained that if I drew the short middle
flight in its entirety I could use the angles of the railing to suggest the other
flights. The ascending angle of the topmost section indicated how the final
flight climbed, even though one could only see the lowest treads. And anyone could imagine the long flight going down on the left if the uppermost
steps were indicated as they joined the descending railing.

The massive stairway had no finicky details, and I was fully prepared to make the drawing standing up, holding my sketchbook in my hand. But Don Gabriel refused to accept my assurance that I would be all right. He went in search of something for me to sit on and returned with the box I had used in the cloister. After seeing I was settled, he withdrew.

The stairwell is amply proportioned for the ordinary purpose of going up and down, but I felt my quarters were very cramped, for I judged them from the standpoint of one wanting a long-range view in order to get all the elements properly scaled. The crampedness can be realized by imagining a wall rising from the front of the square landing suggested at the bottom of the drawing. I was seated in the corner with my back to that wall.

The stone ball on the top of the newel was very close, and being close it looked large. So did the nearer fleur-de-lis. The temptation was to do them almost life size. My chief problem in blocking in this sketch, therefore, was drawing the ball and the stone lilies small enough so that room was left on the paper to get in the rest of the staircase. By careful checking of relative dimensions, though, I managed to get my whole composition on the page with each element properly scaled.

Then came the problem of creating the illusion of depth. Those seven steps directly ahead receded into the background at the same time as they went up. That railing turned at a ninety-degree angle at the newel. And those two archways at the head of the stairs were set at right angles to each other, because each gave onto a different cell corridor. Getting my lines to suggest the solidity and the direction of the forms required more careful checking, for, as usual, I was bound I was not going to take the easier course of resorting to shadow.

But this sort of care was different from the picayune attention to detail enforced by the altar and ceiling drawings. I enjoyed its particular challenge, and I was not made tense by the consciousness that every tiny line had to be delicately right. This stairway was old and battered. I knew that a freer, rougher style would convey its character more faithfully than the style I had used for the church.

It was pleasant sitting where I was. The stairwell was not a bit stuffy, for the windows that lighted it, like most windows in the building, were empty of glass. I was beside the largest of them, a rectangular opening, marked B on the plan (page 296). And not only was that window big by design, but it had been smashed larger in one of the monastery's sieges. I had only to turn my head to see out, and if I had not resolved against doing any landscapes, I would have been tempted to draw the scene through that jaggedly picturesque frame. Not only did one see La Pastora, the ruined chapel, and beyond it the red hills, but squarely in the foreground was the circular pond of the village fountain. As always, it looked more beautiful for the trees that shaded it.

Often, as I had come up the first flight of the stairway, I had been struck not only by the beauty of this view, but by the way its effect was the result of conscious planning. Clearly, it was no accident that the fountain, the window and the stairway's first long flight were all on the same axis. The fountain had been deliberately placed to form the centerpiece of the vista.

The planning behind that sixteenth-century "picture window" made me remember those three arches, now vanished, which had been set in the western wall so they could frame the sunset. They were evidence of similar planning. So this was another vital realization about the monastery. Not only did it present a handsome appearance from outside, but its apertures were so planned that those who were inside received a sense of architectural beauty as they looked out.

Then a book memory stirred. In his *Mexican Architecture of the Sixteenth Century*, Kubler, with his gift for understanding the psychological factors behind the Conquest, stresses the totality of the missionary effort of the Mendicant Orders. The Franciscans, Dominicans and Augustinians did not merely build churches, they also laid out towns; and besides providing the Indians with a new religion and a new ceremonial basis for ordering their lives, they also provided them with a civic administration and a new pattern of secular living.

The integration of that missionary effort, the way it was material as well as spiritual, seemed to me wonderfully illustrated as I looked out on that fountain. The fountain was the source of the sixteenth-century town's most fundamental physical need—water. And the town was laid out so that its water supply system was at the very heart of its plan. Yet, as I could see clearly, that fountain was also an essential part of the monastery's plan. And seeing the role of the fountain in the two plans made me realize how those plans were interlocked. The master plan of the community, obviously, had been drawn up with the idea that the monastery and the town should be interacting, interdependent parts of a single unit.

I turned back to the drawing. But presently my attention was drawn outside the window again by a childish voice that was hollering up a greeting. It was Arturo, the older son of El Presidente. He and his brother Jorge, it seems, had been passing round the back of the monastery and looked up at the window and seen me working inside. That the formerly shy youngsters should be calling and waving in this friendly fashion delighted me. Fortunately, I had a couple of candies in my pocket. I chucked them down to the boys, who scrambled to retrieve them from the grass. As they unwrapped them, they called *"gracias"* and continued homeward.

The market was still going on and I could hear its sounds as I drew. Above the occasional calls of men and women and the hee-hawing of burros came that awful canned music from the top of the truck. Over and over the same few hoarse musical selections, interrupted regularly by the same overamplified voice: "Iris and Corona. None better. The best soaps in the Republic. None better. Iris and Corona." But the truck was far enough away that its raucous sounds blended with the other sounds of the market, and after a while I even came to feel a sort of affection for those repetitious records. They kept me aware that though I was drawing in the quiet solitude of the stairwell I was yet in touch, through my ears, with the life going on in the square. I did not feel as apart from the village as I had when I had been working on my drawings on previous days.

By this time I was giving the various elements their heavy, final overlines. Darkening the upper newel, I received a new lesson in observation: how knowledge of a complete form will enable one to see a fragment with proper comprehension. It worked this way: drawing the intact finial on the newel below had made me so familiar with its form that I was able to recognize the repetition of its base on the broken newel above. This, in turn, made me realize that the upper finial, too, must have resembled a stone ball on an inverted apothecary's cup. Could one say the same of the ruined finial at the foot of the stairs? Glancing down, I saw the conformation of its stump also indicated a ball on a cup.

Between this other broken finial and the point where the ascending stairway passed under the arch was another fleur-de-lis. This gave the first flight three of the stone flowers, the middle flight one and the top flight two. Most of them were chipped or in some way broken. I knew their inspiration from all the Dominican coats of arms I had seen throughout the monastery. And with my memories now being readily accessible, the logic of that particular symbol became plain. Dominic was a Spaniard, but his early work was preaching against the Albigensian heresy in southern France, and it was in France that he founded his Order.

APPARENTLY the Presidente's two young sons were not the only villagers who had spotted me in the stairwell. Juan, the *campesino* I had met at the dance, must have seen me too, for he made a point of coming into the monastery and up the stairs in order to watch me work. He was delighted in matching the fleur-de-lis in the sketch with the ones before his eyes on the railing. I, in turn, was delighted to see the whiteness of his teeth in contrast to his mahogany skin when he smiled. I showed him the other drawing I had done. He could not identify all the doorways and when he saw the drawing of the vaulting in the cloister he exclaimed, *"Altar mayor!"*

Other villagers had made the same mistake, and the source of the error now dawned on me. For them vaulting was inextricably associated with the high altar. Therefore any representation of vaulting automatically flashed the altar into their minds. Since other villagers, too, had failed to recognize some of the doorways, I realized Juan was like one of many in the town. He had taken the monastery so much for granted all his life that he had hardly looked at it.

Leafing further back in the sketchbook, we came to the drawing of the porthole (page 72). I saw it gave me a chance to give him a little instruction. That window (marked *A* on page 296) was near us, so I took him up the seven steps to the next landing and pointed to the window's interior aspect in the wall on our right. Its placement, I showed, meant it provided illumination for the final flight of steps on our left. I could tell from his expression that he agreed it was ingenious.

"But wait," I said. "Come with me." And I led him up that last flight and through the arch until we were part way down the cell corridor. Then, with the air of a magician pulling a spectacular trick, I told him to turn around and see the thing I had discovered my second day in the monastery: the way that very same window, designed apparently only to light the stairwell, also provided a beautiful circular vignette of hills and sky, squarely at the end of the corridor. He was properly impressed.

Then I led him back to the stairwell and directed his gaze up to the magic lantern window in the western lunette under the barrel vault. When he nodded to show he had taken it in, I pointed out how it illustrated the diversity of the monastery's windows. It was not a circle like the double-duty porthole. It was a diamond.

Juan was not a talker, but I could tell I had made him realize there was more to the monastery than he had thought. He left, shaking his head in the way that a person does when he has received a lot of exciting new knowledge that is a little too heady to be absorbed all at once.

Don Gabriel returned just as I put the finishing touch on the drawing. *"¿Le gusta?"* I asked, meaning "does it please you?" *"Perfecto,"* he said.

He was a little surprised when I announced I was finished for the day. Since I was drawing the stairway, wasn't I also going to draw the mural of St. Christopher?

I understood his query, for that mural, besides being one of the major sights of the monastery, is certainly an important part of the stairway. But it was five-thirty and I had already decided to let the mural go.

"Perhaps some other day," I said so he would not feel disappointed. "In the meantime, let's get to the upper flight so we can get a good look at it."

I specified this particular site because those uppermost steps were on the other side of the well. We had to cross over to look at the mural, which, being on the south wall, had been behind me all the time I had been sketching. Also we needed the height. The vast mural is two stories tall and a viewer must have an elevated position to take it all in.

At that time I had little taste for the folkloristic strain that many consider one of the charms of Latin American colonial art. One reason I did not want to draw the mural was that I did not think much of it artistically. But because it was original sixteenth-century work, and therefore of historical importance, I was willing to study it.

My own difficulties in the stairwell enabled me to view it with more sympathy. The artist, obviously, had not been able to get far enough back from his work to see that all its proportions were right. He had drawn the top half of the giant in one scale, the bottom half in another.

I suspected that he had done the bottom half first. Then, when he had got as far as the waist, his scaffold had been raised a story and he had set to work on the top half. Knowing how easily such things can happen, I could picture him outlining that big head, fully confident that he was still working on the same massive scale as those enormous legs. Then I could see him doing the rest of the upper part in proportion to the head. In the affectionate care lavished on the top details—particularly on the little adult he made of the Christ Child—I could sense his pleasure as he worked. I could understand, too, how he could persist in his error. After all, those huge legs, below him, were hard to see, and being at least ten feet down, they undoubtedly looked smaller than they actually were.

He must have discovered his mistake when he came to join the two halves at the belt. Remembering how I felt when I discovered I had made the cloister's classical doorway too narrow, I could sense his consternation.

The more I studied the mural the less I felt anatomical disproportion mattered. The hugeness of those legs fairly bowled you over with their size and strength. They gave an emotional impression of St. Christopher that was more powerful than mere correctness would have been. This giant was truly one who would have needed a tree for a staff.

I was starting to like the mural. The lower left corner seemed to have been destroyed, but I could tell the incompleteness of the leg in this part was deliberate. The artist had chosen to illustrate the moment in the legend when the burly saint was stepping out of the raging river across which, unknowingly, he had carried the infant Savior to safety. The missing shin, obviously, was still under water.

The cloaks revealed the artist's attempt to depict the velocity of the gale the saint had buffeted. The saint's cloak, too voluminous to be lifted completely, was nevertheless well puffed out, and the Child's was blown as horizontal as a wind sock.

The saint's cloak was blue and he was dressed in earth brown. The Child's gown was blue, while the cloak was a dull red. And these heavy tones stood out against the unrelieved white of the stairwell. The colors, then, were few and crude, and all rather somber. But the artist had made an attempt at liveliness in the slashing of St. Christopher's trousers. The segments were blue, red, white and olive green. And those trousers were a particularly endearing touch. They were not a bit Biblical. Instead, they brought back a picture I had loved as a small boy, for they were identical with those worn by Sir Walter Raleigh as he spread his cloak across the mud puddle for Queen Elizabeth.

Had I noticed the friar in the right-hand corner? Don Gabriel asked. This was the most faded part of the mural and I had not. But I discerned the little monk when the query made me search for him. He was standing in front of a little building and he was holding a lantern. His smallness added still another element of disproportion to the mural, but this was a lovable one which made the giant seem all the more towering.

"That," said Don Gabriel, "is Fray Bernardino de Minaya, the founder of the *convento*." Then he added with a note of pride: "He was the man

who went to Rome and obtained the Papal Bull affirming the rationality of the Indians."

Having learned from the "Códice" in Blom's library that there had been two Dominican settlements in Yanhuitlán before the third one that built the monastery, I asked Don Gabriel in which group Fray Bernardino had come. "The first," he said. "He came in 1529. That is the original *convento* behind him."

This seemed a peculiarly local application of the St. Christopher legend, but it charmed me. And there was something especially fitting about that little friar holding out the lantern to welcome this black-bearded, Spanish-looking saint who had carried the Christian faith on his shoulders in striding across the ocean to the New World.

This touch completed my conversion to the mural. What picture could be more suitable for such a monastery than one of a friar welcoming the precious symbol of his faith, brought safely through the raging waters to the new home he had built for it in a strange land? How often friars trudging up and down that great stairway must have had their own enthusiasm refreshed by the examples of the giant saint and the tiny monk!

When we had looked our fill, Don Gabriel suggested a visit to Felix Palma's for a *refresco*. On the way, we met a town burgher whose name I did not catch. He was a short, egg-shaped man with a long gray moustache, pouches under his eyes and a hooked nose with especially large round nostrils. Since I had my sketchbook with me, I used them as a device to improve the acquaintance.

The little man was worse than Juan in identifying features of the monastery. But when I exposed the page with the sketch of the north portal he was relieved. He knew what it was. "*Campo santo,*" he exclaimed.

Don Gabriel laughed and corrected him. When we had separated, Don Gabriel said: "He's like many of the villagers. He hardly knows the monastery." Then he laughed again at the boner. "*Campo santo,*" he repeated.

I thought it was funny too, but a realization made me more tolerant. The portal to the cemetery, or *campo santo*, is a free-standing arch. My drawing, in abstracting the north portal from its context, presented that portal as a free-standing arch. It was this that led the burgher to connect the two archways and to confuse one with the other. He was not so dumb after all. His trouble was that he was not a trained observer. He probably had looked at few pictures in his life, certainly few of an architectural nature. And I comprehended for the first time the degree of visual sophistication needed to look at the abstracted design of a doorway and to recognize it as a representation of something one had always seen in three dimensions as part of a great unit.

When we got to La Providencia, we did not have our drinks outside. Felix invited us in and gave us seats. The floor was more raised than I had realized and the extra foot of height gave the big booth the air of a grandstand box. With such a view of the plaza, no wonder Felix liked to keep his store open at all hours.

Felix gave me some apple cider and Don Gabriel some mezcal. Then he looked at the drawings I had done since his last viewing. He was interrupted, though, by the arrival of three men in a big truck. They had salt to sell. This meant bargaining, and Felix left us to talk with them.

The drink of mezcal was not Don Gabriel's first of the day, so he was in a more confidential, slightly less controlled mood than I had ever seen him before. He launched upon a subject I have said is a favorite of Mexicans—warning against the dishonesty of other Mexicans. "*Gente mala*," he said, meaning, "bad people." There were many *gente mala*, he repeated. Then he confided the sort of person he had expected when he had received his letter about me from the head of the Institute. His picture, he said, was of a very large, dignified, self-important man with a beard of the French type. He chuckled to think how differently I had turned out. His loosened tongue next turned to something he had tried only once or twice during my visit—English. For the first time he had the nerve to try most of the words he had learned in California. "You want?" was a phrase he was particularly sure of. "How are you?" was another.

Having agreed on terms for the salt, Felix turned back to us, while his wife, the plump little ex-maid, set about feeding the three men from the truck. The familiar way they sat down at the table in the narrow room at the back of the booth showed it was regularly used for serving meals. Felix, then, did a little restaurant business on the side.

By this time darkness had fallen and Felix had lit a coal-oil lamp. Having no further work at the moment, he poured himself a jigger of mezcal and sat down to join us. Don Gabriel, being in a humorous mood, told him how the old villager had got eight pesos out of me by driving a hard bargain for the head of the little football player.

"Are you interested in *idolitos?*" asked Felix. Smiling at his diminutive, I said I was. Thereupon he went to a drawer and took out a little stone, which he handed to me. Holding it close to the soft light of the lamp,

I saw it was another head. Its style differed from the others, though. The features were not carved from the stone so much as they were indicated by lines engraved on it. And in place of crescents the eye-centers were depicted by a bold line cut across the whole face. The severe stylization was surprisingly modern. And the stone itself was striking, for it was smooth, hard and so dark a green as to be almost black. And I learned later that the spinach-colored stone was a type of jade.

I commented to Don Gabriel on how the head lacked the modeling and the scooped-out crescents of the others. "That's because this stone is harder," he explained.

The pre-Cortesian inhabitants of Mexico, I knew, had no steel-cutting tools. Remembering this, I saw the force of Don Gabriel's remark. The carver probably had to rely on shallow nicks, most of them cut in straight lines. The stone was so hard he could not make a mark on it in any other way. The explanation that this particular stylization was forced on him by his intractable medium and his limited tools seemed more likely as I examined the head closely. It had the same straight lines framing the jaws, and the same headband across the brow, as the head Don Gabriel had given me earlier in the day. Perhaps it was meant to be like that other head, but it was less naturalistic because the carver was thwarted in getting the little stone barrel closer to human contours.

Aldous Huxley has an illuminating passage in *Beyond the Mexique Bay* in which he says primitive work often has a chaste simplicity, not because native taste has the severe restraint of an Archipenko, say, or a Modigliani, but because inadequate techniques frustrate native artists from doing anything more elaborate. This head, it seemed to me, was an excellent example of his point.

Turning the head over I saw two interconnecting holes: one on top of the head, the other just below it on the back. The football player had

been drilled with similar holes. I asked Don Gabriel about them. They were for string, he said, for the ancient Mixtecs wore the little heads around their necks. I gathered, then, that each head was a sort of amulet.

I was interested in obtaining the jade and as casually as possible I said to Felix, "*¿Se vende?*"

It was for sale, he answered. The bargaining began. Felix asked the sum I had paid for the other head in the church—eight pesos. Since I had been laughed at for paying that much, I was a little at a loss how to proceed. Without committing myself I merely said, "*Es muy caro.*" (It is very expensive.)

I heard Don Gabriel mutter something that sounded like "five."

"*Siete,*" said Felix, coming down to seven.

"Five," repeated Don Gabriel. I was so unaccustomed to hearing him use an English word that I was not sure that he was not employing a Spanish word that sounded like the English "five."

"You mean *cinco pesos?*" I asked in a verifying tone, using the Spanish word for five.

That let the cat out of the bag. He had been coaching me in English, knowing Felix would not understand. But there were no hard feelings. Five was the figure we settled on, and, when Don Gabriel and I got home to dinner, the story of how I had embarrassed my mentor by revealing his coaching made a fine anecdote for Lupe.

At the end of this meal I accepted a second cup of chocolate, for the after-dinner feeling between us had subtly changed. I knew they no longer felt constrained with me; and I, on the other hand, no longer felt I must clear out as soon as possible, for I had become aware that I provided company they enjoyed. Besides, no dance was scheduled tonight, and we could relax.

I persuaded Don Gabriel to fill in the framework of his life. He had been born in Yanhuitlán, he said, and had been raised as a field worker. But in 1926, when he was twenty, he wanted more education. He went to Oaxaca and finished two years of high school. Then he went to Coyoacán, on the outskirts of Mexico City, and taught school. But he gave it up after a year. "Why?" I asked.

"*Lucha,*" he said, meaning struggle. "It was struggle with the children, struggle with the parents, struggle with the government authorities."

"What did you do next?"

"I moved in to Mexico and worked in a drugstore. I gave injections."

At the age of twenty-nine he came back to Yanhuitlán to marry Lupe whom he had known as a girl. They were married on June 9, 1935, and the next year they went to Veracruz. After two years there, they moved to Mexico City where they stayed for nine years. In 1943 they came back to Yanhuitlán. Between August 9, 1944, and November 28, 1946—Don Gabriel was very exact about dates—he was in California. And then, after working for a while as a fiscal inspector in Nochixtlán, he had got his job as caretaker of the monastery in the fall of 1950.

Had he and Lupe been interested in the monastery when they were children, I asked. No, they said, they had been like all the other villagers. They took it for granted. Besides, they were living out on ranchos most of the time, working in the fields. But Don Gabriel remembered that when he was a boy the monastery had been a scary place. It used to be filled with bats and they would fly out at night.

Since it was past eight when his story was done, I said I would like to return to my room.

"Don't you want your money back?" Don Gabriel asked. I hadn't given it a thought, but, after he had taken the key from the wall and unlocked the army trunk, he returned the pocketbook and the traveler's checks.

I strolled to my room with an easy mind. With the drawing of the ceiling and the stairway, I felt I had completed the last of the monastery's major features. All I had left were smaller odds and ends. And, because of my decision to extend my stay until Friday, I had three and a half more days in which to polish them off.

The knowledge that the hardest part was over, my sense of achievement and the fact that I could contemplate so much time ahead in a place where I was so content conspired to make me feel tranquil, happy and very much aware of the Everlasting Wings.

When I took out my diary I noticed a new effect of Yanhuitlán. There were no numbered circles on top of the last entries. I had ceased counting the days.

XVI
SERENATA FOR DON MIGUEL

I GOT INTO my pajamas. But Lupe's dinner had restored me and, when it came to actually turning in, I found I was less tired than I thought. For the time being, the counter was more alluring as a drawing table than as a bed. I wanted to clean up the stairway sketch by erasing the lines that had proved falsely placed. And here I discovered a new advantage to the mirror I had bought in the market. By propping it behind the candle, it served as a reflector and increased the light falling on my sketchbook.

Shortly after nine I heard music, followed by the sound of a rocket zizzing up and exploding. I went to the peephole to see if I could learn what was happening. I could, because the festivity was in front of the big white house where I had taken candy to Paco and his brothers the day they were bold enough to shout at me, but not bold enough to leave the safety of home.

My view can be judged from the town plan (page 60). The house of the festivities is marked 4. It was up the slope and at right angles to the Blancos. The music was being provided by the village orchestra that had played at the dance. I could recognize the musicians because a member of the party was holding up a Coleman gasoline lamp, which scooped an area of startling whiteness out of the jet darkness of the night. Men on the periphery of the group kept setting off firecrackers. The rockets went corkscrewing up with noisy tails of orange gold.

A moment later I was startled by a knock at my door. When I opened it, I found two villagers. One was Refugio Rendón, the smiling greeter at *el baile*. The other was a stranger. Both were a little unsteady. But thanks to that dance, these men did not seem like menacing conspirators, as the emissaries had seemed the night before.

"*Buenas noches,*" I said, and invited them in.

Refugio introduced his friend. His name was José and he was a *veterano*. I threw him a fast salute, which José returned with the swift instinct of the trained soldier. My salute was American style and his Mexican, but in the exchange we had the flash of recognition that makes friends of all ex-soldiers. He said he had been in the army six years. I told him my term had been three.

The men had come from the group setting off the fireworks. They were holding a *serenata* to honor Don Miguel because tomorrow was his saint's day. Would I join the fiesta? Would I! It was the sort of opportunity I'd been hoping for all during my visit and here it was, dropped in my lap when a long eventful day seemed finally over. I assured them I'd be honored to come and asked if they could wait a moment while I re-dressed.

I had heard about such serenades and knew that the fiesta is the Mexican equivalent of a birthday party. In Mexico people do not celebrate the actual date of their birth. They celebrate the day near it chosen by their parents as their saint's day. Generally, too, they are named after the saint of the chosen day. Tomorrow was St. Michael's day and consequently the occasion for Don Miguel to acknowledge he was a year older.

I was in such a hurry to get to the party that I didn't bother to put on socks, I just whipped on a shirt and pants and was ready.

We joined the other serenaders as the first piece was ending. This gave me a chance to shake hands with Don Venustiano, for, as the cornetist of the band, El Presidente naturally was present. Vicente Gutiérrez, the *síndico*, was also in the party. As in the municipal office, he was dressed very correctly in city clothes. I think he was both surprised and pleased that I remembered his name. I had not seen most of the other men before, but I smiled and nodded at them. One with a beard came over and shook my hand. He said he knew who I was. Then he explained to a friend that I was the man who had given candies to their children. That immediately placed me for the other serenader. He smiled, and he, too, shook my hand.

More rockets were shot up and the orchestra began another piece. I had a curious sense of being part of a painting of Mexican life. In the white glare of that gasoline lamp, the group seemed made up of Mexican types, rather than of individuals; and because the lamp was on the upper side of the party, we cast fantastically long shadows that stretched down the slope and then bent upwards on the white walls of the continuous houses of the Blancos' street.

Perhaps it is traditional that serenaders should not be acknowledged too quickly—that is, they should be given time to actually do some serenading before being officially welcomed. The people inside Don Miguel's house must have heard us sooner, but not until the second piece was nearly finished was one of the big wooden doors opened. Don Miguel stepped out. I recognized the swarthy, chunky figure from the night before. So the man we were serenading was Miguel Gómez, the rich farmer who had been one of the four worthies who had escorted me home from the dance. He greeted his old friends among the serenaders and invited all of us in.

The drummer had to dismantle his traps, but moving was easy for the rest of the musicians. Since they had been playing from memory, they had no stands to bother with. Besides the drummer and El Presidente, the orchestra included the blind guitarist and two saxophone players—in other words, everyone who had played at the dance except the third saxophonist who had doubled on the trombone.

The door opened athwart a long, bare, whitewashed room which was so large it suggested a rural Spanish inn. As we filed in, a relative collected the men's sombreros. Taking advantage of their high peaked crowns, he stacked one on top of the other like so many doughnuts.

The room had a beamed ceiling and a red tiled floor, and its sparse furniture was ranged against the walls. Two large wooden beds at the far end were the most conspicuous items. The womenfolk clustered there, including the small girls in the family. Some of the girls were cradled in the women's laps, while the tiniest ones were already sleeping under the sheets of the huge beds.

Don Miguel's womenfolk must have known his friends would not fail him on his saint's day. Guest chairs were set out along the north wall of the room. They were small, unpainted and upright—identical to the one the Blancos had turned over to me. I had seen such chairs in the market and I knew they were made in Tlaxiaco. Seeing so many in this house, I realized they were the characteristic chairs of the region. It was to the row of Tlaxiaco chairs that we went after the sombreros had been collected and we had been welcomed by Don Miguel. Because I felt a little strange among so many people new to me, I was pleased to see that the luck of our order of entry had placed Refugio on my right and the bearded man on my left.

There were more upright chairs in front of the wooden partition at the west end of the room, and the men who came in last sat on them. Thus we were divided into two camps—women at one end and men at the other.

The orchestra began to establish itself near the partition on the opposite side of the room.

As the musicians arranged chairs and set up their equipment, the women went into action. The drinks were stored in the area behind the partition, and the women went to fetch them. As they crossed the room I was glad to see another familiar face—Leonila, the girl dressed in mauve at the dance who had asked if I thought Yanhuitlán was *triste*.

"She is the sister of Don Miguel's wife," Refugio explained. That enabled me to recognize the wife of the host, because a rather heavy but very pretty woman looked very much as Leonila was bound to look four or five years hence. Refugio confirmed my guess that she was the señora.

Mezcal and beer were the drinks offered the men. Most of them took mezcal, but, gauchely, I declined both. I had not had enough experience with the hospitality of the Mexicans to realize that to them declining liquor on the grounds of being a nondrinker was incomprehensible.

They kept pressing me and I kept explaining. Finally, Don Miguel himself came over to see what was the trouble. I repeated that I never took any hard drinks. Hearing that, he issued an order, and an older woman, perhaps an aunt, fetched a bottle of what turned out to be a mild golden wine. Seeing my mistake, I accepted a glass with relief. "Is this a special drink?" I asked Refugio when the servers were out of earshot.

His reply contained no mockery, but it showed I had got what my pigheadedness deserved. "It is the drink for the señoritas," he said.

The musicians were ready by this time. But first there was a speech delivered by the drummer. It went on for quite a long time and I judged it was about the momentousness of the occasion—the saint's day of one of Yanhuitlán's leading citizens.

Then the orchestra struck up a *selección*, and we all listened dutifully, as if at a concert. Having paid the musicians the courtesy of silence during the first piece, though, we felt freer to talk during the second. Where was my home? inquired Refugio. And when I replied New York, he asked for my *motivos* in coming to Yanhuitlán.

"To draw and study *el convento*," I answered. Then I told a white lie. I said Yanhuitlán's monastery was famous in the United States. And not a qualm did I have in speaking thus of a place that most North Americans have never heard of. If it wasn't famous, I felt, it deserved to be.

"*Famoso*," he repeated. And I could see it represented an idea new to him, one he liked. Who could have dreamed that hulking building in the

WEEK IN YANHUITLÁN

center of his little village was famous in a place as far away as New York?

Shortly thereafter, conversation was cut short by speech No. 2. This time the orator was Sr. Gutiérrez, the very correct attorney general. He was obviously accustomed to public speaking, for he was professional in manner, and his words were slow, carefully chosen and inflected as if he were addressing the members of the Senate. It was a pleasure to hear the language spoken with such resonance and with such distinct pronunciation of each syllable.

He spoke of the "transcendent moment" we were privileged to enjoy. The occasion of the saint's day of one of the most illustrious citizens of Yanhuitlán was indeed an occasion to remember. Then the praise was piled high on Don Miguel's head for all he had contributed in the past.

The seriousness of the *síndico's* speech had struck me at first as almost ludicrously out of proportion to such a neighborly gathering. But as his orotund phrases continued I began to see him differently. His manner of speaking showed unmistakably that he was a man of culture. Contrasting his face with those of the farmers and field hands who listened to him so respectfully, I saw he was far better educated than they. Probably he was sometimes lonely in the village, with great poetic thoughts rumbling in his head and no one around with whom he could exchange them in casual conversation. Small wonder he took advantage of the occasion to don the mantle of the prophet.

At the end of his peroration on Don Miguel's virtues came all his wishes for the host's continued health, prosperity and noble service. When he finished talking, he first shook Don Miguel's hand and then embraced him. The members of the band got up and did likewise. And then all the other men got in line, and, one after the other, we hugged the chunky farmer.

When all of us were back in our seats, the orchestra played again and once more the women moved forward to look after the needs of the men. They set up a huge kitchen table in front of those of us who were sitting along the north wall. Then they brought on plates piled high with thumping big buns. After placing these on the table, they distributed soup plates of thick white china. The men against the partition were motioned to bring their chairs and sit before the places represented by soup plates.

To my surprise, there was no soup. The hot drink was chocolate and it was served in handleless bowls, which were placed in the soup plates as if the latter were saucers. We were to reach for the buns as we drank the chocolate. Glancing to left and right, I saw dunking was permissible. This was lucky, for the buns, though sweet, were dry and icingless, and there was no butter.

The orchestra played as we ate and it continued when we were through. Meanwhile, relatives and other members of the family had gathered in the patio to listen. At first they hovered shyly at the doorway which made a dark frame in the opposite wall. But as their numbers increased those in front were pushed forward into the room. I noticed Paco, the bantamweight, and I grinned at him. There were several other boys, too, most of them a little older.

A little later, I was surprised to see Juan, the *campesino,* standing in the doorway. He looked more than ever like an idealized Indian type, for he was wearing a black and orange poncho with the colors indiscriminately mixed like the darks and lights of a crackled surface. "Is Juan a relative?" I asked Refugio.

"He is Don Miguel's brother." Again I was surprised. I did not think that in the same village a single family would have two brothers as far apart in status as a field hand and a rich landowner.

Another familiar face appeared in the doorway: that of Ester, the plain woman with the transfiguring smile. When she had edged forward to a seat vacated for her, I noticed that, late as it was, she was carrying that indispensable adjunct—Hugo, her infant son.

"Is she a relative too?" I asked Refugio. "Yes, she is Don Miguel's sister-in-law."

The music consisted of commonplace melodies carried by the brasses over a rum-tee-tum base. It did not hold the mind's attention, and my eye wandered. It looked with interest on one of the few big pieces of furniture in the room—a sideboard with a mirror above it. Fixed in one corner of the mirror was a U.S.-style birthday card with a sentimental cottage on it. In another corner was a photograph of a man laid out in a coffin. Above the mirror, in a heavy frame, was a large, full-length photograph of an elderly man dressed in the white cotton *calzones* of the Indian. Could it be Don Miguel's father? And perhaps the picture in the mirror was taken at the time of the old man's death. The only other adornment of the bare walls was one of Felipe Cruz's calendars. It showed a very white-skinned *señorita* in a mantilla, flashing a set of perfect teeth.

Next my eye moved to the women sitting on the beds. How apart they kept! If this had been a party in the United States, the men and the women would be mingled. They would be sitting or standing together in talkative, laughing groups, and there would be circulation from one group to another. But these women, from grandmothers to little girls, were part of one static camp, and the only ones who left it momentarily were those with duties to perform in serving drinks or food. No wonder the girls at the *baile* had retreated so quickly from their partners, when they had been brought up as children to remain always safely and quietly with the womenfolk at one end of the room.

Some of the small girls were getting bored. From the way they rubbed their eyes, I could see they would have liked to crawl into bed with the babies who were already sleeping. On the whole, though, the women had an air of composure. It was the men at the other end of the room who looked ill at ease. Seeing them sitting in a row on the upright chairs in a whitewashed room with a beamed ceiling. I again had a sense of being part of a painting that had come to life. Only this time I recognized the painting.

With their oddly mixed native and modern clothing, their work-thickened fingers, their look of being outdoor people who were unaccustomed to being indoors in such a situation, and their general feeling of constraint in being out of their element, the men reminded me irresistibly of Ernest L. Blumenschein's large canvas in the Museum of Modern Art, *Jury Trial of a Sheepherder for Murder.*

With the recollection of that picture, too, many impressions clicked into place. Blumenschein's sheepherders were New Mexicans, and that provided the clue to something basic about Yanhuitlán.

In many ways Yanhuitlán had been different from other places I knew in Mexico. The school with its Presbyterian principal, the prevalence of store-bought clothing and the casualness about Catholicism—all indicated the influence of the United States. None of the vegetation in the high mountain valley suggested a tropical country. And the people themselves were more thrifty, hardworking and reserved than the expansive, more artistic Mexicans I had known elsewhere. The recollection of the Blumenschein painting enabled me to lay my finger on the salient characteristic of Yanhuitlán that had eluded me. It was like a community in New Mexico. And with this realization came the memory of where I had seen long white houses like the Blancos' and Don Miguel's—in the paintings of Georgia O'Keeffe.

The musical selections allowed the women time to wash the white soup plates. Then they set them at the table for a second sitting. This was for the members of the band and those men who had not yet been accommodated. To give them room at the table I moved to one of the other chairs.

Before long Paco and the other boys were sitting beside me. They had grown tired of standing and had come to the chairs deserted by the men who were now taking their buns and chocolate at the big table. I asked the boys their names. Two of them, Bertaldo and Adán, were Paco's older brothers. They must have been about ten or twelve. Were the others also sons of Don Miguel? No. Hector, a lad who was also about ten, pointed to the bearded man. That was his father. The fifth boy was Guadalupe, a cousin, and he might have been thirteen. He was wearing a poncho and his close-cropped hair grew forward like a cap on his finely shaped head.

I don't remember which boy started it, but in a short time they were asking for the English equivalents of some of the most common Spanish terms. "*¿Cómo se dice, sí?*" was one of the first questions. "How do you say *yes?*"

"Yes," I said. "Yess," they repeated, hissing the s's.

No, of course, was easy, being the same in both languages.

"And *buenos días?*" they asked. "Good morning," I replied. And these sounds they loved. "Gude morning. Gude morning. Gude morning," they said to each other, delighting in the odd syllables. And I was struck by their quickness and by how good their ears were, for they caught the sounds perfectly and pronounced them very well.

And *buenas tardes?* How did one say that? "Good afternoon," I said. And this was difficult. They couldn't manage the explosive "t" right after the "f." After a few stumbles they passed to something they hoped would be simpler: *buenas noches?*

"Good night," I said. And they got their wish. This was easier. "Gude night. Gude night. Gude morning. Gude night," the childish voices piped up.

"*¿Cómo se dice, gracias?*" asked Guadalupe. "Thank you."

"Thang kew," he repeated. "Thang kew, thang kew," the others took up in chorus.

And *por favor?* "Please."

"Pleese, pleese, pleese," said Paco, who seemed especially delighted with this word.

It seemed time for a test. So I asked them how you said *sí* in English.

A puzzled silence ensued and they looked from one to the other. Then Guadalupe gathered his nerve and put the question. Was it "yess?" "*Perfecto,*" I said and patted him on the back, A smile lit his delicate, rather shy, brown face.

"How do you say *gracias?*" Paco knew this—or so he thought. "Pleese," he volunteered with confidence. The others laughed at his confusion when he found he was wrong. So we began again until yes, good morning, good night, please and thank you were fairly well planted in their minds.

"*¿Cómo se dice, bueno?*" asked Hector. Perhaps I should have been more scrupulous about imparting elegant English, but the equivalent I gave them for *good* was *O.K.*

If the scarcely learned "good afternoon" was included, that meant eight phrases the boys had learned in a remarkably short space of time. And I decided it was a long enough list. I spent the rest of the time in review. Paco hugged Guadalupe as I tried to catch them one way or another. Sometimes I would say the word in Spanish and ask for the English translation. At other times I'd say the word in English and test their understanding by asking for the Spanish word. They remembered pretty well. And often they came out with the new phrases just for the delight of saying "O.K.," "thang kew," and "pleese."

The adults sitting around the room seemed to enjoy the lesson as much as the boys did, and I can certainly speak for the delight of the teacher. Always I showed my pleasure when the boys gave right answers, and surreptitiously I reached in my pocket to see if I had enough rewards to go around. Isolating the candies one by one, I counted them by touch. Luck was with me. I had exactly five—one for each pupil. So I produced them with the words: "*Su ganancia para la lección.*"—Your profit for the lesson.

Taking the candies, the boys flew off like a covey of birds. They headed for the patio and as they reached the sheltering darkness where politeness could be thrown aside they were shouting "Gude morning. Gude morning. O.K. Thang kew." The pronunciation was far better than that of many Mexican adults. Hector's father, the bearded man, congratulated me on my *discípulos,* and Refugio said I was a good teacher. I made learning enjoyable.

The second sitting broke up; we reassembled at our old seats and soon the orchestra was playing again. The piece was a mournful one, with an important part for El Presidente. As he lifted his fingers from the valves of his cornet, I noticed only one valve was capped. The two absent caps, though, did not bother Don Venustiano and he made the most of his solo opportunities.

"I think this is a sad piece," I said, to make conversation. *"Agonía,"* said the blind guitarist, who had overheard my remark. The others all laughed at the quickness of his wit. The song was about dying.

In the lively pasodoble that followed, the drummer was the man in his element. As well as working the big drum's thumper with his foot, he used his sticks on a snare drum, on the wooden side of the big drum and on a hanging, horizontal cymbal. One of his whacks on the cymbal was so exuberant that the brass disk danced right off its hook. He did not falter in his rhythm, however, and I was amused to see what happened. El Síndico, without any loss of dignity, leaned forward, retrieved the cymbal from the floor and carefully rehung it. And the drummer began hitting it again—all without the loss of a beat.

I greeted the next piece like an old friend. It was *Over the Waves,* or, as the Mexicans call it, *Sobre las Olas.* The lesson-game with the children had melted much of my feeling of being strange and as I listened to the familiar waltz and looked around at the good people lining the walls I was full of contentment and gratitude. Some almost forgotten lines from a prayer by Rabindranath Tagore came into my head. And I said the first verse to myself: "Thou hast made me known to friends whom I knew not. Thou hast given me seats in homes not my own. Thou hast brought the distant near and made a brother of the stranger."

Not remembering the exact words of the second verse, I could not recite them verbatim, but their meaning was very much part of my consciousness: "I am uneasy at heart when I have to leave my accustomed shelter; I forget that there abides the old in the new, and that there also thou abidest."

As it turned out, *Over the Waves* was the penultimate piece, for, when it was over, El Presidente rose and said there would be only one more number. But before that final piece, he said, he would like to add his words of praise and thanks to the host. This was speech No. 3.

After the last piece came speech No. 4. It was delivered by Hector's father, the man with the beard. As he was finishing, the relatives grew poised to leave and one man went for the stack of sombreros. But El Síndico couldn't resist the opportunity to make just one more little peroration. He was on his feet before the breakup had a chance to gather momentum. So

WEEK IN YANHUITLÁN

we all relaxed back in our seats for a while longer. Again there were fine rolling periods and a wealth of lofty sentiment, and again he went on a shade too long. But when he finished at 11:15 the party was definitely over.

Many of the small girls were already asleep. The relatives drifted away, and one by one the serenaders diminished the towering stack of sombreros. When each man had claimed his hat, we lined up to give Don Miguel a farewell hug.

Refugio and José, the two who had called for me, also saw me home. I asked them in and showed them the drawings. Refugio was especially impressed and he repeated several times how deeply, how very deeply, he appreciated my interest in their town.

As they left, I shook hands with Refugio. But José and I exchanged salutes.

XVII
EXPLORE WITH PLANS

When I told of discovering the passageway to the patio, I mentioned the large empty room behind mine. The next morning there was evidence this room was about to play a larger role in the visit. The first indication came when Don Gabriel brought over José Ortiz, the intelligent, broad-cheeked teacher. Don Gabriel apologized for the intrusion, but he explained the teacher was thinking of renting the room. After José had decided it would be suitable for his family, a plump, jolly man was brought in to clean the ceiling. That ceiling was similar to the one in my room, for its roofing, too, was supported by beams and closely packed sticks. The cleaner tied a feather duster to the end of a long bamboo pole and began whisking the sticks. As the man was dusting, Don Gabriel fixed a loop of twine on my side of the interconnecting door and caught the loop over a nail, which he drove into the wall. With this device, he explained, I could still get through the room by unlatching the twine, but persons on the other side could not get into my room.

The renting arrangements meant breakfast was delayed. I put in time by writing some notes at my little table. It was so quiet and peaceful that almost any untoward sound was startling, and the first sound that hit me as a surprise was one of the small monastery bells. Clank, clank, clank it went, as someone rang it in a fast unrhythmic manner. The priest, I assumed was about to say Mass, and it sounded as if he wanted to hurry the villagers. It was already 8:30. The way the bell was being rung suggested a note of exasperation with a flock so hard to summon.

The next startling thing was a small apparition wearing a bright pink false face surmounted by brown curls. It poked its head around a corner of my door and shouted "Boo!" Remembering my childhood delight on Halloweens when adults had led me to believe my masks had filled them with terror, I let out a sharp cry of fright and beat a hasty retreat to a place of safety near the counter. A moment later the owner of the mask poked his real face around the door to see the havoc he had wreaked. As I had guessed, it was Paco. A smile filled his whole brown face when he saw me cowering in the corner.

Knowing a candy would not be unwelcome, I took the opportunity to see how well the boy had remembered his English lesson. Under the circumstances, the obvious test word was "please." So half holding out the *dulce* I asked if he could tell me the English equivalent for what one generally said in asking for something. He gave me a confident smile that had just a trace of relief that I had asked him something he could answer correctly. And out it came, ever so brightly: "Good morning." I had to disillusion him. Then I gave him the candy, but as he took it I asked in Spanish, "How do you say thank you?" This time he had to think, but again there was a smile when his memory brought the answer. "Good night," he said.

As he scampered off, I realized I had congratulated myself too soon on my prowess as a teacher. The boys had remembered the phrases but they hadn't connected them in their minds with the right Spanish equivalents.

Bertaldo, one of Paco's brothers, passed a few minutes later. He was only about twelve, but he illustrated the way older brothers have to work while younger ones are still free to play. He was coming from the direction of the plaza and he was laden with two tins of water that he was carrying home to the family. I took a candy out to him too.

As I came in to breakfast, Lupe's first piece of news was that Don Gabriel had been called during the night. A woman was sick, and at 3:30 they had come for Don Gabriel to give her an injection. Lupe, I could tell, was proud of the Angel of Mercy to whom she was married. But as one who had worked almost five years in a drugstore, Don Gabriel made light of giving a hypodermic to ease pain. The village had neither a doctor nor a nurse, he said, so he was often called to give *inyecciones*.

Breakfast proved worth waiting for. It was enormous. First there was hot chocolate with sweet bread. Then steak with fried potatoes, and, as if this were not enough, Lupe produced two more chunks of lamb in that superb dark red sauce she had served the day I drew the cloister. Again I was struck by its ambrosial flavor and this time I asked which herb was chiefly responsible. It was *cilantro,* or coriander.

I wanted to give Lupe a particularly glowing compliment on the sauce, but when I began to frame it I found myself temporarily frustrated. I did not know the Spanish word for masterpiece. But after a moment's thought I saw how I could convey the idea. This sauce of hers, I said, stood in the same relation to the other things she cooked as my drawing of the church's altar did to the lesser drawings. She caught my meaning right away, but Don Gabriel was puzzled. She interpreted it to him by saying, "He says my sauce is my high altar."

Then Don Gabriel asked what I planned to draw. "Nothing," I replied. "I'm going to take the morning off." After this burst of independence I added, "I want to explore the monastery with the aid of the Institute's plans. Will you come with me?"

Although Don Gabriel had been guarding the monastery for three years, until I arrived with the tracings provided by the Institute he had never seen a plan of the establishment. Thus he had never explored it plan in hand. He liked the idea.

As he ate his breakfast, I watched the passing parade. It contained more animals than usual. Two yoked oxen, one black and one tan, were driven by a sandaled boy with a battered old sombrero. There was a brown calf, but this animal was not being led. Instead, it docilely followed another boy who came from the plaza with two yoked tins of water. A burro passed, laden with two big sacks. The donkey was being switched on by a man whose slate blue shirt hung loose over his white cotton pants.

The parade reflected clearly that this was the first day of school. Youngsters, who had played freely during the last week, were headed for their classes. Two brothers, clad in identical blue overalls, went by, taking their ball with them. Then came Angelita, accompanied by a boy and another little girl who was probably her sister. All three carried schoolbooks. I gave them candies to ease the pain of returning to the scholastic grind.

At 9:10 the monastery bell began ringing again. Another Mass, no doubt, and I wondered what had given the easygoing padre such a spurt of energy.

I slid the plans of the monastery out of the green tube and was ready to start when Don Gabriel finished his breakfast. The open chapel was the first thing I wanted to inspect. And this being our goal, we had to skirt the long ruined wing projecting to the south.

With no drawing to do, I felt like a boy let out of school and I was keenly aware of enjoying my stay in Yanhuitlán. Don Gabriel also seemed lighthearted, and it dawned on me that perhaps he might be enjoying the visit too. Till then I had thought of his feelings as being merely those of a man doing his best to carry out the Institute's instructions of making my visit "the most profitable possible." Should I ask him if he was happy? The fear of embarrassing him if the answer was "no," gave me pause, but I blurted out my question anyway. His unexpected answer came with such conviction. *"Más que feliz,"* he said, and he repeated the phrase, "more than happy," to show how much he meant it.

Suddenly I saw how lonely he had been in his devotion to the monastery. No one had cared about it the way he did, and his job as its caretaker had been isolating. In coming I had brought enthusiasm, curiosity and that source of the most abiding companionship—community of interest. The surprising realization that I had been able to contribute something to his life deepened my sense of friendship; for I was keenly conscious of all he had done for me, and somehow people grow closest when they understand fully how mutually agreeable is the interchange of riches each brings the other.

When we reached the open chapel we found the first floor plan had been rolled in the tube so long that it would not stay flat. Being on tracing paper it tended to be floppy, and it was too large to be held in one hand. Before we could utilize it comfortably, we had to put it on the ground and pin down its corners with four little stones.

During the morning I was to discover that many more doors and windows of the monastery had been blocked up than I realized. And at the open chapel we were confronted with one of the major efforts to prevent the entrance of vandals.

The doorway leading from the chapel into the monastery is one of the chief entrances to be sealed up. It is marked A on the section of the ground plan shown. In the previously free space between the jambs, I have placed an X, the symbol I have used throughout to indicate the passageways and windows that have been shut up with latter-day masonry.

To imagine the open chapel, provide a flat roof over the projecting side walls, and, having created this imaginary porch think of it as resembling a deep stage. I say this because the open front of the porch, with its basket-handle arch, resembles a proscenium. Standing in front of it, as Don Gabriel and I were doing, it was almost impossible not to think: If only that blocked door at the back could be opened to allow the actors to get back and forth from their dressing rooms, it would be a perfect place for ama-

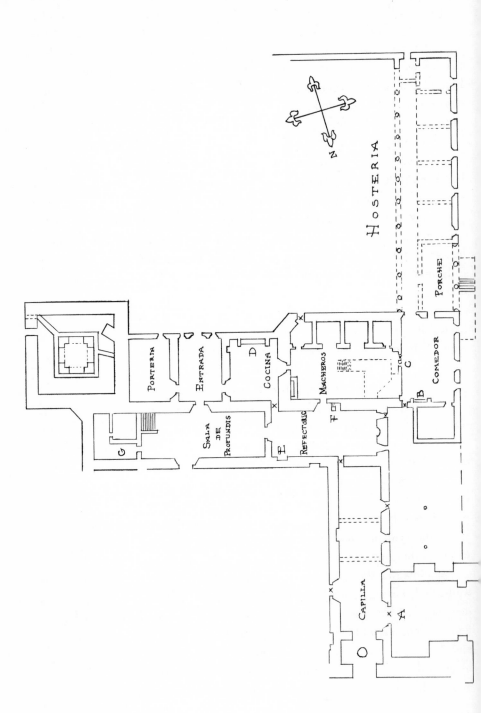

242

teur theatricals! And this thought was intensified by the ease with which a curtain could be rigged across the opening, and by the realization that the audience could either sit or stand on this grassy area outside.

As this passed through my mind, I had the first experience of a type of enlightenment that was to come to me several times during the morning. To explain, I must make a confession. This was the first time I had ever explored a building with its plan available whenever I wanted to refer to it. What the plan did for me was this: it made it possible for me to bring two separated mental pictures together by enabling me to join to what was before my eyes the remembered image of something I could not see.

To be specific about this first instance, the plan made it possible for me to visualize simultaneously both sides of the blocked door. It did this because that word "*capilla*" and the long narrow chamber outlined on the plan were enough to enable me to conjure up the interior in my mind. And with the mental picture of the chapel came the vision of the baptismal font, whose position I have indicated by the circle.

The unseen baptismal font, then, was in a place where in former days it could be reached readily from the open chapel. This realization was the starting point of many others. Together with the memories they touched off, they crowded to my mind so swiftly they tumbled over each other.

One memory was of a mass baptism in the Cathedral in Mexico City. Hundreds of parents had assembled in the huge church. Holding their infants in their arms, they stood in line to pass in front of three priests. The three worked with the efficiency of a well co-ordinated team and the baptized babies had come from their hands like finished products from an assembly line.

At the same time as that scene sprang to my mind's eye—and to my mind's ear, for many of the babies had been crying—I remembered Motolinía's account of how he and other Franciscan friars had conducted mass baptisms of Indians in the early days of the sixteenth century. A single friar often baptized as many as two thousand Indians in a day, and in one case a team of four friars polished off sixty thousand baptisms in five days.

Thanks to that scrap of history and the contemporary scene in the Cathedral, I was suddenly able to imagine a vast assemblage of patient Indians standing outside the open chapel, some waiting to be baptized themselves, others bringing their children. And I could almost see the line moving slowly through that blocked door to the team of Dominican friars inside at the font.

Recalling the little football player and the other heads the ancient Mixtecs wore as amulets, my imagination embellished the scene with a fresh touch. How many of those Indians, I wondered, were playing it safe? As they moved in to get the magical protection of the new religion, were some making doubly sure of their luck by having *idolitos* concealed on their person?

With this vision of the half-pagan converts queued up for baptism came the recollection of perhaps the most penetrating of Kubler's many insights into sixteenth-century Mexico: his singling out of the truly revolutionary element in the Indians' conversion to Catholicism. It was not the introduction of crosses, religious statues and incense. The pre-Conquest religions had all three. It was not the introduction of a series of holy days rigidly fixed by the calendar. The Indians had that too. It was not the imposition of a forceful and authoritarian priesthood on the people. That was standard in the pre-Conquest religion. It was—and this is a point I have seen no other writer make—the shifting of worship from outdoors to indoors.

This was the really enormous change brought about in the religious lives of the Indians. Before the coming of the Spaniards, the only Indians who ever entered the small temples on top of the high pyramids were the priests. The congregations performed their religious exercises in the vast open courts in front of those pyramids.

This chapel that I was looking at then—this deep porch that suggested amateur theatricals—represented a transitional point in the great turnover from worship under the open sky to worship within the confines of a temple. Perhaps the chapel was built before the church. Perhaps the friars had it built as soon as their own living quarters were finished. The probable sequence was that they used it to house their altar in the days before they had an auditorium large enough to house the congregation too. With such a porch they had a covered sanctuary in which they could carry on the most sacred part of the service, and hundreds of Indians could attend because there was space enough for them on the wide lawn in front. And it was likely that the use of the chapel declined once the church was completed.

How this speculation seemed to alter the aspect of the chapel! Earlier in my visit I had written it off as having little aesthetic appeal, and thereafter I had scarcely bothered to look at it. But now it seemed one of the most interesting parts of the monastery. I was more than ready to accept Don Gabriel's suggestion that we go in for a closer inspection. He said he especially wanted me to see the inscription over the door.

Almost hidden in the shadows of the deep chapel and cheapened by

pink and blue paint, the doorway had failed to engage my interest. I had dismissed it as a sort of outsize mantelpiece, but when I was standing within a few feet of it I realized how wrong I was. It lacked heavy accents to make it look dramatic from a distance, but its detail was remarkably fine. I especially liked the way the designer, when he neared the floor level, had swelled out the chief ridge of the molding into little bases to balance the bases of the colonnettes on the sides. And then there were all the flowers! Not only were there roses growing wild, as in the alcoves and bosses of the cloister, but a number of bouquets were heaped in graceful vases.

Even adding that archway leading to the choir, then, I had not exhausted the monastery's notable doorways. This door of the vases needed to be added as No. 7. And I had a fresh sense of the wealth of the catalog when I thought how different this door was from any of the others. It was not like the shell or the classical doorway, nor was it like Santa Catalina's portal; and, even though it shared a flat top with the doorway of the diamonds, it was different in every other way.

EXPLORE WITH PLANS

The inscription was on a broken stone scroll above a fine coat of arms. I could not decipher the Latin, but I copied the printing and I have since found that it read *Nos autem praedicamus Christum crucifixum*. It means "But we preach Christ crucified" and is taken from the twenty-third verse of the first chapter of First Corinthians. It is a fitting inscription for a Dominican house, since the order is one of preachers. A present-day Dominican identified the text for me.

As we left the open chapel, I noticed the masonry to the right of its proscenium arch projected in an irregular fashion, almost as if it had once been connected to another wall that had been clumsily shorn away. Could there have been a further building here? I asked Don Gabriel. He nodded. Then he told me a significant fact. The monastery had been a novitiate in colonial days. It was his belief that some building used by the novices studying for the order had been adjoined to the foundation at this particular point. It might have been the dormitory.

As I knocked away the stones and gathered up the plan, Don Gabriel pointed to a pit sunk in the ground in front of the platform. Although it was overgrown with weeds, one could see it was rectangular and its walls were of stone. It suggested a dried reservoir or perhaps the cellar of a wooden farmhouse that had burned down long ago. Did I know what it was? No. *"Una alberca."*

"A swimming pool?" I repeated, hardly believing what I had heard. "Yes," affirmed Don Gabriel, a swimming pool for the novices. And I had a nice vision of the neophytes splashing happily about, forgetting for the time being their books, their theological examinations and such matters as mortification and penance. At such moments the monastery must have seemed almost like a country club.

From this point on there will be many references to the plan on page 242. What I would like to call attention to first are the two small circles between the open chapel and the ruined wing to the south. These represent holes in the flat roof over two stone chambers which are submerged so deeply that only the tops of their windows appear at ground level. I was not to understand fully the significance of the chambers till the afternoon, but they were cisterns. By crouching it was possible to get through the windows and Don Gabriel took me into the first of the chambers, holding my arm, lest I step in too far and fall into the black waters of the subterranean tank below. The footing was precarious and the vaulted cistern, in its gloomy darkness, sent a chill through me. I wanted to get back into the sunlight. But

Don Gabriel insisted that I look at a clay duct coming down through the wall. The duct, he said, was the terminal point of a system of drains leading from the roofs of the monastery. That stepped up my interest. I had read of other monasteries whose roofs were constructed to serve as catch basins for rain water, and I realized these cisterns were tanks to store water ingeniously captured from the skies.

One reason I was exploring without sketching was because I wanted to see what drawing still needed to be done. As we moved toward the ruined wing, the ground sloped down so that by the time we were abreast of the spot where we had come with Alfonso to watch the sunset we were a whole story below it. I looked up at the gap. With the broken stumps of its lost pillars, it was a pitiful, rather than a beautiful, sight, but I resolved to make a record of it a day or two later. I kept that resolution and the result is shown below.

The plan, once it was unfurled and anchored again, proved exceptionally helpful here. The parallel lines projecting from the wall indicated a stairway. With this clue I looked at the now almost formless little pyramid on the right. It ceased to be puzzling. Surely it represented the start of the steps. Don Gabriel confirmed my supposition. Then he swept his hand in a rising curve to indicate that the steps had been carried up over an arch to the massive chunk of masonry on the left. That explained the mysterious chunk, and why it curved out so curiously at the top. The fallen arch was not hard to re-create in the mind's eye and for a moment I had a vision of what the impressive stairway must have been like. But it was quickly dispelled by a reminder of reality that dashed diagonally across the base of the ruined steps. It was that symbolic haunter of decayed palaces—a lizard.

Consulting the plan again, I spotted something that brought just as much illumination as the indication of a stairway. It was the word *porche.* The triple archway above, then, was built not merely to provide a picture-frame opening in the wall, as I had thought, but to serve as the entrance of the inn's front porch. Naturally, a porch that high would have required steps to reach it.

The drawing shows two doorways at ground level and each is attended by a window to the left. To gain an idea of the rest of the first floor of the ruined wing, imagine a sequence of five more such doorways, each with its attendant window in the same relative position—that is, above and a little to the left. Don Gabriel showed me how each of the seven doorways led into a vaulted stone chamber. These, he said, were used to store grain. They were spacious and made of finely finished stone; and because they were not submerged they were not dank or gloomy. That even the granaries should be so beautifully constructed was still another evidence of the lavishness of the monastery.

Because the old stairs were in ruins, we could not get to the inn the way colonial travelers did. We had to walk to the last of the storehouses, round the wing and proceed along the outside of the southern wall. On this side the path sloped upward so we were at the level of the inn by the time we reached the end of the wall. This wall, it will be remembered, ended across from the *entrada,* for it was at the wall's end that the priest, thwarted of keeping his car in the monastery, had built his crude garage.

The whole *hostería,* or inn-wing, is now roofless. The walls indicated by lines of hyphens are gone too. Thus, the only rooms with walls left are the *comedor* and the little room behind it. The *comedor* was the inn's dining room and as I entered I was struck by how the three windows in its outer wall framed the western hills.

The enclosure's most conspicuous object was against the northern wall. It was the fireplace, indicated as *B* on the plan. The chimney breast and the mantelpiece are still there. The cut stone mantel, with its handsome side consoles, suggests both the nature of the friars' hospitality and the caliber of their guests. With such a fireplace, the *hostería* could not have been a common inn. It must have been a luxurious resting place for important personages on their way to Oaxaca or Guatemala.

The stone of the dining room was white, with just enough green in it to suggest pea soup heavily diluted with milk. Seizing on the unaccustomed color, I called Don Gabriel's attention to what I thought was a revelation: that this part of the inn was built with a different type of stone.

"No," he said, "it's the same stone." He took me to the outer wall and showed how this stone, which seemed so white on its inner side, was pink on its exposed outer one facing the road. And light dawned. Obviously, the dining room had not always been roofless, and it was because a beamed ceiling had sheltered its inner stones from the elements that they were so whitish. The green white, then, was the original color of the monastery's stone. Conversely, it was weathering that accounted for what I had always thought had been the stone's natural distinction—its lovely sand pink.

My thought was that the porous stone was a kind of sandstone. But a geologist, to whom I sent a sample, has since assured me it is the rock composed of stream-deposited volcanic debris that is known as tuff. And because it contains calcium carbonate, it is calcareous tuff.

One intriguing feature of the dining room was especially puzzling. It was a little window with an ogee arch that was next to the blocked door leading into the *macheros* or stable. I appealed to Don Gabriel for help. He did not know what it was either, so we unrolled the plan and tried to figure it out together. The window is marked *G*, and I found a clue in the fact that the room beyond the stable was the *cocina* or kitchen. Perhaps, I suggested, this opening was a serving aperture. And I acted out how the lay brothers might have brought the food from the kitchen and set it on the little shelf in the tiny arched window for the servants in the dining room to pick up and serve to the guests at the table. Don Gabriel liked the explanation and he recalled the confessionals. If my hunch was right, this was another ingenious arrangement whereby friars and laymen could communicate, without one leaving the monastery or the other entering it.

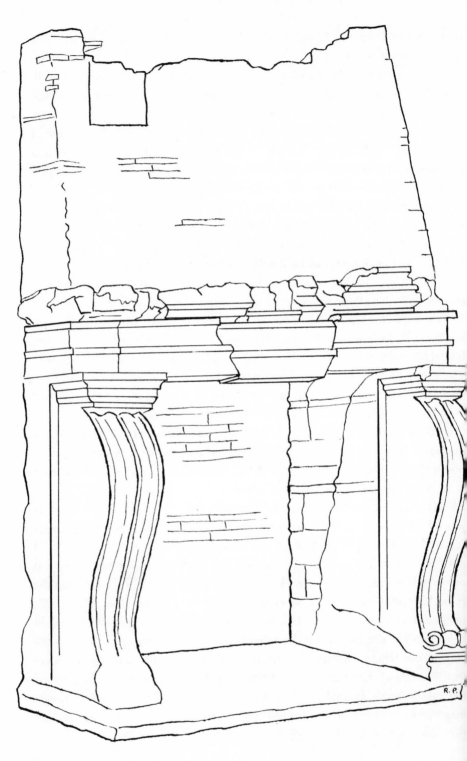

With the porch and the dining room of the inn, the remaining elements were sufficiently substantial for one to visualize their original appearance. But with the sleeping quarters this was not so. Of this wing, only the long west wall and part of the southern corner were standing. And even though the stone flooring remained, it was difficult to tell where the room partitions had been. We unrolled the plan once more to see if it could provide the additional information to make a fragmentary appearance intelligible.

The plan showed there had been a row of five rooms of nearly equal size. Looking at the now incongruous freestanding wall, we saw this division was confirmed by the presence of five windows. The first three rooms did not interconnect; but the last two did. What is more, the coupled chambers had a little anteroom. I went to this apartment at the corner to see if I could find traces of the wall to confirm the plan. I did. And walking from one room to another I decided the rooms must have been a suite for family groups. Don Gabriel agreed it was likely. The three single rooms, we decided, were for solitary travelers.

It did not take us long to figure out the long narrow strip in front of the rooms. Those two circles between the hyphenated lines at the porch entrance, we knew, indicated pillars. The similar circles along the front of the rooms obviously indicated pillars too. A row of ten pillars so close together could only mean an arcade. That strip, then, had been a corridor with one side an open colonnade. I walked along to see if it was still possible to make out where the pillars had been. It was. The shafts have vanished, but with a little imagination and weed clearing one could distinguish each base from the slight swellings inset in the pavement. These remains, too, suggested the colonnade was of stone rather than of wood. Was it arched or flat topped? At the northern end, imbedded in the wall, I saw the springer of a stone arch. And I fancied the eleven arches of this arcade must have matched the three that had stood in the ruined gap which had been the inn's main entrance.

Walking down the corridor to see if I could account for each pillar, and conjuring them up as resembling those of the porch, stimulated my visualizing faculties. The stimulus, in fact, was so great that the arcade seemed to rise before me, and as it rose I saw the red, eroded hills to the east from under that sequence of beautiful frames.

In a flash I realized this colonnade was planned to frame the sky colors at sunrise as the triple archway of the porch had been planned to frame the sky colors at sunset. Knowing how Spanish travelers rose at daybreak for a journey, I suddenly seemed to see a young Spaniard waiting in that corridor as his servant prepared his horse, and I knew he was thinking how lovely were those pale colors of dawn, showing over the crests of those hills under the arches of the colonnade. And those eastern hills were the hills behind which the moon had risen the night I had watched it dispel the engulfing darkness! Suddenly the scene in my mind changed. I heard the sound of a guitar and I knew my traveler was relaxing in the evening and marveling at how beautiful was the zebra moonlight, making alternating black and silver bands as it shone through those arches into the loggia. And as the vision faded I gave a huge sigh of regret—that such an inn should now be nothing but a ruined wall, a stretch of weed-grown pavement and the scarcely discernible stumps of ten vanished columns.

IT WAS NOT POSSIBLE to enter the stable from outside, since both the door by the serving pantry and the door at the corner near the kitchen were blocked. Thus Don Gabriel and I had to go first to the *entrada*. From there we were able to get into the kitchen. Here the only barrier was a padlocked wooden door and Don Gabriel had the key. The *cocina*, like the *portería*, was being used as a storehouse for old monastery stones. They were piled high over most of its floor and the place was dark because its two windows were filled in.

From the hint provided by the two lugs with the line between them in the dining room, it is easy to puzzle out the nature of the larger but similar formation marked *D*, which projects from the south wall of the kitchen. It was a fireplace and its inner walls were still blackened with the soot from the fires that had cooked who knows how many meals in past centuries. It was so wide it occupied nearly the whole wall. Its mantel, too, was unusually high, and the front stones of its shallow chimney mounted to the ceiling like the stepped pyramid of an outdoor fireplace. When I told Don Gabriel that Americans built barbecue hearths with just such stepped chimneys, he laughed and said the projecting stones were not intentional. They had been pressed forward by the movement of earthquakes.

The location of the kitchen on the plan shows how it was designed to be doubly useful. Besides its capacity of serving the travelers in the inn—it could serve even more readily the friars who ate in the refectory.

We passed through into the stable. It was like coming outdoors again, for most of the area was roofless. Had the roof fallen in? I asked. No, said Don Gabriel. It was a courtyard meant to be open to the sky. But protection was provided for the horses and the burros, he explained, for the three well-

WEEK IN YANHUITLÁN

roofed stone rooms on our left were the stalls for the animals. "And that's the drinking trough?" I asked pointing to a stone tank in one corner. He nodded.

I went under the archway leading into the vestibule through which the *macheros* must have brought in their animals. Knocking through the blocked entrance in fancy, I could easily imagine grooms and muleteers leading in their animals.

Returning to the courtyard I looked at the rough open stairway indicated in the plan. It has no railing, but its eroded treads and risers still are usable and it mounts up over an arch and turns to the right where a second flight takes it to the upper floor. It suggested a Gordon Craig setting for a Shakespearean tragedy. Somehow its existence surprised me. But I should not have found it unexpected. After all, that monumental stairway with the stone fleur-de-lis was obviously too grand for servants carrying slops. Even a monastery has to have its back stairs.

We went into the refectory by climbing over the stones partially blocking the doorway. Again I was impressed by the spaciousness of the long, barrel-vaulted hall. Even a pile of building lime in one corner could not take away its essential dignity. The lime and the absence of all furniture, though, did underline how unused the hall was. The effect of whitewashed bareness, too, was emphasized by the emptiness of the pedimented niche at the far end of the room.

The niche was something I had glanced at in the past, but being in an appraising mood I looked at it this time with an assessing eye. As I studied its Renaissance details, and as I realized the nice composition it made with the two deeply splayed windows, I saw the niche was far finer than I had given it credit for being. I came to understand, too, why it was that I had underestimated it before. It was because the window on the left was blocked up.

With one blind window, the balance of the ensemble was difficult to discern. Even worse, the light was curtailed, increasing the gloom and making the niche hard to see. Imagining the refectory as it might have been with light streaming in from both windows made me recollect all the other blocked doors and windows of the establishment. With a rush, I realized the great rooms of the monastery, which now seem musty and almost cellar-like, were once far airier and better lighted. With no doorways or windows walled up, the place must have been far more sunlit and cheerful than it is in its state of decay.

In the wall near the main entrance was an arched niche that I have marked *E*. A friar would pass it on his right on entering and Don Gabriel said it formerly held the basins in which the Dominicans washed their hands before sitting down to eat.

Beside the doorway from the stable the plan shows a puzzling little projection (*F*). I had hardly noticed it until Don Gabriel climbed the few stairs cut in the wall and took his seat behind a sort of ruined stalagmite that previously must have been a stone lectern. I noticed it was ingeniously lighted by a small window behind it. Don Gabriel held up the palms of his hands as if they were they pages of a big book and then he moved his eyes from left to right, back and forth, as if he were reading. In monastic life talking was discouraged and the campaign for silence was carried so far that one of the greatest of pleasures—conversation at meals—was forbidden. Not content with imposing muteness, the rules of most orders made doubly sure that minds should be kept on heavenly things by obliging the friars to listen to reading of sacred writings as they ate.

Suddenly, in my imagination the deserted refectory was filled with friars eating silently at bare tables, while an old Father droned dully at the lectern. And this vision was even sharper than the one of the friars chanting

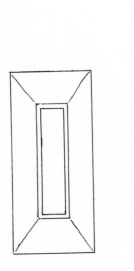

in the choir, for this time I was one of the friars myself. I was a rather cynical young scholar, fresh from Spain; I was thinking what a bumbling old ignoramus Father So-and-So was, reading such outdated theology.

The vision was so intense, in fact, that I'll swear I heard a ghostly burro hee-haw in the deserted stable just behind the reader. What a critic! I exclaimed to myself, feeling the donkey had provided the most appropriate comment.

The vision was so real, I could not help conjuring it up for Don Gabriel too. It sprang to his mind just as vividly—as I could tell by the way his face lit up. But in his imagination he was a jaded friar of a still more rebellious and scornful nature. *"Los dos burros,"* was his comment. It revealed that in his mental picture the burro and the old friar were both jackasses.

We laughed heartily at our responses, and the fact that we both had imagined the scene with equal vividness gave us a happy feeling. We knew that we were enjoying the exploration in the same way. We also knew we had another joke to treasure and take home to Lupe.

We had often passed through the Sala de Profundis, but this time we looked around more carefully. The refectory had accustomed my eyes to dim light and because of this they were caught as they never had been before by the doorway between the two rooms. Once more I saw I had to revise my estimate of the doorways upward. This was an eighth notable one. It was square-topped, like the doorway of the diamonds and the newly acquired doorway leading into the baptistery; but, with its concave niche and its rich molding that projected like ruffles on the sides, it differed as much from them as they differed from each other.

With the Sala de Profundis, the plan helped again. It made me aware how well the hall was related to its neighboring parts. The plan, for instance, showed how this vaulted hall united with the *entrada* to form a symmetrical T. On the opposite side the cloister provided a source of light and a glimpse of green. And because of the width of the refectory doorway, there was a magnificent sweep of space from the monumental stairway to the empty niche at the end of the dining room. Even bare and whitewashed, the Sala de Profundis was still a remarkably handsome hall.

I knew why it had its name. Dominican friars customarily pause for prayers before they go in to eat, and before each meal they pray for the souls of members of the order who have died. The text they use is the *De Profundis* psalm, the one that begins "Out of the Depths I cry to Thee." This scrap of knowledge, returning to me just as I came from the refectory,

enabled my imagination to do some more conjuring. I could see the friars
in their white robes coming down the grand stairway, two by two, in orderly
procession. Then I could imagine the way they paused to pray, and how at
the end of the psalm for the departed brothers they intoned: "Eternal rest
give to them, O Lord, and let perpetual light shine upon them." Finally, the
prayer for the dead finished, I could see how the light of the refectory shone
on the living friars as they filed in, washed their hands on the right and then
took their places at the tables against the walls.

Looking about, though, I could not reconcile myself to the fact that so
noble a hall had been used only for a prayer or two before meals. Didn't it

have some other purpose? I asked Don Gabriel. His answer summoned up another vision. "It was used," he said, "for the laying out of the dead."

Suddenly I saw a high, black catafalque in the center of the hall, and on it rested a dead friar, a rosary in his folded hands. Tall candles in high bronze candlesticks stood lighted at each corner of the bier. And I thought of that body lying there as darkness descended and the candles grew brighter in the gloom. I could see friars keeping vigil, the peaked hoods of their black cloaks drawn up over their heads. And as the time for the Requiem neared I could hear the subdued chanting of the unison male voices of the dead man's friends as the monastic community gathered in the hall to carry the body to the church for the last rites.

And the ghostly impression supplemented my knowledge that the Sala de Profundis was the hall in which the dead brethren were remembered before each meal. Now I understood why the friars had chosen that particular place for such remembrance.

UNDER THE GRAND STAIRWAY was a new wooden door. The plan revealed it led into a fairly large room (*G*). Wanting to poke into every nook and cranny, I was curious to see it. But Don Gabriel said we could not get in. The priest used it as a private storeroom and he was the only one with the key. Accordingly, I wrote it off my list, just as I had written off the Sacristy, which the priest also held under personal lock and key.

We explored the cells on the second floor, but their description will come in a later chapter. This leaves the exploration of the *excusado* as the final sequence of the morning's story. The outward aspect of this semi-detached edifice is shown in the sketch on page 53. There it looks like a perfectly simple cube, with two little windows near the top of the second story. Its interior, however, is so complex that I have abstracted the plans of its upper and lower floors and placed them side by side.

And here another indelicate matter arises. Friars, no less than visiting sketchers, must dispose of human waste. *Excusado* is the extremely tactful word Spanish-speaking people use for the toilet. And the one at Yanhuitlán, because of its particular structure, is what we, in our more vulgar speech, would call a privy.

At the heart of each plan is a square. In the plan of the upper floor it is completely outlined; in the plan of the lower floor, for a reason to appear in a moment, the square is indicated chiefly by small dashes. These squares are the same size because they represent the same thing: the free space in a brick

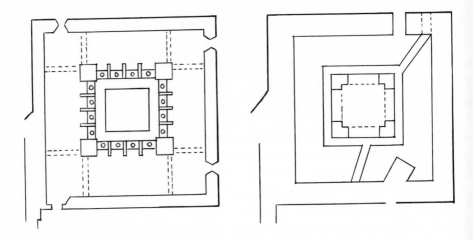

air shaft. That shaft rises from the building's foundations and is open to the sky at the top. As can be seen, its dimensions are so generous it forms a cube within a cube.

We visited the upper floor first, coming upon it when we turned to the left after ascending the grand stairway. Its flat roof was carried on corner arches whose inner haunches were supported by square brick pillars. The windows were arranged to give light to each ambulatory.

Because they are arched at the top, the stalls suggest niches. As the plan shows, there are sixteen of them, four on each side, with each stall backing against the air shaft. The partitions between them extend out so far that front doors are not necessary. Even if every stall were full, not one friar would be able to see another. They would all be looking outward. Presumably in going to their places, the friars would pass the occupied stalls with downcast eyes. As an ex-Army man who got so used to lines of open toilets that he came to enjoy the chummy familiarity that was unavoidable when seated with one's brothers carrying out a function underlining one's common humanity, I felt a pang of regret at what the friars had missed through such ingenious seclusion.

The plan of the lower floor showed an entrance. I told Don Gabriel I would like to go in. He demurred, saying it was not a very nice place. But my zeal for architectural investigation was strong. I said I was willing to face it. More than sixty years had lapsed since any friar had visited the *excusado*, and, as I discovered with Don Gabriel's help, there was an excellent drainage system which had kept the offal from accumulating. The system is indicated by the double-lined frame that seems to have two handles. This frame, which

WEEK IN YANHUITLÁN

runs round the inner cube, is a trench. According to Don Gabriel, water flowed continuously through it, entering from the sluice represented by the lower handle and flushing out through the lane suggested by the upper handle.

The lower part of the air shaft seemed to be supported by table legs rather than by walls. This was because each side was pierced by a Gothic arch as wide as the hyphenated lines show. Since these arches reached high and the shaft was open at the top, plenty of fresh air was let in. The place, in consequence, was as excellently ventilated as it was drained.

Never before had I been in a privy from below looking up. It was a unique experience, and as I saw four round holes high above I had another vision. It was quite the most irreverent I'd had, for truth obliges me to reveal that I saw the exposed bum of a good friar. And something impish from my boyhood burst out of me. I envisaged the pink hams suddenly leaping up with a sharp cry at the shock of a toy arrow let fly in their direction. Again the vision was so real I could not resist passing it on to Don Gabriel. Again he saw it instantaneously and he laughed till the tears came to his eyes. "*Una flecha,*" he kept repeating, using the Spanish word for arrow.

It was almost lunch time when we emerged from the *excusado*. The plans had helped Don Gabriel as much as they had me. We had learned a lot about a place we had both come to love. And as we made our way down the slope we were chuckling still.

"*Una flecha, una flecha,*" Don Gabriel kept repeating. I knew he was polishing the anecdote so he could pass it on to Lupe with the maximum of comic effect.

XVIII
THE WALK TO THE MANANTIAL

As WE ENTERED the Blanco home, we heard guitar-accompanied singing coming from the Gómez house. Don Miguel's saint's day, it seems, was still being celebrated.

Lunch's first course was a plate of rice, and when Don Gabriel saw I was comfortably seated he asked to be excused. It was time to give another injection to the woman he had attended during the night.

Green beans and squash followed the rice, and Lupe told me the broth was *caldo*. There were tortillas for all these courses, and then came the omnipresent frijoles. As I was drinking my coffee, Don Gabriel returned. "The baby died," he said.

So the woman's sickness was pregnancy. She was someone I had never met, but I felt sad for her loss. Don Gabriel said she was about twenty-eight and this was her second child. It was a boy and he could only have lived about five hours, for when he got there the baby had been dead some time.

A little knock sounded on the door of the outer storeroom. It was Nahum, the fourteen-year-old brother of Alberto, the water carrier. The Blancos invited him in and Don Gabriel introduced him as another of his nephews. I explained I knew him already because of the dance.

Since I was about to retire to my room, Don Gabriel asked my plans for the afternoon. "I'm not sure," I replied.

"Would you like to walk to the *manantial?*" he asked.

The *manantial*—that was the spring in the mountains that provided the village's drinking water. In all my thoughts of returning to Yanhuitlán I had wanted to visit that pure source. But on my second morning I had regretfully crossed it off my list. For then, not knowing I was going to extend my stay,

Don Gabriel's information that it was four miles away had made me calculate that it would take more time than I could give it.

And here I was presented with the chance of seeing it! It was a thread from the first stopover that I might be able to pick up after all. Why not, I asked myself, make the day a whole holiday?

The happy thought tipped the scales. The walk was decided upon, and Nahum eagerly accepted our invitation to come along. But since Don Gabriel had to eat first, Nahum and I went to my room to wait.

Almost immediately the boy produced a small apple from one of his pockets. He gave it to me. Then, when I asked if he minded if I shaved, he insisted on holding the mirror as I went about the operation. It complicated the process a bit, for I had to direct him how to move the glass when I wanted better light to see different areas of my chin. But the companionship was pleasant and I learned more about him. I found he was the member of the family singled out for education. He was studying to be a chemical engineer and he was attending the Army College in Oaxaca, where he lived as a boarder. He was home now because of the Independence Day holidays, but on Thursday he would be going back to Oaxaca.

As I was drying my razor, he produced a second object from his pocket —a small round mirror. I could have it as a gift, if I would like it. A little time passed and he produced gift No. 3, another apple. The generosity puzzled me. I think it was partly because he did not quite know how to carry on a conversation with a stranger. I lit on a display of the drawings to put him more at ease. It was what he wanted, though he had been too reticent to ask to see them. As we were going through them, an emissary came from Don Miguel with an invitation to come over and have a drink. Wanting to see as much of the saint's day celebration as possible, I gladly accepted.

We were not ushered into the long room of the night before, but to the room at the corner where I had gone to give the children their candies. The man playing the guitar was the old shepherd who had sold me the stone head in the church. And I recognized the three other men sitting in a circle around Don Miguel. One was the jolly man who had dusted the back room for the schoolteacher. The second was the egg-shaped burgher with the gray moustache who had mistaken my drawing of the north portal for the free-standing arch of the cemetery. The third was Pedro, the large policeman who had been a little maudlin at the dance.

They were all drinking mezcal and I could see they had been at it for quite a long time. Don Miguel's eyes were bloodshot and I got the impression he was wishing his well-wishers would pack up and go home. I think by this time he was a little bored with his saint's day, especially since it meant doling out free drinks over such a long period. These particular hangers-on, I felt, too, were not his close friends. Yet he was too polite to deviate from the custom of offering unlimited hospitality. He saw that Nahum got a bottle of Spur, and this time he was perfectly content to have me drink Spur too. Perhaps he was even grateful that I did not further deplete his dwindling supply of hard liquor.

The well-wishers, though, were oblivious to the feelings fairly apparent in their host's face. They were having too good a time and they were obviously settled in for a whole afternoon's drinking. The old shepherd occasionally raised his voice in song and he strummed away on his guitar without anyone paying much attention to him.

The group was picturesque enough, but I was ready to leave when Don Gabriel came after us.

I expected our excursion would be a rather aimless walk into the hills to see a spring. I was wrong, for, as it turned out, our walk traced the whole course of the town's water supply system. But I did not understand this until later, for Don Gabriel did not tell me his scheme and, from the point of view of easy comprehension, we began at the wrong end. Thus for quite a long time I was guided toward an unknown goal, passing things en route whose interconnectedness I hardly grasped.

I do not want the reader to be similarly puzzled, though, so I will reveal here what only became clear to me at the end of the outward lap of our walk: namely, that the village water is transported all the way from the *manantial* in a conduit that was built in 1950, and that this new conduit follows the same route as the original conduit built by the Spaniards during the colonial era. I might add, too, that the route the Spaniards discovered gave evidence of their skill as hydraulic engineers. Because it hugged the hillsides, it was long and a little circuitous, but it enabled them to bring water to the town almost entirely at ground level. At only three points was it necessary to carry the duct across small ravines.

The sight-seeing began in the plaza. Here, it may be remembered, a grassy shelf projects from the back wall of the platform. This was where the burros had grazed on market day, and the first thing Don Gabriel took me to inspect was the terrace's retaining wall.

I should have known from its rounded cap that it was not merely a confining wall to hold back dirt. But observing other things had kept me

WEEK IN YANHUITLÁN

too busy to speculate about it. Don Gabriel's pointing finger, however, obliged me to look closely. Because most of the cap had caved in, I could see that the upper part of the wall was grooved with a channel to conduct water. Straddling the wall at a point not far from the Palmas' *tienda* was a stone edifice that looked like a dog kennel with a domed roof. The kennel— or perhaps the word "shrine" suggests the appearance better—must formerly have had a dual purpose. It had been a vent for the covered stream running through the wall, and a fountain into which the villagers could dip their jars to draw water.

"Do you see *El Rey?*" Don Gabriel asked. I did not know what he was talking about. Even when he pointed to the right side of the vent I was no better off. But when he mentioned *"escultura Mixteca"* I saw what he meant. There, in relief so low one could easily miss it, was a carving of a Mixtec warrior. He was advancing in profile with his right hand raised, while his left arm carried his shield. The size of his headdress indicated he might indeed have been a king.

The figure amazed and excited me. I knew the Mixtecs excelled in jewelry, pottery and picture writing, but all the sources I'd read, admitting this, had pointed out these were minor arts. The Mixtecs, they said, were gifted only in small decoration. One authority had stated flatly there was not a single known piece of Mixtec architectural sculpture.

Yet here I had stumbled on one. What is more, *El Rey* was two feet tall. My hope was fulfilled: I had found further evidence of the region's pre-Conquest civilization. And the evidence was of a particularly exciting kind. It was not a further example of well known facts. It was proof that the textbooks had to be revised. I felt like a genuine discoverer.

But why, I wondered, had the Spaniards, who wanted to stamp out the old cultures, given this pagan sculpture a place of honor on a fountain the villagers frequented every day? As usual, Don Gabriel had the answer. But it was not what I expected. The bas-relief of the warrior had not been honored in being placed there. It had been used merely as a building stone. And by chipping at its edges he showed that the stone had formerly been covered with stucco. It was only when some of the stucco fell away that the existence of the figure became known.

Later on, said Don Gabriel, along the route of the old conduit we would see several more of these shrinelike vents. Meanwhile, our course lay along Hidalgo in the direction of El Calvario, the gabled chapel at the northern end of the town.

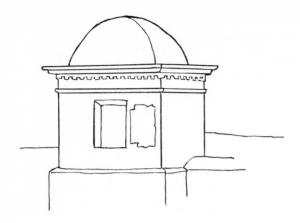

Passing the cross streets, we saw faucets mounted on cement stanchions. Remembering how Alberto had drawn water from a similar faucet the day I sketched the north portal, I realized these corner faucets were the modern equivalent of the colonial fountain-vent. Aesthetically, the colonial solution was the more comely. The stone shrines were handsomer than the cement obelisks. But undoubtedly the faucets, spurting water under pressure, made it easier to fetch the family water.

Since stating that the priest was the only man in town rich enough to have an automobile, Don Gabriel had told me there were four villagers who owned trucks. I had met one of the two men who owned a single truck—Gabriel Sánchez, the gray-haired storekeeper of the Guadalupe calendar who had motioned me to come and sit beside him at *el baile*. I had also met the still more prosperous Felipe Cruz Soriano, who, like Sr. Sánchez, was one of the worthies who walked me home after the dance. Don Felipe had two trucks. The fourth man was even richer. He was Angel Pérez and he had three trucks.

The name Pérez had stuck with me, for it, too, stared at me each day from a calendar on the Blancos' walls. In consequence, my interest perked up when Don Gabriel pointed to large house on the right and said: "This is the house of Angel Pérez." Above the lintel of the main door was a large carving of a couchant lion. The beast was so flat and its features so nearly human it suggested a Thomas Nast cartoon.

Don Angel, who looked like any ordinary foreman, was standing in the doorway, directing the loading of one of his big trucks. Manufacturing soft drinks must have been one of his interests, for the wooden boxes the men were piling into the truck were filled with bottles of soda. Don Gabriel introduced us and after a few polite words we passed on.

After the houses thinned out we came upon the tank of the new water system. Though it was nearly all underground, I could see it was a brick structure with a flat cement roof. I felt it was a pity they had not made the tank larger while they were at it, for it was overflowing and the water it could not hold was making rivulets in the dirt road. Being keenly aware of Mexico's shortage of water I felt sad to see that waste. At least, I thought, some of those people living in the thatched huts nearby could have dug a ditch to see that the overflow reached their plots of corn.

El Calvario was in sharp contrast to La Pastora, the ruined chapel in the heart of the town. This chapel was not colonial in style. In fact, with its little bell on one side of the roof, it looked rather like a one-room schoolhouse one might find in the Midwest. It was so well kept up, too, that it was hard to credit Don Gabriel's statement that it had been built in 1805. Because of its fine, raised site, I regretted it was not more beautiful, but it was interesting as an example of the way Indians will neglect a handsome old place of worship in favor of something relatively crude they have set up for themselves.

Because he was the town's most revered holy personage, I was naturally curious about El Señor de Ayuxi. When we entered the chapel, I felt let down. Outwardly El Señor had nothing to distinguish him. He was one of the village's life-sized *barrio* Christs, and I had already sketched two of his type on either side of the altar's triumphal arch on page 151. Why, I wondered, did this particular crucifix deserve such a fanciful, if tarnished, silver crown? And why was it placed behind a glass frame in a special shrine of its own?

"It is believed to have more miraculous power than the other Christs," Don Gabriel said. And the chapel contained evidence of the fervency of that belief. Not only were there many flowers on the altar, some withered and some fresh, but an elderly woman was heaped on the clean tile floor in front of the huge crucifix and she was sobbing her heart out as she prayed for whatever it was she wanted.

Turning to leave, my breath was caught by the beauty of the scene from under the round arch of the chapel door. The door framed the monastery so perfectly that I could not resist making a sketch after all. And I began the one used as the frontispiece of this book.

As I worked, the narrator in me rejoiced at all the scene showed. For one thing, it encompassed the church's north side, which I had not depicted in its entirely in any of the other drawings. But more importantly, the scene showed, as words could hardly do, how under an ample sky the church stood against the hills of the valley, and how it rose above the roofs of the village, lifted so high on its huge platform that it was utterly unobstructed.

I reflected, too, that from the standpoint of the monastery's preservation, it was really a stroke of fortune that Yanhuitlán, through the years, should have dwindled to almost nothing. If the tide had run the other way— that is, if Yanhuitlán had grown ever larger and more prosperous—the monastery would have suffered. Not only would it have become engulfed in surrounding buildings and perhaps been layered with grime and soot from the smoke of industrial plants; but a large and rich body of worshippers would probably have changed its original form by all manner of drastic rebuilding.

WEEK IN YANHUITLÁN

Don Gabriel and Nahum had stretched out on wooden benches and fallen asleep. The drawing went easily and I had a curious sense of harmony between the four of us. The woman was praying, I was sketching and the man and the boy were sleeping. Each was in his own interior world, and each world allowed the others to exist without interference. My feeling for the woman behind me struck me as being especially curious. I knew, somehow, that because I was going about my business quietly I was not intruding on her devotions. So I was not uncomfortable on that score. Nor, strangely enough, did awareness of her grief make me feel uncomfortable either. What I recognized in both of us—in her grief and in my contentment—was that we were each filled with very human feelings. Perhaps we were each in our own season. For her it was a time to weep, for me a time to smile. And it was part of the rightness of things that our differing attitudes should not be jarring to each other.

Don Gabriel and Nahum woke before the drawing was finished and by four o'clock we were on our way again.

Once beyond the chapel we were clear of the town. For a while, our course continued parallel with the colonial wall that bore the old conduit. Trees known as *huajes* shaded the wall and formed a feathery screen through which we saw the wide ploughed fields on our left.

I had a mounting sense of elation. And as the town dropped behind, I realized this was the first time since arriving that I had been more than two hundred yards from the monastery. It felt good to be free from the dominance of so imposing a presence.

Another shrinelike vent stood where the wall ended, and here the conduit went underground. But its course was not totally lost. Stretching ahead were a number of widely spaced clay pipes, which projected from the earth like the periscopes of a long file of submarines. The file curved in an arc that followed the contour where the flat land ended and the sloping land began.

Don Gabriel bid me look at the first pipe. A piece of tin had been cemented like a drumhead over the top, and the tin diaphragm had been punched as if by a can opener. The perforations let air into the conduit, Don Gabriel explained, and the air aided the flow of the water. "Listen," he said, and he laid his ear over the perforated diaphragm. I followed suit and heard what he wanted me to hear—the gurgle of the water as it flowed in the conduit below. It was so clearly audible one could tell the pipes were hardly more than six inches below the surface.

Looking ahead at the file of pipes, I had another aesthetic pang. These modern vents were utilitarian too, but, like the faucet-topped stanchions, they were much uglier than their colonial equivalents.

The fields we were circling had been planted not long before with wheat. From a distance they had seemed bare, but as we walked beside the furrows we could see the tiny, pale-green spears of the young wheat. Most of the plantlets were two or three inches high and they looked terribly delicate and unprotected. The fields were very large and surely they must have been plowed by machinery to have their particular look. In the Mexican fields I had seen plowed by oxen, the furrows had been wide apart and the high ridges between them had been chunky with grassy clods of unbroken earth. But here the entire topsoil was broken. The red-brown earth was all loose and crumbly and it was remarkably uniform in color and texture. And this soft, porous soil was neatly tracked with close furrows whose parallels, perfectly aligned for long distances, swept around gracefully at the turns.

It was beautiful soil, but I felt that because it was so completely worked over the speed of its being swept away by wind and water would be accelerated. Even now one could see smoky wisps of red dust blowing from some of the crests. The soil, however, appeared to be enormously deep. Where that deep deposit of red loam had come from was all too obvious. One had only to swing one's gaze around the denuded lower slopes of the hills. The color of that red sandstone told the story. Clearly this was slope wash that had been piling up in the flat bottom of the valley as the hills grew barer and barer.

The sight of the fields prompted questions about their ownership. Many Mexico villages, I knew, owned corporate land that was inalienable. That is, individuals could possess and work it during their lives, but they could not dispose of it. It was village land. Was Yanhuitlán, I asked, a village of this type? "No," replied Don Gabriel. "There is no communal property. All the land is in private hands."

This suggested another question. In many parts of Mexico most of the best land formerly belonged to the haciendas. After the Revolution, though, the haciendas were broken up and their lands made available to small owners. Were any of the fields we saw once part of a large hacienda? "No. There were never any haciendas around Yanhuitlán. Always the land has been held by free farmers."

The seedling wheat before our eyes had obviously been planted that month, so I asked if September was always the month for sowing wheat.

"Yes, the wheat is planted in September. The corn in February and May. The corn in the fields now is May corn."

Two crops of corn a year and one of wheat. The advantages of not having a winter! And how, I asked, did the people dispose of their crops?

"They keep nearly all the corn for their own use. For their tortillas and the like. But they sell the wheat."

"In Mexico City?"

"No, in Oaxaca."

"How do they transport it?"

"In trucks."

"But most of them don't have any trucks."

"Yes, that's the trouble. They have to sell it to the men who own the trucks. Two men have a monopoly."

It wasn't hard for him to name them. One was Angel Pérez, the soft-drink magnate whom we had seen not long before in front of his house. The other was Felipe Cruz Soriano, the husband of the postmaster's daughter, who owned two trucks and a grocery store.

The hills on our side of the valley were to the right and as we neared them I could observe the ravages of erosion more clearly than when I had seen the hills only from the distance. From my memories of cornfields on other Mexican hillsides, I could reconstruct what had happened.

Centuries back these naked hills must have been forested. But as the population of the valley had grown larger, men seeking land not already claimed must have begun going into these hills to clear plots on which to grow corn. In doing so they had cut down the trees and broken up the sod cover. Then they had planted their corn in rows that ran up and down the slopes, as I had seen near Tamazunchale. The ditches between the rows of corn had provided watercourses for the rains, and the washing down of the loosened unprotected soil had begun. As one plot after another became use- less for the growing of any more corn, new sections of the forest were cleared, and as the lower slopes grew depleted, the men began making clear- ings higher and higher up. Until now. . . .

And I looked with distress at the bare, runnelled hills. Now it is doubt- ful if even desert shrubs could find much foothold on them. And the bedrock of gray limestone on the upper slopes was as pitifully exposed as the red sandstone of the lower slopes. And down those slopes ran deep ramifying creases that in their multiplicity of branching filaments suggested great nerve systems.

"Can't anything be done about it?" I ask Don Gabriel.

"Nothing," he said. "There is no money."

"But couldn't the Federal Government supply money?"

"The Federal Government isn't interested."

As we walked along, I was struck by the way small sections of erosion formed perfect miniatures of vast sections. Flights over badlands, canyons and deserts had taught me how these things look from the air; and I saw their forms reproduced on a tiny scale as I looked down at the eroded edges of the path. There were grand canyons with upright, stratified walls. There were buttes and mesas. And the slopes of the miniature mountains were engraved by watercourses that formed the same leaf vein patterning as the great channels that cut down the sides of ranges towering ten thousand feet.

Soon the fields were left behind and we were walking upward along gentle slopes. There was a little more vegetation. When we passed a *casahuate*, Don Gabriel said the small tree had a baleful shade. Anybody who fell asleep under one was sure to be ill.

As we climbed we could look back and see further down the gentle rolling valley. Yanhuitlán looked smaller as it seemed to sink into a slight depression, and beyond it, on hills that appeared to rise, we could see two of the other towns of the valley, Suchixtlan and San Mateo.

In the past Don Gabriel had frequently mentioned Yanhuitlán's rivers. It had been puzzling, for to me a river means a broad stream at field level with trees shading its banks and every now and then a gleam of silver to reveal its presence. In the week I had been in the village I had seen no sign of such a thing, and I had wondered what he was talking about. But within a few minutes I was to discover there were rivers. For we came upon our first one.

But we did not see it until we were almost on top of it. Like Yanhuitlán's other rivers, it had disappeared to horizontal vision because it had cut its way down so deep. This river—and it was really only a small stream —flowed through a fairly wide, winding barranca. Don Gabriel said it was called Rio del Pateón because it went toward the cemetery.

The little river also settled another puzzling matter. Don Gabriel had kept mentioning the colonial aqueduct. This, to me, had meant only one thing: arches carrying a stream of water over a valley. Not knowing Don Gabriel had been referring to the whole system, I had kept wondering when we were coming to the promised arches. As the walk had grown longer with

no evidence of them, I started to think they did not exist. And I had been
disappointed, for the colonial aqueducts had been among the loveliest sights
I'd seen in Mexico.

Yet here my spirits rose, for the river was one of the three places where
the Spaniards had to transport their water across a gap, and the conduit was
carried from one barranca rim to the other by four arches. It was a short
arcade compared with those in Zacatecas and Querétaro, but it was lovely
in its own right and I was thrilled to come upon so massive a work just when
I had come to the conclusion that, architecturally, I had exhausted Yanhuitlán's resources.

The aqueduct was still in use, Don Gabriel said. The fact that its arches,
like the stream meandering under the highest of them, had been totally concealed by being below ground level indicated the barranca must have been
deep even in colonial days. A barranca is a gorge with more or less upright
walls that has been caused by a stream that has eaten a deeper and deeper
bed. Young barrancas are generally V-shaped, but, with the attrition of the
water, the upper slopes are undercut. In time they collapse into the stream
and their earth is borne away, leaving the characteristic perpendicular walls.
Barrancas are a sure sign of land in the course of destruction.

Recent rains, I could see, had been eating back the rims of this barranca. How much longer, I wondered, would the earth at its edges last?
Surely chunks kept breaking off regularly and slipping down the sheer walls,
to be borne off toward the sea by that innocent-looking little stream that
hardly deserved to be called a river.

Seeing soil that could still be preserved, I told Nahum I hoped he would learn how to combat erosion in his engineering study and that he would return to Yanhuitlán with that knowledge to help the village. He said that was why he wanted to be an engineer.

To cross the barranca we had to scramble down one side, make our way across the level bottom and climb the other side. Thereafter our route continued in a northerly direction, but, as by this time we were at the end of the valley, the path began to veer toward the west as we followed the line of the encircling foothills.

At the chapel I had been able to see only the church's northern flank, but from where we were now I could get a three-quarter view that included the western façade. From this distance the church looked unwontedly small, but I saw that one of its attributes I had admired from close up—its ability to take light—was just as striking from far off. The late afternoon sun was hitting it from the west and because of the sharp angles of its planes some faces were in strong light, some in dark shade, and one extreme dramatized the other.

As I was looking back in admiration, I heard Nahum exclaim: "¡Mira! Dos pastores."

I wheeled to see the sight that had excited him. And there was cause, for two shepherds were driving a flock of goats down from the heights above. The young men and their stream of goats might well have come from the second chapter of St. Luke.

They passed us with a cheery "¡Buenas tardes!" and as I watched them grow smaller in proceeding along the path by which we had come, I had another realization. Animals, by eating earth-protecting plants, are a factor in erosion. So part of Yanhuitlán's erosion was caused by the grazing of such flocks on its hills.

A few hundred yards more and we came to the second barranca that the Spaniards had been obliged to span with a series of arches. Here the scene was triply sad. Not only had the water cut deeply through this foothill soil, but its action had been such as to destroy the aqueduct built by the Spaniards. Only the ends attached to the side walls remained upright. The central arches had crashed down, and the great chunks of broken gray masonry lay tumbled where they had fallen untidily into the gorge.

Reassembling so massive an edifice obviously had been too big a job for the people of Yanhuitlán. Not having the advantage of old arches to carry their new duct, as at the first barranca, they had been obliged to do some building of their own. What they had stuck up were three tall brick piers with an exposed lead pipe laid across them.

The square piers enabled them to take the pipe across the barranca with a central support to save it from sagging in the middle, but the pipe, alas, was of fairly small bore. This was where the third element of sadness came in. The pipe was too small to accommodate all the water passing through, and the water that could not crowd into the pipe was escaping down the banks of the far side. As it escaped, it was not only washing down good earth, but it was beginning to undermine the new piers. Someday, I felt sure, they too would be toppled in the gorge. It was sad to think that scarcity of funds had forced the townspeople to build so poor a makeshift at such a vital point.

"Who was the engineer for the project?" I asked. Don Gabriel's answer went right through me. "There wasn't one," he said.

"How was it built then?"

"The men of the village built it. They hired four or five bricklayers, but otherwise they did all the work themselves."

Remembering how they had all pitched in to repair the church tower, I asked if this job had been done on a volunteer basis too. "Yes," said Don Gabriel. "The men divided themselves into four work gangs, and the groups took turns laying the pipes. The job took almost two years."

After that, the leaking pipe resting on the brick piers looked different. What had seemed merely shoddy work was revealed as a major community effort.

Beyond this second barranca we came to a stretch between spurs of the hills where fields washed in like the waters of an emerald-green bay. Again we could see a file of pipe vents curving ahead, and in these fields there was a crop of corn. Nahum broke a big stalk in three. He gave one piece to Don Gabriel, and, after he had peeled back the middle piece, he handed it to me. He bit off the tip of his own piece, to show me what to do with mine. To my surprise, I found it as sweet as sugar. After grinding out the cane's moisture, though, one had to keep spitting out the pulp.

By this time all the foreground of the valley, up to and including the *convento*, was in shadow, but the long stretch of the valley beyond was still bright.

Once across the bay of cornfields, the path grew quite steep, and here the untillable slopes were overgrown with bushes. Many bore bright flowers and Nahum and Don Gabriel began picking them. The sweet-smelling, orange-colored flowers with the long narrow bells were called *chepitos,* they said, and made an excellent tea. The flowers that looked like dark-blue pods on very delicate strands were *chepiles.* Those with big pods like Chinese lanterns were *bombitas.* The deep-purple flowers were Flowers of Death, and the yellow flowers that grew so thickly on bushy branches were Flowers of the Mountain.

At a point where the path was so steep that we had to go up sideways, clearing the bushes as we went, we came upon the third place the Spaniards had spanned with masonry. It was a defile so narrow that a single arch did the trick. The arch was strong, heavy and handsome, and buttressed by stone piers that went well down the mountainside so there was little chance of destruction.

Don Gabriel was all for passing it casually, but I wanted to climb up for a good view of the arch. My pertinacity led to a discovery that was new even to Don Gabriel. On the wall of the arch facing in toward the defile was a finely carved stone plaque. Its principal motif was a big flower resembling a squash blossom. Don Gabriel, I was glad to see, was sufficiently excited by the unsuspected plaque to call Nahum up to inspect it too.

Again I contrasted colonial and modern workmanship. This beautiful stone arch further exposed the poor quality of those brick piers; and the Spaniards, not content with constructing so enduring an arch, had also ornamented it with fine carving on the side passersby were least likely to see.

The walk had been full of surprises and shortly after we rounded the spur of hill we were negotiating we were confronted with the biggest surprise of all—the Rio de las Canicas, the greatest of Yanhuitlán's hidden rivers. But we could hardly see its stream, so wide and deep was the barranca it had cut. That barranca yawned before us, making a ravine almost a quarter of a mile wide that separated us from the highway winding down from the pass on the far side. And here I had true evidence of the amazing depth of the deposit of slope wash that had been scoured from the hillsides. The upright walls of the barranca cutting through it were almost forty feet high.

Looking downstream towards the village I saw that the earth was being cultivated right to the barranca's edge. But again I had a sense of resources that would not last forever. Bites from the field edges showed where sections of field had already collapsed into the ravine, and there were other edges due to cave in.

Soon, I thought to myself, this valley will be able to support even fewer people than it does now. And I wondered if Nahum would really come back after his education was complete, or would he join the steady stream of young people leaving the village to find jobs in Mexico's few big cities.

Don Gabriel, however, cut melancholy reflections short by pointing up towards the barranca head and exclaiming: "See—the *manantial.*"

There, gleaming over the rounded surface of bed rock, was evidence of water. It had taken us about forty minutes to come within sight of the promised land. It took another quarter of an hour to reach it, for we had to proceed along our side of the barranca until we came to a place where we could get across. As we skirted it, we saw the colonial aqueduct, which at this stretch was like a retaining wall preventing the earth from slipping into the gully.

At the point where we could cross the ravine there was a stand of corn growing on flat land that had formerly been part of the river bed. There we saw two burros and a woman with wild hair, who was gathering corn with the help of three boys.

The woman was so blackened that she might have been a widow who burned charcoal to eke out her subsistence. Don Gabriel knew her and she smiled at us with a cordiality that totally belied her wild, witchlike appearance. She showed us her corn and I did not wonder at her pride. Never had I seen any corn like it. Not only were the ears large and heavy, but the kernels were like jewels. Most of them resembled rubies. But some ears were encrusted with kernels like amethysts, and some blue cobs had kernels ranging from night-blue opals to moonstones. And the resemblance to precious stones was not just in color. The kernels seemed to have the translucence of cut stones too. She gave me three cobs as a present.

From where I had first seen the gleam of water I had thought the river was the overflow from the *manantial.* But here, standing at the edge of the shallow streamlet, I saw differently. The overflow of the *manantial* undoubtedly had contributed to the river—and surely it was that overflow that had washed the bedrock bare—but the river's source was somewhere back in the hills, as I could tell from the way the stream meandered from them.

The *manantial* was above and to our left, and as we made our way up to it I came to understand that Don Gabriel had been pointing to a little gabled edifice, and not to the water that trickled over the rocks en route. The edifice looked like a small, partially submerged house. Its roof, at least, was quite modern, for it was made of molded cement. The house, Don Gabriel said, sheltered seven springs. Would I like to go in?

He pushed the door open and I saw that steps cut in the rock made it possible to get down to where the water stood. In one corner of the bare house stood a stone cross. On its base was a date. The numerals were so ancient they were hard to decipher, but as nearly as I could make out the year was 1673. By this time I was accustomed to early dates in Mexico, but I must confess that under so modern a roof this date surprised me. The people of Yanhuitlán, then, had been drawing their water from these unfailing springs since twelve years before the birth of Bach.

The water was utterly clear and so still that one could scarcely detect the ripples beneath the surface that indicated the constant replenishment. The water-covered floor of the house was the natural basin of the spring, and growing from a sandy hillock in one corner was a delicate plant of the palest green. It was *culantrillo,* Don Gabriel said. It had medicinal properties and would grow only where there was perpetual shade.

Didn't I want a drink? Don Gabriel asked. And he indicated it would be all right to scoop up the water with my hand.

As I drank, I thought to myself: so this is the water that runs across the four arches, curves round the wheat fields and drains into the tank in front of the chapel before it becomes available at will to the villagers who turn on the faucets at their street-corner stanchions; this, then, is the head of the water system that ends in the plaza fountain, where it bubbles from the central post with the sound of a burro munching.

As I cupped my hand into it I had a feeling of a pilgrimage accomplished. I had finally come to the source of that sweet, refreshing water that Ricardo had ladled out to me on a hot September afternoon three years before. And I blessed the water, conscious of my continuing indebtedness to it, for its known purity had helped bring me back to Yanhuitlán.

The first stop on the return journey was a short way below the *manantial.* Here was another natural basin that had been modified by men cutting steps down to it, and a little water rested in its hollow. This was the earlier *manantial,* Don Gabriel said, and it was used before they discovered those more productive springs higher up.

Since we were now on the highway side of the barranca, we decided to take advantage of the fact and walk home the paved way. This meant ascending the slope to a higher level where the road curved round the hill. On the way up, Don Gabriel pointed out where an automobile had gone over the unrailed curve.

After we had rounded the curve, we saw the red valley stretched below. Remembering how I had swooped round that curve in a bus for my first glimpse of Yanhuitlán in 1948, I had a feeling that this was where I came in. And I thought of the curious way the future is veiled from us. If one of the fellow passengers on that bus had said to me: "Five years hence this strange valley, which you are now flashing through, will be a place well and lovingly known to you, and one late September afternoon you will find yourself walking down this highway with two of its villagers as your personal friends"— if such a thing had been said to me, I would not have believed it.

The northern flank of the church looked damlike, as it had that day I saw it first, but only the buttresses were catching the light. The rest of the vast side was dark. The sandy pink façade, on the other hand, stood so squarely in the path of the westering sun that it looked almost white.

And all around were open fields. The earth that persisted looked marvelously fertile. There was a pale-green cast to the fields that had already been planted with wheat, but much of the earth was an unaltered red brown, for ploughing was still under way. Moving along one stretch of earth I saw evidence confirming my guess that machines had worked the land I had seen on the other side. The evidence was an orange tractor. It was scuttling along as it made its way down the stretch.

A little nearer was a man with two oxen who were slowly drawing a wooden plow down a parallel stretch. The oxen had a head start, but not only did the tractor soon overtake them, but it met them on the way back before they had even completed their single furrow. The tractor was too far away for me to count the disks it was dragging, but I could see that not only was it moving much faster than the oxen, but as it went it was making many furrows in contrast to the one of the beasts. How tellingly that picture contrasted the old and the new.

I asked Don Gabriel the number of tractors in Yanhuitlán. Three, he said. They were not sufficiently numerous, then, to make much impression on the landscape, and one of the things that struck me as we descended into the valley was the consonance between the huge monastery and the life going on at its feet. The monastery was not like an ancient edifice in a modern city—that is, a relic of a vanished past surrounded by an environment no longer animated by the same spirit. It was a creation still environed by the sort of culture that had been current when it was built. And I thought that seldom in this modern world does one see an ancient building and a past way of life preserved together simultaneously. In the clear, golden light it was wonderfully beautiful—as if a Breughel scene had been painted by Van Gogh.

As we reached the valley floor we came to a dirt road that ran directly ahead, while the highway curved gently to the left.

"Would you like to visit the *campo santo* on the way home?" Don Gabriel asked. Having seen the cemetery often from afar, I liked the suggestion, so we took the dirt road. It had been worn a little below the level of the fields that stretched on either side. Those fields were bordered with large beaver-tail cacti, and swarming over the bases of the old plants were the purple flowers known as *maravillas*.

In one field we saw one of the other tractors. The driver turned at the edge of the field just as we passed and I could count that his implement had eight disks. Eight furrows at a crack! What terrible competition for the poor men with only wooden plows drawn by oxen!

Finally we came to the straight road that ran from the front of the church. It meant a right-angle turn to the left, and as we headed toward the cemetery I was struck by the beauty of a tall ash tree that stood on one side with the graceful symmetry of a New England elm.

The cemetery had two arched entrances. The first one, to the new forecourt, was dated 1948 and was an ugly affair. The one beyond on the same axis though, was colonial in style and had the beauty of most colonial work.

This was the freestanding arch that had risen in the mind of the little burgher with the gray moustache when he had seen my drawing of the church's north portal. Don Gabriel and I chuckled again as we remembered that particular case of mistaken identity. Then Don Gabriel directed my attention to the dark-gray stone on the right side of the arch that is outlined in the sketch below.

Looking at it head on, I could not discern any reason for special interest. But when Don Gabriel led me under the arch and pointed to the side of the stone, I saw ample cause for excitement. It was a great serpent head, built into the arch in such a way that the fierce reptile was biting the dust.

Obviously, the head was meant to run horizontally and as I bent to study it in its true direction my admiration kept growing. Who said the Mixtecs were masters only of tiny things? This head was nearly four feet long and it was the work of a master sculptor accustomed to working in a monumental style. It was marvelous how much expression and controlled vigor he

278

had achieved with his decisive stylization. I was especially taken by the resourcefulness of the prone S that served to depict both the eyebrow and the top of the head.

"How many teeth does it have?" I asked Don Gabriel, for I could not be sure if there were two or three.

He stooped and pulled out the weeds that obscured the snout. The exact count was still hard to determine. I got out my knife, loosened the dirt and brushed some away. There were definitely three short teeth. And maybe more, for my little digging disclosed that the stone did not end at ground level.

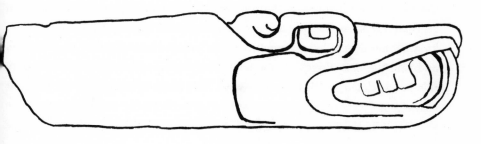

Nahum joined in the digging and soon we had exposed a great curved fang. This was a surprise to Don Gabriel, so we continued excavating until a second fang was exposed. This seemed the end of the stone and we had dug as deep as we could without a spade. With those fangs added to its length, the head was even more impressive. I had made a second significant Mixtec find in one day. And this stone, because it suggested the balustrade of a pyramid stairway, did more than *El Rey* to indicate the character of Yanhuitlán's ancient temples.

I asked Don Gabriel if he knew the date of the cemetery arch. "1878," he said. This surprised me. The arch was not colonial after all. Remembering the 1877 date of the church bells, I realized this arch belonged to the same creative period when the legally expelled Dominicans were still active. I was fascinated by this proof that even late in the nineteenth century, when Mexico was already an independent republic, friars were continuing the practice of their sixteenth-century forebears. That is, they were still building pagan religious sculptures into the foundations of their structures to demonstrate the superior status of the Christian religion. Could it be they felt the old religions retained enough vitality to need repeated degrading?

Passing beyond the arch, we saw two men digging a small grave in the old part of the cemetery. One was an old man, squatting on his haunches, who was giving directions to the young man doing the digging. The young man faced us, but because his head was lowered, his big sombrero concealed his features. "The father of the baby that died," Don Gabriel whispered.

Never before had I seen a man obliged to dig a grave for a member of his own family. It seemed sad enough that the young man should have lost his infant son, but to have also to dig its grave. . . . The earth was hard and stony and the tired digger straightened his back to rest. As he lifted his head I saw beneath the brim of the obscuring sombrero. It was Herminio, the young man of the dance I had nicknamed Hatchet-face. The father who had lost the child, then, was someone I knew—a friend. One nearly always feels tongue-tied and helpless in the presence of grief. I felt both handicaps with especial keenness because of my poor command of Spanish. But I have known what it is to have sympathy extended, so I went forward to Herminio and said the only thing I knew how to say: *"Lo siento mucho."* Generally this is translated as "I am very sorry," but its literal meaning is "I feel it very much."

The three of us moved away. And as we passed the crowded graves

Nahum reminded us of another infant death—but one from which the passage of time had drawn much of the sting.

"*Mi hermanito,*" he said, pointing to the small undated stone that covered the remains of his little brother. There was a date on the tomb of Lupe's father. It was 1947. "*Mi tío,*" said Nahum, meaning "my uncle." The grave was particularly well tended and I detected Lupe's loving hand in the marigolds growing beside the marble slab.

The ruins of a small chapel stood at the end of the cemetery. From the stumps of the pillars and the fragment of back wall, I judged it must have been like a porch with an open front.

Near the ruins was a particularly odd stone—as if an Indian sculptor had tried to reproduce a Victorian monument. "*El último fraile,*" said Don Gabriel.

The last friar! My imagination was immediately captured. How much I wanted to know about him! But Don Gabriel could tell me little more than that his name was Pedro. He had given up his priestly duties and stayed on in the village long after the other friars had left. He lived to be an old man and died just after the turn of the century. Remembering how the friars used to be buried with such solemnity after services in the great hall of the monastery I felt a pang of regret for poor, lonely old Pedro, dying like an ordinary villager, with no monastic comrades to chant his last rites.

As we retraced our steps we were heading straight toward the monastery. The entire western front was bathed in light like golden wine. More than ever, the gap in the wall, where the three arches of the porch had been, suggested a missing tooth. It was so black in contrast to the luminous stone. And in that clear, clear light how beautiful that towering façade looked! I realized I had never fully appreciated it before because I had never been far enough away from it to see it properly.

Recognizing its grandeur, though, was disconcerting. I had been trying to duck the responsibility of drawing it. All through the visit I had been telling myself the sketchy suggestion of the façade in the first drawing was sufficient. I had rationalized away the need for a detailed drawing by arguing that the façade was not important. But seeing it rising so splendidly in front of me, I knew I could no longer believe this. I accepted the inevitable and resolved that tomorrow I would face up to the task I had shirked.

As we walked toward it, I kept on the alert for the best point from which to start the drawing. I knew it when we reached it, for at a given moment I could suddenly see the detail of the carving more clearly, and yet at this point the total composition still was distant enough to be taken in with a single look.

"Tomorrow afternoon," I said to Don Gabriel, "I'm coming back to this spot to draw the façade." And largely to fix the place in my memory, I noted the thatched huts to the right and traced an imaginary line stretching from them across the road.

When we reached the huts at the highway, I remembered little Ricardo, struggling under those heavy tins of water as he came down the steps in front of the monastery. And for the first time I understood why he had been obliged to carry the water so far. In this part of the village there were no stanchions with faucets. To obtain water he had to take his yoked tins to the faucet on the street corner on the northern side of the church.

The surprises of the walk were still not over. As we started up the slope by the ruined wall of the monastic inn, I was struck by the rich dark foliage of a big tree on our right. I asked what it was. "A mulberry," said Don Gabriel.

More excitement stirred my imagination. I had read that the Dominicans had introduced silk culture into the Mixteca Alta and that it had become a flourishing industry. Silkworms fed on mulberries. "Was Yanhuitlán one of the places where they cultivated silk?" I asked Don Gabriel.

"Yes," he said. "It was one of the richest silk centers all through the sixteenth century. But you know what happened. The opening of trade with the Philippines meant Mexico was flooded with Chinese silk. The Mexican silk industry could not meet the competition and when conditions got bad the Spaniards exploited the Indian silk workers cruelly. In many places the Indians retaliated by destroying the mulberries. That is one of the few surviving in the whole region."

Lupe was at the front door on the lookout for us when we finally got home. Nahum took his leave, but Don Gabriel and I paused on the threshold to tell her about our walk. Our backs were to the street so that we saw nothing, but Lupe suddenly pulled us both into the house and shut the front door. In being practically yanked inside I got a glimpse of the danger.

"*Los borrachos*," she said. And this confirmed my guess, for the group of men I had seen coming up the street from Don Miguel's were undisguisably drunk. I gained two impressions. One was that the put-upon host of the saint's day had finally succeeded in tactfully getting his hard-drinking friends to leave the house en masse. The other was that these men were in a state where they would try to draw us into their party and there might be trouble if we declined to go along. After allowing sufficient time for the group to get well past, Lupe opened the door again and then we saw what I assumed was the sufficient reason for setting the drinkers on their way. On the upper level was a party headed for the church, and rockets were being fired as they went. At the heart of the party walked a group of women, one of whom was carrying a carefully bundled baby.

"A baptism," said the Blancos, and they explained there was a new baby in the Gómez house. Don Miguel had chosen his own saint's day for the child and the group was taking the boy to the church to also receive the name Miguel.

I felt glad for the chunky farmer, but I could not help remembering that the day he was having his child baptized, Herminio was burying his.

Lupe's dinner consisted of two eggs, tortillas, frijoles, a piece of sweet bread baked in a triangular shape and hot milk. As I lingered over the latter, my thoughts turned back to the town's water supply system.

"Where did the Mixtecs get their water from before the Spaniards came?" I asked Don Gabriel.

"From the *manantial*. But then they had to carry it to the village on their backs."

Being aware now of the length of the walk, I immediately saw the labor and trouble involved. And the realization of the boon bestowed on the natives by the aqueduct was a new piece of mosaic to fit into my story of the Conquest. On the basis of superficial knowledge, it is almost impossible to credit that so few Spaniards should have held so many Indians in peaceable control for so long. But thanks largely to Kubler I had come to understand one of the great explanations. The Indians had reached such a high point of technological progress that they were not only ready for, but actually reaching out for the technological improvements Spanish civilization was able to bring into their lives—things like steel cutting tools, draft animals, and wool-bearing sheep. And here was another example of a welcome gift from a more technically advanced culture—a water supply system that saved that weary walking to the springs and all the still more tiring walking back. Not only this, but a system that provided more abundant water in the heart of the village than had ever been possible when all the water had to be carried in clay jars on men's backs.

"Who built the aqueduct?" I asked. "The Dominicans," said Don Gabriel.

The Dominicans! I thought the afternoon had been a holiday away from the monastery, but I had not been far from it after all. I remembered those cisterns I had seen in the morning. They were another aspect of what the Dominicans did to see that the town had water. Then I remembered how the village fountain was lined up on the same axis at the first flight of the grand stairway so that it formed the centerpiece of the vista as one mounted those stairs.

Not only was the fountain integrated with the plan of the monastery, then, but the whole of that water supply system, including the four-mile aqueduct with its three arcaded crossings, was integrated with that plan. And I saw more clearly than ever the totality of the missionary effort. It was material as well as spiritual. Then I recalled the mulberry tree and the introduction of silk culture. That was part of the missionary effort too, for the friars were concerned that their charges should be fed in body as well as in spirit. Not only did they want to create the physical plant of a town, but they wanted the town to have the means of sustaining itself. The unity of concept of town and monastery, then, was even more far-reaching than I had thought. Whatever developed in reality, I saw the clear shining of the medieval concept of a peaceful Christian community living within the sheltering aegis of a benevolent and loving monastic foundation.

Though I had finished my hot milk, the Blancos were in no hurry to have me leave. Indeed, Don Gabriel delayed my departure by starting to teach me a song. It was *Canción Mixteca*, a song of homesickness by José López Alavez a man of the Mixteca, who wrote its words and music early in this century when he was far from his beloved region. At the time it was unknown to me and I thought of it as a folk song, composed by someone long forgotten and handed down from generation to generation. Its true role comes later, but because of subsequent events I need to report that it was on this evening that I had my first lesson.

When I finally got back to my room I found that all the walking in the sun I had done during the day had made me thoroughly ready for bed. But I cannot say what time I turned in. Because I had forgotten to wind it, my watch had stopped.

XIX
ESCUDOS

THE NEXT DAY WAS WEDNESDAY, the day I would have left Yanhuitlán had I stuck to my original plan. When the rackety beat of the corn mill woke me some time after six, I remembered I did not have to leave. I murmured to myself: I have all today, all tomorrow and half of Friday. Blessing the extension, I turned over for a little more of that sweetest of all sleeps, the self-indulgent sleep after the first waking.

When I later passed through the back room to get to the patio, I saw that José, the teacher, had already assembled his furnishings in the room he and his family were to occupy. He had been so neatly dressed in city clothes that I had assumed his circumstances were fairly comfortable. But the goods showed the schoolteacher was hardly better off than the average villager.

The only big item was the metal bedstead and it had nothing to cover its taut chain mail but a palm-leaf mat. There was no other furniture except the upright wooden chairs. They were from Tlaxiaco, like those we had sat on at Don Miguel's. I counted fourteen of them—twelve for adults and two miniature ones for children. Three large cylindrical baskets and two wooden boxes held all the household goods except a tin oval wash tub, some pots and pans, a fibre bag full of empty bottles, and a flit gun.

Ordinarily the door to the patio stood open, but José had safeguarded his precious belongings by bracing the door closed with a sturdy log. When I returned, I propped that log back, taking the utmost care that it was jammed immovably so no robber could push his way in.

When Don Gabriel came to escort me to breakfast, he explained he would be away for a while giving another injection to the woman who had lost her baby.

After six beautiful days, the weather had turned a bit cold. Lupe was wearing a black sweater over her orange dress, and Hambre, the kitten, was crouched against the portable stove for warmth. The cold, however, did not keep the little cat at the fire when there was food to be had. She came to my feet and set up her old "whah-whah" crying, all the time looking at me with green eyes, whose vertical pupils she kept narrowing. Did I notice how Hambre had been scorched? Lupe asked. Sure enough, the ordinarily gray fur on the kitten's left side had been burned a yellow brown as she curled around a corner of the stove. I gave her a piece of steak, and some of the meanness went out of her expression.

Meanwhile Bobby had stood patiently by, a kind look in his brown eyes. He got a piece of meat too. I asked Lupe which she preferred, the kitten or the dog. Unhesitatingly, she picked Bobby. He was *más correcto*. I smiled to hear the term for good manners applied to a dog, and it seemed characteristically Mexican that Lupe should place politeness so high in the scale of animal virtues.

As she sat by her stove, Lupe looked remarkably young. Her hair, parted a little left of center, was hanging down in pigtails and in the lobe of each ear was a small golden bead—all one could see of her earrings.

Because Don Gabriel was absent we were free to discuss him. I told her the government was lucky to have such an intelligent and conscientious man to look after the monastery. She agreed, but sighed that sometimes the job was hard on him. It was very monotonous. Weeks might go by without a single visitor.

I asked if she sometimes grew dissatisfied with her own job. No, she said. It was not like Don Gabriel's. It did not depend on visitors. It was the work of the house, and that went on the same whether there were *turistas* or not. She was always busy.

Didn't she sometimes get bored doing nothing but the work of the house, day after day? No, she said. It was what she was used to. She liked it.

The return of the head of the house ended the conversation, and I rose to leave so they could have their breakfast. I told them I was going to draw the steps at the corner of the plaza. But I warned them I would be back later. Though they thought I was joking, I announced my subsequent project was to draw Lupe's pots and pans.

Before I went, though, could I have the time? The Blancos had an old, square alarm clock that generally lost at least twenty minutes a day. Don Gabriel found it, too, had stopped. He shook it, but no ticking started.

The Palmas had a radio, he said. Perhaps they would have the time. The hint was welcome, for the Palmas' stall was at the foot of the steps and I could ask Felix for the time en route. Meanwhile, I added "alarm clock" to my mental list of presents for the Blancos. It already contained knives, forks, plates, flashlight batteries and another blanket.

In small towns in North America people without watches often keep track of the time by the sound of familiar trains. A farmer in the fields will straighten up and say: "It must be 3:38. There's the whistle of the afternoon train from Pittsfield." In Yanhuitlán there are no trains to mark the hours, but there is an equivalent: the morning plane for Oaxaca.

Morning after morning, I had heard its drone in the sky and I had come to realize its punctuality by noting that each day it passed at 8:10.

On the way to the Palmas', my ear caught its drone once more, so my time query was practically answered. But I checked with Felix anyway. He said it was 8:25, and he was sure of this because he set his clock when he heard the eight o'clock news.

"Then the plane for Oaxaca was a little late this morning," I said. "Yes," he replied. And I felt pleased he had noticed the plane with the same thoughts.

The steps leading up to the archway had first appeared to me in the sort of flash I have called picture vision the morning Don Gabriel and I had tried to deliver the president's mezcal. The flash had occurred just as we left the arcade in front of the school. Knowing it is wise to be loyal to vantage points that have provided pictorial inspiration, I went to the center of that arcade to find my sketching position.

As I was sizing up the best place to take my stance, Fausto Cervantes, the Presbyterian school principal, came along. He was about to have his breakfast. Would I join him? I said I would be glad to.

Being a bachelor, the teacher had no wife at home to cook for him, so he took his meals in the narrow little dining room in which Sra. Palma had served the three men who sold Felix the salt.

Sra. Palma insisted that I should eat some of the main dish too. It was green squash and I could see why her husband, her three children and herself were all so plump and healthy. She was an excellent cook. Seldom, if ever, have I tasted squash done so deliciously.

Fausto had a Spanish grammar with him and he spoke of it with an air of discouragement. Yes, this was what he had to teach—just the rudimentary things. And in his tone I heard the voice of the young intellectual who found it drudgery to drill elementary rules into students' heads by repetition and more repetition.

Something set Trinidad, the younger Palma girl, bawling. I had a cure for that, so I went and gave her a *dulce*. Unwrapping it gave the child a fresh interest and when she had it in her mouth, her tears were forgotten. But, of course, I couldn't give a candy to one member of the family and not to the others, Accordingly, I produced one for Graciela and another for Jorge, the baby brother.

Sra. Palma made each one say *"Gracias"* and she made three-year-old Graciela do something more. She stood her on a chair, whispered some instructions, and first thing I knew the tot was reciting a poem. It was something about a little parrot, and as she recited, she waved her baby hands back and forth, as she had been taught to do. I applauded as if she had been a soprano at Town Hall.

Felix asked if I had attended the baptism of Don Miguel's child. Then he put his hand on the black-haired reciter's little head and announced she had never been baptized. What about the others? I asked, indicating Jorge and the now contented Trinidad, who were hanging at their mother's skirts. "Not one of them," he said.

"I haven't been baptized either," chimed in Sra. Palma. I think one reason she volunteered such information was so the children would not feel badly. But I also detected a note of pride. It was partly pride in being a maverick and partly pride in feeling united with her children in a sodality of the unchristened.

Baptism, I had read, was the church rite the Indians cherished above all others, so I asked Felix why he had not insisted on it for his children.

"It costs too much money," he replied.

I asked what a christening cost. A thousand pesos, Felix said. But it turned out the priest's fee was only a minor part of the sum. The big baptismal expense was the fiesta that had to go with it.

Fausto excused himself because he had to get to his classroom. Felix then loaned me an upright chair, and I took up my drawing position at the corner of the school. The stairway was the one leading up to the arch at the back of the church. Its larger setting can be seen in the frontispiece.

The drawing (page 168) required time, but it went with the ease of all such flash-seen subjects. A good many school children passed as I worked. I was too busy to pay much attention to them. But I was charmed at how cleanly they were dressed and I was certainly impressed by their good

WEEK IN YANHUITLÁN

manners. They did not swarm around noisily, and those whose curiosity I satisfied with a showing thanked me most politely. Even the youngest seemed to take the responsibility of going to school seriously. The presence of so many alert youngsters, all with their books, seemed to me as excellent as the absence of beggars.

I GOT BACK to the Blancos around ten o'clock. Don Gabriel was off somewhere and secretly I was rather glad. I had enjoyed my chat with Lupe earlier in the morning and I was grateful for the chance to be alone with her again. I was glad, too, that because the day had grown warmer she had opened the big doors to the patio.

When Lupe understood I was in earnest about drawing her pots, she fetched some and posed them around the portable stove. She was puzzled when I asked her to take them away, and I realized she had expected me to draw a single still life with a number of objects heaped together. My scheme, however, was to sketch each item separately, scattering them around the page.

The stove was the central instrument of the cuisine, so I had no hesitation about where to start. Clearly the stove should be in the middle of the page. It was a simple up-to-date version of a medieval brazier, and Lupe had no difficulty lifting it to a position where the light was good. Having large handles, it was easy to carry, and, being made of tin, it was light. It reminded me of a big biscuit tin with a flaring top. Lupe always cooked with charcoal, which she placed on the grill fastened across the top. And she got the most out of each piece of charcoal, for it did not fall into the box below until it was burned away to sufficient thinness to pass through the slits in the grill. Lupe said the stove was called an *anafe*.

"Where does it come from?" I asked. She laughed and said it didn't come from anywhere. What she meant, of course, was that it was a standard, machine-made item that was not associated with any one town. I could tell, too, that she felt anything that was not handmade in a distinctive style did not deserve to be honored with the name of the place where it was assembled.

Besides being the only item in Lupe's equipment of machine manufacture, the stove was the only thing made of metal. Thus, when it was sketched to my satisfaction—and, incidentally, to Lupe's—the problem was to choose among the various handmade clay vessels she used. I had often fancied the shape of the bulbous little pitcher with a squat cylindrical neck in which she would heat the milk or make the hot chocolate. So it was my second choice, and I sketched it above the stove to the left. Originally it was a dark brown, but it had been placed on the coals so often that it was now practically black.

The word for pitcher in Spanish was *jarro*, Lupe said. This particular *jarro*, being made by hand in a recognizable shape, clearly came from somewhere. Where? I asked. And Lupe answered without hesitation. It came from Tlaxiaco.

Next I picked a second graceful pitcher, which had a rounder body, a narrower neck and a more pronounced lip. Its shape and red-brown color made it like the ware from Santo Domingo Tonaltepec I had seen at the market. Lupe confirmed the attribution. This pitcher was used mostly for water and because it was not put on the fire, it had retained its original color. It was as innocent of glaze, though, as the Tlaxiaco one. To achieve a balance between the two pitchers, I drew the second *jarro* on the right. And it was not by accident that I depicted it as if it were rocking back. Its bottom was not leveled off and it never did stand up straight.

When I had the three objects on the page, Lupe finally understood my alternative to a still life. Seeing she grasped my plan, I asked her if she had some object that would nicely fill the space between the two pitchers. Being most co-operative, she went to her storeroom to investigate.

Would this do? she asked, handing me a large orange-ochre pan with handles at each end. I said her eye was perfect and placed it on the table in front of me. Pans with handles at the two sides like this were called *cazuelas*, she said. This one came from Puebla. It had some crude ornamentation, roughly sketched in black, and its interior had a transparent glaze that gave the appearance of a slapdash varnishing job. This, too, did not sit quite level.

As I sketched, Lupe sewed. She was working on a little cloth like those she always set out for my meals. It was called a *mantel*, she said, and was for covering tortillas in a basket. I admired the flowers she was embroidering and asked if she liked fancy sewing.

Not as much as crocheting, she said. Would she show me some of her crochet work? She was pleased to be asked and produced some fine doilies with very complicated patterns.

"*Muy bonita*," I said, and asked if it wasn't very difficult work. Not when you understood how it was done. And did she use the doilies much? Hardly at all, but she enjoyed making them.

Next I needed something tall and narrow that would fill the space under the tilting pitcher. "What about that?" I asked, pointing to something Lupe

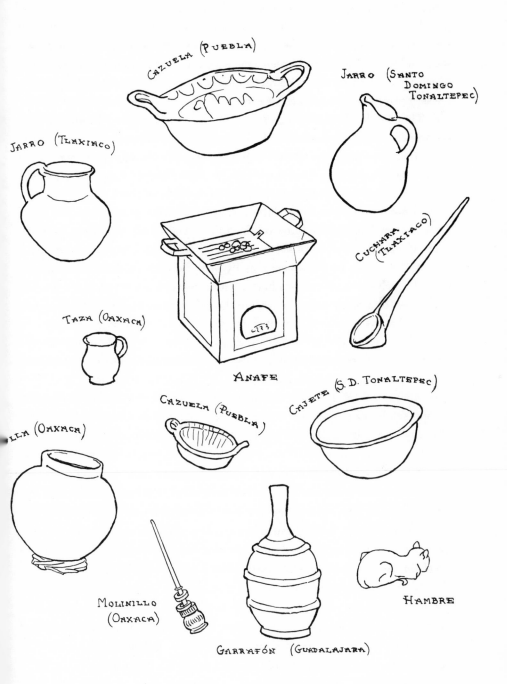

CAZUELA (PUEBLA)

JARRO (SANTO DOMINGO TONALTEPEC)

JARRO (TLAXIACO)

CUCHARA (TLAXIACO)

TAZA (OAXACA)

ANAFE

CAJETE (S. D. TONALTEPEC)

LLA (OAXACA)

CAZUELA (PUEBLA)

MOLINILLO (OAXACA)

GARRAFÓN (GUADALAJARA)

HAMBRE

291

often used to stir her sauces. *"La cuchara,"* she said, and she gave me what turned out to be a long wooden spoon from Tlaxiaco.

I wanted to draw one of the cups in which she had served hot milk, and I saw it would fit on the other side of the stove. So I asked for a *taza,* and she handed me the glazed green one with the cream-colored interior from which I had often drunk. It came from Oaxaca, she volunteered, for she saw I was writing the provenance of each item beside its name.

The simple objects were wonderfully easy to draw and I enjoyed both the work and Lupe's company. I also enjoyed the cheep-cheep of the little black turkey as it moved about the room, generally chasing, or being chased by, the brown chicken. That the turkey was now bigger than its companion made me aware that it had grown in the week I'd been there.

"Look," I said to Lupe, "the turkey is growing faster than the hen." To my astonishment, she burst out laughing. And I saw why when, between gales of chuckles, she managed to get out, "That's not a hen. It's a rooster."

As I worked, I looked occasionally at the room's calendars. I smiled at the lady picador on the brown horse, whose fearless lance was about to stop the onrush of a black bull. She was on the calendar of Angel Pérez, the truck owner with the couchant lion over his door. She was Mexican enough. So was Felipe Cruz' "Pietá," which showed an athletically built Jesus, slumped against the red-draped knee of a blue-cloaked Virgin. And of course Gabriel Sánchez' out-of-date calendar of the Virgin of Guadalupe couldn't have been more characteristic. But the other three! The one advertising Sidral Mundet, a popular Mexican apple cider, had three U. S. college girls sipping bottles of the beverage in question. The one of a Oaxaca restaurant had an exultant blonde standing on a beach, clad only in the briefest of bikinis. And the Coca Cola calendar showed a pretty North American housewife putting some cokes into a well-crammed refrigerator of enormous proportions.

I couldn't help contrasting her facilities with Lupe's. Never using ice, Lupe didn't have an icebox, much less a refrigerator. And Lupe was no more likely to have that much food on hand than she was to go cavorting on the beach in the nearly nude state of the blonde in the bikini.

Next I did another two-handled *cazuela,* but a small one this time. Then another vessel from Tonaltepec—a chrome-brown bowl that looked like a sandhog's helmet. It was called a *cajete.* And as each new item was added to the page I could see Lupe's amazement grow. It had never occurred to her that her cooking things could look so pretty or interesting.

In the silence as she sewed and I sketched strains of music drifted to us from Don Miguel's house. A group was singing to the sound of guitars. I perked up my ears.

"Isn't that *Canción Mixteca*, the song Don Gabriel began teaching me last night?" It was. So the celebrating was going on for a third day. I wondered if this was still in honor of Don Miguel's saint's day, or if it was a new fiesta for the baptism. I had a vision of the bored farmer still being obliged to give out mezcal to all comers. If he had been tired of the spongers yesterday, what must he feel about them today? It led me to remark cynically, "I think more of them come for the free drinks than for love of Don Miguel." Perhaps the truth wasn't customarily put so bluntly. At all events, Lupe laughed heartily. And when Don Gabriel returned a moment later she explained her continuing laughter by repeating the remark.

Naturally, she wanted her husband to see how handsome her cooking things looked in the sketches. He, too, was delighted as he recognized each item.

"Don't you want an *olla?*" he asked. And I was glad of the reminder. He led me out to the storeroom and we looked over several sizes, all brick red, with olive-green interiors. I picked the one I liked best and he brought it into the living room, together with the straw ring to keep it steady. *Ollas* are storage vessels, and they are generally used for corn kernels. As I arranged this particular one for drawing, I saw the handiness of those straw rings. I could move the almost spherical jar on it as easily as if it were a ball bearing, and the jar would stay at almost any angle. A cook, then, could readily place it where it was easy to reach into.

Next Don Gabriel suggested a chocolate beater, and I was glad to get it included too. This required a little more care in the drawing, for I had to indicate the loose rings that fly around as the cook holds the beater upright in a *jarro* and rotates it between her palms, as if she were making a fire with a stick.

The water carafe was Don Gabriel's next suggestion. I had never been much taken with this heavy barrellike jar. But it came from distant Guadalajara and I could tell from his tone it was a family treasure. So down it went.

"Aren't you going to draw Hambre?" Lupe asked. I realized the kitten, who hugged the stove so closely when it was cold, would be the perfect final touch. Fortunately, she was lying in the doorway, taking advantage of the sun. So into the last free corner she went.

Then I held up the completed page. I had to admit I was surprised myself at how well everything looked. Another lesson: drawing could induce

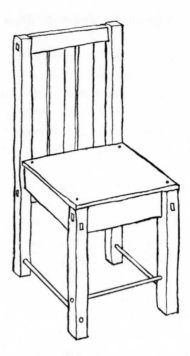

vision of pots and pans, no less than of architectural details. And I was glad that once again it had forced me to look carefully at things I had only observed casually before.

I still had some momentum, and, since I was doing household objects, I could not resist sketching something else. The chair the Blancos had lent me had helped my work so much I had become attached to it. And at Don Miguel's and again that morning, in seeing the schoolteacher's things, I had received ample proof that it was characteristic of the region. Why not draw a Tlaxiaco chair? The Blancos' other one was at hand. So down it went into the book too.

As I was drawing it, Don Gabriel made me aware of a feature of its construction I had not noticed. The whole frame was fitted together without a single nail. The joints were strong, though, because the tenons at the ends of the boards fitted so tightly into the slots in the uprights.

Don Gabriel had been very good about helping me draw Lupe's cooking things, but the thought occurred to me that perhaps his feelings had been a little hurt that I hadn't drawn anything of his. It would certainly do no harm to include one of his possessions, so I asked if I could draw his hat.

This was the hat whose orange band had caught my attention the Sunday he had showed up dressed in pink. I had admired its lines ever since and so it wasn't just tact that gave me the idea. Besides, it was a type the men of Yanhuitlán seemed to like particularly.

Mexican men wear many different sorts of sombreros, and I knew each style had its own name. Don Gabriel said his was a *fieltro vaquero*. I could understand the logic of *vaquero*. It meant cowboy, and the sombrero was like a cowboy hat. But *fieltro* meant felt. Why did he call it a felt, when it was made of straw? The explanation was simple. It was because the sombrero, with its two oval dents at the front, resembled hats commonly made of felt.

Don Gabriel's pleasure in the finished drawing showed I had been right to render the same homage to something of his that I had rendered to Lupe's possessions. And the household things being done, I was free for my next big project.

IN DESCRIBING my first stopover in Yanhuitlán I spoke of the monastery's wealth of minor detail. I mentioned especially the medallions carved over the doors of the friars' cells. Because many of them carry coats of arms, those medallions are known locally as *escudos,* or escutcheons. It was the *escudos* I wanted to draw next.

In previous chapters I have noted how Helen Griffith's book helped explain symbolic features of the monastery. Actually, these instances were more or less accidental. Where I had planned to use the book—and the reason I had sought it out and brought it to Mexico—was to help interpret the *escudos*. Before starting off with Don Gabriel for the cells, I went to my room to fetch it.

As we reached the top of the slope, we saw the priest backing his automobile from the shed. He was off for Oaxaca, and he waved jauntily as he drove past. This was the first occurrence to give me a sense of a weekly cycle. It was Wednesday, and the week before, when the priest headed for the big city, it also had been Wednesday.

ESCUDOS

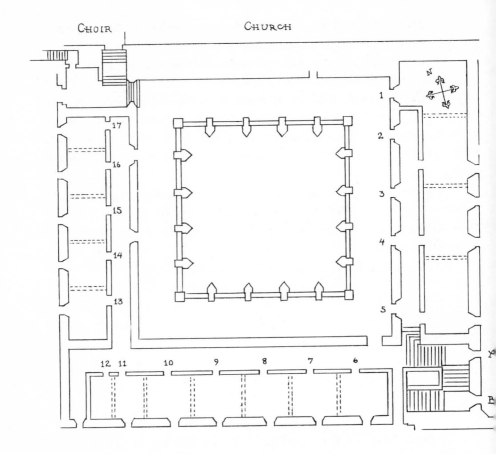

Above is the plan of the monastery's second floor to which I have referred several times. The former walls between the cells are indicated by the
hyphenated lines. The locations of the *escudos* are shown by the numbers
which run clockwise around the sides of the cloister bound by cellblocks.

The reader who remembers the visit to the priest's quarters already
knows that the four large cells of the east range do not open on the same
line. The first one, where I have placed the compass rose, opens onto the
cloister gallery. The three that have been taken over by the priest open onto
a corridor of their own. Apparently, though, the designer wanted to keep
his medallions in a single plane; so on this side he took the doorway of the
large cell at the top as his starting point and then, instead of placing the
other *escudos* over the cells inside, placed them over the entrances leading
from the gallery into the private corridor.

For me, this was doubly advantageous. On the one hand, I could draw the medallions in the spacious cloister gallery, where the air was fresh and the light excellent. On the other, I was spared the necessity of working directly in front of the priest's doors, as if I were a keyhole peeper.

Before describing the *escudos,* I should explain I was unfamiliar at the time with the chief personages of the Dominican Order. Nor was I aware of the extent to which all monastic orders tend to play up their own saints by reminders of them in their conventual decorations. This lack of knowledge not only inhibited my interpretations of the *escudos;* it allowed me to make wrong ones.

Take the first one, which shows a rather poorly modeled hand holding a pear-shaped object. I did not know then that, of all its female saints, the Dominican Order takes greatest pride in St. Catherine of Siena. I was unaware of the legend of her praying to Christ that he might take her heart and give her his, and of the subsequent miracle of the interchange being made. Further, I did not know that because of this St. Catherine was often depicted in art offering up her heart in her hand. Thus when Don Gabriel said the *escudo* showed San Basilio holding the heart of the world, I accepted his information. Not until later did I veer to the belief that the hand was St. Catherine's.

Similarly, I have since learned St. Thomas Aquinas was a Dominican and I have seen him pictured holding a church on a book often enough to believe the hand in *escudo* No. 4 is that of St. Thomas. But this flashes forward. I prefer to tell the story of the medallions as they seemed to me the day I drew them.

The hand of San Basilio—as I thought of it then—was easy to draw. No. 2 was even easier, for by this time I had sketched so many representations of the cross fluery that I could almost reproduce it with my eyes shut. I noticed some unusual features of this *escudo,* though. It was smaller and rather crudely cut; it was under an ogee arch, and it was on a raised boss, whereas all the others were cut in relief on the flat stones that served as lintels for the entrances.

No. 3, unfortunately, had been destroyed, and by what looked like an act of calculated vandalism, for surely only a man with a chisel could have cut the lintel so clean. As it was, he had not quite eliminated the indications that it was another cross fluery, this one with a shield at its center.

No. 4, the one of the hand holding a book supporting a church, was a beauty. And this one had tiny eight-pointed stars in its border—the only *escudo,* as it turned out, that was not merely circled with a plain ring.

ESCUDOS

Did Don Gabriel know its significance? He wasn't sure, so we hunted through Miss Griffith's book of symbols. We found that a church on a rock was a symbol of St. Peter. Perhaps, then, this was St. Peter's hand and the book was emblematic of the Bible, the rock on which the Church was founded.

The sign book devoted several pages to stars. Don Gabriel, who hunted as I sketched, found one with eight points. What did it say? he asked, handing me the English text to read. It said the eight-pointed star was emblematic of baptism because Jesus was given his name when he was circumcised on the eighth day.

This interested Don Gabriel because of all the eight-pointed stars in the cloister, including those on the bosses. The book further said that eight was the symbolic number for regeneration. This still did not explain why the eight-pointed star was intimately connected with St. Dominic, but we both felt we had made progress in learning that it was not a meaningless decoration.

No. 5 was the loveliest *escudo* yet. It also showed a hand, but one much daintier and more anatomically correct than the two previous ones. This hand was holding a chalice and the fineness of the carving can be judged from the leaves engraved on the cup. Behind the hand was a puzzling object carved at a slant. We suspected that the wafer seeming to rise from the chalice represented the Host, and I was pretty sure the chalice represented the wine vessel of the Last Supper. But because I'd seen a drawing of a cup in the book, I decided to read the entry. It proved me wrong. The chalice, it said, symbolized the agony in Gethsemane because of Christ's cry that the cup might pass from Him. This was news to Don Gabriel too. Excitedly, I read on, and the entry, fortunately, also mentioned the other symbols of the Passion.

This led to an experience I particularly love—in which a word or a phrase suddenly gives you the ability to see something clearly that formerly you could hardly see at all. Here the key word was "scourge." The scourge, the book said, was an emblem of the Passion. With that word I was not only able to understand what that puzzling object was, but for the first time I was able to fully grasp it with my eyes. Thongs—that was what those fine lines were, splaying from the top of the stick. And, to the pleasure of a word illuminating a physical image, was added another pleasurable instance of how knowledge, through providing the ability to interpret, can strike scales from the eyes.

1   2   3

How to convey my discovery to Don Gabriel? I didn't know the Spanish word for whip. I had to act it out; so with one hand I turned away his shoulder and with the other I pretended to bring down a lash on his back. "*Látigo*," he exclaimed. And the way his face brightened showed that all that had flashed through my mind had flashed through his. He, too, had recalled pictures of Jesus being beaten, and understood instantly why that scourge was depicted along with the cup. It was another instance of what makes for the deepest sort of friendship—a shared experience perceived simultaneously with a complete identity of response.

Drawing the *escudo* of the cup and the scourge took time. Its lines were so fine that I had to keep sharpening and re-sharpening my pencil. Don Gabriel was growing a little restless, so I told him I could get along perfectly from now on. He was grateful for the opportunity to leave, for he had promised to give another injection to Herminio's wife.

IN THE SOUTHERN RANGE, the wall dividing the cloister gallery from the cell corridor is pierced only in a single place. Thus in this range, as in the west one, the medallions are all directly over the cell doors. Accordingly, when I began the second lap of my project I was forced into what I had been spared with the first set. I had to work in the narrow corridor, standing directly in front of closed doors.

No. 6, the first of the southern *escudos*, displayed the cross fleury on an ornate shield. As I drew its curling edges, I was reminded of a strip of tin rotated around a key in opening a coffee can. I did not need the book to identify the five heart-shaped charges. From visits to Franciscan monas-

4   5

teries I knew they represented the five wounds of Jesus. It interested me to see a Franciscan coat of arms superimposed on the Dominican one. This was a second instance of close liaison between the two orders, for I remembered Don Gabriel saying that statues of St. Dominic and St. Francis had shared the main niche of the high altar before the priest had them carted away.

The cloister plan shows what happened when the door under this particular *escudo* opened and a woman emerged. She almost knocked me down. The woman was the priest's pigeon-plump little maid, and she was so shy that she was far more embarrassed than I. Through the open door behind her, I could see why she had been in the cell. It is now the priest's kitchen.

I tried to put the *criada* at ease by showing her the drawings of the *escudos*. They helped a little. Then I asked her if she lived in the monastery. Yes, she said. El Cura had taken over the first four cells of this range for the servant's quarters. Then she made her escape, still covered with confusion at having bumped shamelessly into a strange man.

Medallion No. 7, with the triple crown of the Pope above the crossed keys, reminded me of the papal flag. According to the book, one key represented excommunication, or the locking of the door to exclude unrepentant sinners from heaven; and the other absolution, or the opening of the door to admit the penitent. The dove, of course, was a symbol of the Holy Ghost. Like the other *escudos*, it was only about six inches in diameter. As I tried to reproduce the three-pronged bits of the keys, my admiration for the skill of the sculptor kept growing. How could he have carved such fine detail so cleanly and crisply in stone that seemed so soft? Then I remembered the little football player's head that I had bought in the church, and I recalled that its stone was so hard that Don Gabriel could not even mark it with a knife. If the Mixtec sculptors could cut such delicately modeled heads from intractable stone when they had no steel cutting tools, carving these *escudos* with

6

7

Spanish steel must have been relatively easy. Then I remembered the golden jewelry discovered in Tomb No. 7 on Monte Alban. That was Mixtec work, as was the intricate carving on the jaguar bones, and proved how good the Mixtecs were at tiny sculpture. Perhaps the carving of these *escudos* was not so surprising after all. Perhaps it was the work of a native. But since the symbolism was obviously Christian, where had he got his models?

I think the shape of the *escudos* gave me the idea: signet rings. I knew Indians had often based stone sculpture on designs taken from the work of silversmiths. The finials over the doorway to the sacristy (page 97) were clearly modeled on candlesticks. Why not rings? These certainly looked like signets. At all events, it was a conjecture that would be fun pursuing.

In the symbol book most of the sacred monograms were on the same page, so I was able to look up Nos. 8 and 10 simultaneously. I saw the XPS was derived from the first two and the last letters of Xpistos, the Greek word for Christ. And I found an explanation for the line above with the croquet hoop in the center. It was an ornamental version of the overhead bar that customarily signifies an abbreviation. The IHS in *escudo* 10 was based on Ihsoys, the Greek work for Jesus. And with my new comprehension of why bars were placed over letters that did not spell out a complete word, I appreciated how cleverly, and how differently, the designer had handled the abbreviating bar here. He made a Dominican cross out of it.

In this range, as in the eastern one, the middle *escudo* (No. 9) was destroyed. Only a trace of the circle remained and the door beneath was bricked up.

As I was drawing Nos. 10, 11 and 12, I heard a repeated cheep-cheep, very like the sound made by the Blancos' little turkey. There were other familiar barnyard sounds too, and a familiar odor. Could it be? I decided to investigate. These doors were blocked almost to the lintel too, but through a crack over the bricking of one I saw the vision that confirmed my suspi-

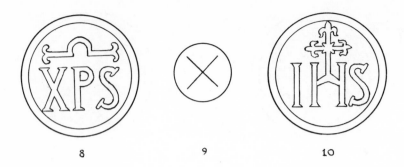

8   9   10

cion. The priest had taken these last three cells and converted them into a hen run. And there, before my eyes, was a young turkey taking a drink from a finely carved font that was lying on the floor. I was swept with the same wave of humor mixed with outrage that had come over me on learning the priest had cut the entrance door wider so he could drive his car into the monastery.

I remembered the insect which killed many chickens that pecked around the common earth, so I could sympathize with the priest for wanting to have his fowls off the ground and in a place where they would be less likely to eat the fatal insect. But did he have to turn the cells into a hen house? I wondered, too, if they were many chickens in the world who drank from holy water stoups, or had beautiful coats of arms carved over their living quarters.

Drawing the chickens' armorial bearings meant doing three more Dominican crosses. Repeating the same form so often, understandably, set me speculating about the effect on the friars of so many repetitions of the cross. How did the sight of that coat of arms, day after day, and in so many places, affect their thinking? I recalled our school crest that had been almost equally omnipresent—on our caps, our stationery, our bulletin boards, our hockey sweaters, our prizes, our china. Did the frequent sight of this coat of arms affect the friars as our crest affected us? It seemed only human to believe it might.

Our school was an old one with a good scholastic record and a high social standing; and, being private, it was outside the jurisdiction of the public school system. This led me to consider Dominican parallels. The Order, being founded at the start of the thirteenth century, already gloried in a three-hundred-year history when the friars came to Mexico. Being organized primarily to equip its members to be preachers, the Order educated its friars exceptionally well. And being a monastic order, its friars were not

11

12

subject to the hierarchy of regional bishops, like the secular clergy. They were subject only to their own superiors under the authority of the Pope. Added to this distinction, those who came to Mexico were white men living in a province whose inhabitants were nearly all brown-skinned natives.

Our crest had good influences. It served as a constant reminder of the gentlemanly ideal. It helped us merge ourselves into a group, and it generated a feeling of loyalty to something bigger than ourselves. But it also had bad effects. It was like an endlessly whispering voice telling us of our rather special position in the world. It tended to make us feel smug and superior. And by overemphasizing a relatively small unit of loyalty, it tended to make us lukewarm about larger loyalties.

Traditionally, coats of arms are signs of nobility. Surely, then, all these representations of the Dominican coat must have engendered a degree of ecclesiastical snobbery. I could see some of the less earnest friars coming to feel in their hearts that they were first of all Dominicans and only Christians incidentally. Indeed, living in such a place, with the escutcheon on every hand, how could the good friars help but be tempted into spiritual pride?

The last *escudo* of the southern range done, I turned my attention to the western range. The whitewashed corridor was austere and narrow; and, like the others, it had a beamed ceiling that was in good condition. But when I looked through the doors I could see why Don Gabriel had said it would be impossible for me to have a cell. The priest had not appropriated any on this side. But they were no longer a row of neat little rooms. Most of the partitions were gone and the long narrow space that remained was filled with rubble and rubbish. The doorway under *escudo* No. 16 was blocked up and three other doors had been crudely cut in the wall, destroying No. 15 altogether. I wondered for what purpose the range had been so barbarously remodeled. Was it to make an orderly room during one of the sieges?

ESCUDOS

13   14   15

The bottom of *escudo* No. 13 had been sliced off in the remodeling, so I could not complete the shield, but I noted it was shaped differently than the more ornate ones. I was interested, too, in the recurrence of the eight-pointed stars—in this case, two stars, one superimposed on the other, with the lower one having wavy points.

My affection for the little *escudos* had been mounting with each drawing, and this sense of personal attachment led me to think of a different effect of the shields—namely, how each friar must have been affected by the particular one that graced his cell. I could almost imagine, for instance, how a friar who lived in this cell might have written back to Spain.

"All the cells," his letter might have said, "have exquisitely carved coats of arms over the doors. Brother Pedro has the *escudo* of the cup and the scourge. Brother Martín has the monogram of Jesus. I have the *escudo* of the two stars. And though my cell is bare and simple, it gives me a sense of coming home when I see the *escudo* as I open my door. Sometimes, too, I think of those carved stars as I lie on my pallet at night and it makes me happy to know they are there."

Each *escudo*, too, I realized, would have a subtle psychological influence on the friar whose cell it distinguished. It would be a constant reminder of an ideal. To live under the monogram of Christ, for example, would be an incentive to keep as near His standards as possible. And perhaps the friar who lived under the first *escudo* would see that hand holding the heart as a constant reminder of how deep his compassion should be for his Indian charges.

No. 14 was another hand, and this one held three lilies. My book said the lily was the flower of the Virgin Mary, for the Angel of the Annunciation carried a lily as he came to her. Later I was to learn, too, that lilies were as closely associated with St. Dominic as the eight-pointed star.

No. 16 was a skull, the symbol of death and sin. And as I sketched it,

WEEK IN YANHUITLÁN

16

17

I saw a new merit in the carving of the medallions. The depth of the cutting varied according to the requirements of the subject matter. The monograms, for instance, were in low relief, but here the sculptor had cut deep into the surrounding stone causing the skull to stand out with an impressively rounded dome. The eerie little death's-head he had created conveyed so much sinister feeling that I felt any friar who drew this cell must have considered it an omen of bad luck.

At this point Don Gabriel returned to say the midday meal was ready. I knew it had been growing late, but I asked if I could finish the last *escudo*. This showed a bird that seemed to be feeding its young. As I sketched, I asked Don Gabriel to see if he could find a clue for the symbolism in the book. He thumbed through the pictures and suddenly gave an excited exclamation: " *El Pelícano*."

Not understanding, I asked to see what he had found. On the open page was a picture of a pelican, and the English text, which he could not read, said the pelican was a symbol of Christ because it was believed that in times of famine this bird tore open its breast and gave its life blood to its young. I explained the meaning carefully and once more it did my heart good to see his face brighten. As we left the monastery together, I promised I would give him the book.

DURING OUR *comida* the little black turkey stepped over the threshold coming in from the patio. *Cheep-cheep*, it went, and the sound reminded me irresistibly of the small turkey I had heard in the priest's hen house. So I looked at the Blancos' bird and drawing a mournful face, I said: "*Pobre pavito, no tiene un escudo sobre su celda.*"

Don Gabriel was exasperatedly aware of the poultry behind the coats of arms in those three cells, so he saw the point right away. Laughingly, he explained that I was commiserating with the little turkey for its poor accommodations. It wasn't like the priest's turkey. It didn't have a coat of arms over its door.

That set Lupe laughing too, and with such encouragement, I extended the disadvantages of the poor underprivileged turkey. *"Pobre pavito, no tiene agua bendito."* That meant it had no holy water. And the mock deprivation brought more laughter.

"Pobre pavito," the Blancos repeated, enjoying the joke further as they joined in bewailing the young turk's social disadvantages.

The entrance of the little brown cock enabled us to go through the whole happy foolishness again.

If only the telling of mental processes could be as swift as the processes themselves! For in a moment I was starting a drawing. But first the stages.

The priest's poultry having coats of arms had caused my mind to leap to that cartoon lion carved over the door of Angel Pérez. His household, then, was a human habitation with the pretense of an escutcheon. The presence of the couchant lion over his door, in turn, made me aware of the total absence of any heraldic bearing over the Blancos' lintel. That was why I was drawing. *"Momentito,"* I said to the Blancos.

First, I outlined a shield. Then, inspired by the crossed keys of St. Peter, I drew Lupe's long cooking spoon at a slanting angle and crossed it diagonally with her chocolate beater. These kitchen items saltire gave me four points to fill. Clearly the stove deserved the honor point, so I sketched it above the beater and the spoon. The carafe was a good candidate for the dexter point, and the taller pitcher for the sinister. In they went, and thanks to the familiarity engendered by the morning's drawing, I could sketch them rapidly from memory. That left only the small space at the bottom where the shield came to a point. A perfect spot for Hambre caboched! I dashed in a full face of the neckless kitten and handed the result to Lupe.

"Su escudo," I said.

Don Gabriel was quick to look over her shoulder. Each of the pictured household objects, named aloud on joint recognition, produced a new laugh, with Hambre making the biggest hit of all.

And I wasn't through yet, for I had more to say to Lupe on the subject. "Now when you go to market," I said, "and when you meet Sra. Angel Pérez, you can say, 'I have an *escudo* too.' " They knew I was referring to that awful lion, so the humor continued to run fresh and clear.

"When you go to market now," I asked Lupe, "do you know what the women will say after you've passed?" She shook her head.

WEEK IN YANHUITLÁN

"They'll say: Poor Lupe, she used to be so nice, but ever since she's had that *escudo* she's had a *cabezón.*'" It was the term for a swelled head.

Could they keep the *escudo*, Don Gabriel asked. "Of course," I replied. And he took down the keys from the wall, opened the army trunk and locked it away with their treasures. In return, he gave me something he had copied for me: the words of *Canción Mixteca*, the song he had started teaching me the night before. Later, he said, he would locate the music. And I returned to my room with the song in my hand.

XX

THE FAÇADE

THE DETAILED DRAWING of the west front was my afternoon project. But because I shrank from the work involved, I welcomed the daily shave as an excuse for stalling.

Juan, *el campesino*, came slowly and perhaps not quite steadily by as I was sitting on the doorstep applying the lather. He stayed to watch. The effects of three days of celebrating his brother's saint's day and his new nephew's baptism betrayed themselves in only one marked way. His right eye had grown smaller than the left. Otherwise, once he stood in one place, he was a model of rectitude. He watched for a long time, unsmiling and without saying a word.

Being busy with my own stubble made me conscious of his beardlessness. His bronze jaws had the fine clear texture of many Indian faces. And, though he was twenty-three, his upper lip had nothing but a little black down. Comparative thoughts must have been going through his mind too, for he finally broke the silence.

"Don't you want a *bigote?*" he asked. Then he stroked that bit of down, as a pointed, but unspoken, way of calling attention to his superb moustache.

"*Bigotes,*" he added, "are the fashion in this region." With that he walked stiffly on.

Don Gabriel was amused when I told him the story, and I guess he understood Juan's aspirations to be hirsute. He was twenty years older, yet his own beard was so sparse he only had to shave every four or five days.

I have told how I rejoice in the elucidating word—the accurately descriptive term that either will make the eye look at something it glossed over before, or will enable the mind to grasp what the eye saw without comprehension. I mention it again because of something I armed myself with before setting out to draw the façade. One of the excerpts Don Gabriel had typed out so conscientiously was Manuel Toussaint's description of the monastery in *Paseos Coloniales*. I had made notes on Toussaint and it was these notes I stuffed in my pocket, calculating they might help my observations when I was in front of the façade.

A bookrest was another item I thought of in advance. I knew I needed support for a drawing that was going to be as carefully detailed as the one I planned to make. So I asked Don Gabriel if we could go to the church first to get the lectern-candlestand I used in drawing the main altar. His answer was the perfectly agreeable: *"Sí. ¿Cómo no?"*

Not only had I been getting to know the people of Yanhuitlán, but its birds had also been growing more familiar. Several times I had been charmed by an especially sweet-noted *whee-wheet,* and when we heard it on the way to the church I asked Don Gabriel to identify the bird.

The *cuitlacoche,* was his reply, and I have since learned this is the regional name for the curved-bill thrasher. In the spring the bird's song was even prettier, Don Gabriel said.

Once we had the drawing lectern, we carried it to the point by the thatched huts I had indicated the day before. And there, almost a quarter of a mile from the church, I began the drawing. As may be seen on page 32, the façade has four stories—three that are richly carved, and a more or less blank one at the top that is surmounted by a triangular cresting. I wanted to make my task as easy as possible, so my plan was to do only the three carved stories. The drawing of the first day, I felt, gave the reader evidence enough to imagine the Baroque gable for himself.

What I had to block in, then, was a three-tiered rectangle. Because of the size of my subject, I decided to utilize as much of the page as possible. I drew the top line just below the rings of the spiral. Then I began sketching in all the main compartments, for I was aware that each one had to be the right size in relation to the others and that the outer frame had to be large enough to accommodate them all. The correctness of the skeleton was essential, for once I moved up close and started to concentrate on detail, I knew I would not be able to keep everything in proper scale if the guiding niches and pillars were not right. Accordingly, I worked very painstakingly. I held up my pencil at arm's length and moved my thumb along it to check my relative proportions. And since I was drawing a symmetrical composition from dead center I measured and remeasured to see that my spaces were always equal on both sides of the center line.

Two barefoot little boys and three little girls in rebozos stopped to watch. I noted that one little girl was carrying a *tenate* almost as big as herself, and that all the scantily clad children looked cold, for the day had never really warmed up. But I was too absorbed to pay attention to them, and they disappeared into the thatched huts without my seeing them go.

As I worked I saw a new advantage of my distant position. The fact that I could not see any small details meant they did not claim my attention. That simplified the task of judging basic relations.

The façade grew on me. There was no doubt about it: the composition, for all its vastness, was beautifully proportioned. It was tall enough to be elegant and the width was calculated to a hair's breadth. Anything wider would have destroyed the elegance; anything narrower would have been too skinny. And there was a subtle rightness about the diminishing heights of the stories as they ascended.

Feelings of affection for the façade began to stir. Could my first indifference have been protective? Had I adopted the attitude to save myself from being overpowered by something too big for me to grasp? I sensed I was on the right track. When my framework was finally finished, I held it out at arm's length, and made an appalling discovery. It looked ugly.

Holding it up against the church and checking the two point by point, I couldn't see where I had gone wrong. Yet my compartmented rectangle was ill-shaped and the façade was not. What was the answer? Then it dawned on me. The triangular top! That gable had to be included. Though it was not a mass of ornament like the other stories, it was integral to the composition. In fact, the composition was not successful without it. And this showed me how seriously I had underestimated the artistry of whoever designed that façade to think I could have dispensed with one of his elements.

What made the discovery so hard to bear was that my page did not have space enough at the top to admit the cresting. If I were to make a drawing including the cresting—and my artistic conscience made this inescapable— I would have to do those three stories over again on a fresh sheet, starting them far enough below the rings to leave room for the Baroque triangle.

It was disheartening, I was already beginning to tire and the afternoon was waning. I knew now that I could not get the drawing finished that day. If only that façade hadn't finally got under my skin, I could have junked

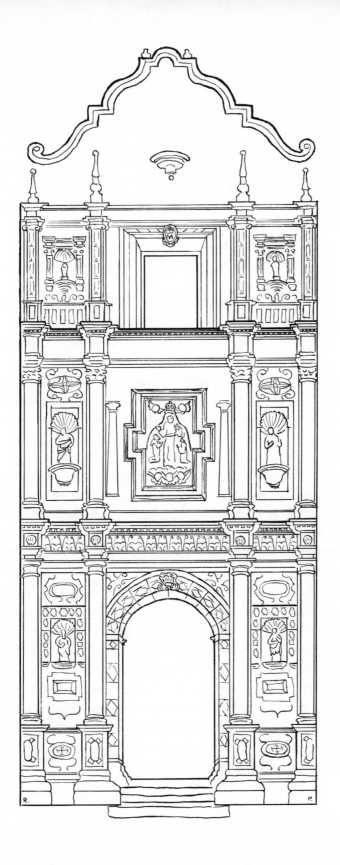

the whole project. But by now I knew I had to have a decent representation of it. I gritted my teeth and turned to the job.

I soon found the situation was not as black as I thought. I wouldn't have to rejudge those proportions. By marking the old measurements on the edge of a piece of paper and using this as a gauge I could reproduce the framework fairly readily. And I could do it without having to look at the monastery. Seeing this was so, I decided to move up to the head of the stairs, where I had known all along I would have to move when the time came to fill in the details. And the steps would provide something to sit on while I finished transferring the old skeleton to a new sheet of paper.

"Vámanos," I said to Don Gabriel. He scrambled to his feet, and insisted on carrying the stand for me.

The transfer did not take very long and the new version had the advantage of being cleaner. And the difference made by outlining the cresting on top proved the rightness of my decision. Soon I was on my feet again, ready to start the details.

At this point I am faced with the same dilemma that arose in the church. And I am solving it in the same way. I am giving the finished drawing here so the reader can have it before his eyes as I had the actuality before mine.

Before beginning the details, I got out the Toussaint notes to help organize my observations. Being close, I could see well enough to appreciate the distinctions he made between the paired uprights of each story. He was right to call those at the top pilasters, instead of columns, for they were square. And as one who has groped for terms to describe unusual physical appearances, I admired the word he found for the carving of those pilasters. They did look "cushioned."

The uprights of the middle story were different in that, being round, they were real columns. And Toussaint made me aware of the acanthus capitals by classifying the pillars as Corinthian. Then he made me see the uprights of the lower story were different yet again. Having no leafy capitals, the columns were not Corinthian. "Doric" was his term. And here he stimulated me by stirring a contradiction. These columns weren't fluted, they didn't flare at the base, and they didn't have the typical padlike Doric capitals. The smooth shafts and those isolated rings below the capitals made them Tuscan. And I thanked the famous Mexican scholar for forcing me into even closer observation by his slip.

I was stimulated, too, by his conjecture that the façade was not contemporary with the rest of the building. Its arrangement of parts, he argued, was typical of Dominican façades known to have been built at a later date. I was not scholar enough to verify this, but his suggestion of seventeenth-century work was enough to make me aware of how different in style this façade was to other parts of the establishment.

The difference was not merely in the decorative motifs employed, but in the whole principle of their organization. Elsewhere the carved stonework had been trimming applied to plain walls to make apertures more handsome and interesting. But no one could say this façade consisted of the trim around the choir window and the main door. It was an elaborately carved, ornamental wall which happened to have voids where the window and door were. And its difference from the rest of the monastery was emphasized by its color. Enough sand and pink were in it to harmonize with the older stone, but its complexion was more swarthy, for it contained more brown, and a hint of olive.

Benefiting from past experience, I began at the top. The cresting was easy, but once I came to the first cornice the minute work began. As I drew the oval medallion over the rectangular choir window—a monogram of Mary, surmounted by a crown—I realized it had some of the same exquisite quality as the *escudos*. The niches were remarkably good too, and the paneled pilasters were work of the most beautiful finish and refinement. Why, then, had I underestimated this carving? It was a question I was too busy to answer. But I remember thinking the two top figures were unworthy of their niches.

Frankly, I felt no regret that the one on the left had lost its head. Even with its head, it would have been as poor as the characterless figure on the right.

Then came the second cornice, with five bands of molding to worry about and dentils to indicate. It was pernickety work. But by now I was a little more accustomed to it and Don Gabriel helped by seeing my pencils were kept sharp. Every time I would lay down a blunted one, he would pick up the razor blade and repoint the lead.

In the central panel was a large carved tableau which showed the Virgin Mary holding the infant Jesus with one hand and blessing two kneeling suppliants with the other. She was standing on some knobby clouds supported by cherub heads. There were two more winged cherub heads in the upper corners. In proportion to the human figures, the cherubs were enormous.

The way the Virgin's cloak was looped up to make a canopy over the heads of the suppliants identified her as the Virgin of Mercy. Kelemen's *Baroque and Rococo in Latin America* had made me familiar with versions of her in Peru and Ecuador. Thus on first glimpsing this tableau I had been interested to see a more northern version, but because of the disproportion of those cherubs' heads I had dismissed it as an inferior rendition. In trying to reproduce the tableau, though, I was forced to linger long enough over its various parts to see it was beautifully carved.

Perhaps I had just been snobbish about those heads. As I outlined them, I saw that their being drawn in a different scale than the full figures was an example of the folkloristic aspect of Latin-American art I had encountered in the mural of St. Christopher. And as the outsize cherubs became more endearing I began to understand better why Kelemen finds that folklore quality charming. I also found myself in a better position to appreciate his point that it is this folk quality that makes colonial art a distinct branch, rather than a straight, and inferior, imitation of Spanish work.

Often in versions of the Virgin of Mercy the figures kneeling under her sheltering mantle are popes and kings, and they are clearly proclaimed as such by their tiaras and crowns. But these two suppliants obviously were simpler folk. Don Gabriel knew who they were. The man on the left, he said, was a Dominican friar. The woman on the right was a Dominican nun.

In drawing the figures in the niches flanking the tableau, I saw these figures were every bit as inferior as I had thought. Then, dropping my eyes to the figures in the two bottom niches, I saw they, too, were as crude as they had seemed at first. And with that confirmation came another effortless realization. My North American artistic environment, with its fine museums and its relatively few important early buildings, had developed my sensibility for figural sculpture, but it had given me practically no opportunity to develop an appreciation of architectural sculpture. In consequence, those six crude figures and the disproportionate cherubs had leaped out at me and prejudiced me against the whole façade.

My relative indifference to the façade, then, had not all been protective. It was partly due to an unequal development of my powers of perception. I had been able to see the faults clearly in the one part of the work that was weak, while I had been nearly blind to the merits of the major part which was strong. The effortlessness of this comprehension reminded me of the similar ease with which I had realized that so many representations of the Dominican coat of arms would make for spiritual pride. In neither instance had I been deliberately trying to analyze effects. On the contrary, I'd been narrowing my eyes and concentrating on putting on paper just the lines I saw in front of me. The realizations had swum to the surface of their own accord.

But I knew it was not accidental. And I apprehended still another beneficial result of drawing. Most of those I had become aware of stemmed from drawing's enforcement of careful observation. This new benefit arose from the very factor in the nature of drawing I had tended to resent—namely, that it took time.

How is it those thoughts about spiritual pride had come to me as I was drawing the *escudos*, when they had not come to me on the many occasions I had seen those *escudos* in passing down the cell corridors? And there had not been a day that I hadn't looked at this façade. Why hadn't I understood sooner that I had been overly prejudiced by the crudeness of the figures in the niches?

It was because in the corridors and in front of the façade I had been too hurried. My mind—and I mean the subconscious part too—had not been given sufficient time to operate on either the *escudos* or the façade. But the physical necessity of drawing them had held me prisoned in front of them long enough for reflections to begin.

As I thought about those reflections, examples of others of the same kind came to me. One was how I thought of the friars coming to the choir to chant the Divine Office. Another was the train of thought following the discovery that the town fountain was integrated with the monastic plan. Correlating them, I saw that it is in the nature of the mind to start thinking about the things that come before the eyes—that is, if the mind is given a free space of time in which it is allowed to operate spontaneously. Put another way, one can say that, if the mind is not loaded with new problems that the will insists be solved, the mind moves of its own accord on material brought to it by the eyes. And often these unwilled thoughts prove to be the most important ones of our lives.

In general terms, then, I saw that not only do we observe carelessly, but we turn away too soon. And drawing is a discipline that enables us to overcome both bad habits.

Discipline was certainly the word to describe the way I had to direct my seeing and govern my penciling in drawing the cornice of the lowest story. Sometimes, to give myself a rest, I would let my eyes play over the whole façade. Man and the elements had treated this more kindly than the north portal. The upper triangle was rather battered and the cornice and capitals of the top story showed signs of erosion. But the only other marked evidence of destruction was a largish bite out of the cornice under the choir window. I decided that in the various sieges in which the monastery was used as a fortress the attackers must have made a point of not aiming their cannons directly at the façade.

Mention of that bite from the second cornice might have led the reader to look for it. It is not in the drawing, for I took advantage of my freedom as an artist to restore it. A photograph, I realized, would perhaps have more value in preserving each little nick. This did not make me feel my work was inferior. On the contrary, the thought of the photograph made me aware that I was depicting the façade in a way that no single camera could do. I was presenting it from two points of view simultaneously. Its general conformation was depicted from a quarter of a mile away; its detail from a distance of about thirty feet. And the result was not a double exposure. The mind was clever enough to see to that.

My eye level was just below the base of the Tuscan columns. Thus from my close position, when I looked directly ahead, I could not see the tableau of the Virgin of Mercy at all. Yet the Virgin is in the picture, to say nothing of the Virgin's monogram, which is still higher. This anomaly showed me that not only was I depicting the façade as no camera could, but I was also depicting it as no human eye could see it. By this, I mean no physical eye, for when the eye is far enough away to encompass the whole outline it is too far away to see this much detail; and when the eye is near enough to discern, say, the ribbing of the shells in the niches, it is too close to take in the whole façade with a single look. In other words, the façade could not possibly look to any one's actual vision the way it looks here. This is a composite picture that depicts the door as it exists in the mind's eye.

Remembering my experience with the north portal, I realized that only when they are seen with the mind's eye can one ever fully appreciate these great Spanish portals. Always knowledge of the total design must be brought to inspection of the parts. This may be a fault in the genre, but I'm inclined to doubt it. To be properly known, all important music has to be doubly comprehended—in total structure as well as in felicity of detail. Surely it is no reflection on an architectural creation to say it cannot be swallowed in a single visual bite.

Though I was fairly isolated in my thoughts as I drew, I was not isolated in human terms. Fausto, the principal of the school, and José, the teacher who was moving into the room behind mine, had come to the front of the church, and I could hear them chatting pleasantly together as they sat at the head of the steps behind me. Other villagers, too, paused to watch. One was the old man with the staff and the big bandage around his gray hair who had sat on the steps of the unused pulpit during the Sunday Mass. Now he was more picturesque than ever, for he had draped a blanket over his shoulders against the cold. He was a Ribera model if ever I saw one.

When I paused in my drawing to show him all the other sketches, he thanked me with a gentleness and sweetness that exceeded anything I had experienced in the village. As he smiled and shook my hand as his expression of gratitude and farewell, I had a strange sense I had been touched by pure goodness. The feeling was so strong that I asked Don Gabriel who the man was. His name was Felix Soriano and for many years he had been the sacristan. Now he was too old for the tasks of the post, but he still haunted the church like a loving spirit.

Ordinarily, Don Gabriel did not introduce villagers, so my curiosity was piqued when he made a point of introducing Juan Santos, a man with a lean, alert face. When the man was gone Don Gabriel supplied the explanation on his own initiative. Santos, he said, was Yanhuitlán's Protestant pastor. The presence of a minister suggested a Protestant church. Was there one in the village? I asked, surprised at this new turn of events.

"No," said Don Gabriel. "There are congregations big enough to have churches in Teposcolula and Tejupam. But here the Protestants hold their services in groups that meet at each others' homes."

The Tuscan columns were not the only features making the first story different from the others. The style of the sculpture was different, too. One might almost say the stone was brocaded. Nearly every element was covered with an over-all design, finely carved in very low relief. Even the frieze under the cornice was decorated. And the ornamentation included scallop shells on the entablatures of the four pillars.

As I was working on the frieze I heard behind me a heavy, unforgettable, lowing, clomping sound. I turned and saw one of the most wonderful sights of my life. Eight pairs of brown oxen were being driven home after the day's plowing. The yoked creatures were so big the highway was not wide enough for them all. Several teams walked along the green margins of the road. And the dignified beasts, who had dragged their wooden plows behind them all day, were now carrying them home, hooked to their wooden yokes. Most of the men in sarapes who herded the oxen were on foot, but the rear of the main herd was brought up by a man on a gray burro. And trailing the great procession was a man in blue driving a ninth team. One of his beasts was brown like the rest, but the other was coal black.

Added to the sounds of the oxen were the occasional hisses of switches and the joking shouts of the men. Clearly, they were relaxed and happy that the day was over. And I think I loved the scene as much for its symbolism as for its actual beauty, for in the procession of the animals and the sounds of the men's voices I heard deep and ancient undertones. I heard the sounds of a way of life that went back at least to the lean and the fat kine of Joseph's Egypt. I heard something of the earth's music and of what it means to till it. I heard a motif that had been constant for so many centuries, yet which evoked the changes of the cycles—winter, spring, summer and autumn; morning, afternoon and night. And I heard the sound of what it means to go home in the evening at the end of a day's work.

It was a quarter past five when the men and their beasts passed out of view. I turned back to the façade, for I wanted to finish as much as possible. The keystone of the doorway took time, for it was carved in the same delicate manner as the *escudos* over the cell doors—and with some of the same symbols, for against the background of a shell were a lily and a book.

Over the doorway was a painted inscription. All the letters were intact except the one ending the last word. A modern Dominican later recognized the Latin text and supplied the missing "e." The text was *Introite Portas ejus in Confessione.* It is taken from the Psalms and means "Go ye into His gates with praise."

When a building is faced with pillars that do not reach the ground, architects have a term for the space below the columns. They call it the basement. And when I had finished the keystone, I paused to study this façade's basement. It was finely carved, too, but here the style differed once more. It was not like brocade, for there were many flat surfaces and the raised parts suggested welts. For the moment, though, I couldn't put my finger on what it resembled.

The basement contained a number of Dominican symbols, including multipointed stars and lily crosses. But the most striking were the dogs. There was one seated on a book in each of the oval shields adorning the two pedestals closest to the door. Each dog held something in its mouth resembling a dish mop. This was one emblem I could interpret unaided. The

sight of it on previous Dominican monasteries had led to investigation. I had found a dog was doubly appropriate to represent a Dominican. First there was a pun. *Dominus* is the Latin word for God. *Canus* is the Latin for dog. Dominicans, therefore, suggest "dogs of God." The second reason arises from the prophetic dream St. Dominic's mother had shortly before his birth. In her dream she saw her unborn son in the form of a black and white dog that ran about dispelling the darkness by the flaming torch it bore in its mouth. I knew then that what looked like a dish mop was meant to be the torch of faith. The symbolism of the torch touching the cross-tipped globe, of course, was that of faith igniting the world.

As I studied the panel, I suddenly got the phrase for the carving. It resembled embossed leather. And I wondered if among the objects that inspired colonial carving, such as candlesticks and signet rings, one could include the richly embossed binding of Renaissance books.

The dogs, I decided, were too low in relief and fine in detail to include in my drawing of the façade as a whole. But meanwhile other details had to go in. I worked a little longer, but shortly after six the failing light made me realize the ornamentation below the arch of the door would have to wait till the next day. However, I was pleased with the progress I had made. I had got further down the façade than I expected.

When I indicated I was knocking off, Don Gabriel started to pick up the drawing lectern. I planned to carry the other end, but one of the watching villagers came forward with a gesture which said "allow me." I gratefully acceded, and I recognized the extent of my tiredness in the relief I felt in being able to walk beside them, carrying nothing more than my sketchbook.

Once the stand was back in the church, Don Gabriel and I headed for home. We overtook the Widow Isabel. It was the first time I had seen her since the ball, but she nodded and crinkled her humorous old eyes at me in the friendliest way. I should stay in the village and marry one of the local girls, she said. "Well," I said, "I like María Luisa very much. And I like Leonila. But I think I'll wait till Serafina grows up."

I had some cards to mail and Don Gabriel volunteered to come with me to the post office. Again we had to rouse Don Patricio to open the door, and again I was struck by the old man's parchment-colored face, cross-hatched with wrinkles. Since Mexican politeness insisted that we engage in a little courteous palaver instead of just dropping the cards and running, I showed Don Patricio my drawings. He was so unfamiliar with the monastery that he could scarcely identify anything. And when he saw the sketch of the north portal he made the same mistake as the egg-shaped burgher. He, too, exclaimed, *"Campo santo,"* taking the doorway for the arched entrance to the cemetery.

When we came away, Don Gabriel and I chuckled over the old postmaster's unawareness of what lay under his nose. Jokingly I explained his ignorance of the church by saying, "He must be a Protestant."

"He was once," said Don Gabriel, taking me seriously. Then he added an interesting fact: the old man had reverted to Catholicism.

Don Gabriel had not forgotten his promise about the music for *Canción Mixteca*. Shortly after my return he brought over a frayed and yellowed piece of sheet music that he had borrowed. It had the song's treble part. And I realized how bent he was on my having the music to take home with me. He had also managed to rustle up some lined music paper to help me transcribe it.

"When you are back in New York," he said, "you will be able to play it on your piano. Tonight we will have another lesson."

I put in the time before supper by copying out the music and making a word-for-word translation of the song. Here is the Spanish text he had given me:

> *Qué lejos estoy del suelo donde he nacido*
> *Inmensa nostalgia invade mi pensamiento.*
> Refrain: *Tal verme tan solo y triste cual hoja al viento*
> *Quisiera llorar, quisiera morir de sentimiento.*

O tierra del sol, suspiro por verte
Ahora qué lejos yo vivo sin luz, sin amor.
Tal verme tan, etc.

And here is the translation:

How far I am from the region where I was born,
Immense nostalgia invades my thinking.
On seeing myself as alone and sad as a leaf in the wind
I would like to weep, I would like to die of longing.

Oh land of the sun, I sigh to see thee.
Now how far away I live without light, without love.
On seeing myself as alone and sad as a leaf in the wind
I would like to weep, I would like to die of longing.

Because they knew I was staying for the projected song lesson, Don Gabriel and Lupe took their own supper seated by the little stove as I lingered over my hot milk at the table. And as the lesson began Lupe washed the few dishes.

The song was in six-eight time and it was in the key of D major. Don Gabriel was a tenor, and although his voice was a little quavery he always sang exactly on pitch. The high note of the song was the A at the end of the phrase *"O tierra del sol."* Nearly always Don Gabriel's voice cracked just a little on this, but he was not self-conscious about singing in front of a music critic. After all, his purpose was not to show off, but to teach a song. And he knew the way it went. Having gone over it several times with him the night before, I was able to start singing along with him. I, too, had to gulp a bit before that high A, and we would look at each other with pleasure when we both got it.

He was seated on the bed and I had drawn my chair over to the corner of the table so we could have the words and music where we both could read them. The candle stood so close it almost dripped on the music. After several duets, he asked me to try a solo. I needed a lot of coaching, for I was still singing most of the Spanish syllables by rote and I was not yet sure how the syllables were distributed over the notes. He saw I was not yet ready for solo work, so we reverted to singing in unison.

When I felt fairly confident, I asked to try it again by myself. I didn't have it as right as I thought. By this time the melody was fairly well fixed in my mind, but, as Don Gabriel showed me, I was distorting the rhythm by stumbling through it so slowly. My tendency was to give each note the same time value.

"Faster," he said as he beat out the rhythm in the air. And he worked with me till I sang the eighth notes more rapidly and drew out the dotted quarters long enough.

The thought went through my head that it was a pity he had given up teaching after that one year of it in his twenties. He was a good teacher—patient, firm and watchful. He did not hesitate to interrupt me when I was singing incorrectly, and he was ready to repeat and repeat a phrase till I got it right. His tenacity interested me, for it was part of the same pattern as his concern in seeing that I had the music to take home with me. At first I had been puzzled and even a little amused at his earnestness in the matter. But as the meaning of the song grew clearer to me I knew why he was taking such pains. The song was something intimately associated with his region. He wanted to fix it in my mind so it would always be there, carrying its charge of nostalgic overtones whenever it came back to me. And I knew from his reference to the piano that he hoped when I was back in New York I would sometimes play the song and think lovingly of him and his wife and of the visit to Yanhuitlán.

The musical phrase that came most easily to me was the straight ascent on the chord of A major that went with the words "O tierra del sol." Here I also had the easiest time singing the words meaningfully, for the translation "Oh land of the sun" was easy to hold in my consciousness as I articulated the Spanish syllables. Finally, I got through a whole solo without a mistake. Don Gabriel applauded.

After this, we took more pleasure in our duets and began to sing with more expression, lingering with especial feeling over the "miento" of the final "sentimiento."

"Don't you want to sing with us?" I asked Lupe. She laughed and shook her head.

"Why not?"

"I've got a voice like a frog," she said.

After one or two more run-throughs, the lesson ended and Don Gabriel saw me home. The night was so black that he lit a match so we could see our way from one door to another.

Before turning in I could not resist propping up my sketchbook in the light of the candle and looking at the unfinished drawing of the façade. Away from that towering west front, I was less conscious of where the representation fell short. In fact, I had the contrary feeling of surprise in finding it had captured more than I thought.

Clearly, the façade was the monastery's architectural climax. And to think I might have been too lazy to draw it!

XXI

THE LAST COMPLETE DAY

THE DAY ITSELF decided this title. Lacing through it were threads that would be broken by the isolation of parts of the day into separate chapters. And the day's pattern, besides being interwoven with threads already laid down, ended with unworked threads that reached to the day ahead.

The familiar thread with which it began was the throbbing of the corn mill, which greeted me when I woke at six-thirty. I heard a bird whistling prettily and my sense of being among familiar things was increased by being able to identify the bird as a *cuitlacoche*.

When I opened the door to light the room I saw the sky was gray and overcast, and the clouds were so low they cut off the tops of all the hills. Most of the time the atmosphere had been so clear I had tended to forget that the valley was more than seven thousand feet up. But today there was the near-drizzle in the air that is common at high altitudes. It revealed the logic behind the name for the people of the region, for in translation the word Mixteca means "people of the mist."

One of those people, equipped with a knotted rope, was herding turkeys not far from my door. From the crackled black and orange poncho I guessed it was Juan, *el campesino,* and when I called out *"buenos días"* he turned and confirmed my supposition. The three-day spree was definitely over. Not only was he back at work, but the effects of the alcohol had worn off, for his smile had regained its flexibility and his right eye had opened to normal size.

Bobby was the next old friend to be greeted. And since the dog had paid me the honor of a visit I wanted to show my hospitality by offering a tidbit. But on consulting my supply of candies I found I was down to my last sack. Clearly, I had to go easy on the dwindling treasure. Accordingly, I offered Bobby a piece of one of Nahum's apples. It was not to his taste. And when the dog refused it I saw I could not get away with that particular economy. I parted with a *dulce*.

On my way to the Blancos for breakfast I heard singing and music coming from somewhere on the far side of the plaza. It sounded like another *serenata*, and Lupe said it was. Today was the saint's day of Angel Pérez, the soft-drink magnate. The repetition of the custom prompted me to put a question to Don Gabriel.

"Do the neighbors come to your house and serenade you on your saint's day?" He chuckled as he replied in the negative. "Why not?" I asked.

"I don't have enough money. I can't give a fiesta."

There was a knock at the outer door. It was Nahum, who, because he was going back to school, had come to say good-bye. Lupe asked him in and he was there when she set two fried eggs in front of me. The presence of the boy made me feel shyer than usual, so instead of speaking the grace aloud, I said it to myself. I asked Nahum when his bus left. Half-past twelve was the time, and he left after Don Gabriel and I promised to see him off.

After breakfast, I had to run to my room, for the near-drizzle had turned to rain. From my doorway I scanned the sky to see if the day might clear. I hoped it would, for I was anxious to finish drawing the façade. The prospect did not look very encouraging, but I did not feel downhearted. I've learned not to despair too early, and, even if the rain continued, I was endowed with that great substitute for patience—an intervening project.

"*Buenos días*," a tiny voice said at my elbow. It was Angelita, the little girl with the bare legs and the pigtails who always resorted to some form of greeting if her silent passing was not sufficient to catch my attention.

I gave her the candy she was after. But this time she did not go skipping away after saying "*gracias*." Instead she looked up with big black, appealing eyes and asked in a tiny wisp of a squeaky voice: "*Tiene usted dulces para mis hermanitas?*"

Did I have any candies for her little sisters? The question led to an inquiry as to how many little sisters there were. "*Cinco*," came the wispy reply, and she held up the five fingers of her hand to make sure there would be no misunderstanding. I was not surprised that she had so many sisters— I was used to Mexican families—but that was a large order when I was on my last sack. Still, I was taken by her generous spirit and I couldn't resist those eyes. Five I gave her. And she ran off in the rain.

My intervening project was to make a tour of the altars in the church. Since they were ornate, complicated and not related integrally to the architecture, I had deliberately checked myself from giving them more than cursory glances. But now that my main work was done I was ready to look at them with an interested eye. I mentioned the tour when Don Gabriel arrived after eating. He was more than ready to conduct it.

To save ourselves from getting soaked, we ran up the slope and across the weed-grown yard to the entrance. Don Gabriel was wearing his dark-gray poncho and he ran with his knees close together in the way I had seen Indian boys run. Those flying ankles and the nearly knocked-knees made me see something about him which I had glimpsed only occasionally—namely, that the little boy in him was only superficially buried. That strain of melancholy I had detected in his face was an overlay from the way life had turned out. It was not so much part of his true nature as this boyishness which had seemed to be rising more and more to the surface in the last few days.

Once we were in the church, I paused to make a rough plan of the altars. To keep them distinct, I numbered them in advance, as is shown here, and I indicated to Don Gabriel that I would like to start at No. 1 and continue round the circuit until we came to No. 13.

The first one was under the choir on the left. How it held together I do not know, for many of its sections were missing and some of the tiers seemed on the verge of toppling. The low-relief bust of God the Father that leaned forward from the pinnacle was especially precarious. Don Gabriel, as I was confident he would, provided the explanation for its ruined state. The altar, he said, was dedicated to Saint Augustine and what was left of it had been salvaged from the ruined chapel, which we had seen on a hill beyond the cemetery the day we climbed to the roof.

The gilded carving was of good quality, the two matching pillars of the first tier being especially fine. Each began enchantingly with the figure of a cherubic angel, while the rest of the shaft was elegantly fluted. To have possessed such an altar the *barrio* of San Sebastian must have been rich. The evidence of so prosperous a suburb in a district where now not a habitation remains gave me a sharper sense than before of what Yanhuitlán must have been like in its palmy days.

When I described the support for the organ, I said it suggested an immensely tall fireplace. Altar No. 2 was set in the recess where one would have made a fire if the support had really been a working chimney. One

326

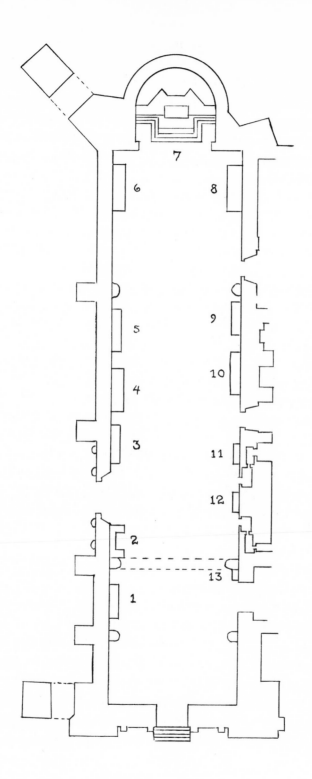

could tell by the ugly lemon-yellow paint that the altar was a relatively modern makeshift. It consisted of little more than a glass case to house another of the *barrio* Christs. This dead Christ, Don Gabriel said, was El Señor de Xaayucu. He was similar to El Señor de Ayuxi, which we had seen two days before, but clearly he did not inspire the same devotion as the Christ in the separate chapel. But the candlestand I had used as my drawing lectern was evidence that he was not entirely neglected. I had found it in front of this dark figure.

The Baroque Spanish altar generally takes the form of a great triptych, with its outer wings two or three stories tall and the central panel one tier higher. Commonly, too, the central panel is equipped with projecting bays or platforms to hold statues, while the side wings have oil paintings. The pillars, cornices and frames that create the compartments are apt to be elaborate and fanciful, in some cases amounting to a riot of ornamentation that overwhelms the figures and pictures.

Altar No. 3 on the other side of the north doorway was the first one of this type that we came to. It had Solomonic pillars and a decoration known as strapwork because its curving, intertwining lines suggest men's belts. On the whole, though, the ornamentation was relatively reserved. Saint Bartholomew was on the first platform. On the second, the gold niche behind him slipping away, was a young friar whose stance was so characteristic one could recognize him as St. Anthony of Padua, even though his book and his bambino were missing. A painting of the Virgin of Carmen topped the central panel. A stretcher of one of the side paintings had snapped. But the crumpled canvas, one could see, like the other paintings, showed gray human beings standing waist-deep in orange flames. "The Altar of the Souls," said Don Gabriel. And I recognized that the gray mortals were all suffering for their sins in an afterlife.

"But one is a bishop," I protested. "Bishops go to Hell too," said Don Gabriel, a hint of relish in his voice.

On the altar tour I was to discern all sorts of strange heads peeking out from the ornamentation, including mermaids with foliage tails, sturdy infants, doll-faced cherubs, and evil-looking old men with grotesque double tongues running off into scrollwork. But here, thanks to Don Gabriel's pointing finger, I saw the oddest thing of all—turkeys. There were four of them, and the plump birds, with pomegranates bursting on their chests, were serving as caryatids at the base of the reredos.

Altar No. 4 had three tall side tiers, and the pillars that framed the

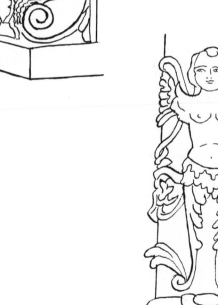

329

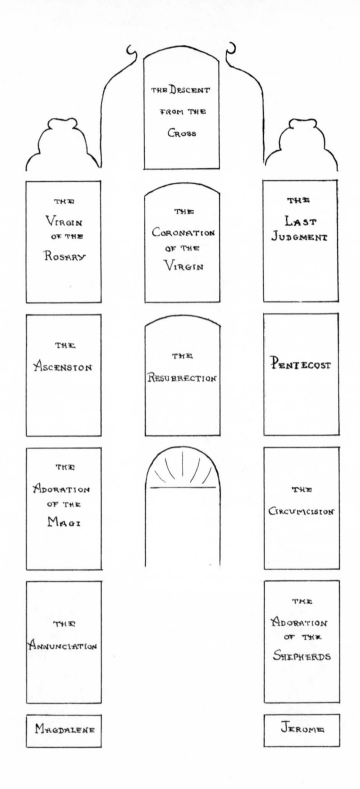

THE DESCENT FROM THE CROSS

THE VIRGIN OF THE ROSARY

THE CORONATION OF THE VIRGIN

THE LAST JUDGMENT

THE ASCENSION

THE RESURRECTION

PENTECOST

THE ADORATION OF THE MAGI

THE CIRCUMCISION

THE ANNUNCIATION

THE ADORATION OF THE SHEPHERDS

MAGDALENE

JEROME

four-storied central panel had life-sized angels for shafts. The angels had billowing skirts and upraised arms and the topmost one on the left was so out of line that he suggested a tightrope walker flailing wildly to regain balance. It was apparent even before Don Gabriel spoke that this altar was dedicated to the Virgin of Guadalupe. The side paintings depicted four familiar scenes from her legend, ranging from her first appearance to the Indian, Juan Diego, to the consternation of the ecclesiastics when her picture was seen on his cloak as the roses tumbled out.

When we paused in front of No. 5, I saw that the scheme was to make the altars increasingly gorgeous as one approached the high altar. I was impressed by the psychological insight that conceived such a series as a means of developing an emotional crescendo. "El Padre Jesús," said Don Gabriel to identify the altar. And I could see how it earned its name. The grayish paintings, now turning a dark red-brown, were devoted to the Passion. In a manner suggesting the influence of El Greco, they showed Jesus chained to the column for the flagellation, Jesus in Gethsemane and Jesus being nailed to the cross. The Passion theme, so dear to Mexican hearts, was further underlined by the central bays. In the glass-enclosed lower one staggered a morbidly realistic statue of Christ carrying His cross. On the open bay above was a statue, even more gruesome, of a Christ who, under the weight of the cross, had fallen to His knees. Both figures jarred with the elegant architecture of the altar, for here the twisted gold columns were set in pairs and domelike canopies sheltered the niches. Under one of these half shells was a figure more consonant: a jaunty St. Christopher whose red and gold cloak was flying in the wind.

No. 6, the final altar against the north wall, was the most splendid yet. It was dedicated to La Soledad, or the Virgin of Solitude, who is the patroness of the state of Oaxaca. A crude statue of the crowned and black-cloaked Mary filled the glassed bay in the place of honor. In the bay above stood a crucifix which I recognized as another *barrio* Christ. At the top was a painting of the Resurrection.

One of the paintings of this altar bore a signature which Don Gabriel proudly pointed out. "Villalobos" it read, and because of this I was able to identify the author as Juan de Villalobos, a Puebla painter, who was born in 1687 and lived until 1724. His works were done with the easy skill of a professional. Their pretty blues and reds, though, rather belied the grimness of such subjects as the Crowning with Thorns, Christ Carrying the Cross and an angel displaying Veronica's veil with the face of the suffering Jesus.

A portrait of a Dominican bishop hung in a lower frame. It did not fit its space and its style differed from that of Villalobos. Don Gabriel confirmed that it did not belong to the altar. The original painting had been cut from the frame and stolen. A further evidence of vandalism was the square hole where one of the sleeping apostles had been cut from the Agony in the Garden.

Nearly every Mexican church has its Santo Entierro, a realistic, life-sized version of Christ lying dead in a glass coffin. Yanhuitlán's was at the bottom of the Soledad retable, and here the body of the corpse was covered with a scarlet shroud.

Since I described the main altar when I drew it (page 151), all I want to do here is comment on what I neglected then—the paintings by Andrés de la Concha. With Don Gabriel's aid, I charted them.

Concha was one of the best Spanish painters who came to Mexico in the sixteenth century. His pictures had considerable virtuosity, but they reworked familiar themes without strong individuality. Time, too, had dulled their colors, leaving mostly ochres, slate greens and blacks. The paintings at the top had suffered most. Being nearer the large windows, they were more faded than the lower ones.

The Ascension showed only Christ's feet, leaving the viewer to imagine the rest of the body above the top of the frame. It interested me especially, for this was the first time I'd seen an artist use this somewhat naïve device in trying to convey that the Lord was on the way up.

Pointing to the painting of the Virgin above the disappearing feet, Don Gabriel said she was the Virgin of the Rosary. Because he had once had the benefit of field glasses, he was able to identify the medallions that formed an oval around her as small pictures of the rosary's fifteen mysteries. The Virgin of the Rosary, he explained, was especially dear to the Dominicans because it was long believed the Virgin had given St. Dominic the inspiration to invent the rosary.

Then Don Gabriel approached the altar and beckoned me to follow. To the left of the little panel devoted to St. Jerome was an opening I had never noticed. He led me through it and suddenly I was behind the great sevenfold screen. There I discovered something I should have seen was apparent in the plan—namely, that there was quite a lot of space at the back of the big M of the retable.

The stone work of the inner wall of the apse was finished to a beautiful smoothness and it was painted a pale blue-green. On it were two identical orange medallions. Each carried a coffee-colored chalice remarkably like the one carved on the fifth escudo over the friars' cells (page 300). The unexpected decoration gave me the clue that in the early days the friars had used the curved wall as a backdrop for the altar table, much as if they were knights in *Parsifal* and this was the cyclorama of a modern opera house. "Do the medallions mean this ornate retable was not in existence when the friars first conducted services in the church?" I asked.

"*Sí*," replied Don Gabriel, and his expression showed he was pleased I had understood the import of his revelation without its being put in so many words. I got the impression that he looked on this area behind the retable as his own discovery. Why, I wondered, if he was so proud of it, had he not brought me behind the altar before? In my eight days in Yanhuitlán there had been opportunities enough. It occurred to me that he was chary about the monastery's secrets and only revealed those he treasured most to friends whose interest in the monastery he fully trusted. Perhaps there were still other features he knew and had not disclosed. Certainly his alacrity in identifying every picture had more than justified my hunch that he would be able to tell me nearly all I wanted to know about the altars. And all these facts about the retable had only come out on direct questioning. He had never given them to me spontaneously and I had seen him even less communicative with others he was guiding.

Often in the church I had been delighted when, in looking upwards, my eye had been caught by the clear blue of the sky showing through those great high windows of the white nave. On those occasions I was glad they had no glass. Panes so inaccessible would be virtually impossible to wash and with the passage of time they would grow opaque and dusty. Such enchanting, unobstructed glimpses of the purest blue would be denied. But when we ducked through the retable in returning to the church I was struck by a disadvantage of that glasslessness.

So much rain had blown over the altar on the left that it made a dark red stain on the ordinarily brick-red floor. And the idea of rain falling on that particular altar was especially saddening. No. 8 was the most gorgeous of all the side altars, even outstripping *Soledad's*.

"The altar of the Virgin of the Rosary," Don Gabriel announced with a flourish.

The fullness of his explanation of that Virgin among her oval of mysteries in the main altar paid dividends here. Her importance to the Dominicans accounted for her having the side altar of the greatest splendor. It towered five stories high in the center and four at the sides and there was not an inch of its gilded surface that was not elaborately carved.

The figure of the Virgin in the place of honor was a doll with a pretty china face, a wig of human hair and clothes made especially for her. The pretty child in her arms held a globe surmounted by a silver cross.

The paintings of this altar, said Don Gabriel, were attributed to Juan de Arrua. Whoever the artist was, he also appeared to have been influenced by El Greco, though his pictures were finer than those of the other El Greco disciple who had done the paintings for the altar dedicated to Jesus. The fact that the four paintings in the lowest tier did not fit their frames any better than the Dominican bishop across the way led me to believe that they also were stopgaps. Don Gabriel confirmed this. Here, too, the originals had been stolen.

No. 9, the smaller altar on the far side of the shell doorway, had far more undercoated flat surfaces than the other altars and its gold was an almost buttercup yellow in distinction to their darker, almost red golds. This, said Don Gabriel, was the most recent of the major retables, and it was the only one that bore its date.

"Where," I asked, expecting to find something like 1903. "See, in that panel," and he pointed to the writing.

It was 1789, the year of the French Revolution. That such a date should make the altar comparatively new dramatized the age of the others.

"This is dedicated to Saint Gertrude," Don Gabriel said. "You can see that four of its paintings have been stolen too."

In this case, the stolen pictures were taken from the top. Two remained on the left: one showing a young novice having her hair cut by a nun, the other showing a nun raising her lips to a Christ leaning forward from the cross to kiss her.

It was the picture remaining on the right, though, that had the most historic value. Pointing to the oval painting, Don Gabriel said: "That is Don Juan de Mata, who gave the altar as a thank offering when his son was baptized."

I looked with especial interest, for I had been hoping for evidence of individuals associated with the monastery, and this was the first portrait I had seen of any of its historic figures. I judged it was an honest portrait, for there was no attempt to idealize Don Juan. He had a gray peruke, lace at his throat, coat and breeches of bottle-green velvet, white stockings and buckled shoes; but, for all the finery, there was no disguising that the plump little man with the worried look in his dark eyes was a provincial squire. His wife, wearing a black dress with a red shawl over her head, was also a little dowdy. They were shown standing near the baptismal font as a priest was christening their infant son.

Altar No. 10 was dedicated to St. Peter Martyr. He was unknown to me then, but I have since looked up his story. He was born in Verona about 1206 and he grew up as a devout Catholic, even though Verona was then a center of the Manichaean heresy. At the age of fifteen he went to Bologna to study at the University. There he heard St. Dominic preach and he was so impressed that he joined the order Dominic had created a few years before. Just as Dominic had preached against the heretics in southern France, Peter preached against those in Lombardy and Tuscany. He was so zealous and successful, in fact, that, after Pope Gregory IX had set up the Inquisition as an independent body, he made Peter its head. As Inquisitor, Peter not only preached against heretics, but he had them seized and brought to trial. Finally, some influential heretics decided to do away with Peter. The Saturday after Easter, 1251, while on his way to Milan, he was ambushed and killed.

In this Yanhuitlán altar, set among gold pillars encrusted with gilded grapes, were paintings depicting Peter's story. One portrayed him listening to Dominic preaching, and the preacher's words flowed from his mouth in a ribbon of letters. Another raised my hackles. It showed a priestly court passing judgment on a poor man whose dunce cap and sandwich boards slashed with a great red X proclaimed him a heretic. And tracing the life of the Inquisitor, I found myself so out of sympathy with him that I felt in the final picture he was getting his just desserts—an ax in the center of the head.

On the cement block in front of this retable was a figure group that stood in gentle contrast to the fierce story of persecution and retribution above. I had already marked it down for depiction: a saint towering beside a small angel, who was holding a wooden plough drawn by miniature oxen. Don Gabriel said the saint was San Isidro Labrador.

Altars Nos. 11 and 12 were placed where they could be studied by those waiting to go into the confessionals. They consisted of large paintings in identical gold frames that rose behind gilded shallow tables the way big mirrors rise behind old-fashioned dressers. The canvases were by Villalobos, who did the Soledad altar, and the common authorship was apparent in the pretty blues and reds. Each depicted a mystic marriage to Christ. In both cases the rite was being watched by several holy personages on earth, while the dove of the Holy Ghost, a head representing God the Father and assorted cherubs looked down from the sky.

The mystical bride in No. 12 was being married to Jesus as an adult. She was wearing a crown of thorns and the black and white habit of a Dominican nun. Don Gabriel identified her as St. Catherine of Siena. The mystical bride of No. 11 was being married to Jesus as a child. In the picture the infant was seated on the Virgin Mary's lap and was stretching out the ring to His kneeling betrothed. She was a girl of winsome beauty, richly clothed in an olive-green dress and a red cape; and her air of splendor was increased by her golden crown and the pearl earrings that hung from her ears. She, said Don Gabriel, was Santa Rosa. To identify the brides further, I later studied records of the Dominican saints. I found Don Gabriel was right about the nun being married to the full-grown Christ. She *was* St. Catherine of Siena. But whoever "Santa Rosa" was, she could not be St. Rose of Lima, the one Dominican saint with the same name. Rose of Lima was not of royal blood.

Who, then, was she? Remembering that many Renaissance paintings depicted women saints being married to Christ, I searched through art books. Whenever I saw Mystic Marriages that looked anything like my puzzling Yanhuitlán one—whether because the attending figures were the same or the bride had a crown or a similar kneeling attitude toward the infant Christ—I eagerly read the captions. Soon all the evidence pointed to one figure: our old friend of the doorway to the cloister, Santa Catalina, the Alexandrian princess, who, supposedly, had hacked off her father's head. Then I learned that, besides Mary Magdalene, the Dominican Order had a second great patroness in Saint Catherine of Alexandria. That both clinched the identification made through the paintings and explained why that particular saint should be twice honored so conspicuously at Yanhuitlán.

The final altar, No. 13, was just under the choir loft. It, too, resembled a dresser, though here the high back was divided into two sections. The upper compartment contained an oil painting of two men with triangular halos. Obviously it was a study of the Trinity, for the men were God the Father and God the Son and between them hovered the dove of the Holy Ghost. Along the bottom of the canvas was some writing. I asked Don Gabriel if I could climb up on the altar table to read it. He gave me both the permission and a hand up. The lettering, fortunately, was clear and the Spanish easy to translate: "This image of the Most Holy Trinity, was painted for a widow of this town very devoted to this sacrosanct mystery called María de la Trinidad. Year of 1784."

Unexpectedly, I had found evidence of a second parishioner who had worshipped in the church in colonial times. And the date revealed she was a contemporary of the periwigged Don Juan, who had given the altar of St. Gertrude. Had she, I wondered, attended the christening?

I examined the lower compartment with special interest. It had another representation of the Trinity. Again the Father and Son had triangular halos, but here they were not paintings. They were exquisite little dolls that emerged from the background in almost complete relief. And though they were protected by glass, the dove between them had disappeared, leaving only the outline where it had been stuck to the back of the case. This representation, too, had writing. I scanned it eagerly. The date showed this gift to the church had been made nine years later. Again the widow María was the donor—proof that her devotion to the most Holy Trinity had retained its old affectionate warmth.

"What happened to the dove?" I asked Don Gabriel. "It was stolen." Then he added: "It had diamonds for eyes."

The devout widow, I realized, must have been very rich. That she and the chunky Don Juan could both make such lavish gifts to the church at the same time revealed that even as late as the 1790's Yanhuitlán must have had a wealthy community of cultured Spaniards.

Maria's unwavering devotion to the mystery after which she was named had come through to me. I wanted to know more about her. But, alas, all Don Gabriel knew of the widow's history was that she had lived in the *barrio* of St. Sebastian.

I looked across to the first altar we had examined, the toppling one dedicated to St. Augustine which had been salvaged from the ruins of the chapel of the decimated barrio. "The same *barrio* as the altar?" I asked.

Don Gabriel nodded his head. So now, besides knowing of the barrio's wealth, I knew one of those who had lived there. The social life of eighteenth-century Yanhuitlán rose in my imagination with a vividness it had never had before. And the intensity of the vision made me feel all the more sharply what time, the war against Spain and cholera had carried so completely away.

When we left the church I was struck by the way the colors of the hills had been intensified by the water that had soaked into them. Their reds fairly leaped out. And I use the plural because the intensification of the hues made obvious a difference I had scarcely noticed before. There was more purple in the red of the hills on the west; more brick red in those on the east.

But the rain, to my delight, had stopped. There was even evidence that the sun was struggling to get through the overcast. I would be able to finish the façade that morning after all. But since the air was still heavy with moisture, I decided not to risk smearing my detailed drawing by working on it just yet. Clearly, the day was going to get dryer, so in the meantime I would make that less exacting drawing of the ruined porch, which I have used on page 247.

As I drew, Don Gabriel read at the window of the former dining room that can be seen at the upper left. We exchanged smiles as we occasionally looked up from our preoccupations at the same time. And every now and then he would call down to ask how the drawing was going.

"*Bien,*" I would reply. And really that was an understatement. It was going more than well. Or perhaps I should say I felt more than content. And I wondered why I should have such a deep sense of well-being. I saw it was partly because of the nature of the work. It was work with my hands and I saw that the effect of nine days of work with my hands—especially as a relief from so much brain work—was tranquilizing. Then I saw that for more than a week I had been standing at the confluence of two tranquilizing streams: the tranquil environment of Yanhuitlán and the tranquil nature of the occupation.

Then I thought of an explanation that went even deeper. My newspaper work has always interested me, and often, when I have contrasted reporting with the sort of drudgery other men have to slave at, I have thanked my stars for such an enjoyable way of earning a living. But the true work of my heart has been, not journalism, but the research, thinking and drawing that are part of writing illustrated books. Yet nearly all my adult life, because breadwinning has had to come first, I have only been able to do that other work late at night, on days off and in odd chinks of time between assignments. And often it has had to be laid aside for weeks or even months.

What I saw was this: for almost the first time since I had stepped on the wage-earning treadmill twenty years before I had been able to devote myself uninterruptedly for nine whole days to the work of my heart. And the continuing joy of this, I am sure, was even more important than the physically calming influence of work with my hands.

WEEK IN YANHUITLÁN

So much observing, too, must have played its part. For the cycle of observation I have mentioned—from seeing to knowledge, from knowledge to understanding, and from understanding to keener seeing—is not the only virtuous circle that vision describes. That cycle might be called the intellectual. The other, which I have already hinted at, is the psychological. Close observing, in fixing the attention on something external, disengages the consciousness from preoccupation with anxieties and cares. Disengagement from these leads to calmer inward states. Improved inward states allow for less beclouded vision. Less clouded vision means seeing more. Seeing more leads to self-forgetfulness in the excitement of discovery, to the awakening of curiosity and to a deeper awareness of life's interest. And these, in their turn, lead to a still more liberated and harmonious inward condition.

When the drawing of the ruined porch was finished, the air was clear and dry. Don Gabriel and I went to the church to get the candlestand and I resumed my work on the lowest story of the façade. Again it was a painstaking filling in of details and by 12:20, when Nahum's bus was almost due, I welcomed the excuse for a break.

Don Gabriel and I went to the cantina by the highway where the bus would stop. Waiting with Nahum were his brothers Raul and Alberto, the butcher's helper and the water carrier, and two girls. "¿Sus hermanas?" I asked Nahum. And he nodded his confirmation. They were Rosalía and Alva and it was their deerlike eyes that identified them so surely.

Eliel, Alfonso's little cousin, was also there. He looked adorable in a poncho and a sombrero turned up sharply all the way round. Vicente Gutiérrez, the dignified speech-making síndico, was there too. When the bus arrived the boy and the civic official got on together and sat side by side.

"Is Eliel Don Vicente's son?" I asked Don Gabriel, for it was hard to believe so happy a spirit was the child of the elderly man. "Yes," said Don Gabriel.

The twelve-year-old was obviously happy and excited at the thought of a visit to Nochixtlán. And some veil of melancholy had fallen from the little man in the correct suit. I saw a tie of compatibility between them that I could not have guessed if I hadn't seen them about to leave together on an outing.

I shook hands with Nahum and said I hoped to meet him in Oaxaca. Then he hugged his Uncle Gabriel and each of his brothers and sisters and boarded the bus. As it drew off we turned away, and, as there had been at Alfonso's departure in the opposite direction, there was a sense of loss.

The façade took another half hour to finish and I breathed a sigh of relief when it was done. We returned the candlestand and then went home for the midday meal.

Food is one of the great gifts of life and probably there is no time when one appreciates it so much as when one is tired after the completion of a major effort. Counting the false start, the façade had taken almost five hours of the most concentrated sort of looking, so I felt most grateful when Lupe set before me one of those white soup plates filled with rice, with a few slices of squash on top. Accordingly, before picking up the blue tin spoon, I began my grace. "*Gracias a Dios* . . . . "

Then I had the first indication that my saying the grace meant anything to the Blancos. "You forgot it this morning," Lupe said. So she had noticed my silence—and remembered.

"No," I explained, "I said it, but to myself. Because Nahum was here, I felt *tímido*."

As I was shaving after lunch, my mirror warned me Angelita was approaching. Having given her six candies in the morning, I had the impulse to make her work for her noonday *dulce*. She slowed down as she drew near. I pretended I was so engrossed that I did not see her. Her pace became even slower. Still, I did not look up. And she was the first to crack, for when she had already passed me she could stand it no longer. "*Buenas tardes*," she said. I looked up in feigned surprise. "*Buenas tardes*," I said and made no move. But when she stood stock-still, too shy to actually ask for a sweet, I relented and gave her one.

The shaving finished, I came indoors. Adán, Bertaldo and Paco, the three sons of Don Miguel, ran past my door with a noisy rush. The sound subsided the moment they were gone, so I was sure they were waiting quietly in hiding around the corner. I went out and discovered them. As I expected, they were having a hard time choking back the laugher that might betray their ruse.

I decided I'd make them work a little for their candies too. "How do you say *por favor* in English?" The awful thought passed through all three faces. Perhaps they wouldn't get a candy if they didn't remember. There was a pause, and then Bertaldo remembered. "Pleeze," he said. That meant all three were saved, and each got his candy.

"Now," I said, "how do you say *gracias?*" "Good morning," said Paco, and the three bounded off.

As I had been giving them their candies, Alicia, one of Angelita's little

WEEK IN YANHUITLÁN

sisters, watched from a distance, one bare foot crossed over the other. Since she had never been bold and I could not bear to see her watch others get candies without getting one too, I took one out to her.

Back at my table I heard another noisy rush. It was the three boys again, but this time they were carrying little Tlaxiaco chairs like helmets on their heads. "Thank you," they called out as they passed. "Good-bye" they shouted as they passed again.

Because I had let the diary lapse for several days, I had to concentrate to remember. I did not hear anyone approach, so I was surprised when a little voice at the threshold inquired, *"¿Blanquitos?"*

It was Angelita, back again. She had three little white eggs in a basket. I gladly bought them and gave her another candy for her pains in bringing them. But she did not turn away. Out came her question of the morning: did I have any candies for her little sisters. The sack was two-thirds empty, so I demurred. But the sad expression in her eyes was too much for me. I decided on a compromise. "I'll only give you four," I said, "for I've already given one to your sister Alicia."

"Alicia isn't my sister," piped the wispy voice. "But I've seen you with her," I said.

"She's only a friend, not a sister," the child repeated. "I have to have five." I gave in. Five she got. I returned to my book and she returned to her home.

When Don Gabriel came over I gave him the three eggs. In doing so I explained how the little salesgirl had obtained the five extra candies for her *hermanitas*. "What was her name?" he asked. "Angelita," I replied.

"Angelita?" he repeated with a question in his tone. "Yes, Angelita."

He shook his head. "Angelita hasn't got five little sisters. She's only got one sister, an older one, Serafina." The little imp had invented five imaginary *hermanitas* so she could get six candies at a crack.

I heard a little cough behind me. It was a boy I had not seen before. *"Buenas tardes,"* he said, for it seems other had told him the password.

"¿Una dulce?" I asked. He nodded his head. I gave him one. *"Gracias,"* he said with a smile, and scampered off.

"I think the candies have been a success," I said to Don Gabriel. "A great success," he said. And as we strolled towards the monastery he made me realize the *dulces* had been more of an inspiration than I thought. In Yanhuitlán, he said, the children scarcely ever had candies. When the stores did stock them, the sweets were poor, and always very expensive.

Lupe was waiting at the entrance, her arms full of the pale mauve lilies she had called *reginas*. Apparently her day to decorate the altar of the sacristy chapel had rolled around again. Once more I had a feeling of the weekly cycle.

Once Don Gabriel had unlocked the grilled wooden doors leading into the cloister, Lupe went one way to her chapel and we went the other to ours. My remaining project was to draw as many of the figures as time allowed and the first one I was after was an example of a *barrio* Christ. Don Gabriel had said the unattached one in the western chapel would be the easiest to do, so our quest was to find it.

Since we were to spend almost all afternoon in this chapel I have saved its description until this point. A glimpse back at the Institute's plan on page 12 will show one essential difference between this chapel and the one on the east that had the Descent of the Cross. This one is more open. As can be seen, the *sagrario* has a definite anteroom, but this other chapel presents a clear sweep of space from the church nave. The sweep, though, is not quite as unobstructed in reality as the Institute's plan shows. That plan leaves out the two stumpy side wings that I have drawn in the plan on page 242.

My own plan also shows a circle at the center of the open foyer created by those side wings. I hope the reader will remember what the circle represents—the baptismal font. And this reveals the nature of the foyer. It is the church's baptistery.

Two other features heighten the apartness of the baptistery bay. It is roofed with fine ribbed vaulting, and its side walls have murals. One shows Christ's entry into Jerusalem on Palm Sunday and the other Christ driving the money changers out of the Temple. They are dated 1882 and are naive work painted mostly in olive greens. The real treasure of the baptistery is the baptismal font, which stands directly under the central point of the vaulting.

The font, which is carved from a single huge stone, is one of the establishment's most amazing works. When we had first looked at it Don Gabriel had said he did not understand the symbolism of the serpents supporting the great basin. Looking closer, I had seen that the projecting heads were swallowing other serpents, who, in turn, seemed to be swallowing others. Knowing that the serpent swallowing its own tail is a symbol of eternity, I had suggested this explanation. Don Gabriel had been dubious. He was pretty sure the serpent was a representation of the plumed serpent, one of the great gods of Middle American culture.

When we paused to examine it, I saw those serpents certainly had plumes growing from their sides. And I now had two memories as interpretative aids: the figure of the Mixtec king that the early friars had stuccoed over in their conduit vent, and the big serpent head that later ones had set face down in the cemetery arch. Perhaps, I said to Don Gabriel, they made this font as proof to the Indians that the holy water of the Catholic Church was superior to the power of the ancient god. Perhaps, like the building of the monastery on the pre-Conquest platform, this was symbolic of the triumph of the new religion over the old.

An advantage of observing the world carefully is that one stores up visual memories that often, at unexpected moments, come back, heightening the pleasure of new things and sometimes enabling one to make unanticipated discoveries. An instance of fresh dividends from past observations occurred as I studied the font. Weren't its big leaves like something I had drawn elsewhere? I had my book of "Details" and I ruffled back through it to check. I was right. These leaves on the great stone basin were remarkably like those carved on the tiny chalice of the fifth *escudo* (page 300). This, in turn, made me remember the leaves on the capital of the diamond doorway (page 129). The three sets of leaves were enough alike to suggest that font, *escudo* and doorway were all works of the same unknown master. And those squared flowers under the font's flaring lip were not unlike the flowers that framed the confessionals (page 134). Their central petals formed a cross in the same way.

The chapel that extends beyond the baptistery is now a bare, white-washed chamber, but looking back from its center I realized how it provides another example of beauty arising from relationships.

Church and chapel together, in fact, form one of the most beautiful sights in the whole establishment. For the chapel is long enough to provide a true vista, and beyond the narrowing frame of the stone-ribbed baptistery one sees the ampler, better-lighted nave; and the part of the nave revealed is that which is roofed by the gorgeous coffered ceiling under the choir gallery.

The charm of the vista is heightened by the sheeted figures that stand, like momentarily frozen ghosts, ranged on either side of the baptismal font. In actuality, the figures are angels. There are eight of them and they were conceived as attendants for the barrio Christs—one for each Christ. They form one of the treasures of the monastery and it is to save them from dust, fading and misuse that they have been fitted with baggy slip covers that make them so irresistibly reminiscent of Halloween.

They really suggest a family of ghosts, for one, being so much smaller than the others, appears to be a child. And there is variety in the clan, for five are sheeted in white and two in mauve. The one which is exposed— perhaps its delicate, wide-spreading wings made a covering unfeasible— gives the clue that his fellows are angels in disguise.

The whereabouts of five of the barrio Christs has already been indi-cated. El Señor de Ayuxi is in that chapel of its own on the outskirts of the town. Two hang on either side of the triumphal arch, as shown in the draw-ing of the main altar. And two stand in altars on the north side of the church: El Señor de Xaayucu in the niche under the organ, and the other above the Virgin of Solitude. That leaves three to be accounted for. No. 6, Don Gabriel told me, hung in the anteroom to the *sagrario*. No. 7—the small one which had the small angel for its attendant—was kept in a private home. And No. 8—well, here it was. And he pointed to a crucifix stacked in a corner with three or four other large crosses.

This figure, stored so unceremoniously, was El Señor de Tico. All we would have to do, said Don Gabriel was to lift it up and carry it across the chapel where we could prop it against the wall, facing the light from the western windows.

The figure was more than life-sized. Wasn't it too heavy for two men to lift? I asked.

"Oh, no," said Don Gabriel. And he rapped a knuckle on one of the legs to show how light it was. I recognized the almost hollow sound, so I knew the figure was not carved of solid wood, as I had thought, but was made of *caña de maíz*. This is a substance made from the pulp of corn stalks which, when moist, is as malleable as soft clay. It was used extensively in the construction of large religious figures that had to be light enough to be carried in religious processions. The technique was similar to stuffing dolls. First the figure was made, glovelike, from limp cloth. Then the cloth figure was plumped up with the malleable *caña de maíz*. Once the figure was filled, a sculptor modeled the soft image until it looked like a wood carving. Then it was left to dry. In setting, the pulp grew hard, strong and light.

Before we could move El Señor de Tico, we had to lift off the other crosses. One bore a man with long drawers, who was missing both forearms. The Good Thief, explained Don Gabriel. The second had a figure whose head was gone: the Bad Thief. The figure on the third cross was unmistakably Jesus.

"Look at the eyes," said Don Gabriel. They slanted as if the Christ was a Chinaman. "It came from the Philippines," Don Gabriel explained.

The figure, about half life-size, was exquisitely carved of white wood. I felt a particular sense of tender responsibility as I helped shift it. After all, the Philippines were also a major part of the Spanish empire in its days of glory. A Manila galleon must have brought this crucifix to Mexico. Besides thinking of it as a work of art, I felt it was a token of a romantic era. It was proof, too, that even if Chinese silk helped destroy Yanhuitlán's silk industry, the once flourishing trade between the two great colonies brought compensatory enrichments.

Lupe, having arranged her lilies in the other chapel, arrived as we were about to move Tico. And Don Gabriel was right. Between the two of us we were able to carry it. But it was heavy, nevertheless, not because of the figure, but because of the big wooden cross. When we had propped it against the eastern wall, Lupe told us to shift it first a little to the left and then a little to the right until we had it as nearly upright as possible. But it had to slant a little so one arm of the cross could serve as a brace.

Lupe, as it turned out, stayed with us all afternoon. I was glad that she did. It was good to have her sharing our pleasures directly, and I liked the sense that we were a happy threesome. She and Don Gabriel sat behind

me on the sill of the window that was providing most of the light. As I blocked in the sketch, I liked the sound of their quiet whispering.

El Señor de Tico's skin was as brown as Don Gabriel's. But the figure was not an Indian Christ. Its features were European, and that thick, black beard cultivated into two points was most un-Indian. The discoloration must have been time's work. Probably its cloth skin had once been white pink, just as the tarnished fringe of the mauve waist wrapper had been gold.

When Don Gabriel and I had moved the image, I had assumed the cross was made of a particularly knobby wood. But when I came to draw my permanent lines I was forced to observe that the cross was an astonishing performance in its own right. At the junction of the beams was an exquisite carving of Christ's head on Veronica's veil. The ends of the arms were tipped with yellow crowns, and the whole cross was a solid mass of black flowers. What I thought were knobs were so many bulging petals.

Since I could not hope to draw all the flowers, I indicated a few and then turned to the problem of the final lines of the Christ. I'm sure I don't need to tell those familiar with Mexican Christs that the drops from the wound in the side were painted red. The lines running down the arms from the nailed hands and the lines from the lacerated knees were also blood red. And blood welled at the shoulders. So a strong first effect was of depressing goriness. But as I sought to match my lines with the lines of the figure before me, I began to be aware of its remarkable grace of outline. And as I worked on the beautiful head I found myself close to tears.

The wig of real hair and the crown—so like a circle to support an *olla*—were non-sculptural additions, but in their naïve way they made even more apparent how much fellow feeling for the dead Jesus had gone into the work's creation. Clearly, too, there must have been a good deal of self-identification for the sculptor to have achieved so moving an effect; and just as surely many Indians must have gazed on the figure with the same feelings of love and pity that it was rousing in me.

I worked silently on. And as I did my best to capture the curves of the hollowed cheeks and the whole general expression, I had another experience of effortless understanding. It concerned that incredible Conquest of some ten million Mexican Indians by a mere four or five hundred Spaniards, and the even more incredible consolidation of that Conquest. And the new understanding occurred because this was a subject on which I had enough information for my mind to be at the point of crystallization.

When the Spaniards came to Mexico in 1519 they reached a land that had only recently been conquered by the Aztecs. Those Aztecs offered human sacrifices to their gods, and they did it, not out of sheer brutality as has been so often claimed, but out of a deep religious conviction that is not without its symbolic beauty. Their idea, as George Vailliant has pointed out, was a twofold one. The first was that the gods could not survive without humans helping to sustain them. The second was that those gods "received their best nutriment from the most precious of offerings, the hearts of men." The deduction, of course, was that the gods should be offered human hearts.

The horrifying thing from a modern standpoint is that the Aztecs took this belief literally. They actually cut the hearts from living men as their supreme act of devotion. Huitzilopochtli, their chief god, was a god of war. Since they had embarked on the conquest of Mexico, they desperately needed his favor and strong right hand. They felt, in turn, that he had to have more and more living hearts.

But they needed to conserve their manpower. The result was that, in order to have an increasing number of hearts to offer Huitzilopochtli, they sacrificed more and more of the prisoners they took in their wars of conquest. First they conquered the tribes around their capital and then in 1456 they began their conquest of the Mixtecs. As the goodwill of the war god grew ever more vital, the Aztecs even began to conduct military expeditions primarily for the sake of gathering sacrificial victims. Tradition has it that once the mass butchery reached a staggering total of twenty thousand in a single ceremony.

The conquered tribes, understandably feeling less sympathetic to the nourishment of that enemy god, dreaded having their captured warriors killed in this way. And this wholesale sacrificial killing was one of the chief reasons most tribes hated the Aztecs so intensely that they were willing to side with white Spaniards against people of their own brown skin.

So much for what was in my mind as I began sketching. What came to me as I worked was that on the eve of the Conquest, because of existing conditions, the Indians of Mexico were used to the idea of their best young men dying for their sakes to appease a wrathful god. Put another way, they were accustomed to death, if not on the cross, then on the sacrificial stone.

Then what happened? And here I state it as the Indians must have seen it. White men came who had a chief God greater than Huitzilopochtli. Was not this proved by their military conquest of the worshipers of Huitzilopochtli? And after the Aztecs were overcome, the friars arrived with the assurance that no humans ever had to be sacrificed to this new chief God. And they had a most convincing reason. The killing of Jesus on the cross was a sacrifice so enormous, so completely satisfying to the new deity, that no further human sacrifices would be necessary. And the reason this one sacrifice was enough for all was because of the goodness and eminence of this Jesus. Like Quetzalcoatl, he was a god in human form and he loved his people so much that he willingly let himself be killed on the cross because he knew that by sacrificing himself he could spare all men from ever having to be sacrificed again, either on the cross or the stone.

In other words, thanks to the intensity of feeling behind this sculpture, I suddenly saw Jesus as he must have seemed to Indians who were still living in the shadow of the Aztec past. No wonder he was a figure they could rush out to with love. Because they were used to human sacrifice, he and his death were both easily intelligible. And the magnitude of his gift in dying to spare them was such as to endear him to them forever. With this comprehension I saw the wholesale conversion of the Indians to Christianity as readily understandable, and I saw further why they were ready to remain peaceable subjects of the men who introduced them to this generous and loving God in human form.

I saw, too, a possible reason why Mexicans seem to love the dead or suffering Jesus so much more than Jesus in his other aspects. After all, in dying he didn't merely save them from sin. He didn't just redeem them in a general sort of way. He saved them from ever being killed similarly themselves. To the Mexican Indian there is special poignance in the words, "Surely he hath borne our griefs and carried our sorrows."

When I had finished the Tico crucifix, Don Gabriel led me to another reminder of Christ's Passion. This was a statue against the wall near the altar which depicted the Man of Sorrows standing with a bowed, thorn-crowned head, with blood running down his face. The inert figure was dressed in a white nightshirt, and Don Gabriel began fishing up under its clothes as if he were a valet about to pull down the back of a coat.

To my horror, the ghastly figure suddenly raised its head and looked me straight in the eye. And in the terrible pain of that face I almost heard the unspoken question: "How could you have done this to me?"

It was a startling illusion. Involuntarily I drew back. And that reaction made both Lupe and Don Gabriel laugh. The trick had worked. I had been frightened. Then to set my mind at rest, and to prove that the figure was not alive after all, Lupe lifted the nightshirt high enough so I could see Don

Gabriel's hand tugging on the rope that made the head nod up and down. The realism of the head and its motion was quite uncanny and I could see how the figure might have been used unscrupulously in the past to strike awe and terror into poor natives who did not know the secret of its operation.

The fact that this was the first time Don Gabriel had shown me the figure confirmed my guess of the morning that he had not revealed all he knew.

The chapel's altar was relatively modern. It was a neoclassic affair of white and gold, which had hearts all over it. They were crudely made things that might have suggested red pincushions if the gold rays, curving half limply from them, had not made them look more like big red spiders.

The altar was set up in 1922, said Don Gabriel. And my curiosity about the chapel's past led him to reveal more of his secrets—secrets that can be most easily followed by glancing back to the plan on page 242.

The plan shows two hyphenated bands. These represent former walls and the marks of them can still be seen in the barrel vault of the ceiling. What Don Gabriel disclosed was that in monastic days the end of the chapel in which we were standing had been partitioned. The room between the hyphenated lines, he said, was the *sala de espera,* or waiting room, and the room that now has the altar of the red spiders was the *locotorio,* or visiting room, where friars could receive secular visitors. The reader who remembers that the x's on this plan signify blocked-up doorways can readily see how this worked. The friar, permitted to have visitors, could come out to join them through the doorway from the refectory, and the visitors could enter the locutory either directly from the outside or from the waiting room in which they had been biding their time.

After a last look around we left the chapel. It was about four-thirty so there was still time for another drawing before the light failed. And I had no hesitation about which one it was to be. I wanted to draw San Isidro Labrador, the benign saint in front of the altar of the less tolerant Saint Peter Martyr.

San Isidro was dressed in a long smock of yellow-gold velvet, mauve pants, and a blue cloak which had been lovingly draped over his raised arm. *Labrador* means tiller of the soil, and Don Gabriel explained he was the saint of farmers. His day was May 15, and on that day farmers of many villages decorate their oxen and bring them to the priest to be blessed. An upsurge of fondness had made me want to sketch this particular group. And as I drew the yoked oxen and the details of the plough I realized they had

stirred so much affection because they had been carved with affection. Since most of the people of Yanhuitlán tilled the soil as the angel was doing, I could understand the loving familiarity that went into the work.

Suddenly, into the quietness of the nave came a sound that thrilled me. It was that heavy, lowing, clomping, unforgettable sound I had heard the afternoon before. And I knew that, as I was sketching these sculptured oxen, outside the great church those many teams of live oxen were being driven home. The sight of the brown, lumbering, dignified beasts and the joking men, relieved that the long day's work was over, sprang to my mind's eye. And I got a hint as to why I had responded so to San Isidro. In contrast to many of the stiff, neglected dusty figures that stood on other altars, he was still an object of living devotion.

The next figure I wanted to draw was the Jesus riding into Jerusalem on the papier-maché ass. Lupe and Don Gabriel accompanied me to the *sagrario* as I went to examine it. But I saw this project would have to be left till the next morning. It was now so late in the afternoon that not enough light was entering the darkening chapel.

As the three of us walked home together I got my first real sense of how small the couple were. They were both so well proportioned that I had assumed we were all more or less the same size—and there had been no full-length mirrors to remind me of the contrary. Yet Lupe must have been well under five feet, for she only came up to my shoulder. Don Gabriel was not much taller.

SHORTLY AFTER I RETURNED to my room, José, the schoolteacher, came to make another inspection of the quarters into which he was to move. When he was through, he stayed for a talk and we sat together on the threshold of the door as dusk gradually deepened in the overcast valley. How old were his children? I asked. Five-and-a-half and one-and-a-half. And did he like Yanhuitlán? Well, for himself and his wife it was all right and for a while it would be all right for his children. But when they were older he wanted to move to where they would have more educational opportunities. He said he had been a teacher for ten years. I asked if he wanted to teach at the university level. To my surprise, he did not. He wanted to work with children. He was interested, he said, in theories of pedagogy.

"Do you know John Dewey?" he asked. "Of course," I replied. His face brightened, but it dimmed when I had to explain I only knew Dewey through his writing. He had thought my answer indicated personal acquaintance. He was disappointed, for he greatly admired Dewey and his educational ideas.

"If you like teaching children, you are probably happy with your work in Yanhuitlán," I said. He answered, "Not very."

"Why not?" He replied with the identical word Don Gabriel had used when he explained why he had given up teaching. "*Lucha*," struggle, was the key to the trouble. There was struggle with the children, struggle with the parents and struggle with the authorities.

In his voice I caught the sound of nostalgia for life in a larger city where he could teach in a progressive school and have the companionship of those with similar intellectual interests. I thought of my own position: living in a large city and wishing I could have his tranquility in a small town. I pointed out the irony of the contrast. Fate had made the wrong disposition of lots.

I could tell he found it hard to understand why I should be so happy in Yanhuitlán. Why was it? he asked. "Well, basically, it's because of my feeling for Mexico."

"Why do you like Mexico so much?"

"There are many reasons." And I made the reply general and noncommittal, not because I wanted to be evasive, but because of the limitation of my Spanish vocabulary.

"What are some of the reasons?"

I saw he was genuinely interested. I saw, too, that perhaps I could slightly alter his own outlook if I gave him mine. Clearly, he was feeling a little exiled and discouraged, and perhaps he had lost some realization of how much good there was in Mexican life in being so aware of its handicaps. But where to begin? It was a subject I had probed fairly thoroughly, for my response to Mexico had been a constant source of surprise to me. Why, I had asked myself again and again, should this Indian-Spanish country far to the south, that by all rights should be most alien to my cold, northern Anglo-Saxon upbringing, seem like my spiritual home?

Obviously, I could not give José all the reasons. I lacked the linguistic resources to tell him that somehow the whole foundation of my life had been shaken by Mexico, and that, instead of feeling panic, I had rejoiced that so hard a base had been finally broken up so I could start living in a more loving and humane way. But I did have the words for the bud metaphor, and that conveyed something I knew he could understand. There was a catch, though. It meant using a simile that north of the border might seem too unmanly to be permissible. Yet I decided to risk it, for I was confident José would not find it affected or silly.

Holding up my clenched fist to indicate a tightly closed bud, I asked him if he had ever watched a rose open. The outer petals, I said, did not just fall back, they were forced back by the swelling of the centre. And I opened my hand slowly to show how this happened. Finally—and here I splayed my hand wide—the whole flower opens easily.

Thanks to the understanding and affection of his people, I said, something like that had happened to me. It was as if—and here I had to use the word *alma*, meaning soul, for I did not know what other term to describe my inner being—it was as if in Mexico that *alma*, which had been a tightly closed bud for so long, had unexpectedly opened into flower.

My confidence had not been misplaced. I could tell by José's expression that he knew and respected what I was talking about. It encouraged me to go on, for I had also worked out a theory as to why that feeling of flowering had taken place. I had to review the theory in my mind, though, to see how much of it I had the power to describe.

The theory is that each of us lives at the center of three major concentric circles. The innermost circle is what people have come to call the inner life—the life that we lead when we are alone and have no need to consider the opinions of others. The second circle is the circle of our associates. It is the area that includes our life with those we love, with our friends and our acquaintances and with those with whom we work. The larger circle, in which the two smaller ones are set, is the circle of our environment—and this embraces our life among those people we don't know personally.

Most men and women, I have found, struggle to get their two inner circles right. By this I mean they consciously work to establish an inner life that gives them a sanctuary of tranquil retreat, and they work even more deliberately to surround themselves with congenial associates. But their attitudes toward the third circle is generally to accept it as something imposed by fate, and the average person tries to ignore it if it happens to be uncongenial.

When I went to Mexico I stepped into a new third circle. One of the chief effects of this was to make me more conscious of the nature of the outer circle I had left behind. What I had more or less taken for granted as being part of the air I breathed was suddenly seen to be, not the whole world's atmosphere, but a very special environment that could be scrutinized like an entity isolated in a laboratory. The nature of my new specimen—the cultural environment of Mexico—stimulated me to notice features of the old specimen with fresh eyes.

One marked thing about Mexico that struck me was the harmony between the people and the environment in which they moved. They seemed related to their landscape in a way that North Americans were not. And as I saw this harmony between people and environment year after year in one new Mexican place after another, I became aware of how much disharmony there is in the United States between the people and the environment in which they live, especially in cities. I came to realize, too, how much I suffered in my psyche from that disharmony. For disharmony in the hearts and minds of the people who are all around us is like noise. It can be shut out so we don't think we are hearing it, but when we come to a quiet place we know how much we have suffered from the apparently unheard noise and what it has cost us to achieve its exclusion.

By the time I began going to Mexico regularly I had achieved a fair degree of harmony in my inner and my middle circles and those two circles, in turn, rotated harmoniously together. But I had never lived in a place where there was equal harmony in the outer circle surrounding the two inner ones. In Mexico I found it, and I am sure it was this harmony prevailing in all three at once that allowed that effortless opening up I have tried to describe.

Instead of feeling merely like a person who lived in a safe house in a safe quarter of the city, I felt as if I were in a wholly safe world, where I could let my sensibilities roam to the furthest horizon without danger of being hurt or misunderstood. Not only had I found this wonderfully liberating, but when I had sometimes lost some of the harmony in the two inner circles I had been able to get them retuned, as it were, by transporting them to Mexico and setting them within the movement of that larger circle whose steady, harmonious turning transmitted itself to the smaller wheels so that they, too, became balanced and peaceful again.

Even drawing three circles with a stick on the ground, though, I felt I could not explain all this to José. But I saw I could tell him one particularly vital part if I knew one word more—the Spanish word for harmony.

By means of questions I set out to pinpoint the word I wanted. "What is the word for one of the chief things in music?" I asked.

"*Melodía*," he volunteered. I shook my head. "*Ritmo*," was his next guess. Again I shook my head. Then he thought a moment and said "*armonía.*"

It was the word I needed. From then on it was easy. I told him that in the United States there was constant *lucha* between the people and their environment. But that in Mexico there was *armonía* between the people and their *tierra,* and that I found that Mexican *armonía* made me feel happy and tranquil.

Shortly after this, José said he felt it was time to go home. As we parted I had a sense of wonder at the relative ease with which we had been able to converse on fairly abstract matters. It was largely because of José's intelligence. He had spoken slowly so I could understand him. His quick mind had reached out so he could understand me. And since he had a mind trained in academic matters, we had a meeting ground in a common level of culture.

I think he enjoyed the conversation as much as I did. I saw, too, how important like-mindedness is in communication. Even when words are scanty, people with the same basic orientation towards the world can share their thoughts with each other better than they can with people of their own tongue who live in different mental worlds. I think it had been a long time since José had found someone with whom he could discuss John Dewey.

For my final dinner Lupe had prepared some of the superb *cilantro* sauce she knew I liked so well. Besides the pieces of meat in that sauce, she served eggs scrambled in tomatoes, tortillas and frijoles. And there was hot chocolate both at the start of the meal and at the end, and with the final chocolate there were cookies.

After dinner, too, it was understood that I would not go back to my room. It was our last evening and we wanted to be together. Don Gabriel and I reversed seats. This time I sat on that thinly covered bed while he ate at the table. The sight of them eating by the light of the one candle was like a scene from Millet.

When Don Gabriel had given me the Mixteca pieces, he had told me there was a man in the village who had *idolitos* he was willing to sell. His name was Romualdo Ceballos.

Since tomorrow was my last day, I asked if it would be possible to see Sr. Ceballos' collection? Don Gabriel said it would be and that the best time was before breakfast. My hope, of course, was that the collector would turn out to be the man with the club foot who had limped off to fetch his idols three years before.

Was I satisfied with what I had achieved during my visit? Don Gabriel asked.

Yes, I said, but there was one disappointment. Because the priest had the keys, I had not seen the sacristy.

As I talked, Lupe did the dinner dishes. What I noticed was that she had hardly a thing to wash. Because there were only the two spoons and the two soup plates, she had washed them between courses to use them over again. Thus at the end of the meal she was not confronted with a stack of dirty dishes from each course. For the first time I realized that one reason North American housewives suffer so much from the burden of dishwashing is because their shelves are so abundantly stacked with dishes. Having so many, they use so many, and there is always that nightmare of washing them all up, meal after meal. I struck the set of china from my mental list of gifts for the Blancos. Meals were less of a chore for Lupe for the very reason that she did not have many dishes.

Towards the end of the evening came the question I expected. Would I like to go through *Canción Mixteca* again? Of course, I replied. So Don Gabriel got out the yellowed sheet with the words and we began singing. I still needed quite a lot of correcting. But as I became surer of the tune I was freer to think of the meaning of the text.

"*O tierra del sol, suspiro por verte.*" Suddenly my mind leaped forward to the coming winter in New York. Often, I said to myself, I'll be thinking of this valley—the land of the sun. And I'll be sighing to see it.

"*Inmensa nostalgia invade mi pensamiento.*" The words were in the present tense, but these, too, evoked the future. Flowery language or no, I couldn't resist telling the Blancos what I had come to realize.

"Do you know what will happen to me back in the United States?" I asked. "Often I will think of Yanhuitlán, and an immense nostalgia will invade my thinking."

When it was obviously bedtime for us all, I said good night to Lupe, and Don Gabriel saw me to my room for the last time.

XXII

THE FAREWELL

FRIDAY, OCTOBER 2, 1953, was my last day in Yanhuitlán. It began when I woke at a quarter to seven. And this morning I got up right away. At seven, when Don Gabriel came over, I was dressed and ready to go to Sr. Ceballos' home to view his collection of idols.

His house is marked No. 5 in the plan on page 60. To reach it we turned our backs on the monastery and headed south. At the end of Don Gabriel's street we cut across the village green. We walked swiftly because it was drizzling.

Sr. Ceballos' house was pink and it was toward the end of its block. When we entered the front room, I discovered he was one of the town butchers. The giveaway was a pig's head, hanging by its snout from one of seven iron hooks over a big carving table. The room had an earth floor and, except for that scrupulously clean table, was completely bare.

The door at the back led to a courtyard where we could see a closely tethered red-brown bull. Don Gabriel said it was to be slaughtered that morning.

Presently a woman came to see what we wanted. When she learned our mission, she ordered her daughter to bring in two chairs so we could sit down. Her husband, she said, would be ready shortly.

His arrival brought a surprise. He was not the man with the clubfoot, but an old friend. Sr. Ceballos, in fact, was none other than the egg-shaped burgher with the long gray moustache who had mistaken the north portal for the cemetery arch on my first meeting, and who had been enjoying Don Miguel's free drinks on my second. He went off to fetch his idols.

Sr. Ceballos returned with his Mixteca treasure knotted in a bandanna.

He untied the red handkerchief and when he spread the little objects on the table, I felt I was seeing things. If I hadn't known they dated back five or six centuries, I would have sworn they were sculptured versions of William Steig's "Lonely Ones."

Most of them were heads, but there were a few complete figures, including a squatting man sculptured in pure white stone. It was obviously the finest piece in the lot, but Sr. Ceballos wanted seventy-five pesos for it. Don Gabriel, who was behind the little butcher, frowned and shook his head. I took his silent counsel and passed it up.

My second choice was a small praying man carved from an almost cylindrical piece of white-green stone. Here the resemblance to a Steig figure extended even to the posture. He was so like the lonely one sitting in the box with the caption "People are no damn good." Yet his expression was more benign. Irresistibly, he suggested a pious pilgrim. That look of a Pilgrim father reminded me of the head Don Gabriel had given me; and when I laid that head beside the Pilgrim I could understand how Don Gabriel had known his head was broken. It resembled the head of the complete figure so closely in size, style and notching at ear level that obviously it, too, had once had a stumpy body with bent-up knees and hands clasped in prayer over a self-contented stomach.

Looking at them side by side, I was struck by the vivacity of expression in the faces, and I marveled that such variety of character could be con-

veyed by crescents and lines. The variety was especially remarkable because both sculptors were clearly obliged to work within the limits of a rigid convention.

When I turned the praying figure over, I saw two holes angled to meet each other at the back of the neck. As I turned the head over, I received a fresh instance of what has always fascinated me: namely, the way vision is sharpened when different but related objects are seen side by side. Suddenly I could see something I had never noticed in the head before: the top arches of what must have been two interconnecting holes. And with vision came understanding. Obviously, the figure broke off at the neck because the holes weakened the stone at this point.

The holes meant the praying figure could be threaded on a cord, so I asked Don Gabriel if the figurines, too, were worn as amulets around the neck. He said they were. And I learned later they are characteristic of the region. They have been given the name *penates*, after the household gods of the Romans. In late periods of the Mixteca civilization the dead were buried sitting upright, with their knees drawn up. This has led to the belief the *penates* are little figures of the dead.

Sr. Ceballos was a model of patience as I compared his figure with my head. When I asked how much it was, he said fifteen pesos. Don Gabriel nodded to indicate the price was fair. With this approval, I cheerfully paid out the money and pocketed my tiny Pilgrim father.

Then Sr. Ceballos surprised me by throwing in another object as a gift. This was carved of the same fine white-green stone as the pilgrim. It was a head with so much hair on either side that I took it to be a woman. I could not help smiling at her expression. She reminded me vividly of another of Steig's lonely ones—the crazy dame leaning out from behind a subway pole, showing by being entirely nude how true it was that public opinion no longer worried her.

As we left the butcher's street and turned back towards the monastery, my breath was caught by how majestically the building rose ahead. I also got a flash as to why Sr. Ceballos and Don Patricio, the postmaster, had failed to recognize the north portal. They both lived on the south side of town.

The drizzle turned suddenly to rain and we ran the rest of the way home. Lupe had a big breakfast ready, which included steak and fried potatoes, as well as eggs and tortillas. As I tucked in, I realized the punctuality of the meal was characteristic of Lupe's home. And I crossed another item from my gift list. Obviously the Blancos knew how to keep time well enough—despite their unreliable alarm clock. I certainly was not going to do anything to impose on them the time slavery we suffer from, partly because our hideously shrill alarm clocks never lose a minute.

I decided to cross off the flashlight batteries too. Giving anything so minor might have the effect of saying: See, I realize how poor you are. I did not want to affront them in this way. But even more important, my attitude had changed. I still was going to send them another good blanket, but fundamentally I no longer thought they were poor. They had taught me you do not really need many of the things whose absence spells poverty in the United States.

In many respects, I saw that, in terms of the true wealth of affectionate contentment, they were richer than most of us. And I felt this particularly at this moment, for the rain outside had made that big, hospitable room cozier than ever. Or did it merely seem so because I would be leaving it so soon?

Whatever the explanation, we were all together, for the rain had driven the little black turkey and the brown chicken indoors. Delightedly, I watched them peck the drops of moisture from their feathers. I could judge the growth of the cock during my visit by the new redness in the hint of comb on its head. I became conscious, too, of another household bird—a dove in a little wooden cage.

Lupe was sitting by the warmth of her stove, Don Gabriel was stroking Hambre, who rested contentedly in his lap as he sat on the bed. And Bobby was standing by my knee, waiting politely for whatever he might be given. The only thing needed to complete the scene was a framed sampler with the words HOME SWEET HOME.

At the end of the meal there was a discreet knock at the outer door and I was familiar enough with the routine of the household to know it was a tradesman's knock. It was the milkman, or rather the milkboy, for he was a shy, lean youth with a lovely smile. He filled his measuring can to the brim and then dumped it into Lupe's pitcher. His measure held half a liter, the Blancos explained. And then, as if they wanted to oblige me by telling me as much about marketing as possible, they showed me how the transaction would have taken place if the tradesman had been selling corn. From one of the shelves Don Gabriel took a square box which he said was called a *maquila*. And I was able to understand its use, for in markets I'd seen such boxes being leveled to the top with corn kernels as they were employed both to measure and to transfer corn from the salesman's pile to the purchaser's sack. The present price of corn, said Don Gabriel, was four and a half pesos a *maquila*. He added that nearly every household had its own *maquila*, for there were some corn merchants whose measuring boxes were a little on the small side.

He and Lupe both laughed tolerantly at such shortchanging. It was the sort of thing you would naturally expect from human nature. And I thought how wise and friendly was their way of circumventing it. You did not haul the merchant into court and you did not think any the less of him for doing the natural thing. You just took your own *maquila*.

Mexicans have a way of transforming every religious figure into a *santo*. A peculiar result of this habit is that the most popular religious personages become a variety of different *santos*. Mary, for instance, becomes a different *santo* in each manifestation. Thus Guadalupe is one, Soledad another, and so on. Jesus as a child is Santo Niño. Jesus nailed on the cross is Santo Cristo. Jesus laid out in a glass coffin is Santo Entierro. And Jesus riding into Jerusalem on an ass is Santo Ramos.

I learned this last name when Don Gabriel applied it to the first of the figures I wanted to draw that morning. "Why is it called Santo Ramos?" I asked, as we stood before it in the *sagrario*.

"Because of the *ramos* of *Domingo de ramos*." Seeing I still did not understand, he touched the long branch of real palm the figure held in its left hand. "*Un ramo*," he said. So that was it. Christ on the donkey was called *Santo Ramos* because of the branches, or *ramos*, of palm associated with Palm Sunday.

As I drew the figure on the papier-maché burro I grew increasingly charmed by it. But I think "figure" is really a misnomer. I did not have the temerity to lift the bright red robe, but I think those feet are merely hung over the back of the brown burro like a pair of stirrups. If there is a figure,

it is surely only solid from the waist up. The long hair of the *santo* is human hair and the violet cloak, like the robe, is sateen.

As I was completing the donkey, I heard,the braying of a distant burro. It gave me the same curious feeling I had when I heard the oxen being driven home as I was drawing San Isidro's oxen. Again I felt the rightness of the particular *santo* for Yanhuitlán. And I received the same clue to the appeal of Santo Ramos. Heaven knows he didn't represent great sculpture, but perhaps he, too, was the object of a living devotion. When I had finished him, I printed his name clearly at the foot of the drawing.

A glance at my watch showed I had time to draw one more figure. I wanted to do one of the eight angels, not only because of the group's relationship to the barrio Christs, but because I wanted to show an example of Yanhuitlán's statuary at its best. Which angel, then, was the only matter to be decided. Don Gabriel and I returned to the baptistery to make the selection.

I had not seen all the angels uncovered—just hints of gold and ravishing colors and beautifully modeled limbs when Don Gabriel had lifted corners of their ghostly sheets. But I was beginning to feel time was short, and rather than asking to have them all uncovered so I could make a judg-

ment of Paris, I decided to draw the exposed angel with the delicate tin wings. It was beautiful enough to suggest the quality of the series.

The angel, though, had to be brought into the nave, for the vaulted baptistery, having no windows, was too dark for decent visibility. The angel was mounted on a low sturdy table, which, because of projecting handles, could be carried like a litter. But when Don Gabriel and I lifted our upright patient I had occasion to appreciate the lightness of the corn-pith Christ. The solid wood angel was smaller than the Christ, but it weighed much more. I was glad we didn't have to carry it far to get it into the light.

Tinde, according to Don Gabriel, was the name of my chosen angel. Its head, arms, knees and toes had the natural pink of a skillfully painted doll. The true beauty was in the colors of the sculptured clothing. The lining, which showed where the sleeves were rolled back and where the skirt billowed from the legs, was a damask rose. The dress itself was gold—but it was not an ordinary shining gilt. Red flowers with black foliage had been painted over it, and because some of that paint had worn thin the gold showed through the scarlet and black in a subtle and enchanting way.

Thanks to Felix Palma's hard pencil and the candlestand pressed into service for the last time, I was able to outline the whole figure with the faintest of lines. And it seemed as if I could not make a false stroke. The fingers came out as neat and correct as could be. I even caught the doll's likeness, which was no mean feat, considering how little individuality it had.

María Luisa, looking charming in a green dress and a rose rebozo, entered the church. She came over to see the work in progress. Then she went towards the sacristy. Shortly thereafter, another woman in a black rebozo opened the north door. Three old women came in, followed by Felix Soriano, the former sacristan with the staff, the bandage round his head and the blanket over his shoulders. They, too, made their way towards the *sagrario*.

It looked as if there was going to be a service. But this was strange. The week before the priest hadn't come back from Oaxaca until Saturday, and here it was only Friday. I couldn't resist leaving my work for a few minutes to find out. So I tiptoed to the entrance of the *sagrario* to have a peek.

Sure enough, the priest was celebrating Mass at the altar at the foot of the huge sculptured Descent from the Cross. Three candles stood on the altar, and, on the floor in front, another candle flame wavered in a ruby-colored glass. The women worshippers were on their knees a little to one side, with María Luisa's rose rebozo making a lovely contrast to the black ones of the older women. The gentle old sacristan, looking like a shepherd, knelt on the other side, his staff resting on the red tiles of the old floor.

It was a scene so beautiful I tiptoed away as quietly as I had come.

When the lines of my drawing were so securely established that I had nothing to worry about except darkening the contours, I began to be a little curious about the angel's attitude. Why did it have its hands up like that? Don Gabriel's answer gave me much more than the brief explanation I sought. In fact, it provided one of my deepest insights into the people's lives.

Each year on the Thursday before Good Friday, he said, the angels and the barrio Christs were taken out in a procession. Each angel preceded its Christ, carrying one of the instruments of the Passion. The angel that went before El Señor de Ayuxi, for instance, carried the pincers. The angel in front of El Señor de Xaayucu carried Veronica's veil. Others carried the nails, the crown of thorns and so on. Tinde's burden, he said, was the ladder. It was laid across the outstretched arms.

"At what hour did the procession start?"

"About eight or nine o'clock at night."

"Then it was dark."

"Yes, they carried candles."

The scene flashed on my mind's eye: the women in black, the men with their sombreros in their hands, the wavering candle flames, the towering crucifixes at varying angles, and the angels that must have bobbed unsteadily, since they were so heavy to carry.

"Was there music?" I asked. "Yes. Sometimes the people sang and there were a few mournful instruments. They went very slowly. They used to go as far as El Calvario, the chapel on the hill at the edge of the village. The procession would take about seven hours, and they would not get back to the church until three or four in the morning."

"What did they do on Good Friday?" I asked. "They crucified Santo Entierro."

"The image in the glass coffin?" I asked incredulously, remembering that prone figure lying under its red shroud in Soledad's altar. "How could they do that?"

"Its arms move. And once they fix it to the cross they take it on another procession. They used to carry it to La Pastora, the chapel at the corner of the plaza."

"Do they still follow these customs each Easter?"

"Not all of them. They have given up the big procession on Maundy Thursday. I don't think they have had such a procession since 1902. But they still crucify Santo Entierro, though now they don't take him so far. The roof of La Pastora, as you know, fell in 1927. Now they only take the Santo to the baptistery and back. And on Saturday they take him down from the cross and lay him in the coffin."

I returned to my sketching, considerably sobered. The present villagers might not be very religious compared with those of former generations, but they still marked Easter in a way that made the blood run cold.

As I finished off Tinde, my curiosity stirred about the figure's baldness, especially since the top of the skull was not painted as the face was. Again Don Gabriel had the explanation. When fully rigged out the angel had a wig of real hair and a silver crown with big plumes. The information about the missing headdress gave me the clue to what the angel resembled. Before I had not been able to place it, but when I envisaged the plumes, I had it: a dancer in one of Louis XIV's court ballets.

"Where is the crown now?" I asked. "It has precious stones so it is kept under lock and key."

Since Tinde represented the end of my project, I was loath to put my pencils away, but after a little unnecessary fussing with the stylized cloud on which the angel stood, I faced the inevitable and gathered up my drawing things.

Don Gabriel replaced the candlestand in front of El Señor de Xaayucu and we were about to take a last look around when the worshippers emerged from the chapel. One of the older women, I saw, was the Widow Isabel. Since pride in my latest drawings made me want to exhibit them, I took my book to her. The others wanted to see the previous drawings too. So I began at the beginning.

The priest, having finished his backstage duties, came out and joined the group of viewers. He nodded in evident pleasure at the windows, the doorways, the coats of arms; and like the rest of the group, he exclaimed in audible surprise and delight at the page of Lupe's cooking things. But at Santo Ramos he frowned.

"No," he said, almost vehemently. "Not Santo Ramos. El Salvador." Apparently, turning Jesus into a mere saint and dividing him up into different saints for each major representation was something he had fought hard and long in his congregation. He ordered me to write "El Salvador" under the figure. I did, carefully printing the name. But this was not enough for him. He insisted I cross out the name Santo Ramos.

This hint of altercation aroused the curiosity of old Isabel. Apparently up to this time she had not been seeing very clearly. But now she got out her glasses—a small iron-rimmed pair—set them crookedly on her nose and looked more closely at the figure that had caused the dispute. "Oh," she said, looking up brightly, "Santo Ramosito." Thereby compounding false doctrine with the local habit of adding *"ito"* to make everything diminutive.

Perhaps at this point the priest gave up. To think he should have made so little impression on one of his best customers. Changing the subject, he came out with a most unexpected suggestion. Could he show me through the *sacristía?* The sacristy—the one part of the building I had not seen. So I was not going to miss it after all.

It was a lofty square chamber with two especially striking architectural features. The most surprising one occupied a third of the west wall. It was a big ornamental alcove to house the basins in which the priests washed their hands. This alcove, a stunning Renaissance performance, was another doorway of the diamonds.

In one sense it outdid that doorway in its multiplicity of diamonds.

Not only did they surround the frame, but they filled the rear wall of the alcove too. And here the pyramids rising in each panel were dramatized by paint. Pink coated some of the triangular faces, and cream and dark brown heightened the tonal contrasts between the facets in light and those in shadow. Such painting was charming in its way, but it seemed more appropriate for a harlequinade than for a niche for sacramental washing.

Resting on the alcove's counter was a large basin covered with a square of fine linen. The priest lifted the cloth. What he wanted to display was the blue figuration of the precious Talavera bowl from Puebla; but what I noticed most was that nearly all the holy water had developed a white crust.

The ceiling was the other striking architectural feature. Not only was it lighted by those oddly shaped windows—the diamond and the hexagon shown as they look from the outside on page 73—but the ceiling was superbly vaulted. Ribs sprang from each corner, and superimposed on the arching Greek and St. Andrew's crosses was a circle of intermediate ribs. There were bosses at the points of intersection and all the bosses were carved. I recognized a Dominican cross and another hand holding a pear-shaped heart. The boss in the center of the web had a rayed sun. It was painted red.

I think El Cura was pleased at my surprised delight in the great room. While I was still examining the four-foot crucifix standing on the big central vesting table, he went to one of the magnificently carved bureaus against the east wall, pulled open a drawer and lifted out a cross even more gorgeous.

"El Señor de Expiración," he said, holding it up for my admiration. The figure of Jesus was relatively small. It was the carving of the cross, with many angel heads and the fancy INRI scroll at the top, which made it notable. I exclaimed in sincere wonder and the priest warmed to his task under the encouragement of my enthusiasm.

"*Otra curiosidad*," he said, as he selected one of the two big keys dangling at the waist of his black cassock. The key went into a carved cupboard door in the north wall. Its opening exposed a number of shelves and from one of them the priest gently lifted a silver chalice with a gold-lined cup.

"Look," he said, and pointed to the engraved base. It bore a date— 1773—and a name. Because of my desire to have some record of those associated with the monastery, I copied down the name, though I knew nothing about the man. It was Padre General Francisco Ayala.

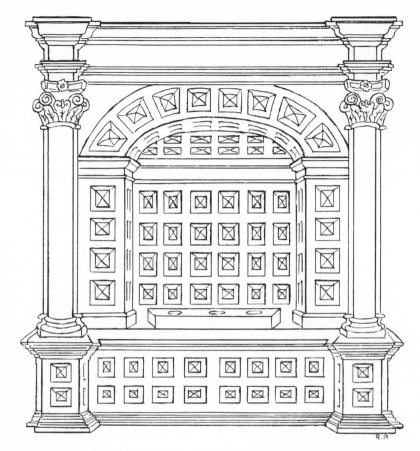

The final object Father Lorenzo showed me was a crucifix which he said was a companion of the silver chalice. The cross was black and the figure was ivory, with its bloodstains looking very red on the white carving. The body was all one piece and revealed the slight curve of the original tusk. It was so exquisitely carved that it was possible to trace each interweaving line of the crown of thorns. I felt a pang that one of the points of the forked beard was chipped off.

Around the upper part of the room's whitewashed walls were oil paintings. Most of them were portraits of Dominican friars and nuns. I could not study them, however, for after putting away the ivory crucifix El Cura was ready to lock up. The only canvas I remember distinctly was an Ascension, which, like the one on the main altar, showed only the lower legs of Jesus. In this case there was an added touch to show the almost vanished Christ had once been on the ground. On the little mound at the bottom of the painting were his footprints.

THE FAREWELL

As Father Lorenzo locked the sacristy, I felt grateful that he protected its treasures so scrupulously. After he took the shortcut up to his quarters, Don Gabriel and I went back to the church for a final loving survey.

The rain had stopped and again blue sky showed through the great high windows. I stood a moment appreciating the white walls, the cool height and the gold of the organ. And in the quietness of that moment a rooster crowed somewhere in the village.

I turned back for a last look at the high gold altar, recessed in its night-blue apse and framed by the sea-green triumphal arch. Then we passed through the portal of Santa Catalina to where the sun shone on the green leaves of the apricot tree in the cloister. How dark in contrast was the foliage of the ancient cypress! Lovingly my eyes fell on the two battered lady saints in their niche at the end of the ambulatory; lovingly my eyes rose to a last glimpse of the brick tower as we passed along the arches of the east side of the cloister.

The doorway of the classical pediment, the doorway of the diamonds, the box I had sat on to draw, the long Sala de Profundis, the grand stairway leading up to the left, the empty niche at the end of the refectory on the right—these were among the things I saw for the last time, and as their beauty came home to me I wondered if they were really so beautiful as they seemed in this washed sunlight after rain, or was part of the beauty they trembled with merely the projection of what they had meant to me?

Leaving the friary for the last time, I had a flash of insight. I had come to Yanhuitlán to draw a monastery; not to enter one. Yet, in a way, hadn't the visit as a whole been an experience of monasticism? The hard bed, the early rising, the simple meals, the daily round of gentle and unchanging activity within the church close, the seclusion from the world—all these were features of the monastic life. My thoughts had seldom been specifically religious. But perhaps one of the lessons I'd learned was that monasticism works on a human being in certain beneficial ways, independently of what he believes.

At least, I was sure of one thing. In becoming aware of the monasticism of the stay I had isolated another factor contributing to the feeling of tranquil well-being I'd tried to account for while drawing the ruined gap. And I smiled at the irony and unexpectedness of the situation. Without having any such intention, and without knowing what I had done, I had made what my Catholic friends would call a retreat.

Once outside, I saw the clouds had lifted from Jazmín and San Pedro and the hills were very red after the rain. On the way home I saw more things with a new comprehension of their beauty—the twenty-one white arches of the arcade in front of the municipal palace, the circular fountain in the plaza with the trees circling it like Matisse dancers; La Pastora, the roofless ruined chapel on the far corner. And I felt sad.

I began to pack. First I put my keepsakes together: the big blue ribbon that had been pinned on my lapel at the dance; the wooden comb I had bought at the market, Nahum's little mirror; the corncobs like rubies and opals given by the friendly woman on the walk to the *manantial;* the clay whistle of the dog-faced king, the jade bead, the football player and the other little idol heads.

Ironically, I picked up the three books I had brought—Thomas à Kempis, Wordsworth and H. M. Tomlinson's *The Sea and the Jungle.* And I smiled that I, the compulsive reader, had not read a line of them. I opened à Kempis at the place where he wrote, "But if it please you to hear news of the world, you must always suffer disquiet of heart as a result." His words made me realize I had not read a newspaper in almost ten days; nor had I seen anyone else reading one.

I smiled as I set aside the medicine I had brought. I had not touched it either, for the water was indeed pure.

I put aside a shirt and a pair of suntan trousers as a gift for Don Gabriel; and for Lupe the soap I had left and the mirror I had bought at the market.

As I was getting everything assembled a familiar little figure passed. It was Angelita and I could tell she was on her way home from school, for she had a book under her arm. *"Buenos días,"* I called out to her. And when she stopped for a candy I could not resist my opportunity.

"¿Cómo se llaman sus hermanitas?" I asked. And her face disappeared behind her schoolbook. She knew my request for the names of her little sisters meant she'd been found out.

"You have only one sister," I said, "an older sister, Serafina. Take this candy home to her. And here is one for yourself."

I placed most of my clothes in the orange brief bag. After leafing through the two well-filled sketchbooks I put them in the striped fiber bag, from which the plans projected in their green cardboard tube. By ten minutes past twelve I was ready to leave. But I could not bear to go without looking once more at everything—at the big counter with the black and gray sarape, at the table with the little patchwork cloth and the two containers of flowers, at the upright Tlaxiaco chair, the gin bottle with the drinking water, the gray graniteware wash basin, the bucket with the water for washing, the tin holding the candle, the three benches against the walls, the beamed ceiling, the brown bricks of the ancient floor, the arched peephole, the log for jamming the doors; and, when I finally locked up, the leather thong that enabled me to draw the doors to.

I had about half a dozen candies left, so I walked over to Paco's house and gave them to the bantamweight and his brothers and sisters. Returning, I encountered Gabriel Sánchez, the dignified little man I had sat beside at the ball. He invited me to join him for a *refresco*, but I begged off because my bus would be leaving soon.

Being barely past noon, the hour was early for the *comida*, but Lupe, as I knew she would, had a nourishing dinner ready. There were two eggs on rice; meat, potatoes and squash; tortillas, of course, and, just as inevitably, frijoles. There was cheese to garnish the latter, and hot milk.

As I was drinking the milk, my curiosity got the better of me. I knew I was the first North American who had ever stayed with the Blancos. They must have had preconceived notions about *gringos*. What I wanted to know was if I had turned out differently than they had expected. I asked if I had been a surprise.

Lupe shook her head. All human beings, she said, were the same.

Don Gabriel elaborated. I am sure he had never read *The Merchant of Venice*, but sitting on the bed he gave me what in substance was Shylock's famous speech. All humans, he said, had souls. All had sensibilities. All had intelligences, and here he tapped his brow. Then he pinched the skin of his hand to show that all people felt pain if they were hurt. All laughed at what was humorous. And feeling perhaps his own authority was not sufficient, he went to his small bookshelf to get a quotation.

What he produced was a Bible and I am afraid my desire to see something in that Bible was so intense I hardly heard the text he used to prove all men were alike under God. What I wanted was the translation of something I had tried to translate into Spanish myself—the Twenty-third Psalm.

It began "*Jehová es mi pastor.*" I read on past the green pastures and the still waters and I came to the phrase "*confortará mi alma.*"

"*Confortará mi alma . . . .*" That was where I stopped. In a flash the phrase told me the essential thing that had happened to me in Yanhuitlán. My soul had been restored—or, in this particularly beautiful way of putting it, comforted.

And with that comprehension my almost forgotten book came back to me. I did not have to junk the idea of a Yanhuitlán book after all. Through the days I had scarcely been aware of its process, but something important *had* happened inside me. And in the restoration of my spirit the deep sense of failure had vanished. Gone too was the bitter taste of rejection, and the feeling that I had wasted my life in a vocation for which I did not have the necessary gifts.

Excitedly I realized that, even though the outward events had continued to be mild, there had been an inner drama of some significance. A heart had been unhardened, an inner circle retuned, and a man had emerged from the prison of self and self-doubt into a world in which he felt at peace. I had a story worth telling. And, as an additional gift, that flash from the Bible had furnished one of the hardest things any author has to work out— a closing scene with a proper climax.

I did not tell Don Gabriel all that had gone through my head. Instead I handed back the Bible as reverently as I could. The way he received it almost as if he were a preacher, gave me a clue.

"Are you a Protestant?" I asked. "Of course," he said. And we shook hands.

Then he indicated it was time to leave for the *cantina* where the bus stopped. He did not know the exact time it passed, and it would be better to be early than late. This meant I had to ask how much I owed them. In view of the way they had begun calculating exact costs when I had broached the matter at the start of the visit, I expected a neatly totaled bill. No such thing was forthcoming.

"Whatever you choose to pay," said Don Gabriel gently. And Lupe seemed embarrassed even at that modest request.

Thank heaven I had discovered how much the Institute paid him. That ninety pesos every two weeks gave me a guiding figure. I knew, then, that by all Mexican standards, one hundred pesos was a fair price. And I hesitated to go higher for they had refused to accept ten pesos a day, saying it was too much. But perhaps, I thought, they might consent to a little more if I phrased it differently.

"Let me see," I said. "I have been here eight whole days and two half ones. That makes ten. Let me give this."

And I handed them a bill of the denomination mentioned. To my relief, they accepted it. Then, with apologies, I gave Lupe the cake of Palmolive and the standing mirror, and I gave Don Gabriel the shirt and pants. They were both delighted with the pants, but when Don Gabriel held them up in front of him, it was plain they were too large.

"I am fatter than you are," I said. "Lupe can fix them," said Don Gabriel proudly, and Lupe nodded in agreement.

After this I handed Don Gabriel his *propina*, or tip—another hundred-peso note. He refused to accept it.

Why not, I asked. The Institute, he said, had specially instructed that he should not accept any money for his services.

Then, since the farewell at the bus would be more public, we had our real good-byes. First Lupe and I hugged each other. Then Don Gabriel and I exchanged the same *abrazos*, with the accompanying pats on the back.

Lupe stayed behind, but Don Gabriel and Bobby came with me to the bus stop. And here three loose threads were unexpectedly tied up. When it began to rain again we took shelter in the little brick *cantina*, and who should be behind the counter but Soledad, the plump girl with the kind face who had danced with me so willingly and then left me with such alacrity as the music stopped. That was thread No. 1.

No. 2 was tied off when Don Gabriel pointed to a youth coming from a thatched hut near the cantina. He was Jerónimo, the brother of Cutberto. So that explained why the friendly youth with the wavy hair had been coming by that particular spot three years before. He had been returning to this hut, which was his home. And Jerónimo, on being introduced, furnished the final thread. Yes, he knew Ricardo, the boy who had given me the water. There was a reason I had never seen him on this visit. Ricardo, too, had joined the ranks of those young men who had left the village in the hope of a livelier future in Mexico City.

A few minutes before two o'clock I spotted two things simultaneously: the bus winding over the pass into the valley, and Lupe standing in the gap of the ruined wing where the three arches had been. I waved to her and she waved back.

Don Gabriel saw that I got a seat up front near the driver and he put my luggage in the overhead rack. And this time when we said good-by we merely shook hands.

When the bus pulled away I waved back to Lupe at the gap and to Gabriel and his dog by the road. And they stood waving till we lost sight of each other.

I settled back in my seat. The rain grew heavier, and I was sorry to see it carrying away more of the red soil of the valley I was leaving.

"*Inmensa nostalgia invade mi pensamiento,*" the words came as the tune rose spontaneously in my mind. So it had started already. But the nostalgia I felt was one of heart-easing love, rather than of longing. And mingled with the words of *Canción Mixteca* came another Spanish sentence I had caught further down in the Psalm—the one just after the anointing with oil.

"*Mi copa está rebosando.*"